D1528470

Disciples and Friends

Disciples and Friends

Investigations in Disability, Dementia, and Mental Health

Essays in Honor of John Swinton

Armand Léon van Ommen and Brian R. Brock

Editors

BAYLOR UNIVERSITY PRESS

Book design by Baylor University Press
Typesetting and cover design by Kasey McBeath
Cover art: Lightspring via shutterstock.com

The Library of Congress has cataloged this book under hardback ISBN 978-1-4813-1700-9.
Library of Congress Control Number: 2022940197

Contents

Introduction

What Does It Mean to Be Human?

Armand Léon van Ommen

In my first week as a new lecturer at the University of Aberdeen, I was provoked into thinking about the importance of the question, What does it mean to be human? In saying this, however, my mind travels a few months further back than those first days of teaching in September 2016, specifically, to my interview with John Swinton for the post of Christ's College teaching fellow in practical theology. At the end of the interview, I asked the panel members if they could tell me what courses I might be teaching if my application were successful. John Swinton replied by listing various courses, all of which aligned rather well with my research interests and teaching experience. Except for the course What Does It Mean to Be Human?—addressed from the perspective of disability theology. At this point I had to sheepishly admit that I had not studied disability theology at all. I was so vague about what that field might be that I forgot to mention that during my own doctoral research I had drawn on the book that I was soon to discover would be the course textbook (see Brock and Swinton 2012). John replied with his typical wit: I looked quite human, he said, so he didn't think the course would be too much of a problem for me.

Despite his confidence, I nevertheless felt out of my depth as I led my first tutorial in this class. To make matters worse, John managed to injure his leg to the point of not being able to work, meaning that I would now need to cover the main lectures as well! John apologized, of course, for throwing me into the deep end with a new course, on a topic that I did not really know, and in an educational system that I—coming from mainland Europe—did not understand. Despite the pains of being a new lecturer, I don't regret for one moment facing the steep learning curve demanded by this course. Since my office was situated literally between

John's and Brian Brock's, it provoked many discussions that left me with an enduring interest in disability theology and the heading under which John filed those discussions: what does it mean to be human? Having next gotten to know John and his work much better, I have come to see that this question runs like a scarlet thread through all of John's work. It is this question, then, that lies at the heart of this volume.

This book identifies some of the ways in which John in his theology and practice has answered the question of the meaning of human life in a God-given world or, perhaps better, how he has helped his readers, students, friends, and colleagues to think through this question. John has undeniably put his stamp on practical theology in the United Kingdom and beyond, and he has been especially influential in the areas of disability theology, dementia, health care, and chaplaincy. Readers should be aware at the outset that this volume is not a comprehensive survey of the distinct contributions John has made in all the areas in which he has written. Rather, the contributors have collectively identified several key theological motifs that run throughout John's work and have taken the question of what it means to be human as an entry point to engage with these motifs.

This volume is a celebration of John Swinton's tireless explorations of the question of the human. All chapters were written by colleagues, friends, or former students of John who have been influenced by him as a person or by his writings and therefore approach his life appreciatively. Taking John's work seriously means acknowledging its value while also sometimes gently pushing back and constructively thinking about ways to make new inroads and take next steps. This volume is a celebration of John and his impact on practical theology. Celebration means recognizing someone. This work is a recognition of John as a person, friend, and theologian.

What does it mean to be human? In what ways has John answered this question, and how might we answer this question, reflecting on the themes, issues, and methodologies that John offers throughout his work? This volume is a response to those questions in four parts, the first of which is titled "Practical Theology in a Swintonian Key." The "key" in question is a nod to John's musical abilities, which the editors suggest is an apt metaphor for the interlocking parts that make up John's way of doing theology. This part opens with a chapter on a recent project that John launched at the University of Aberdeen, the Friendship House. The Friendship House initiative is an attempt to form an intentional community of friendship with people with intellectual disabilities situated within the university. Inspired by L'Arche communities (founded in 1964 by Jean Vanier), Friendship House is a telling exemplification of what it means to be human in a wider social context that unduly values intellect. Written by three PhD students who helped set up the Friendship House, Topher Endress, Hannah Waite, and Julie Land, chapter 1 shows that theology for John is always embodied in faithful discipleship. The editors believe it is particularly important to begin the volume here: if one wants to think theologically with John Swinton and understand his writings, one needs to begin from the lived reality of friendship and of creating spaces of belonging for marginalized people. This first chapter is appropriately titled "Enacting a Theology of Disability: Framing Swinton."

The first part of this book continues with what is, to our knowledge, the first systematic scholarly overview of Swintonian practical theology. In chapter 2 Henk de Roest outlines the key methodological choices John makes throughout his wide-ranging body of academic writing. De Roest begins by relating some influential events in John's life that have shaped his way of looking at the world. He suggests that the linchpin of a Swintonian practical theology is John's foundational understanding of the world as God's "strange" world, which one can perceive if only one looks through the eyes of faith. Seeing the world in this way yields a describable set of methodological consequences. This is a groundbreaking piece of research that will be essential reading for any student who wants to understand Swinton's methodology.

The first part of this volume concludes with an exploration of two other themes that run through John's work, without which one cannot understand John's practical theology: worship and discipleship. In chapter 3 Doug Gay relates how John, in his writings, takes us to church. John takes us there with his friend Stephen, who has Down syndrome, and points out that indeed the body of Christ has Down syndrome.[1] In yet another publication, John takes us to church again, and here Gay encourages us to think about John's theology as liturgical theology, turning pastoral theology toward political theology. These accounts necessarily lead to the second theme Gay discusses and which is key to John's theology: discipleship. Gay demonstrates how for John discipleship starts alongside people like Stephen because discipleship is a matter of going at the pace of the slowest. Gay draws out Kosuke Koyama's wonderful insight, elaborated by John in the context of disability theology, that God walks three miles an hour. Discipleship must not be rushed. Gay then outlines a curriculum for discipleship based on John's theology

[1] John makes this claim and tells the story of Stephen in the article with this name (Swinton 2003).

aptly titled "Slow Friendship with Jesus." He concludes the chapter with a challenging reflection on the story of Lazarus, friend of Jesus and brother of Martha and Mary, showing how John's writings have helped him to gain insight on this story and to preach on it. Theology with John is profoundly practical.

The second part's title, "Vulnerability Subverted," signals that this book moves onto a different conceptual register. The theme of vulnerability has often appeared in recent decades among people who ask what it means to be human. There are good biblical reasons for the central place of vulnerability in this discussion, and several disability theologians make vulnerability central to their work. Nevertheless, this trend is not without its critics. Concerning the theme of vulnerability, each of the four chapters in this part demonstrates its role in John's work. As a New Testament scholar who also writes on autism, Grant Macaskill provides an in-depth reading of Paul's subversion of "strength" and "weakness" as a simple binary opposition. A nuanced reading of this reworked binary shows that, in Macaskill's terms, "the binary is not dismissed or rejected, and neither is it destabilized through an attempt to make its elements fluid, but it is reframed in terms of the divine economy and the language that pertains to the binary thus functions differently, altering fundamentally the *evaluation* of 'strong' and 'weak' without altering their *definition*." Macaskill demonstrates how this reframing might (and should) work out for the church community in relation to its autistic members.

With this biblical reframing of strength and weakness in place, Marcia Webb argues in chapter 5 that the human response to vulnerability is not only fear or anxiety but also, at a more fundamental level, dread. Webb builds on psychological literatures on terror management, fear, and anxiety, suggesting that dread takes the reader beyond these responses to vulnerability. She offers a penetrating theological reflection on the impact of the human dread of vulnerability. She relates this to John's work on mental health and what John terms "re-membering" and his proposals for reforming our understandings of personhood.

The next chapter asks a more critical question: is vulnerability really a good starting place to think about the question of what it means to be human? In chapter 6 Hans Reinders and Cristina Gangemi begin some of the necessary but difficult critical work needed to engage with the legacy of Jean Vanier, tainted as it has been by the discovery of Vanier's sexual abuse of several women. Vanier held vulnerability and brokenness as important themes in his writings, and his influence in doing so on many disability theologians, including John Swinton, cannot be denied.

Reinders and Gangemi critically look at the vulnerability trope in disability theology and suggest another starting point for disability theology drawn from the work of Edith Stein. Concretely, they suggest replacing the idea of "vulnerability" with that of "value-ability."

Chapter 7, by Mike Mawson, could be read as a response to the previous three chapters' complex engagements with the theme of vulnerability. Although Mawson himself did not conceive of his chapter as a response to the other chapters in this section, it seemed to us as editors that he offered a rather "Swintonian" reframing of the debate that has so far emerged about vulnerability. Mawson's title states the central point to be kept in mind in the discussion of vulnerability: "Being Remembered When We Forget." Mawson discusses John's insight that the question of what it means to be a disciple of Jesus when you don't know who Jesus is anymore is best answered by confessing that even then Jesus still knows who you are. Theologically and pastorally, this is perhaps one of John's most profound and fruitful insights. Mawson discusses memory and identity in John's work by reflecting on the artwork *Lost Time*. Mawson then turns to the theology of Julian of Norwich to show points of convergence between John and Julian, despite being centuries apart, and he also shows how both have something distinct to offer to the complexity of the experience of dementia.

The third part of this volume picks up on the theme that this volume deliberately foregrounds as a key to understanding John Swinton's theology and work: "Quests for Faithful Embodiment." Most chapters in this volume relate personal anecdotes about John, often with a humorous twist. In this part, however, the personal and theological embodiment takes a more central place, probing questions around how John's explorations of and answers to the question of what it means to be human might be embodied in personal, institutional, and ecclesial contexts. In the first chapter of this part, chapter 8, Aileen Barclay tells her story of accompanying her husband through the long and grueling decline of dementia. Her personal story displays the raw reality that often accompanies this difficult journey. It is also a personal chapter in the sense that John is a friend of the family and Barclay reflects honestly on how she found John's theology of dementia often—but not always—helpful. Nevertheless, "the enormous gift [of] John as my friend" shines through the chapter.

Chapter 9 also offers a personal story, that of Elahe Hessamfar, as she writes of her experience as mother of "Helia, who carries the diagnosis of 'schizophrenia' in her medical files." In her gripping account, Hessamfar does not shy away from the difficult questions about evil in relation to mental health, though she carefully distinguishes evil from demon-possession and divine providence.

Chapter 10 transports us to Australia or, more particularly, to HammondCare, a charity renowned for its dementia care. Stephen Judd, until recently CEO of HammondCare, tells how the organization became John's "laboratory" and his team "willing collaborators." Judd reviews the mutual benefits that John and HammondCare have imparted to each other, those mutual benefits serving as a "site" where theory and practice mutually inform and strengthen each other. Let's call it practical theology!

How John's theology has been embodied in the institutional context of HammondCare is followed by a chapter that looks at how Swinton's insights illumine the ecclesial context. Bill Gaventa's chapter, "All God's Children Got a Place in the Choir," draws out the links suggested by John's work between discipleship, disability, and dementia. Gaventa takes us with him on his journey through disability theology, offering valuable insights into how this field has grown over the years and how John has been an important companion on his journey. In this chapter Gaventa highlights a gift important to John's work and life but one that not many get to see: that is, John's musical abilities. Gaventa makes the provocative claim that "those skills and passions are ones that have imbued his voice with the underlying tones and tunes of pastoral work and a theological harmony." Let the reader listen.

Part 4, finally, contains four thematic essays under the title "Gently Living in a Violent World"—a play on the title of a book John edited, *Living Gently in a Violent World* (2008). This part starts with a central theme in John's work and, according to Benjamin Conner, a fundamental human need—the need to belong. In chapter 12 Conner summarizes important aspects of John's theology of belonging, which positions social practices as central, and he argues that to talk about practices is to insist that theology is always embodied. Conner highlights John's important contribution to the practical-theological discussion about practices, especially their missionary aspect. Nevertheless, belonging is not a practice but a need. Conner shows how John, throughout his work, theologizes hospitality and friendship as practices that create spaces of belonging. The reader will note how these themes of embodiment, belonging, hospitality, and friendship take us back to the opening chapter of part 1 of this volume—Friendship House as a practical outworking of the themes Conner discusses.

The next chapter further explores the theological motif of friendship in John's work. As Andrew Root notes, "For Swinton, friendship is a form of human action that draws us into divine action." That's how high John raises the stakes for this motif. Root explores not only what kind of action human friendship constitutes (building on the work of Erich Fromm and Hartmut Rosa) but also how this kind of friendship, though resisted by the forces of modernity, remains a deep longing of human beings. Profoundly, Root explains how "friendship is a mode of action that seeks not to rush to have the world but share in the world with another." Challenging enough, this requires a deep sense of waiting.

Chapter 14, by Warren Kinghorn and Stanley Hauerwas, explores gentleness, another important theological notion in John's thinking. As the authors themselves state, they "explore what we can learn from Jesus about gentleness, what we can learn from L'Arche about gentleness, and what we can learn from John Swinton about gentleness." They are particularly interested in showing how gentleness might function in a medical context and the difference it makes to clinicians' work. The authors' reflections on gentleness near the end of their chapter relate strongly to Root's analysis of late modernity and the need for deep relationships.

The last chapter is titled "Peace." As explored in the first part of the book, worship is key to understanding John's work. Worship services, certainly more traditional ones, often start and end with peace ("Grace and peace to you from God" / "The peace of God which passes all understanding, keep your hearts and minds in the knowledge and love of God"). It is only fitting, then, that this volume concludes with a chapter on peace. Medi Ann Volpe aptly argues that "even though [peace] isn't a prominent theme, all of what John does is deeply irenic. That's not because he's interested in peace; it is because he is interested in *Jesus*." Volpe's chapter explores three ways in which Jesus and peace are interrelated: Jesus is peace, Jesus makes peace, and Jesus preached peace. Indeed, therefore, "the way to becoming people of peace is by following Jesus." Connecting this back to the liturgy, we might conclude with the final words of some traditional liturgies: "Go in peace to love and serve the Lord." To which the worshiper, and here the reader, is invited to respond, "In the name of Christ. Amen."

WORKS CITED

Brock, Brian, and John Swinton, eds. 2012. *Disability in the Christian Tradition: A Reader.* Grand Rapids: Eerdmans.

Hauerwas, Stanley, and Jean Vanier. 2008. *Living Gently in a Violent World: The Prophetic Witness of Weakness.* Downers Grove, Ill.: IVP Books.

Swinton, John. 2003. "The Body of Christ Has Down's Syndrome: Theological Reflections on Vulnerability, Disability, and Graceful Communities." *Journal of Pastoral Theology* 13, no. 2: 66–78.

I

Practical Theology
in a Swintonian Key

1

Enacting a Theology of Disability

Framing Swinton

Topher Endress, Hannah Waite, and Julie Marie Land

This chapter explores John Swinton's theology of disability in conjunction with his founding role in Friendship House at the University of Aberdeen. First, a brief history of the Friendship House includes his personal and academic involvement with the project. Next, Swinton's practical work is positioned as a natural outflow of his writings on theology. We suggest, finally, that Swinton's practical engagement with the Friendship House highlights the ways in which this theological framework aims to create space for transformative praxis.

In 2018 three incoming graduate research students accepted fellowships through the Centre for Spirituality, Health, and Disability. Arriving in Aberdeen, Scotland, they assumed practical leadership roles in the project within the Divinity Department of the University of Aberdeen exploring the concept of *friendship* as foundational to community. With the addition of a fourth fellow PhD candidate, the first Friendship House cohort was formed. This initiative, spearheaded primarily by the authors of this chapter, was aimed at creating communities where people with learning disabilities[1] and those without can come together to develop Christlike friendships. In UK culture generally, people in universities would rarely mix with people with learning disabilities; fleetingly few social situations exist in which interaction between these social groups would be possible, much less expected. The University of Aberdeen

---

[1] Because we have friends who prefer various terms regarding their relationship to disabling conditions, we will alternate between person-first language and identity-first language throughout this chapter. It is our intention to honor the preferred terms of individuals, but many of those individuals diverge in their terminology.

Friendship House was established precisely to explore ways in which these essentially distinct communities can develop together in a genuine place of hospitality, welcome, and belonging.

Just as individuals in any community are shaped by the presence of friends, institutions, too, deserve to be invited to be transformed by the presence of Christlike friendships. The advantage to the University of Aberdeen is that such presence broadens and deepens its perception of both education and the full meaning of being human through the power of witness across social boundaries buttressed by social convention. But lowering the barriers between the university and society at large, usually crossed only to study those whose lives are lived outside the ivory tower through the lens of research and scientific analysis, requires significant trust in those who are leading the endeavor. However, it was not simply the well-respected name of John Swinton that validated the idea of the Friendship House for the university. His insights into community formation also showed this initiative to be a potential answer to a significant problem faced by many not only in the Aberdeen area but also across the world: namely, that "disabled people are more likely to experience social isolation and emotional loneliness than the nondisabled population" (MacDonald 2018; see also Tarvainen 2020; Olsen 2018).

THE VISION

The aim in forming Friendship House was to explore what community might look like if each person in the community were allowed to shape and form what Friendship House was to become. We were committed to the Friendship House as a constant and never-concluded journey, as the community is continuously shaped by the people who come into it. The aim of Friendship House was to transcend the demand to be just "one more thing to do," or to be yet another line of accomplishment on the CV. The essence of the social space we were seeking in Friendship House was to be one free from the demands to perform and from any culture of competition. Rather, this community was prepared from before its inception as a space in which all are welcomed to come, dwell, and belong—and in that space, encounter one another.

St. Mary's Parish Church, located directly across from the university, graciously offered their building as a hosting site for many of the Friendship House gatherings. It is a community with its own deep history of disability engagement. Its willingness and graciousness allowed this new community the much-needed space to emerge. Other local organizations have been happy to come alongside to participate and aid in this initiative, and the ever-changing array of faces in each meeting ensures that every gathering is a unique and open experience. Friendship House gatherings often include time spent together eating, enjoying a cup of tea, and drawing pictures together. At times we've sung, played American football, and shared Thanksgiving meals. Time is spent with one another in moments of both laughter and tears—sometimes concurrently. A regular practice of dining together in smaller groups helped establish getting to know one another more deeply.

Although disabled experiences are varied, perhaps to the point of being resistant to the same social label, in some real material sense "disability oppression . . . is a logic bound up with political-economic need and belief systems of domination" (Charlton 2000, 22). This is not to claim that any two disabled people will share more in common than any disabled person and nondisabled person, nor that oppression ought to be considered the normative framework for defining disabilities (Swinton 2012, 176). It is primarily an assertion that there are socially expressed beliefs and logics forced on disabled people that lead to negative experiences the church must seek to remedy. In Aberdeen and in Western society more widely, this logic excludes folk with disabilities from social spaces. Those without disabilities likewise must suffer by living in a world bereft of a section of our siblings in Christ. As Dietrich Bonhoeffer (upon whom Swinton regularly draws in his writings) demonstrates, all such "exclusion of the weak and insignificant, the seemingly useless people, from a Christian community may actually mean the exclusion of Christ; in the poor brother Christ is knocking at the door" (Bonhoeffer 1954, 38). This exclusion hurts disabled people and nondisabled people alike, albeit unequally; both are unable to live in the fullness of community and diversity present within the body of Christ. To be part of a solution to this problem, the Friendship House must offer a new hope to the world by practically living an expression of an alternative ethic—a theme found time and time again throughout Swinton's writings.

CHARITY AND REHABILITATION

Not only the written theology but also John Swinton's practical labors have been fundamental to the emergence and continuance of the Aberdeen Friendship House. Without his theological insights into what it means to truly belong rather than to merely be present, this work may have defaulted to the usual ways of articulating the relation of the church to people with disabilities: namely, positioning them as recipients of charity or rehabilitation. Many charity efforts already dot the country, relying on a specific form of instrumentality (i.e., *from* the person with social power *to* the person without) foreign to the concept of a friendship based in mutuality.[2] At their collective root, charity models claim that there is a discrepancy between what various people possess, placing the focus on conditions external to the individual. Given this analysis it is not accurate to label the Friendship House a charity since it does not seek to rectify an imbalanced system. We certainly agree that persons with disabilities need better access to goods most of us value highly (health care outcomes, voting rights, living situations, etc.), but the intent is not to make a broken system work better. Rather, the Friendship House seeks to build a new social economy rooted in presence rather than production. This is not to disparage charities but to practically respond to Swinton's constant challenge to attempt something beyond charity.

Similarly, rehabilitation efforts (by which we mean any program designed to help someone "overcome" a disabling condition through training) are plentiful and often manifest as job training or specialized education. These efforts can be individually ameliorative and useful, but ultimately they derive their power from the promise of transformation of some deficient identity. In the space of the university, most disabled students are offered help to "overcome" their disability and still succeed in their academic careers. Or, if the disability makes them unlikely to study at the University of Aberdeen, some may be offered a job "supporting" the university in the food services or as custodial staff. Again, Swinton's work challenges this framework of production, asking communities to instead acknowledge a call for transformation *into* communities of friends. This is to argue that the aspects of persons *as they currently exist* are worthy of friendship without the need for developing some new skill or way of being in the world. As Swinton (2016, 99) notes, "the pattern of the Gospel is not that we choose Jesus but that Jesus chooses us." Christian friendship, then, isn't based on the premise of a person becoming more useful over time. The Friendship House is instead interested in acknowledging that receiving one another without respect to what can be value-added is a gift. This requires a "divine point of view," which allows for a deeper concept of "vocation" as something not based on transaction but as "a network of neighbourly love wherein God's providential work is carried out" (Swinton 2016, 103, 119).

[2]   Cf. Charlton's critique of charity efforts that make disabled people into objects that reify hierarchies of power; and Beauvoir's contention that charity is an act that forces a recognition of shared and mutual agency (see Charlton 2000 and Beauvoir 1948).

HISTORY

Identifying and planning a practical manifestation of these ideas while avoiding the pitfalls of preexisting methods takes time. And indeed the journey of Aberdeen's Friendship House is one of many years. In 2014, when Stanley Hauerwas served as chair in theological ethics at the University of Aberdeen, he, L'Arche cofounder Jean Vanier, Professor Brian Brock, and John Swinton held a conversation on how university spaces might open up to the message of L'Arche communities.[3] The results pointed Brock and Swinton toward seeking university approval and funding for the Friendship House, to try to concretely and institutionally instantiate the vision described above.

Since its launch, the Friendship House met regularly to build relationships across the community with disabled people, social-support services, students, faculty, staff, and local faith leaders. We were slightly over two years into welcoming people into this communal journey when the COVID-19 pandemic disrupted our standard practices. As such, our terminology and understanding of what Friendship House is, was, and will be, has changed, grown, and deepened in ways no one could anticipate. Just as the specifics of the Aberdeen Friendship House were not immediately apparent to Swinton in his first engagement with it, the future of this initiative is also veiled to all.

It is important to note that the Friendship House is not Swinton's personal endeavor. There are several dedicated leaders, visionaries, students, volunteers, and participants who make up this community and perpetuate the practices and ethos which mark the Friendship House as a site of communal care. Yet Swinton's involvement and continued passion should not be ignored or discounted. The vision of Friendship House cannot be separated from the work that Swinton has done not just overtly in organizing it but also in spiritually and theologically guiding this movement since its inception. In fact, Swinton has been involved in this work for far longer than the official story of the University of Aberdeen Friendship House. In reading Swinton's earlier

---

[3]   We acknowledge and mourn the abuses perpetrated by Fr. Thomas Philippe and Jean Vanier as spiritual guides of L'Arche. It is our intent to name Vanier here to be open and honest about the lived history of the Aberdeen Friendship House, not to valorize his participation. Friendship House is greatly indebted to our friends at L'Arche for both practical help as well as spiritual support, and we continue to celebrate the work they do in creating communities across the globe (see L'Arche International 2020).

academic work, and even before, the same themes on which this community was founded are clearly present.

SWINTON'S THEOLOGY PREFIGURES THE FRIENDSHIP HOUSE

Before his entry into the world of academic teaching, John worked as a nurse for sixteen years, specializing within the areas of psychiatry and learning disability. He also spent several years working as a hospital chaplain, specifically a community psychiatric chaplain. The work of the Aberdeen Friendship House must be explored through Swinton's writings on **practical theology, experience, disability**, and **Christ**. An investigation into his corpus shows how the emergence of the Aberdeen Friendship House, or something like it, has long been a potential outworking of his work.

Practical Theology

Swinton's theology is deeply oriented toward enacted practices and committed to reclaiming practical theology as a field of primary inquiry rather than a list of helpful tips for ministers. In an early article, he notes that "practical theology seeks to utilize the Kingdom of God as a critical hermeneutic, which can be used to test and determine the authenticity and faithfulness of the practices of the church" (Swinton 2003, 66). Swinton's more recent work (Swinton and Mowat 2016, 24) builds on this idea, stating that practical theology is "critical, theological reflection on the practices of the Church as they interact with the practices of the world with a view to ensuring faithful participation in the continuing mission of the triune God," with an aim to not simply "understand the world but also to change it" (Swinton and Mowat 2016, 26). Thus, for Swinton all theology requires engagement with this practical bent.

Certainly, there are aspects of working alongside disabled people that might offer insight into how to care for, love well, and befriend every person, disabled or not. Swinton found in the course of studying L'Arche that "practices [such] as spiritual direction, contemplation, friendship, hospitality and gentleness . . . [open a] balanced, trinity-centred model of pastoral care which is applicable not only to the care of people with profound developmental disabilities, but to all people. This of course is exactly as it should be. In the end, people with profound developmental disabilities are no different from anyone else" (Swinton 2003, 77).

Still, the practices are not simply a list of strategies that describe theology but are deeply theological themselves. Elsewhere, Swinton (2007, 81) refers to these as "communal enactments of God's redemptive movements within creation" and "forms of embodied theology that communicate and reveal meaningful theological truth." Even as far back as his PhD thesis, Swinton highlights how friendship is rooted in an actualization of the *imago Dei*: "The relationship of friendship creates an environment, or better, a space, within which individuals can experience themselves as they are, as whole-persons and learn to understand what it means to relate to others as whole-persons" (Swinton 1997, 232). Thus, friendship is a process, one marked by freedom, mutuality, reciprocity, care over instrumentality, and cruciform sacrifice (Swinton 1997, 236).

Experience

While Swinton (2018, 36) writes that "we assume that certain ways of being in the world are a waste of time," it is equally clear that his life's work and academic focus is consistently critical of this social "disableism" (Swinton 2014). His work as a hospital chaplain and mental health nurse gives credence to his findings, highlighting that his practical theology is not rooted in the *idea* of experience but in lived experience. The personalization of practical theology is another way in which Swinton's work is foundational to the Friendship House. As Swinton himself summarizes,

> we are called to the difficult work of creating good communities. Good communities include diversity and difference based on a conviction that we cannot be whole without others being different from us; in such communities people can be different without regret. In building good communities we must act from conviction deep enough to overcome our fear of difference and safeguard our temptation to either separate those who carry frightening differences away from us or attempt to discipline them into simulacra of a tame and bland normality. (Swinton 2005, 46)

Disability

The experience of creating community among people with serious mental-health challenges, learning disabilities, and other forms of difference actualizes practical theology. This is centered on concepts of disability that must be narrated through the lens of faith (and disability to narrate faith) to refute the world's claims on both the importance of categories of *right* and *wrong*, as well as what fits into those categories (Swinton 2008, 14). Disability, to both Swinton and the Friendship House, is certainly still an important concept that ought not be written out of theological assessment. The negative connotation and oppression must be addressed, but dependence cannot be conflated with these terms.

> In my experience, personal contact often dissolves the perception of difference that separates people on the basis of intellectual disability; unusual movements, unique ways of communicating, strange appearances, and obvious limits in learning often fade when people meet each other in almost any ordinary setting. What does not dissolve is the reality of dependence: This person needs specific and unusual assistance or accommodation from most others every single day. The asymmetry generated by dependence continually tempts those who offer assistance and those who receive it to freeze themselves into postures of power and dependency that obscure gifts and distract from taking the next steps in a shared journey. (Swinton 2005, 49)

Swinton (2012) notes that disability, while impossible to define in ways that don't include and exclude people in problematic ways, can be understood through proper categories. "Elderly people, people with dementia, people with intellectual disabilities, are best understood as *disciples* with a *vocation* that is not invalidated and does not end because we are old or have some degree of brain damage" (Swinton 2005, 189). Thus, disability ought not be placed solely in the realm of *pastoral care* but must instead be accepted as a particular form of "God's choice and command" for the work of our lives (Swinton 2005, 191). This could include, and does so for everyone at various moments, "the vocation to be cared for" (Swinton 2020, 196). Although this is not distinctive to those with disabilities and cannot be used for any sort of definitional work, Swinton's theology is rooted in reading the category of disability as a hermeneutic by which we receive the greater awareness of a creation dynamic in which care, dependence, and friendship are mutually extended within all human relations because these vocations were first given to us by God.

Christ

Swinton's rationale for critiquing independence, a claim central to his understanding of disability, is found in a theology explicitly focused on the practical experience of Christ. Following Karl Barth, Swinton seeks a Christocentric approach to definitions and engagements with disability as a theological concept. In reaching back for Barth's *soteriological objectivism*, Swinton pulls definitions of disabilities (and all truth) away from phenomenology and into the work of Christ (Swinton 2016, 185). Swinton's notion of community, as well, has long been dependent on naming the work of God for its institution. There is simply no community in which one can be dependent freely and safely without the centrality of God's grace. This is a unifying claim, bringing together the disabled and nondisabled alike. Explicitly, Swinton takes Hauerwas to task for maintaining "an outsider role" in talking about communities with intellectual disabilities.

> He does not ask his listeners to consider how to move beyond the separating out of "the retarded" as a group that draw the limits of human community, maybe in part because he has a notion that "the retarded" are somehow a distinct human group. . . . I think the oversimplification matters because it underestimates the role of God's grace in sustaining the hard work of building community. (Swinton 2016, 49)

Likewise, he writes (Swinton 1997, 240) that "all are called to become friends of Jesus, and all find value by reason of their shared humanity. Thus, they become equal, even in the midst of their diversity as each one shares in the common friendship of Jesus." The notion of a Christ-centered community weighs heavily on this account, derived not from a distanced and idealized notion of what community might in principle be but from a deeply rooted understanding of living and praying with people with disabilities. More than mere "christoform," or that shaped like the person and ministry of Jesus, these communities are actively produced by the Spirit through the person of Christ. Christoform community and social structures are those which lend themselves to certain analogies of Christ's life or ministry, such as the practice of itinerant preaching or challenging hegemonic social institutions. In contrast, Swinton's practical expansion of his theology leads not to a modern analog of Christ's life but to a present-day experience *with* Christ.

For some, but importantly not all, the presence of disabling conditions leads to theological questions on the presence of suffering. Some within the Friendship House struggle with some aspects of their disabilities, whether regarding physical pain, social ostracism, or discomfort with the limits of their bodies and minds. Some do not. But for those who do, Swinton reminds us that formal logic breaks down when confronted with experience. His solution is not to explain away evil or suffering but to be reminded of the power and presence of Christ. For Swinton, gestures that are reminiscent of the cross do not adequately explain or eradicate evil but rather prevent it from taking the last word. Swinton's theology ties the experience of the world, especially when heart-breaking and challenging, with the experience of the cross; the cross is not something ideal or abstract but something real in which we can and should participate (Swinton 2007).

Likewise, joy, laughter, friendship, and community are not explained by some expression of logics and ethics. Rather, these moments are marked by the presence of the living Christ, who teaches us how to be friends. Our experiences matter, as does cruciform living. Swinton's written response to theodicy highlights this link, which has been made abundantly true in his own life. What follows below are examples of how the larger umbrella of Swinton's Christocentric, disability-minded, and experiential practical theology unfolds within the Friendship House. These stories ultimately point to other aspects of his theology—worship, personhood, and friendship—which can be seen to fall under this wider rubric.

INAUGURATING THE FRIENDSHIP HOUSE

We hope that it will have become clear why Friendship House was an institutional initiative that flowed directly from the central emphasis of John's theological writings. And at the heart of this body of written theology lies the claim that Christian faithfulness, and indeed theology, is embodied; learned not purely by the reading of texts but also through observing the relationships of our mentors—mentors like Swinton. Swinton's theology of disability and friendship is a theology of practice; and Swinton as a person embodies this theology in his personal interactions. Therefore, for those unable to visit the Aberdeen Friendship House in person, the best way to discuss Swinton's theology in practice is through stories.

The first Friendship House meeting was marked by a time of prayer and worship; a space in which we shared our hopes and dreams for the future over generous pours of coffee. As Swinton led us through worship and prayer, it became apparent this was the beginning of a community of vulnerability, friendship, and belonging. The moments of worship and prayer embodied the ethics and values that the Friendship House was designed to encourage and stood as a foundational moment in fixing our trajectory.

It was clear at this first meeting that Friendship House was a sort of antithesis to the academic world of the university, where a person's "worth" is often conflated with grades, the number of papers published, or the prestige of one's job title. This ideology—that a person's value is tied to their ability to perform—is precisely what the Friendship House was founded to challenge.

The first community event also consisted of worship, with people in attendance from the university, local community, and L'Arche. It was an evening of dining, creating communal art, spending time together, and

Fig. 1.1 A participant places a foot coated in red paint on a white canvas, which shows previous handprints and markings in colorful paints from other participants.

meeting people who would continue to shape and form the Friendship House community. Like most Friendship House events, there was time for people to get to know one another, share food, and take part in activities together. Everyone who came was invited to dip their feet in paint and walk across long strips of paper (fig. 1.1), creating a colorful and messy display of fellowship.

Stephanie, one of the several long-term visionaries of the Friendship House project, offered a speech summarizing the history and vision of the Friendship House to the public who had gathered. She, like many others in Aberdeen, longed for a place where people with intellectual disabilities are not only welcomed and accepted but also seen as essential members of the community. Like John, she believed that to be "included" was far less important than to "belong" (Swinton 2012). Following Stephanie, John led everyone in a time of worship; that both the private and public instances of inaugurating the Friendship House were paired with acts of worship highlights the connection between worship, disabilities, personhood, and friendship in practice.

SWINTON'S THEOLOGIES OF WORSHIP AND PERSONHOOD

In *Becoming Friends of Time* (2016), Swinton draws a deep connection between the act of worship and the necessity of properly defining personhood. In telling of Graham and Elizabeth, two elderly people with dementia living in a care facility (an example similar to experiences John surely has encountered in his past work as a mental-health chaplain), Swinton offers a challenge to the scientific understanding of memory as a necessary component of the self. As dementia impairs memory recall, individuals find themselves "dislocated in space and time" and alienated from the life they once lived (Swinton 2016, 136, 140). However, Swinton's story of Graham and Elizabeth participating in a worship service helps underscore his contention that both memory and worship are always *about* something beyond the autobiographical person. The tactile, embodied, and deeply sensual experience of a worship service points to a truth about the nature of personhood; by worshiping something outside oneself and by making memory and action "*about* something," the human breaks the shackles of Cartesian notions of mind/body dualism (Swinton 2016, 152). If memory involves the whole body and is sustained by God, then that people with advanced dementia like Graham and Elizabeth have forgotten specific things (even very important things) is not dehumanizing in the way that disabilities are often deemed to be in our world. Rather, "our existence is redescribed and reinterpreted as we realize what it means to be in Christ," which is likewise to be included in the worship that all of creation offers back to God (Swinton 2016, 186).

This tie between existence and worship describes a "theological dimension to our understanding of personhood wherein our ultimate value is maintained by God rather than tossed around by the vicissitudes of unpredictable human relationships" (Swinton 2021, 175). To be disabled is, in some sense, to be the vector which highlights the necessary shift in theology from personhood to citizenship. Perhaps, that is as much of a definition of disability as one can truly offer (Swinton 2012, 187). Swinton's work on personhood and disabilities relies on thick descriptions of lives that are not merely political entities or social constructs. Rather, the ways in which all people participate in a worship-filled creation calls us back to the rich description of *politically informed spirituality*. This tasks us with "bring[ing] something of the heavenly into the present" (Swinton 2021, 179), a challenge enacted and embodied by John through his gift-giving practices within the Friendship House.

FRIENDSHIP

It was the Friendship House's first Christmas together and thus our first time hosting a Christmas event. We were fortunate to host a carol service at King's College Chapel, the University of Aberdeen's beautiful

Fig. 1.2 John (left) and Steven (right) play guitar for a carol sing. Both are sitting between the pulpit and altar in King's College Chapel, Aberdeen, UK.

foundational building. We had planned that John would lead music, guiding those in attendance through each carol. In planning meetings leading up to the event, one of the members of Friendship House, Steven,[4] offered to join John and together lead the group in song. Steven was happy to bring his own guitar and mentioned his excitement to lead numerous times before the event. As the guests poured into the fifteenth-century church on the day of the carol service, Swinton took his place at the front of the chapel with his guitar to adjust his microphone and to tune his guitar. Soon after, Steven arrived and set up his place. Both appeared ready to lead, but it quickly became apparent that while Swinton was musically gifted and knowledgeable, Steven was not formally trained in the ways of the guitar. Although eager to be in the privileged spot at the front, his exuberance and joy exceed his training. However, as the two of them sat at the front, strumming away on discordant chords, Swinton continued to encourage Steven in his guitar-playing skills (fig. 1.2). He was quick to communicate with Steven about which carol was coming up next and made no indication whatsoever that the music coming from Steven's guitar was in any way less valuable in that holy space. Ultimately, he made space for Steven to step into a place of leadership, ministry, and vocation. This public witness stood in stark contrast to the historic and powerful church setting around them—a place that is often not welcoming to those who are different.

---

[4] We have used pseudonyms to protect the anonymity of individuals.

As John and Steven continued to lead us in times of worship, carols, and hymns, it became apparent that this interaction was much
more than simply singing together; this was Swinton's theology in
action. It was an action that depicted respect for the other and challenged implicit biases and injustices (Swinton 2000, 32). John's respect
for Steven was evident in the way he welcomed Steven to the front
of the chapel and respected his musical abilities. He did not try to
silence Steven, nor did he try to teach Steven to play the chords or
read the music; rather, John encouraged him to strum along, using the
skills and gifts already present to lead the group. What may in many
ways seem like a small act of inclusion was more than just a practical
way to include Steven; it was an action that shifted and blurred the
boundaries of leadership. It was an activity that demonstrated the core
ethics of Friendship House: that each member has ownership of the
community and what it is, and is able to minister to others. It was an
act of resistance to ableism and to the unjust oppressive views placed
upon friends who live with a disability. In acting so John resisted the
unjust view that those at the front of church, who lead worship and
minister to us, are only those who have a certain level of "ability" and
education. Rather, the opening of space for Steven to lead worship
alongside Swinton spoke of Christian friendship. In this, John was living out the challenge that "the task of the Christlike friend is not to
do anything for them, but rather to *be* someone for them—someone
who understands and accepts them as persons; someone who is with
and for them in the way that God is also with and for them" (Swinton
2000, 143).

Swinton (2000, 39, 43) writes of Christian friendships as relationships marked by unconditional acceptance and commitment to others.
These friendships are radical relationships that transcend relational
boundaries and are a powerful force of liberation and rehumanization
for those on the margins. Unfortunately, those who have an intellectual
disability, physical disability, or mental-health challenge are often the
most vulnerable in society. They are spoken of in tones of condescension, detachment, and pity. Relationships involving disabled people are
not often thought of with respect to equality or mutuality.[5] However,
Swinton's work on friendship and disability makes people confront

---

[5]   "To be a disabled person means to be discriminated against. It involves
social isolation and restriction. This is because of an essentially inaccessible socio-
economic and physical world" (Barton 1998, 56).

their ableist and disableist biases[6] and their unjust views toward those who sit on the margins.

Looking at the interaction between Swinton and Steven through this lens of Christian friendship further highlights the practical application of Swinton's theology. In the moment of the carol service, Swinton has unconditional acceptance for Steven (and his questionable musical abilities). His actions may be small, but they demonstrate that Swinton was not concerned with the quality of the music or how loudly people sang along. This is not because Swinton lacks in care for music or worship, nor because he lacks discernment of which chord progressions fit with "Joy to the World." Rather, Swinton enacted his theology, signifying an intentional privileging of acceptance over a certain accuracy of musical notes. The space for Steven at the front of the service to lead worship was an active and tangible way to show Steven he was seen, accepted, and desired within the Friendship House community. He is not a bystander but an integral part of the corporate body; without his presence, the service would have been different and very likely worse. Through this interaction, Steven is not placed on the sidelines or margins, as is so common for people with his disabilities, but brought to the center. His friendship with John, and, indeed, the rest of the friendship community transcends traditional boundaries and transactional expectations for people who live with a disability. Whom society often deems as someone-to-ignore, the Friendship House made space for at the very heart of the community. It is through the actions lived out by John and the rest of the Friendship House community that Steven's personhood is reclaimed.

Steven is known in this community as someone who loves his local football team, is keen to be a part of the leading of the Friendship House, and thrives when he feels included and seen. This is a far cry from the ways society shuns and dehumanizes disabled persons. It would be unfair to claim that Steven's acceptance is due purely to John himself. However, it is Swinton's definition of friendship and, indeed, his examples of friendship with those on the margins that highlight a radical friendship that truly reflects the role of Jesus; it is this radical mode of friendship that the members of this community follow.

Therefore, when it comes to learning Swinton's theology, it is important to not think of it in a cerebral or detached manner. Rather, Swinton's theology on disability and friendship is oriented toward those who

---

[6]   *Ableist* denotes actions and beliefs which actively privilege those who lack disabilities at the expense of disabled people, whereas *disableism* is defined as attitudes and actions which are actively discriminatory toward people who are disabled.

are marginalized and alienated; it is a theology that stands against such injustice and oppression. It is a theology based not in the head but in the heart. It is a transformative theology requiring sacrifice, evaluation (and often re-evaluation) of the things that we hold on to and the ways we spend time with one another. Swinton's enacted theology of disability does not allow us to think ourselves into a new way of being but requires us to be and act—and in so doing, our thinking is forever changed.

FRIENDSHIPS IN SMALL ACTS

It is evident that Swinton's experience stands in the background of the whole of his work on friendship; for Swinton, friendship must not be an abstract theological concept. Rather, it is crucial that friendship be something embodied and enacted. The church must embody its calling to live as friends of God and one another. In so doing, it may also awaken to its many malformed understandings of what it is to be human and what it means to have value and worth.

Swinton (1997, 57, 77) understands friendship as something located in the context of God's redemptive eschatological movement, and this is important for understanding the significance of friendship in the ministry of the church. For Swinton, the church is called to live in the friendship of Jesus. As Swinton (2000, 142) notes, "Jesus' friendships were always personal, as opposed to instrumental, [and] primarily aimed at regaining the dignity and personhood of those whom society had rejected and depersonalized." More than just patterned after the relationships between Jesus and his friends, this model of friendship finds its place in the life, death, and resurrection of Jesus (Swinton 2000, 9). Friendship sees the other as loved by God and thus resists societal norms that often degrade, stigmatize, exclude, dehumanize, and marginalize people (Swinton 2000, 10, 17). Additionally, friendship fosters a space where people can relate without being bound by false identities but as they are; it is not static but dynamic and ever-changing (Swinton 1997, 78–79).

Swinton's theology requires us as embodied creatures to "be" and act, and not just think ourselves into a new way of being. Likewise, in the Gospel of John there is a repeated invitation to "come and see." It is an invitation to be with, to dwell with, and encounter this person of Jesus. Having explored Swinton's theology of friendship in the specific context of the inaugurations of the Friendship House and the Christmas carol occasion of Swinton and Steven, what follows is an invitation to the reader to come, see, and experience the Friendship House in its everydayness, not as an abstract concept or way of thinking but as human beings encountering one another.

We might say such an understanding is in part what Swinton is pointing toward; that is to say, Christlike friendship that requires an encounter and dwelling with Jesus. One cannot simply "think" themselves into dwelling with Jesus. It takes an encounter with the person of Christ and a true "dwelling with." In befriending those who lacked social space, much like many of our friends in the Friendship House today, Jesus shifted the balance of power from the oppressive center to the margins that redeem the center.

If one were to walk into a Friendship House gathering, one would see people gathered around tables, enjoying tea and biscuits together—a Friendship House staple (fig. 1.3). Tea, coffee, and biscuits are a constant presence at Friendship House gatherings; there is always time to sit down and enjoy a cuppa with someone. You may see that some people have stood up to refill their cups, or maybe they are passing a football back and forth, doing their best to avoid hitting the hanging ceiling lights. Others might be drawing pictures, or just talking. Perhaps you are seated next to Sarah, both of you quietly drawing flowers together. You enjoy each other's presence, and at some point she looks at you, smiles, and quietly reaches out with her hand to touch you gently on the nose. Over the other conversations, you hear Andrew's deep and contagious laughter from across the room. In another moment, he is filled with tears, openly expressing grief over a loss. Now having switched seats, you are sitting next to Carolyn, who has brought her notebook and invited you to read and listen to her latest poem. She shares with you a written prayer, then asks you to gaze at her recent drawings as she explains what they mean to her. Finally, on your way to grab another biscuit, you encounter Peter, who quietly reaches out and greets you by placing his hand over your mouth. The gesture may surprise you if you do not know Peter. But it may also begin to dissolve any distance you felt there was between you and him as he extends his hand toward you to touch your face, and you know that your presence is noticed; you are seen.

At a subsequent Friendship House gathering, a group has come to play traditional Highland music. Glen invites you to dance with him. You hesitate, knowing your own lack of dance experience and rhythm, and you wonder what others will think. You picture how you will appear stumbling along, but you take his hand and agree. You do in fact stumble, trying unsuccessfully to learn the dance as you go, but soon you are laughing and you realize no one seems to mind that you don't know the

Fig. 1.3 Five people are gathered and two hold up a plate with a "birthday donut" while many who are not pictured join together in singing "Happy Birthday."

steps well, least of all Glen. The embarrassment you might have felt in another situation fades away and you start to think maybe your performance doesn't matter, and all that matters is that you are here. The next week, there is a dinner gathering of a few people and Carolyn and Andrew are teaching you how to make their favorite lasagna recipe. You experience the joy of being taught something new from friends, and the joy of seeing your friends excitedly share with you their recipe. You enjoy a delicious meal made together. And then there are no Friendship House gatherings that week, and it's the middle of a very busy season. You are stressed about work when you see you have missed three phone calls in a row from Pauline. Part of you is slightly annoyed and you wonder why your friend can't seem to recognize you might be busy, but then she calls again and this time you answer. She asks, "How you keepin'?" as she always does. And you talk for just a few minutes when she abruptly says "OK, bye" and hangs up. And you wonder why you were ever frustrated and think, why don't more friends call, and call, and call, until they reach you, simply to ask, "How you keepin'?"

These small anecdotes may not offer much. It would be better if readers could simply come along and see for themselves. However, these stories suggest that these Friendship House gatherings are spaces where one's "performance" does not matter. What you can produce is not relevant, though it is still celebrated. The ethos of the community is one where your presence is important; to belong is not about producing or competing or pretending to be someone you are not, but simply to come as you are.

CONCLUSION

The four-part framework of Swinton's theology of disability (practical, experiential, disability-focused, and Christ-centered) challenges the church to take an active and participatory role in creating spaces that can connect worship, personhood as politically informed spirituality, and friendship. Swinton highlights how one must engage in community, offering one's gifts and delighting in the sharing of others', with these experiences informing the theological narratives and questions that the academy seeks. In small actions, and larger stories, Swinton's participation in the Friendship House offers a telling insight into the ways in which disability theology transforms every person involved.

WORKS CITED

Barton, Len. 1998. "Sociology, Disability Studies and Education: Some Observations." In *The Disability Reader: Social Science Perspectives*, edited by Tom Shakespeare, 53–64. London: Continuum.

Beauvoir, Simone de. (1948) 2018. *The Ethics of Ambiguity*. Reissue ed. New York: Open Road Integrated Media.

Bonhoeffer, Dietrich. 1954. *Life Together*. London: SCM Press.

Charlton, James I. 2000. *Nothing about Us Without Us: Disability Oppression and Empowerment*. New ed. Berkeley: University of California Press.

L'Arche International. 2020. "Summary Report." www.larcheusa.org/news_article/summary-report-from-larche-international/.

Macdonald, Stephen J., Lesley Deacon, Jackie Nixon, Abisope Akintola, Anna Gillingham, Jacqueline Kent, Gillian Ellis, et al. 2018. "'The Invisible Enemy': Disability, Loneliness and Isolation." *Disability & Society* 33, no. 7: 1138–59.

Olsen, Jason. 2018. "Socially Disabled: The Fight Disabled People Face against Loneliness and Stress." *Disability & Society* 33, no. 7: 1160–64.

Swinton, John. 1997. "From Bedlam to Shalom: Towards a Practical Theology of Human Nature, Interpersonal Relationships and Mental Health Care." PhD thesis, University of Aberdeen.

———. 2000. *Resurrecting the Person: Friendship and the Care of People with Mental Health Problems*. Nashville: Abingdon.

———. 2003. "The Body of Christ Has Down's Syndrome: Theological Reflections on Vulnerability, Disability, and Graceful Communities." *Journal of Pastoral Theology* 13, no. 2: 66–78.

———, ed. 2005. *Critical Reflections on Stanley Hauerwas' Theology of Disability: Disabling Society, Enabling Theology*. New York: Routledge.

———. 2007. *Raging with Compassion: Pastoral Responses to the Problem of Evil.* Grand Rapids: Eerdmans.

———. 2008. "Introduction." In *Living Gently in a Violent World: The Prophetic Witness of Weakness*, by Stanley Hauerwas and Jean Vanier, 9–20. Downers Grove, Ill.: IVP Books.

———. 2012. "From Inclusion to Belonging: A Practical Theology of Community, Disability and Humanness." *Journal of Religion, Disability & Health* 16, no. 2: 172–90.

———. 2014. "What the Body Remembers: Theological Reflections on Dementia." *Journal of Religion, Spirituality & Aging* 26, nos. 2–3: 160–72.

———. 2016. *Becoming Friends of Time: Disability, Timefullness, and Gentle Discipleship.* Waco, Tex.: Baylor University Press.

———. 2020. "Disability, Vocation, and Prophetic Witness." *Theology Today* 77, no. 2: 186–97.

———. 2021. "Re-imagining Personhood: Dementia, Culture and Citizenship." *Journal of Religion, Spirituality & Aging* 33, no. 2: 172–81.

Swinton, John, and Harriet Mowat. 2016. *Practical Theology and Qualitative Research.* 2nd ed. London: SCM Press.

Tarvainen, Merja. 2020. "Loneliness in Life Stories by People with Disabilities." *Disability & Society* 36, no. 6: 1–19.

2

Exploring the World through a Theological Lens

"Swintonian" Practical Theology

Henk de Roest

INTRODUCTION

I start my contribution to this book by presenting some of John Swinton's personal experiences that have shaped both his faith and the characteristic elements of his theology.[1] I then share what I believe is a critical interview moment in which Swinton reveals, albeit modestly, what he hopes to contribute to the world through his life. Such close examination of these experiences and of Swinton's "disclosure" informs the structure of this chapter. And I seek to answer the following questions: What is Swintonian practical theology? Is there is a distinctly "Swintonian" kind of practical theology, and, if so, what is it?

First, in an interview from early 2020, John Swinton states that "once you hang around with people who are different, you will become different" (Swinton 2020c, transcript). In this citation I hear him say that if you spend time with people you are likely to end up taking on their perspective. "Hanging around with people" implies spending a long time with people, which undoubtedly changes you, and perhaps the more different a person is the more likely they are to change you. During the interview,

---

[1]   I wrote these lines and the first paragraphs of this chapter in the last months of 2020. In February 2021, when I was completing this text, I purchased (for just €39!) an article by John Swinton, which I did not have access to via our library database. The article contained Swinton's keynote lecture, delivered at the twenty-fifth anniversary of the British and Irish Association of Practical Theology (BIAPT). To my surprise, in this text he states, "Practical theology is an organic, contextually defined discipline that is highly dependent upon the formation and interests of the particular theologian" (Swinton 2020g, 164).

Swinton talks about the many instances in his life when he spent time with people who perceived the world in completely different ways than he was accustomed to: "You know, people with psychotic experiences, people who don't have language, people with dementia who really are entering into places that none of us really know" (Swinton 2020c). In my words, they explore unknown worlds and thereby demonstrate how "our world" has its boundaries and how "our perspective" has its limits. Swinton talks about how their perceptions altered his own perceptions, how they influenced his own imagination, and how their exploration of the world led to different stories about the world. In a 2014 article in which he offers some theological reflections on dementia, Swinton writes, "My journey into theology has been an interesting one. For many years of my life I worked *alongside people* [emphasis added] to whom contemporary theology and practice often struggle to understand and respond faithfully—that is, people with enduring mental-health issues such as schizophrenia, and those with profound intellectual disabilities or profound cognitive dysfunction such as stroke or advanced demen-tia" (Swinton 2014b, 160). Here we discover how the people he "hung around with" profoundly influenced his theology, challenging him to "understand and respond faithfully." These experiences had some major consequences. Swinton came to realize that theology is never only about beliefs or concepts, but, rather, as he puts it elsewhere, "the conceptual elucidates the practical" (Swinton 2020f, 104). The way we talk about something, the language that we use, determines "*the way we see it and act toward it*" (Swinton 2017c, 191; emphasis added). In addition, he dis-covered that the people one hangs around with play a significant role in one's own formation. This had consequences for his later view of the local church and his favoring of a high level of diversity within it. Peo-ple with all their different abilities and all kinds of disabilities have a vocation within the body of Christ. Finally, Swinton was struck with awe about the impact of spiritual practices in this specific context. He often refers to his experiences as a chaplain, expressing his wonder about what bodily and soulfully participating in a ritual does for people with severe dementia: "When I offered people the Eucharist their bodies reached out and responded even when their minds no longer seemed able to grasp the intellectual complexities of the practice" (Swinton 2014b, 161).

The second experience also had a formative influence, though in a dif-ferent manner. In an interview from 2011, John Swinton explains how he was a minister's son and that this made it difficult for him to escape from church. There was a time when the church as inescapable reality led to the church having no attraction for him whatsoever: "If you are made to go to church, you learn to associate it with extreme boredom" (Swinton 2011). Yet even here he was "hanging around" with some close friends, and this made him perceive the world through their eyes. In between the lines, we read that he lost the faith of his childhood, but then we also read about how his friends' faith became his faith and that he thus discovered what it meant to live faithfully. "What brought me back to faith was seeing a group of friends suddenly become Christians, for no particular reason I could see. There was a significant change in their lives which embodied a possible transformation that was going on" (Swinton 2011). We see how the people he identified with and felt affection for were people that went through a phase of discovery in which they realized that we are not left alone in this universe and that there is a God. They influenced him in this observation of the world, and they opened his mind to new thoughts. However, this was not just an intellectual matter. Their faith also moved his heart and thus changed his life: "It made me rethink. I'd heard a lot of noise, but only when it touched my heart did it become something in which I wanted to invest" (Swinton 2011). Considering these experiences, we see an attentiveness to the other. The young John noticed a transformation in the lives of his friends, and we see that this transformation made them—–and thus him—take a different stance and take up a different view of things in the world. The effect was not just that he was "struck" by this change, but that it made him "rethink" life. He "heard a lot of noise," but in this "noise" he felt that "his heart was touched." The consequence was that he became motivated to "invest" in faith. It is again evident that understanding—and being touched—elucidated practice. Additionally, we also see how the people Swinton hung around with played a significant role in his spiritual formation.[2]

The two experiences highlighted above are already instructive, but perhaps even more so is a fragment of the last part of an interview from 2011. It is shortly after his fifty-fifth birthday, and all of a sudden Swinton modestly, but frankly, reflected on what he considers his possible contribution to the lives of others. If an epitaph suggests something about the

---

[2]   It is fascinating to see how the two personal, formative experiences and the disclosure come together in Swinton's most recent book *Finding Jesus in the Storm*. In it he describes how people living with unconventional states of mental health might experience God in unique ways "that are real and perhaps even revelatory" (Swinton 2020d, backcover). *Per consequence*, the church should, with compassion, "hang around with" people experiencing depression, schizophrenia, bipolar disorder, and related difficulties and learn from them. I have not included a consideration of this new book in this chapter.

meaning of a person's life, he would like his tombstone to read: "John Swinton made a little bit of difference to people's lives, and *helped them to see the world slightly differently*" (Swinton 2011; emphasis added). The phrase "slightly differently" is a modest expression. What is striking is his hope about offering the world a new perspective. Somewhat later in the interview, it becomes clear how this new perspective differs from other perspectives: "As a theologian, I think our task is to *counter the way most people see the world*, through the media and so on" (Swinton 2011; emphasis mine). I believe the word "counter" is what matters most. Both here and in his earliest writings, we notice how John Swinton was aware of the effect of labeling. Labels, concepts, and understandings—both of ourselves and of the people we "hang around with"—are not neutral or objective but actually *productive* of reality; they affect people's lives. Labels can be attached to people by the media but also by the sciences. Here, too, the lives of people with perceived cognitive deficits, how they are labeled, and how they disclose strange, unexplored worlds opened John Swinton's eyes. It became his conviction that practical theology, as a *theological* discipline, should come up with other terms, labels, and understandings, and he decided to use a more encompassing term, "perceptions." What's perceived is indeed the same world, but it is God's world and that enables people to see the world "slightly differently" and to "counter" other perceptions of the world.

The two experiences and the disclosure discussed above provide us with some glimpses into what I consider to be the core of Swintonian practical theology. This core consists of five elements or aspects that are distinct but belong together. Swintonian practical theology consists, first, of a specific experiential-dynamic understanding of perception, which is explicitly emphasized even as of late (Swinton 2020f, 104). Second, it perceives the world through the eyes of faith as being God's "strange" world. Third, it performs all four methodical steps of practical theology, namely, describing what is going on, interpreting why it is going on, discussing what ought to be going on, and suggesting how we should respond through a theological lens, which means that "finding God" governs the methodological design of every research project from the start. Fourth, it logically prioritizes this perception and understanding over other social-scientific lenses or the lenses of the media. Fifth, practical theology's purpose is to use qualitative research in order to create practical wisdom, not for the sake of knowledge itself but to enable faithful Christian living for the benefit of the world. These five elements will structure the chapter.

WHAT IS "SWINTONIAN" PERCEPTION?

In his opening lecture at the conference of the International Academy of Practical Theology (IAPT) in Oslo in 2018, Swinton compares the psalmist's perception of the world to that of Martin Luther. Following Walter Brueggemann, Swinton states that psalms "restructure" our experience so that we "see the world in quite particular ways" (Swinton 2019, 5). Psalmists can provide orientation, disorientation ("no longer seeing the world in the way . . . used to" [Swinton 2019, 8]), and reorientation, and, within one and the same psalm, the perspectives may shift in profound ways as the psalmist starts to remember God's unending and faithful love. First, there is every reason for lament and complaint, but then there is a memory of God. Swinton asserts: "The horror of the fearful moment remains, but is profoundly re-conceived by the memory of God's unfailing love. The psalmist begins to *perceive* things differently. He looks out at the same situation, but he perceives it quite differently" (Swinton 2019, 8; emphasis in original).

This reorientation leads to a different feeling and a different response. The psalmist does not revert to the first perspective, but rather adopts a radically new perception. It is an "eschatological newness," in Swinton's words, "a newness that respects the significance of what has been, but opens up new vistas for understanding and faithful living in the present and on into the future" (Swinton 2019, 8). Regarding Luther, Swinton underlines this same structure of perception. In Luther's days the church saw itself as glorious and powerful, yet Luther, shaped by an "ongoing emersion" in the "strange world that is revealed within the Bible" (Swinton 2019, 8), perceived the church in a radically new and different way: "Luther's scriptural formation meant that he looked at the same things as everyone else was looking at but perceived them quite differently. His changed perception was intended not to reject all that had gone before, but to reorient it and put it to its proper purposes" (Swinton 2019, 8). For Swinton, perception can imply radically new orientation, but it can also imply disorientation and reorientation, and all three things—orientation, disorientation, and reorientation—affect practice and lead to a reconsideration of the purposes of one's own actions or the actions of others. Thus, according to Swinton, perception is not merely seeing or observing. Rather, it encompasses seeing, feeling, acting, and being aware of the consequences of actions. It reminds me of the German concept *Wahrnehmung*, which holds these same intricate connections between seeing the world, providing it with an orientation, and acting. In an earlier article ᴜɴ ꜱports, Swinton writes that words, concepts, and images are important, and talking is important, but also that language not only describes worlds but also creates worlds. Swinton is not so much interested in the act of *defining* something (providing a precise definition so that we then seem to know what a phenomenon *is*); rather, he states that we come to know a concept by perceiving the impact it has on practice and thus we are able to understand the meaning of a concept. We will see that Swinton follows Ludwig Wittgenstein when we see how this approach functions. I offer four different examples to illustrate this.

First, in his highly acclaimed book *Raging with Compassion* (with theodicy as its basic theme), we fail to find a "dislocated," philosophical, intellectual solution to the problem or conundrum of evil (Swinton 2007b). Such reflection is not unimportant, but it is a "second-order activity." Swinton is less interested in explaining evil than he is in practices of resisting evil, and in how evil and suffering can be overcome, changed into good and well-being, and what a faithful response to evil entails (just as in the Joseph story in Genesis). The book therefore analyzes the practices of lament, forgiveness, thoughtfulness, and friendship.

A second example of this approach is found in Swinton's view on the concept of spirituality. In 2007 Swinton draws on distinctions made by Joanne Coyle to describe two approaches to the concept of spirituality. First, he discusses the "hard science" approach mostly found in the United States, which tries to establish connections and correlations between religion (primarily Christian religion) and health benefits. The second approach is mostly found in the United Kingdom and fits the spiritual climate of a culture that assumes spirituality "relates to values, principles and ideals that do not necessarily relate to belief in the transcendent" (Swinton 2007c, 293). The latter approach focuses on the meaning of spirituality for the client, evident, in Swinton's case, in a 2001research project. This approach is aimed at enhancing good practices of care (Swinton 2007c, 302). Seven years later, Swinton writes that such definitions of spirituality in healthcare do not describe what spirituality is but what it does (Swinton 2014a, 163). In 2020 he nuances his view somewhat, writing that a discourse on what spirituality is can be useful and may provide some intellectual clarity. It may lead to a wide diversity of intelligent understandings, yet he adds that each definition will always be a "narrow understanding." It is more beneficial if we relate it to practice and thus to the impact that spirituality has: "There have been many valuable conversations around what spirituality *is*. However, I think there is mileage in slightly reframing this issue and further drawing out the points I made ten years ago by focusing on what spirituality *does*" (Swinton 2020a, 8).

Swinton quotes Wittgenstein in stating that his "practice-oriented theory of language" enables us to see that "spirituality does not get its meaning from dislocated intellectual reflection alone. Rather, its meaning emerges from the impact that it has on practice" (Swinton 2020a, 11). It is by *engaging* in spiritual practices that we come to understand what spirituality is. In a 2017 response to Edward Frick, Swinton calls it a "practical concept" (Swinton 2017b, 225) in the sense that the concept acquires meaning in the context of specific practices, namely, the practices of a particular community. Swinton references Wittgenstein as he talks again of "key ideas and concepts" that cluster around spirituality—and also around spiritual care—such as meaning, purpose, hope, value, love, and God. But these concepts also "function like a Wittgensteinian language game" (Swinton 2017b, 225). Swinton adds that the same can be said about "elusive" concepts such as care, health, and community. These concepts, which he calls fuzzy and vague concepts, have a "transformative power" (Swinton 2017b, 226). We should add that we do not understand Swinton correctly here if it is about *applying* concepts in practice in order to transform the practice. Rather, the relationship is reciprocal; seeing enables acting, and as we act we learn to see. These "elusive" concepts may teach us to see differently and thereby to act differently.

A third example that has consequences for the critical task of practical theology (to which we will later return) can be found in Swinton's warnings against how we name things. In practice, concepts may function as labels through which people can be framed. Indeed, by its influence on perception, naming is in itself a practice. In 2014 Swinton writes that naming determines how people are perceived and the ways in which they are treated (2014c, 235). Over the years he emphasizes again and again that the act of naming someone a person or nonperson is a "dangerous practice" (2014c, 235). This warning against naming is also explicitly articulated in his reflections on the term *disability*. It may be necessary to use this term, but then "the ways that we use to define disability can simultaneously bring liberation and oppression and sometimes even death" (Swinton 2012a, 173). Definitions can have devastating consequences for practices.

A final example can be found in Swinton's response to Wilco Van Holten and Martin Walton on the concept of God's timelessness, as expressed in Swinton's book *Becoming Friends of Time*. According to Swinton, in this book he was not interested in defining God's timelessness in terms of what it *is*, but rather he tried to explore "what certain experiences look like in the light of Divine timelessness" (Swinton 2020f, 105). Swinton explains that he uses concepts not for clarification, though this is valuable, but "for the purposes of *illumination*" (Swinton 2020f, 104; emphasis in original). He states that he intended his book to be read as an exploration and reimagination of the practices that emerge from certain understandings of time. He goes on to explain how speaking about God's timelessness and using images such as "three mile an hour God" might make a difference in ("illuminate") the practices of chaplains and spiritual caregivers. The concept may have a performative effect on the practices of caregivers, making them respond more empathetically. Here we see that for Swinton it also matters that in these practices one "deals with" the *living* God, "the God whom people encounter in the world" (Swinton 2020f, 106). His interest is not simply in talking about the concept of "God" (Swinton 2020f, 106). According to Swinton, it is "the living God to whom pastoral carers strive to remain faithful" (Swinton 2020f, 106). Also, to better understand the experiences of people with dementia and brain damage, the notion of God's timelessness might *illuminate* "the sense of timelessness" (Swinton 2020f, 109), the concurrency of past and present, that people with dementia experience. This is not a direct comparison, but rather a helpful analogy from which we may learn. Swinton adds that perceiving—which I understand here as believing in and acting in accordance with—God's providence in relationship to dementia, brain damage, and personhood is also illuminating. Here he suddenly turns to a definition (albeit a helpful one): "Providence is God's faithfulness to uphold the integrity of what God has created" (Swinton 2020f, 110). It is a narrative account that makes God's hopeful story trustworthy. God's creative act will not "fall into oblivion" (Swinton 2020f, 110) and therefore neither will we.[3] With these last remarks we turn to the second element in Swintonian practical theology: faithful perception.

---

[3] In a recent article in *Theology Today*, on vocation, discipleship, and disability, we find similar reflections. Following Scott Bader-Saye, Swinton writes, "Providence provides a powerful story that ensures that in the midst of the fallenness, brokenness, suffering and confusion of God's creation, the beauty of God's story is not lost (. . .) Within such a narrative context, vocation is an opening up of our hearts to the callings of the Spirit in order that we can properly locate our narratives, and in so doing be enabled to participate faithfully within God's work in the world. Within this model of providence, all human beings have a vocation and a calling from God in which to participate. However, not everyone recognizes or chooses to respond to that calling" (Swinton 2020b, 190).

PERCEIVING THE WORLD THROUGH THE EYES OF FAITH

I believe it is safe to say that both Karl Barth and Stanley Hauerwas have influenced John Swinton in terms of his use of what we may call "faithful perception" as a core element of his practical theology. We might also call it "biblical perception," since time and again we see him draw from the "strange world" of the Bible. In his appropriation of this Barthian notion, John Swinton emphasizes that this world of the Bible is "filled with odd narratives, sometimes dysfunctional people and dissonant occurrences" (Swinton 2019, 9). Perceiving this strange—and I would add, this newly becoming—world to also be the real world has changed this world; and therefore it has the potential to change it again and again. According to Swinton, it "caused Luther to set in process a reforming dynamic" (Swinton 2019, 9) and it "drove Calvin to try to create 'a small piece of heaven on earth' in Geneva" (Swinton 2019, 9). It also "drives Pope Francis to embrace disabled people" (Swinton 2019, 9). This world within the Bible can "shape and form our perceptions, and transform our intellectual and bodily practices" (Swinton 2019, 9). In this regard, Swinton's *perception* can also refer to a framework, a hermeneutical layer (Swinton 2019, 6), or a Christian map of meanings (Swinton 2019, 11). It is this map or layer that provides orientation to the faithful but also reorientation and radically new orientation for practical theology. In explicit accordance with Barth, Swinton speaks of "an extra level of interpretation" (Swinton 2019, 6): "All events are open to a variety of inter-relations, all of them which may contain truth and significance. The difference is that Christians have an extra level of interpretation which situates all events within a broader, more all-embracing framework. It is this framework that allows them to perceive the event as an act of God" (Swinton 2019, 6). The biblical narrative is continued in the present and has (as I understand Swinton) the potential to transform our world and make all things new both in principle and in practice. This is not just because biblical stories, concepts, metaphors, and the like can shed rich and new light on the world, such as on the world and experiences of people with dementia or disabilities as Swinton demonstrates throughout his work. Neither is it just because such new insights may inform and change our practices of care, love, hope, and compassion. Rather it is also because the biblical narrative enables us to see *God in action*. Accrued over the years, Swinton's basic theological assumptions are that the world is created, that it is fundamentally good, that each human being is God's image-bearer, that the Trinitarian God is relational, and, by implication, that human beings are relational beings that find their goal in their relationships with God, humankind, and the world (Swinton 1997, 23; Swinton 2000; Swinton 2017a, 153–84). God also continues the work of creation. The New Testament narrative also enables us to see that we are not only individuals, each living our lives independently of others, but that on a deep and radical level people baptized into the body of Christ live in God's presence; they belong to Christ and therefore to each other. In his book *Becoming Friends of Time*, Swinton writes:

> As people are baptized into the body of Christ, so they enter into a space of deep and radical belonging. Within the body of Christ, every body has a place, and every body is recognized as a disciple with a call from Jesus and a vocation that the church needs if it is truly to be the body of Jesus. . . . The truth of who we are is hidden in Christ. (Swinton 2016, 208)

I believe that the notions of "being in Christ" or "receiving one's identity in Christ" have become more and more important in Swinton's appropriation of Barthian theology over the years. Indeed, these originally Pauline notions also "refounded" his perception of the world. In his keynote lecture at the opening of the IAPT conference in Oslo, he credits Karl Barth for having introduced the idea of soteriological objectivism as "a way of framing what it means to be a creature" (Swinton 2019, 10). Thus, we see that it is not only the biblical narrative that informs a faithful perception but also what Clare Watkins calls a *formative* theological voice. In an explanation of Charles Hunsinger's soteriological objectivism, it strikes Swinton that this concept "opens up a whole new way of viewing the truth about who we truly are" (Swinton 2019, 10). Who we are, and who we think we are, is not who we have become. Who we are is not our personality, or our character, or the "result of our biography"; it is not the sum or the mean of what others think of us. Rather, who we truly are is given and found in Christ, and Swinton adds that our identity is hidden in Christ. Again, this faithful perception of our identity is not just an understanding or a definition of who we are. Instead, it illuminates our identity and thus it may have a performative effect. This performative effect can be especially observed if it is ascribed to, and "applied" or appropriated by, someone who has experienced a break with his or her past. Such a break could be caused by an accident or crisis, and possibly followed by a change in one's personality. The illumination offered by this understanding implies the realization that ultimately no change in one's personality can affect this "grounded" and "immovable" identity in Christ: "Paul's reminder of the true source of identity refounds this experience and offers a different point of orientation and a different set of responses" (Swinton 2019, 10).

How does this performative effect "work"? What kind of practice is needed for it? In his book *Becoming Friends of Time*, we find texts that Swinton cowrote with Tonya Whaley, who suffered traumatic brain injury. Here she writes that her family and friends told her that her personality had changed. Reflecting on the impact of the brain injury on who she has become postinjury leads to similar thoughts: "There was a fracture in who I was and who I had become"; "there is a mourning for that self-confident person that I used to be"; "you change" (Swinton 2016, 178). In a sense she became a stranger to herself and even speaks of a "live death" (Swinton 2016, 196). Whaley and Swinton speak of an "experiential reality that things have changed, sometimes quite radically" (Swinton 2016, 193). They speak about a "critical tension" between this experiential reality and the "theological foundations of [their] identity," a tension without which theology will become irrelevant and practice ill-informed. Both emphasize that people (such as Tonya) need theological advocates "who can help articulate the complexities of their experiences" (Swinton 2016, 193). However, people can also advocate for themselves, and in both cases practical theologians have something to offer that relates to what Swinton and Whaley (following Susan Marie Smith) call *experiential* effectiveness and *theological* or doctrinal effectiveness. There is the experiential reality that is narrated—speaking about the before and after, the effect of the fracture, the grief and pain that is witnessed and that is listened to—and there is the "hermeneutical layer" of doctrine "which enables Christians to see God more clearly, to imagine God properly" (Swinton 2016, 194). Experiential effectiveness "informs us of what doctrine *feels* like and *looks* like" (Swinton 2016, 194; emphasis in original). It is about embedding and embodying doctrine within one's experience. According to the authors, we need "timefull practices" (Swinton 2016, 194) for this purpose. For Tonya Whaley, keeping in mind the doctrine of our identity being grounded and hidden in Christ, while also being fully aware of the tension or dissonance between belief and experience, turned out to be experientially effective. She took ownership of the fact that she had passed a point of no return. She decided to create a particular form or ritual, namely what she called a "lived funeral" (Swinton 2016, 203) for the "old Tonya," in which friends and family told stories of the Tonya "before" and "after," expressing lament and grief but also their love for her and the hope that the bridge between before and after was the sustaining presence of Jesus. This ritual, with its central liminal phase, helped her to "embody doctrine" (Swinton 2016, 201). Later, Swinton writes that "the theology that suggests that her identity is both held and hidden in Christ has proven to be deeply healing and helpful for her as she works out the continuity of her identity within her new situation" (Swinton 2020f, 112). Clearly it is not that the "horror" of the injury, or even of the perceived reality of personality change, is overruled or glossed over, but rather that a new, helpful perspective was offered *and* experienced in the ritual.

Now, if offering faithful or biblical perception, or even "doctrinal perception," is essential for Swintonian practical theology, and if these perceptions are essential for practical-theological perception to be able to orient, reorient, revision, and refound our identities and our world, then we should also name Stanley Hauerwas as an influence. Even in his first publication in 1974, Hauerwas wrote about the Christian idiom, arguing that in the church we learn "'to see' the world under the mode of the divine" (Hauerwas 1974, 46). Later he further developed this view of Christian perception. In 1987 Hauerwas argued that the church is the continuation of the biblical narrative into the present (Hauerwas 1987). In 2001 we read that according to Hauerwas descriptions matter. To touch on just one example, it matters that the one we care for is a creature of God, or a brother or sister for whom Christ died, rather than just a "person" (Berkman and Cartwright 2001). In his book *Raging with Compassion*, John Swinton refers to Hauerwas' view on Christian parenting, which has important consequences for our attitudes toward children with disabilities (Swinton 2007b, 195ff). Christians do not perceive children as their products or, albeit subliminally, as "customizable commodities" subsumed to parental desire. Instead, children are viewed as gifts rather than possessions. Christians perceive having children as a vocation. In his article "What the Body Remembers," Swinton describes the church as the place where we are trained to be faithful. He writes that when this fellowship consists of the people "we hang around with," then between and among them we get to know the stories of redemption, and between and among them we learn what following Jesus means, what it looks like, and what it feels like (Swinton 2014b). Here we learn the grammar of faithful perception, which informs not only the mind but also the body. This is the language and these are the stories that form us. In accordance with Hauerwas, it is the language and practice of the church as a faithful manifestation of the "peaceable kingdom in the world" (Hauerwas 1983, 99) that shapes our inner selves. According to Swinton, this language has consequences for the deepest levels of our identity, for when we learn this language, sing it, get to know it by heart, and live by it, this is the language that we will always recall and that may revive us, even if our cognitive functions are impeded. Practicing the kingdom means shaping our bodies accordingly: "Such learning contains formal didactic components, but much of the education we receive within the church goes unnoticed—it is implicit, precognitive and subtly physical rather than cognitively formative. As we practice the Kingdom, so our bodies take its shape" (Swinton 2014b, 163).

To conclude this section, and as a bridge to the next, biblical and doctrinal perceptions of the world summon the practical theologian to live, so to speak, in the world of the Bible and the Christian tradition. To be an empirical theologian, one first needs to be a biblical and systematic theologian first! This is what Swinton labels "*refounding*," namely, "returning to our core documents and traditions in order to look differently at situations and experiences" (Swinton 2019, 12). For example, in an article on medication, Swinton dwells on the Westminster confession of faith, stating that "human life before God has a quite particular intention and direction" (Swinton 2018, 308), which informs our faithful perception of human life. Practical theology goes back and forth, from the Bible and tradition to a situation, and from the situation back to the Bible and tradition; the first is foundational for the second. However, what does this mean for the first step in practical-theological research? We need to consider the role of the theological lens in the process of observation.

PERFORMING PRACTICAL-THEOLOGICAL RESEARCH THROUGH A THEOLOGICAL LENS

Practical theology explores the world (Swinton 2019, 12). With this simple statement, John Swinton describes the domain of practical theology. It is neither the church, nor Christian practices, nor religious practices, nor practices related to "the sacred" (to name some of the recent descriptions of the domain of practical theology); rather it is the wide, wide world. In this world, practical theologians are theological explorers. They are on a journey of discovery, and they invite us to join them in this journey. Following Swinton on this journey, we see him exploring the fields of dementia, brain damage, and disability, and of spiritual care as it engages with these fields (but he also analyzes sports and medicine). However, as Swinton writes in 2019, it is not just "the world" that practical theologians explore; it is *God's* world. Earlier, in their well-known and oft-used book, *Practical Theology and Qualitative Research* (published in 2006, with an updated second edition in 2016), John Swinton and Harriet Mowat sketched the domain of practical theology as "the practices of the Church as they interact with the practices of the world with a view to ensuring faithful participation in the continuing mission of the triune God" (Swinton and Mowat [2006] 2016, 24). In the various case studies in this book, the starting point of research is a situation that is explored. A range of different qualitative-research approaches and methods are applied respectively to understand the situation.

Now the question is, How are theological exploration and analysis of a situation precisely related? In their book Swinton and Mowat are not always crystal clear about this, though they primarily locate theology in what they term the "third phase." This is a moment in the cycle of research that occurs after analyzing the complexities of a situation, and after choosing the appropriate method (Swinton and Mowat [2006] 2016, 93). Let me explain by referencing a figure that Swinton and Mowat present, and which entails a refinement of the well-known pastoral cycle that consists of seeing-judging-acting. Here, practical-theological reflection starts with "current practice," namely, the identification of a practice or situation that requires reflection (Swinton & Mowat [2006] 2016, 90). It is an intuitive phase, in which the researcher articulates what appears to be going on, begins to formulate initial observations, and works out some key issues as they try to attain a preliminary understanding. The second stage is the stage of the disciplined investigation called "qualitative research," which helps to develop a deeper understanding. It is also the stage of cultural/contextual analysis. At this stage, particular approaches and methods chosen may differ. For example, hermeneutic phenomenology may be used to assemble a cohort and create interview questions. A hermeneutic approach is chosen to enable participant observation and interviews, while an ethnographic approach may be taken which encompasses telephone interviews, studies at different case sites, and second sets of interviews. At this stage, data such as interview fragments, codes, fieldnotes, and the like are also analyzed, often with the help of computer software. Then, in stage three, "we begin to reflect theologically," though Swinton and Mowat add that "this is not of course to suggest that theology has been absent from stages 1 and 2" (Swinton and Mowat [2006] 2016, 91). However, now it is a "more overt" theological reflection. In stage four, both cultural/contextual analysis and theological reflection are "drawn together" to "produce new and challenging forms of practice that enable the initial situation to be transformed into ways that are authentic and faithful" (Swinton and Mowat [2006] 2016, 92). Somewhat later, and as a structure for the six research projects that they present, Swinton and Mowat summarize the cycle as a pattern: "the situation" is followed by "the method," which in turn is followed by "theological reflection," and finally leads to "suggestions for revised forms of practice" (Swinton and Mowat [2006] 2016, 93).

While in this pattern, theology is firmly located in the third stage; there is a tension here. This is because, as I understand John Swinton, the heart of the "practical-theological gaze" engages the world (and therefore every situation) from the outset of a research project, with theological, that is biblical and doctrinal, attentiveness. Not only does this have consequences for *interpretation*—that is the answer to the *why* question—but it also has consequences for the *observation* of the situation. Theology governs the methodology from the start. In 2012 Swinton is himself more overt about this when he writes about ethnography, claiming that "theologians who desire to use ethnography as part of their theologizing should approach the issue as theologians. Ethnography should be perceived as occurring within a theological context, rather than theology speaking into a context that is already defined by ethnography" (Swinton 2012b, 87). The tone is quite firm, buttressed by the additional claim, "Theology should assume the right to have a methodological voice that is deeply *influential on the process of observation*, the methods used, and the ways in which the Christian ethnographer's look is shaped, formed and practiced" (Swinton 2012b, 90; emphasis added). Clearly, theology is not absent from stages one and two, and in their book Swinton and Mowat should have been more outspoken about the consequences thereof, as we find it throughout Swinton's entire oeuvre. Practical theology has a strong interest in the empirical, but for the practical theologian the empirical world is not conceivable without a theological lens. It is not that practical theology collects and "uses" empirical data to reflect upon interview fragments (or sermon fragments, survey answers, or fieldnotes stemming from one's own observations of practices) and then interprets these data theologically. Furthermore, it is definitely not that practical theology is primarily interested in providing indications about what ought to be going on. The data are not just "given," despite the Latin etymological background of the term. Rather, data collection is steered by perspectives, convictions, and basic assumptions, and for practical theology these are theological assumptions. Therefore, it is not that social-scientific analysis of a situation comes chronologically and methodologically in the first place and theology in the second place. Instead, social-research approaches, such as ethnography, are used *within* a theological framework. It is indeed a conversation, but it is a conversation in which practical theology appropriates social research methods by "converting" them to the service of God. This is confirmed by yet another Swintonian assumption to which we turn next.

Until now, it may seem as if the core elements of Swintonian practical theology primarily consist of elements that are shaped by theological frameworks, layers, and maps of meaning. If that were the case, the focus would then be on what Hans-Georg Gadamer would call hermeneutical pre-understandings (*Vorverständnisse*) (Gadamer 1990, 272f.). However, theological perception of a situation and collected data is not only about frameworks, or even deeper levels of meaning. For John Swinton the theological foundation of practical theology implies a fundamental openness toward at least the possibility of revelation, not only seen in hindsight but in the (perception of the) situation and data itself. Practical theology needs to be open to "finding God" in the fieldnotes. This is not to say that epistemologically speaking, contemporary experiences have a priority over the knowledge of God as it is conveyed in Scripture and tradition—since we've learned that we are shaped by this "strange world" of the Bible, doctrine, and the community of the faithful—but these experiences can teach us something about God in action. Precisely because this world is God's world, *disciplined* perception is needed. As John Swinton writes in a reflection on the practice of taking medicine faithfully, we perceive the world "in the light of what we know and understand about God and by implication what we know and understand about human beings in relation to God" (Swinton 2018, 303). Practices are potentially revelatory. In Swinton's work this is a recurring refrain articulated in its most concise form in an article from 2020: "practices are knowledge of God" (Swinton 2020g, 167; also see Swinton 2020d). From a social-scientific perspective, a helpful confirmation for this fundamental assumption of Swintonian practical theology is to view the domain of practical theology—namely, "practices of the church as they interact with the practices of the world" (Swinton and Mowat [2006] 2016, 24)—as so-called *interventionist* practices. Coined by sociologist Martin Riesebrodt in *The Promise of Salvation*, this term entails a nonreductionist social-scientific view of religion. Riesebrodt calls all practices that aim at establishing contact with superhuman powers interventionist practices. General religious practices are characterized by two major elements: "first, affirmation of the *reality* of superhuman powers; and, second, expressed in different ways, attribution to the practices the *power* to avert misfortune, overcome crises, and provide salvation" (Riesebrodt 2010, 75, 96; emphases added). In his theory of religion, discursive practices presuppose interventionist practices (Riesebrodt 2010, 85). When applied to Christianity, talking about worship, sermons, prayer, chants, and God and God's will and promises (e.g., in Christian everyday discourse or in Christian upbringing and education) presupposes practices in which contact with God is established. What would God want me to do? What is my vocation? What can I hope for? Such questions, and teaching and learning to believe in God, all presuppose the existence of interventionist practices. In Riesebrodt's theory of religion the same goes for normative practices that are regulated by morality and ethics. These practices are also justified by interventionist practices in which people not only "merely" believe in God but also communicate with God: "Without belief in the possibility of establishing contact with superhuman powers, religious discourses are '*relatively insignificant*' and behavior-regulating practices lack a foundation. The meaning of discursive and behavior-regulating practices becomes accessible through the analysis of interventionist practices, not the other way around" (Riesebrodt 2010, 86; emphasis added).

Following Riesebrodt, the existence and presence of God is assumed in practices of the church. This is true in not only worship, sermons, prayer, the Holy Supper, and funerals but also in new practices such as the funeral ritual designed by and with Tonya Whaley and in what I would call "ecclesial-shaped" everyday practices. If the existence and presence of God is not assumed, then these practices become less significant and their meaning is obscured. We understand them better if we presume God at work. For example, in hermeneutical pastoral care and in particular when someone opens his or her soul in prayer, the existence of a "Third" entity is assumed, even though the participants may have their doubts. This assumed "Third" provides pastoral care with a "structure of meaning": "No matter how many doubts an individual believer might carry around, in religious practice the existence of God is presupposed and confirmed in word and deed. This structure of meaning is public, observable, and reproduced over long periods of time" (Riesebrodt 2010, 100). Riesebrodt's theory of religion and the "structure of meaning" of religious practices converges with Swintonian practical theology. Having arrived at this point, we now ask: how does John Swinton himself describe the critical conversation between theological and social-scientific perceptions? We will focus our attention on this in the following section.

THE RELATIONSHIP OF PRACTICAL-THEOLOGICAL PERCEPTIONS TO SOCIAL-SCIENTIFIC AND OTHER "WORLDLY" PERCEPTIONS

In the introduction I referred to Swinton's assertion that practical theology needs to *counter* perceptions of the world and of the other as they are shaped by the media today and have become dominant in our society. As I understand him, perceptions of the media but also of psychology, neurology, and other sciences (and even perceptions born out of everyday family conversations or those we invent ourselves based on our experiential reality) may in our society have received a status of being "obvious" or "logical." Descriptions, such as the so-called personality change of Tonya Whaley, may, for her family members, friends, and also for herself, capture an obvious and true reality. Such perceptions may shape the words we operate with, and these words in turn shape our approach to the world and therefore to our practices. In his book *Raging with Compassion*, we find the term *counter* again. Here Swinton describes *ubuntu* ("I am, because you are") theology and its accompanying words, such as love and relatedness, as advocated by Desmond Tutu as a "useful counter" to Peter Singer's highly influential view of, and criteria for, personhood (Swinton 2007b, 201).[4] The consequences of these criteria are that a severely disabled infant who lacks cognitive ability is not considered a person. In the Oslo lecture, Swinton refers to John Locke who describes a person as a being with memory, imagination, and awareness, "a thinking intelligent being that has reason and reflection, and can conceive itself as itself, the same thinking thing, in different times and places" (Swinton 2019, 10; also Swinton 2017a, 239). Personhood is defined by the cognitive and social capacities that a person "possesses." In this sense, if someone loses these capacities or does not yet have them, this human being is not considered a person. Swinton states that practical theology needs to counter this view which has become a "cultural mantra" (Swinton 2015, 230) in our society and is also influential in psychology and neurology. The critique of this concept of personhood runs throughout Swinton's books and articles. For him, the theological perspective on relationality fundamentally alters our perception. As early as 1997, he writes this

---

[4]   In an article on Christian bodies, diversity, belonging, "we-identity," friendship, and being the body of Christ, Swinton states that the understanding that we are deeply interconnected is "inevitably dissonant with *Western* [emphasis added] understandings and perceptions of self and what it means to be 'me'" (Swinton 2015, 230).

with Esther Mcintosh: "A serious consideration of the relational nature of personhood can '*challenge*' and fundamentally '*reframe*' many commonplace ideas about personhood that derive from modern individualism" (Swinton and Mcintosh 1997, 176; emphasis added).

In a 1997 article in the *Journal of Religion and Health*, we read that "Enlightenment rationalism has taught us that reason and intellect are to be understood as our primary faculties" (Swinton 1997, 23). Regarding cognitive disability, Swinton disputes the suggestion that the inability to reason is incompatible with "spiritual experience and the development of authentic faith" (Swinton 1997, 23). Today, particularly in the public discourse on dementia, Swinton often still encounters—and wishes to counter—the view that "our value is often judged by our ability to think, act rationally, remember ourselves and others and participate productively within society" (Swinton 2020e, 173). He states that this view leads to a commonly held idea that is similar to that in the book he wrote with Tonya Whaley: that a person seems to be gone when suffering from brain damage. In 2007 Swinton writes that people with dementia suffer real loss, and indeed as a medical condition dementia can be defined biologically as a clinical state characterized by a catastrophic loss of function in multiple cognitive domains (Swinton 2007c, 41). Dementia is a "narrative of profound loss for both sufferers and for those who care for them" (Swinton 2007c, 41). Indeed, often "the person-as-we-once-knew-them encounters radical changes" (Swinton 2007c, 58). Yet when the notion of "forgetting" becomes the dominant feature of personhood, it becomes very easy to "forget" the personhood of people experiencing dementia. The view on personhood within liberal society is one of an autonomous, rational individual, but "as we relate, as we love, as we struggle to hold onto one another in the midst of the storms of dementia, we know intuitively that there is something more; that the person before us is of worth, is valued, is a person" (Swinton 2007c, 38). Swinton adds that through faithful perception we can recognize people as fully human, as persons related to and loved by God (Swinton 2007c, 58f.).

In a recent article on vocation, Swinton again counters an influential assumption that is comparable with the liberal, rationality-focused view of human beings. Vociferously he again states that the modern emphasis on reason, free will, and autonomy regarding vocation is a "mode of false consciousness" (Swinton 2020b, 191). Receiving a vocation is completely different from "trying to figure out what you can do with the rest of your life" (Swinton 2020, 192). Rather, vocation can be perceived, described, and acted upon as responding to God's call.

It is important to note that the word "counter" does not *necessarily* imply competitive frameworks of modernity, (social) science, or practical theology, as his discussion of neurobiological and theological discourses demonstrates. Swinton says the latter may be "richer" than what is accounted for in the former, though he adds that "they *can* clash" (emphasis in original). Although the two language domains may *conflict*, they may also "happen to *converge*" (Swinton 2020f, 113). According to Swinton, the phenomenon of personality change due to brain damage can be accurately described both psychologically and neurologically as a change in one's identity. This may seem somewhat complicated so next we will address the question, What do we learn from John Swinton about the relationship and differences between theological and nontheological perspectives? We highlight three aspects below.

First, in his Oslo lecture, Swinton stated that social sciences have their own specific assumptions which influence how a social scientist perceives a situation (Swinton 2019, 6). He goes on to argue that these assumptions, and their accompanying worldviews, limit sociopsychological, historical, ethnographic, medical, or psychiatric perceptions of a situation to "worldly terms," which implies that such perceptions lack a significant layer of interpretation. These perceptions are not necessarily invalid; they can be accurate and correct while still being limited. They often provide a helpful perspective but not the *only* perspective. Swinton is particularly concerned about the possible reductionism present in such viewpoints. As early as 2006, he calls it an "ever-present shadow" when discussing highly technologized healthcare. Interestingly, that article was not published in a journal on practical theology or chaplaincy but on clinical nursing (Swinton 2006, 918).

Second, throughout his work, we find incisive warnings about the strong effect that "overarching," dominating, or absolutizing social-scientific, biological, psychological, or neurological layers of meaning have on how we *value* persons, experiences, and things. These layers of meaning are what Swinton indeed wants to *counter* and *challenge*. In 2002, in a critical article on the relationship between science and chaplaincy, he emphasizes the need for a scientific "underpinning" to chaplaincy and for the need to legitimize its necessity within institutions of care. Thomas Moore uses the term *psychological modernism* to describe the values and understandings that make up the worldview of the modern world. This approach, with its empiricist focus on measurement and the quantifiable, cannot do justice to the "central tenets" of chaplaincy, namely, love, relationship, hope, transcendence, and meaning (Swinton 2002, 226).

Swinton writes that though statistics, numbers, and randomized control trials "offer us knowledge of human beings and human experience" (Swinton 2002, 227), on their own these dimensions of science restrict and narrow what human beings consider meaningful. He asserts that chaplains need to widen the understanding of healthcare "to incorporate the dimensions of being human which often fall outside the standard medical gaze" (Swinton 2002, 227). Chaplains should not surrender to positivistic science but should rather counter this understanding of science and the "techno-medical system," which have come close to being idolized. This scientific methodology is worshiped "at the expense of that which makes human living human" (Swinton 2002, 235). Ten years later, in a 2012 article on the terms *disability* and *inclusion*, Swinton counters political and social definitions of disability. He writes that they are formed on the basic tenets of the philosophy of modernity, which are "too thin to capture and value the richness of the experience that human disability brings to our attention" (Swinton 2012a, 179). Six years later, in a critical essay on taking medicine, Swinton warns against the "epistemological reach of neurology," which he calls "neuromania" following Raymond Tallis (Swinton 2018, 304). Swinton goes on to say that if biology and pharmacology dominate our understanding of mental health, they will lead to what he terms "pharmacomania." In these "manias" basic assumptions about humankind "narrow" our understanding, and "occlude the meaningfulness of people's experiences" (Swinton 2018, 307). Swinton is not blind to the positive effects of medication, and indeed medicine may even help people to relate to God. Mental-health experiences can be spiritually distressing. Yet the language of "neurological defects and deficits" is too limited, too narrow and too "thin" (Swinton 2018, 308) compared with the richness of viewing humankind's goal as the realignment of the human soul toward God's glory. Good mental health is not equivalent to getting rid of symptoms or even the absence of illness. Yet it is not only "thin" neurological, biological, psychological, or medical assumptions and language that dominate and shape our values and our response to the world. In an extensive analysis of sport, Swinton asserts, sport, too, has an absolutist "tendency implicitly or explicitly, to shape and form our perceptions of the value of certain types of body" (Swinton 2017c, 191). The focus in sport on power, strength, success, and competitiveness enforces the "norm of the able body" (Swinton 2017c, 192), and the "successful Paralympian" even becomes a "paradigm for the expectations of disabled bodies more generally" (Swinton 2017c, 192). Recently, in his book *Finding Jesus in the Storm*, analyzing the distinction between "thin" and "thick" descriptions as coined in the early 1970s by anthropologist Clifford Geertz, Swinton again refers to the "thinning" and "flattening" effect of medical and other languages: a thin description offers a "minimum amount of information" to describe a situation (Swinton 2020d, 14). Strange as it may sound, even spiritual language, when bound to the Western emphases on the individual self and self-actualization, can be a "thinning" language (Swinton 2020d, 34ff.).

Third, if practical-theological research helps to *reform* how we go about looking at things, it is structured by providing orientation but also by reframing and *reorientation*. Practical theologians "take a second look" at a situation and allow theology to change one's perspective, thereby enabling participants in the situation to respond differently (Swinton 2019, 8). Theological attentiveness (as Swinton calls it following Alister McGrath) respects and acknowledges other interpretations but opens up "new vistas for understanding and faithful living in the present and on into the future" (Swinton 2019, 8) based upon "the world as God is revealing it to us" (Swinton 2019, 9). As we saw earlier, relationality is a key concept here. For example, practical theologians might ask: what is the impact of medication on the soul? Medication can hinder but also *facilitate* a reconnection with God (Swinton 2018, 316). It is not that there are two realms, a "worldly" realm of the natural, biological, or bodily existence and a realm of the supernatural, God, theological, or soulful. As Swinton states, "God is not in any sense apart from our biological existence. He is the very sustenance that holds it in place. . . . The two are one: the biological is theological" (Swinton 2018, 309). Instead, the "second look" of the theological perspective or "frame" encompasses or *converges* with the biological frame, enabling even pharmacological interventions to be perceived both as a therapeutic means "designed to alleviate symptoms and ease distress" and as an "aid in the process of realigning the soul" (Swinton 2018, 309). Swinton describes reorientation as a process of redirecting the position of God in our understanding of healing from the "optional" to the "central": "Pharmaceutical healing is redirected from a purely biological and therapeutic task within which God is optional, and healing has simply to do with symptom alleviation, toward a theological framework wherein God is central and healing can be understood as an aspect of the human desire to connect with God, that is, to live into our soulfulness" (Swinton 2018, 310).

With regard to the social sciences, the second look of the practical theologian entails taking the results of psychological or sociological analysis, in which an assertion about God or a transcendent reality is not possible, or in which God is indeed only optional, and using these within a theological analysis, in which relational assertions about human beings, the world, and God are central (Swinton 2018, 310). If we understand Swinton correctly here, the "reality" of God, as experienced and understood by people, is a condition for research since faithful practices presuppose relationship with God. In Swintonian practical theology, social-scientific interpretations and theories find their proper place by *serving* practical theology. Using Hans van der Ven's distinctions, it is not an *inter*disciplinary conversation but an *intra*disciplinary appropriation of social-scientific theories and methods (Van der Ven 1993, 97–101). In retrospect we can clearly see this in *Practical Theology and Qualitative Research*. Here, methods and insights from the social sciences are used, interpreted, and evaluated within a theological, fundamentally relational, framework that is "operative" right from the start (Swinton and Mowat [2006] 2016). However, we need to be precise here since, according to recent "Swintonian" formulations, the social sciences should not be used for theological ends but rather should be used to "explore the real presence of God in the world" (Swinton 2020g, 170).

We could call this the "critical ancilla" paradigm, implying that some social-scientific methods, approaches, and theories may be better suited for this purpose than others. While some methods need a fundamental reorientation, others, though seemingly convergent with a theological perspective, need to be complemented by practical-theological perception. A good example of the latter is seen in the relational approach to personhood in dementia as advocated by neuropsychologist Steven Sabat (Swinton 2014c, 238), philosopher Robert Spaemann (Swinton 2014c, 242)[5], and psychologist Tom Kitwood. Swinton calls Kitwood's book a "classic" in which his definition of personhood ("a standing or status that is bestowed upon one human being by others, in the context of relationship and social being; it implies recognition, respect and trust") is considered important and "helpful" (Swinton 2020e, 173; 2007c, 45f.; 2014c, 242).[6] According to Swinton, Kitwood's definition "captures nicely something of . . . personhood as a gift that we bestow upon one another; it is

[5]   Robert Spaemann offers what Swinton calls a very important and "useful distinction" between properties/capacities and persons: "Human beings have certain definite properties that license us to call them 'persons'; but it is not the properties we call persons, but the human beings who possess the properties" (Swinton 2014c, 242). Spaemann also states that personhood comes with belonging to the human family.
[6]   Swinton refers to Kitwood 1997.

the product of being incorporated into a meaningful community that values *you* and cares that *you* are there" (Swinton 2020e, 173f.). Yet he hastily adds that this approach is problematic, because if people do not value specific human beings they *do* lose their personhood. If personhood is bestowed upon one human being by others, then a loss of community implies a loss of personhood, and then the people "who have lost their value in the eyes of many within society are in trouble" (Swinton 2020e, 174). Swinton asks with concern, How can we ensure that people are "committed or even obligated to offer the gift of value and relationship"? (Swinton 2020e, 174). We should not make personhood wholly dependent on human relationships and individual choice; it also requires legal structures and stable social structures (Swinton 2020e). Yet for Swinton a theologically informed understanding (read: perception) of personhood is also indispensable. It is a perspective in which "our ultimate value is maintained by God rather than tossed around by the vicissitudes of unpredictable human relationships" (Swinton 2020e, 174).[7] Regarding Robert Spaemann, who holds that personhood comes with belonging to the human family, Swinton writes, "One objection to Spaemann's position might be that whilst we may all be family, bound together by relationships of kinship, it is not immediately obvious why we should acknowledge these biological bonds in any kind of meaningfully positive moral way" (Swinton 2014c, 243). The reorientation provided by a theologically informed understanding entails that we care because we are loved and we love because we are cared for.

Interestingly, we also find the *reorientation* that practical theology can provide within the discipline itself. Swinton speaks of "category realignment" (Swinton 2020b, 188). Disability, aging, and dementia are often placed in the subdiscipline of pastoral care in theological education and research. Yet if we place the same "subjects" within the field of mission, community development, or youth ministry, the perception changes radically. Then the understanding becomes grounded in the enduring faithful practices of the body of Christ, in which all participate and learn from each other. Here Swinton shifts his focus to discipleship and vocation so that they may receive new meaning in the context of dementia and disability.

---

[7]   Swinton adds that if we would stick to an immanent conception such as Kitwood's then this requires legal and social structures, simply because "people do not inevitably gravitate towards the vulnerable. If people are left to choose, they often do not choose for people with dementia" (Swinton 2020g, 4).

Discipleship and vocation are profoundly important aspects of the Christian life with which we all need help in recognizing, nurturing, and sustaining throughout our lives. When we think in such a way the questions we ask are changed: What does it mean to love and to follow Jesus when you have forgotten who Jesus is? What does it mean to be a disciple with a vocation when you do not have the intellectual capacities that religion often demands for participation in the faith? If we miss the significance of this category realignment—from pastoral care to discipleship—we miss something crucial to the experience of disability and something vital for the enduring faithfulness of the Body of Christ. (Swinton 2020b, 188)

Pastoral care is still important since we all need to be cared for, but it is encompassed by a wider and richer understanding, a wider—and profoundly biblical and theological—perception of the body of Christ. Earlier, in *Becoming Friends of Time*, Swinton wrote that membership and discipleship in the body of Christ are the same thing, and that we need to rethink or reimagine discipleship. In contrast to the intellectualist or activist narrowing of the concept, we need to rethink discipleship in a way that truly recognizes that people with intellectual disabilities are disciples: "The pattern in the gospel is not that we choose Jesus but that Jesus chooses us" (Swinton 2016, 99). In this book he reflects extensively on vocation, calling the vocation of the profoundly disabled slow and gentle discipleship (Swinton 2016, 121ff.).

DOING PRACTICAL THEOLOGY THE SWINTONIAN WAY

Swinton does not aspire to offer a definition of practical theology, but rather he focuses on what practical theology does, the questions that it asks, what it works out, and the impact that it has on practices. For Swinton, gaining understanding is not enough. Keeping in mind this focus on the impact of practical-theological research on practices—and therefore the impact of perception in the sense described earlier—we can now properly understand Swinton when he asserts that for him practical theology is fundamentally action research (Swinton and Mowat [2006] 2016, xvi). According to Swinton and Mowat, action research is "a method of enquiry and practice which encourages controlled and focused change using the knowledge and expertise of those involved in the research setting" (Swinton and Mowat [2006] 2016, xvi). They connect "focused change" with the aim of practical theology, thus creating new modes of faithfulness. In 1946 one of the school's founding fathers, Kurt Lewin, stated that action research started with questions by practitioners from schools, minority organizations, and government institutions that approached him to do research on such topics as improving intergroup relations. Research reports focusing on description and explanation were only likely to mirror the surface and thus were not considered helpful. As Lewin wrote, "Mere diagnosis . . . does not suffice" (Lewin 1946, 37). Today, action research still investigates issues related to the concerns of practitioners and addresses them by planning and implementing changes. Reflection and action, and research and practice are held in tension, each informing the other. We have seen how this relationship "works" for Swinton. Seeing things more clearly enables acting more faithfully, and acting more faithfully leads to learning to see a phenomenon properly (Swinton and MacKinley 2016, 6). Although important to Swinton, diagnosis or (as his discussions of spirituality, spiritual care, theodicy, and vocation demonstrate) concept-clarification is not enough. Practical theology should enable, support, and lead to faithful practices. The discipline moves back and forth from practice to reflection to create practical wisdom and discernment, which enables faithful Christian living and the exploration of the world as God's world. Even in 2006 Swinton writes with Harriet Mowat that the purpose of practical theology is to ensure "faithful participation in the continuing mission of the triune God" (Swinton and Mowat [2006] 2016, 24). They also speak about a "movement towards faithful change" (Swinton and Mowat [2006] 2016, 25). We mentioned earlier that practical theology explores the world, but based upon the previous four core elements of Swintonian practical theology we need to add that theological perception or attentiveness indeed opens up the world in a faithful and even revelatory way. Theology may find traces of God and help people to see God's new world, that is, "what God is doing" amid practices.

Exploring the world in the light of the strange world of the Bible or of doctrine can entail countering the assumptions of social-scientific or neurological theories, of philosophical concepts—such as of personhood. And it can also lead to challenging cultural assumptions as expressed by the media or even other theological assumptions. Practical-theological perception implies a "slightly different, second look," trying to offer a thick, or even thickening description (Swinton 2020d, 79). In a recent article in line with Stephen Pattison's approach, John Swinton summarizes his view of what he considers to be the crucial task of practical theology: to ask questions that "deconstruct the world" and to counter and challenge assumptions and presuppositions that "undermine people's ability to see God's Kingdom" (Swinton 2020g, 166). As he gets older, Swinton uses the aforementioned "counter"-approach more and more since he is becoming increasingly concerned about the modern tendency today to "*frame*" (emphasis added) people both individually and communally. He adds that "deconstructive questioning" is "absolutely vital" in a culture in which we find a dominant "pathogenic anthropology" and in which people tend to use reductive frames and labels to describe people's identities (Swinton 2020g, 167). Thin concepts tend to impose a stigma on people (Swinton 2020d, 14). Earlier, we saw how critical Swinton is in terms of mainstream conceptualizations of personhood. He expects practical theology to ensure a deep reframing of some of the key assumptions that lie behind these philosophical conceptualizations which he believes are highly influential in determining what people in our societies currently fear most: namely, dementia. Both *de-* and *re*-construction need to be practical theology's top priority, which will turn practical theology into a "prophetic discipline" with an orientation toward "truth-telling" (Swinton 2020g, 167). It is precisely this orientation that requires both a faithful openness toward God and a position of nearness to the poor, excluded, and marginalized, which, in Swinton's pathway into practical theology, implies a nearness to people with mental-health challenges, dementia, or disabilities (Swinton 2020g, 168). According to Swinton (in accordance with Pattison, Lartey, Watkins, and others), prophetic practical theology also requires collaborative, conversational, or relational research approaches such as action research, participatory action research, theological action research, and collaborative ethnography. Swinton finds the development of international research networks such as the Ecclesiology and Ethnography Network highly promising.

As this book amply demonstrates, the major fields of research for Swinton are spirituality ("an appropriate subject for serious empirical research" [Swinton 2020a, 7]), healthcare, spiritual care, mental and physical health challenges, dementia, and disability. For a long period of time, he has been interested in the formative power of spiritual development, the impact of spiritual care, and the performative effects of participating in rituals. He is also more and more interested in congregations that, while acknowledging and honoring diversity and personal vocation, represent the body of Christ as communities of belonging. Finally, he calls on practical theology to take up a prophetic task in taking a stance against reductive frames, labels, and perceptions that affect practices of dealing with and caring for one another. Practical theology should perceive human beings and the world from the perspective of being created and loved by a truly relational God, and of being sustained through his salvific providence. This second look will help people to see each other and the world . . . slightly differently.

WORKS CITED

Gadamer, Hans-Georg. 1990. *Gesammelte Werke*. Vol. 1, *Hermeneutik. I. Wahrheit und Methode. Grundzüge einer philosophischen Hermeneutik*. Tübingen: Mohr Siebeck.

Hauerwas, Stanley. 1974. *Vision and Virtue: Essays in Christian Ethical Reflection*. Notre Dame, Ind.: Fides.

———. 1983. *The Peaceable Kingdom: A Primer in Christian Ethics*. Notre Dame, Ind.: University of Notre Dame Press.

———. 1987. "The Church as God's New Language." In *Scriptural Authority and Narrative Interpretation*, edited by Garret Green, 179–98. Philadelphia: Fortress.

———. 2001. "Must a Patient Be a Person to Be a Patient? Or, My Uncle Charlie Is Not Much of a Person, But He Is Still My Uncle Charlie." In *The Hauerwas Reader*, edited by John Berkman and Michael Cartwright, 596–602. Durham, N.C.: Duke University Press.

Kitwood, Tom. 1997. *Dementia Reconsidered: The Person Comes First*. Rethinking Ageing. Buckingham, UK: Open University Press.

Lewin, Kurt. 1946. "Action Research and Minority Problems." *Journal of Social Issues* 2, no. 4: 34–46.

Riesebrodt, Martin. 2010. *The Promise of Salvation: A Theory of Religion*. Chicago: University of Chicago Press.

Swinton, John. 1997. "Restoring the Image: Spirituality, Faith, and Cognitive Disability." *Journal of Religion and Health* 36, no. 1: 21–28.

———. 2000. *From Bedlam to Shalom: Towards a Practical Theology of Human Nature, Interpersonal Relationships, and Mental Health Care*. New York: Peter Lang.

———. 2002. "Rediscovering Mystery and Wonder: Toward a Narrative-Based Perspective on Chaplaincy." *Journal of Health Care Chaplaincy* 13, no. 1: 223–36.

———. 2006. "Identity and Resistance: Why Spiritual Care Needs 'Enemies.'" *Journal of Clinical Nursing* 15, no. 2: 918–28.

———. 2007a. "Forgetting Whose We Are: Theological Reflections on Personhood, Faith and Dementia." *Journal of Religion, Disability & Health* 11, no. 1: 37–63.

———. 2007b. *Raging with Compassion: Pastoral Responses to the Problem of Evil*. Grand Rapids: Eerdmans.

———. 2007c. "Researching Spirituality and Mental Health: A Perspective from the Research." In *Spirituality, Values and Mental Health: Jewels for the Journey*, edited by M. E. Coyte, P. Gilbert, and V. Nicholls, 292–305. London: Jessica Kingsley.

———. 2011. "Interview: John Swinton, Professor in Practical Theology and Pastoral Care." *Church Times*. November 2, 2011. https://www.churchtimes.co.uk/articles/2011/4 -november/features/interview-john-swinton-professor-in-practical-theology-and -pastoral-care.

———. 2012a. "From Inclusion to Belonging: A Practical Theology of Community, Disability and Humanness." *Journal of Religion, Disability & Health* 16, no. 2: 172–90.

———. 2012b. "'Where is Your Church?' Moving towards a Hospitable and Sanctified Ethnography." In *Perspectives on Ecclesiology and Ethnography*, edited by Pete Ward, 71–92. Grand Rapids: Eerdmans.

———. 2014a. "Spirituality-in-Healthcare: Just Because It May Be 'Made Up' Does Not Mean That It Is Not Real and Does Not Matter (Keynote 5)." *Journal for the Study of Spirituality* 4, no. 2: 162–73.

———. 2014b. "What the Body Remembers: Theological Reflections on Dementia." *Journal of Religion, Spirituality & Aging* 26, nos. 2–3: 160–72.

———. 2014c. "What's in a Name? Why People with Dementia Might Be Better Off without the Language of Personhood." *International Journal of Practical Theology* 18, no. 2: 234–47.

———. 2015. "Using Our Bodies Faithfully: Christian Friendship and the Life of Worship." *Journal of Disability & Religion* 19, no. 3: 228–42.

———. 2016. *Becoming Friends of Time: Disability, Timefullness, and Gentle Discipleship*. Waco, Tex: Baylor University Press.

———. 2017a. *Dementia: Living in the Memories of God*. 2nd ed. London: SCM Press.

———. 2017b. "Response to Eckhard Frick's Reflections on Spiritual Care." *Spiritual Care* 6, no. 2: 225–27.

———. 2017c. "Running for Jesus! The Virtues and the Vices of Disability and Sport." *Journal of Disability & Religion*, 21, no. 2: 189–200.

———. 2018. "Medicating the Soul: Why Medication Needs Stories." *Christian Bioethics* 24, no. 3: 302–18.

———. 2019. "Reforming, Revisionist, Refounding: Practical Theology as Disciplined Seeing." In *Reforming Practical Theology: The Politics of Body and Space*, edited by Auli Vähäkangas, Sivert Angel, and Kirstine Helboe Johansen, 5–12. Oslo: International Academy of Practical Theology.

———. 2020a. "BASS Ten Years On: A Personal Reflection." *Journal for the Study of Spirituality* 10, no. 1: 6–14.

———. 2020b. "Disability, Vocation, and Prophetic Witness." *Theology Today* 77, no. 2: 186–97.

———. 2020c. "Embracing Difference: Interview with Sarah Kift." Sanctuary Mental Health Ministries. Released January 30, 2020. Podcast, 46:07. https://www.sanctuarymentalhealth.org/2020/01/29/john-swinton/.

———. 2020d. *Finding Jesus in the Storm: The Spiritual Lives of Christians with Mental Health Challenges*. Grand Rapids: Eerdmans.

———. 2020e. "Re-imagining Personhood: Dementia, Culture and Citizenship." *Journal of Religion, Spirituality & Aging* 33, no. 2: 172–81.

———. 2020f. "A Timeless God? A Rejoinder to van Holten and Walton." *Health and Social Care Chaplaincy* 8, no. 1: 103–15.

———. 2020g. "What Comes Next? Practical Theology, Faithful Presence, and Prophetic Witness." *Practical Theology* 13, nos. 1–2: 162–73.

Swinton, John, and Elizabeth MacKinley. 2016. "A Word from the Guest Editors." *Journal of Religion, Spirituality & Aging* 28, nos. 1–2: 2–6.

Swinton, John, and Esther Mcintosh. 2000. "Persons in Relation: The Care of Persons with Learning Disabilities." *Theology Today* 57, no. 2: 175–84.

Swinton, John, and Harriet Mowat. (2006) 2016. *Practical Theology and Qualitative Research*. 2nd ed. London: SCM Press.

Ven, Johannes van der. 1993. *Practical Theology: An Empirical Approach*. Kampen, Netherlands: Kok Pharos.

3

Worship and Discipleship as Meta-Themes in the Theology of John Swinton

Doug Gay

Festschrift is a word I have always liked. Writing to celebrate the life and work of someone is a warm and affectionate task; in terms John Swinton would relish, we can say it is a gesture of friendship. It doesn't, of course, have to be anodyne. A real friendship is one which can survive and even thrive on friendly challenge and vigorous disagreement, gentle leg-pulling, and mischievous "slagging off" (as we sometimes call it in Scotland).

I don't remember exactly when I first met John, only that when I first heard him speak he referred several times to how good-looking he was, in a way that surprised us, made us all laugh, and put us at ease. Although he was humorous and self-deprecating, there was no sense that he meant us to think he didn't mean it. He meant it with the same seriousness he showed when writing in 2017, "My mother is ninety and very beautiful" (Swinton 2017, 165). John has made me laugh many times. He has also made me cry at least twice. I have a long association with Greenbelt Festival and had recommended him to them as a speaker, as I'm sure many others had. In 2016 I sat in a venue at Cheltenham racecourse, along with hundreds of others, listening to his talk on living with dementia, "Who Am I When I Forget Who I Am?" Many of us sat there with at least something in our eyes, if not openly weeping, as he reflected on the testimony of those living with dementia, speaking gently but powerfully of "a God who would not forget about us, even if we forgot about God." It is a line I hope to take with me to my grave, but if I forget it (as I may well) I have told my wife and kids they have to remember it for me.

Reading and rereading my way through John's work to write this chapter, I have been struck once again by the hospitality of his writing.

It is not always easy, because he is a theologian who writes with depth and sophistication, but it is never showy or needy; it never tries to obfuscate or complicate to impress the reader. Near the beginning of *Church Dogmatics*, Karl Barth claims, "The whole Church must seriously want a serious theology if it is to have a serious theology" (Barth 1975, 76–77). John's work is serious theology in a way which puts the question to many of us in the churches, as to whether we are serious enough people, serious enough disciples, to want a theology like this and to understand what it means to belong to the whole church?

Those of us who have been reading and writing theology for several decades now have witnessed a good few theological waves breaking across the academy, some of them building into storm conditions; driven by intellectual moods and movements, theoretical trends and tastes . . . Some of them were prophetic, though many weren't. Some *were* both showy and needy, reveling in complexity and desperate to demonstrate their critical virtuosity as they raised the linguistic and conceptual bar for entry into theological discourse and debate. A common factor would be that most of them announced themselves by proposing some new starting point for theological reflection. John Swinton's theological originality and freshness as well as his spiritual and ethical seriousness have developed from what might seem like a familiar and even "conservative" theological palette. We could see him as a proponent of what, after Hans Frei, many have termed a "generous orthodoxy." I think John would be quite comfortable with the term *orthodoxy* being attached to him, and when I consider the other adjectives sometimes paired with that term in recent theology (e.g., "subversive" or "radical"), his own work also has things in common with the projects those terms identify. But in respect of the tone and texture of John's writing, generous or gracious orthodoxy seems a good fit.

If the palette were familiar, his starting point was not. In his contribution to a collection of essays on liberation theology, Oliver O'Donovan wrote that "theology must be political if it is to be evangelical," observing in the same article that "the *regula fidei* does not prescribe a single starting point for theology; but it warns against making any starting point the stopping point" (O'Donovan 1999, 241). John Swinton is that welcome thing among both theologians and politicians, someone who has had another job outside their current profession. He was an RMN (Registered Mental Nurse) and RNMD (Registered Nurse for People with Learning Disabilities) before he was a BD (Bachelor of Divinity), and that life and work experience has formed a starting point for much of his life and work as a theologian. While he is not often described as a Scottish liberation theologian, or even as a "political theologian," his "method" as a practical theologian offers a striking illustration of what O'Donovan insists upon, "that evangelical theology must be political"; as well as an apt example of not stopping where we start. John is for me a theologian who is both profoundly political and evangelical because of his decision to elect a different starting point from many other theologians. From almost the first page of any of his books, his theology offers an unsettlingly obvious demonstration of that most basic axiom of a sociology of knowledge, that where we sit affects what we see. In Lucan terms, it makes a good deal of difference whether our line of sight begins with Dives or Lazarus. Or to draw on a Scottish musical reference John will appreciate, it's as Ricky Ross said, "I've found an answer/ I don't think you don't care/ You just laugh 'cause you're loaded, and things are different from there" (Deacon Blue).[1] What we have with John is the lived and worked example of someone who discerned a continuity of vocation between his life and work as a nurse and his life and work as a theologian. I am being careful to say "life and work" here because John is consistently wary of invoking professional boundaries where they might inhibit our understanding of what we share with those they may distinguish us from.

John's starting point in theology, as I understand it, has been to resist and refuse thinking about worship and discipleship, about vocation and ministry, and about church and society, in ways which are not in loving communion with sisters and brothers who have disabilities or who live with challenging mental-health conditions. When we hear it spelled out, it seems like such a small and obvious thing, such a low threshold for any serious church to reach if it were to be taken seriously in respect of its theology. Hardly the heady stuff of revolutionary, emancipatory theology, we might start to say, until we hear the words come out of our mouths and swallow them again as we reflect on what Nicholas Healy might call the "chastening" realities of our existing ecclesial communities (see Healy 2012). In that same piece, O'Donovan suggests that "to speak of the authority of God's rule is to speak of the fulfilment promised to all things worldly and human; and to measure the exercise of political power in its light is to make its world-affirming and humane character a test for all that is authentically political in human communities" (O'Donovan 1999, 246). We.could repeat the sentence with the word *ecclesial* in place of *political*.

---

[1]   *Loaded* is Glaswegian/Scottish slang for being wealthy.

John's move, making his work as a theologian a continuous piece of discipleship with what came before, has been simply to carry on attending to developing a serious theology for the whole church, not just those temporarily able-bodieds (TABs)[2] among the baptized. And that has made all the difference . . . because "things are different from there" and from here. It is a simple insistence, a practical prolegomenon for dogmatics, which turns out to be deeply challenging and disorienting for dominant modes of theological thinking. My late mentor, the distinguished Scottish practical theologian Duncan Forrester, was very fond of quoting whenever the opportunity arose a flipped Scripture verse: "without them ye shall not be made perfect."[3] This is an apt description for John's way of doing theology: "no us without them" or, more accurately, no "us and them." Having made that his starting point, in the spirit of Matthew 6:33, we may then hopefully and joyfully expect that all these other "theological" things shall be added to us. My sense, reading across two decades of John's writing and into a third, is that having taken us patiently and unapologetically to this starting point, he then says, "OK, now that we're all here in the room, let's think again together about . . . [insert your dogma/doctrine/theological theme of choice]."

In the rest of this chapter, I want to explore with you something of how I find that developed in John's writings in relation to the two defining themes of worship and discipleship and to reflect on what that has provoked and nourished in my own thinking.

WORSHIP

When trying to explain the peculiar methods and insights of liberation theology, Gustavo Gutiérrez often used the illustration that historically, and particularly since the Enlightenment, the main interlocutor for Western academic theology had been "the nonbeliever," whereas for liberation theology the interlocutor was "the nonperson" (Gutiérrez 1990) As someone whose work includes the fields of liturgical and homiletical theology, I sense a parallel with questions that John puts to these fields about how their discourse has been structured and who has been seen and heard within it. We might say that for the most part liturgical theology, when it goes to church to worship, does so in the company of an ideal type of TAB worshiper. By contrast, in line with what I have said above about John's "starting point," we find that before he engages us in any kind of conversation about "the shape of the liturgy" (Dix 1945) or

2   For his use of the term *temporarily able-bodied*, see Swinton 2017, 7.
3   A reversed riff on Heb 11:40.

"getting the liturgy right" (Jasper 1982) he insists that we talk about who gets to church, and why and how, and how they are treated when they get there. An unwary liturgical theologian might be tempted to bracket these as "practical concerns'" in a way which limits their value or importance. My advice to them would be to keep reading.

It seems to make a difference to our liturgical theology when "the action" starts.[4] Does it start at eleven on a Sunday morning, when the Presbyterian beadle solemnly carries in the Bible, or does it start at half past nine in the morning when the wheelchair accessible minibus leaves on a pilgrimage around several local addresses in the parish to call for folk who need this means of mobility to get them to church in the first place?[5] Once we arrive at the building, our liturgical theology may have to also reckon with which entrance is accessible for us and whether there is a handrail for us to hold, before considering how easy doors are to negotiate, whether wheelchair users can sit in ways integrated with everyone else, whether the hearing loop is working, and whether there is an accessible loo if we need to pee before, during, or after the service. Behind the ritual "call to worship" ("Let us worship God"),[6] there lies a set of political, social, and material conditions and decisions, which determine who will make it into the *ekklesia* on any given Sunday morning and who will feel comfortable there.

From his very earliest publications, John has never been afraid to take us to church in his academic writing. But what is most significant for me as a reader is that if I go to church with John I do not go alone, prepared to engage a TAB ideal type of worshiper. Instead, I go with sisters and brothers whose gifts and callings, and bodies and brains, may immediately and drastically "reframe" my liturgical theology.[7] One of the first times this happens is in his 2001 article on "Building a Church for Strangers," which uses a mix of ethnographic and autoethnographic writing as it moves into theological reflection (Swinton 2001). The decisive starting point for liturgical theology here is that we go to church with John and with his friend Stephen, who has Down syndrome. Already, with this innocuous and mundane piece of information we have reframed our liturgical ecclesiology. "The Body of Christ," John says, "has Down's

---

[4]   In some schools of Scottish Reformed communion theology, the ritual element of The Lord's Supper is referred to as "the action."
[5]   The introduction of the theme of time here reflects the central themes of John's 2017 book, *Becoming Friends of Time.*
[6]   *Let US worship God?*
[7]   For an introduction to his use of reframing, see Swinton 2007, 15–17.

Syndrome" (Swinton 2001, 47). In fact, John takes us to two different worship services with Stephen. The first is in the familiar setting of the small hospital fellowship which is Stephen's spiritual home. Because we go there with John, we get to know what John feels. This is not the mystical hush of a perfectly executed liturgical ritual in which each syllable of the Cranmerian collect is enunciated and savored for its theological aptness and poetic sensibility and every microgesture unfolds in a perfectly ordered sequence. This liturgical assembly is sweaty, affectionate, lusty, and lively as Stephen and his friends enjoy the music and shout out their praise to Jesus (Swinton 2001, 28). John feels an unprecedented sense of acceptance and community as he worships here alongside Stephen and invites us into his own feelings of wonder and shame as he reflects on what he understands of how Stephen is worshiping, of how Jesus is with Stephen in bread and wine. I'm not sure this is what Oliver meant when he said that our starting points should not be our stopping points, but it seems like a fine example of it to me. Going to the Supper with Stephen has reframed our engagement with sacramental theology, our centuries-old debates about real presence, our wary Presbyterian concerns about "fencing the table," our retentive obsessions with the wording and placing of the epiclesis. Our fierce catechizings into what these mean and why these matter has been unsettled by the difference of Stephen's participation in the body and blood of Jesus. As we are taken to church, the sinking feeling we begin to experience through John's heart and mind is not about Stephen's ability to "discern the body"; it is an anticipatory look beyond this holy, graced, and blessed *ecclesiola* and a shudder of apprehension about the wider church's "learning abilities" with respect to folk with learning disabilities (Swinton 2001, 28). It is as he feared. Supporting Stephen's move to live in the community, he goes with him to a new church near his new home. As Stephen, eager to participate, cries out the name of Jesus loudly for the third or fourth time, he and John are asked to leave or go out to the Sunday School so the others can "worship in peace." They leave, but the looks on parishioners' faces stay etched in John's memory (Swinton 2001, 35).[8]

This kind of autoethnographic writing is deeply distressing to read. Writing about someone with limited or no language abilities, John's

---

[8]   Of course, the body will still have Down syndrome even if Stephen were not in church, because he would not have ceased to be part of the body. But it would truly be tragically misknowing itself and in terms of Matt 25 and 1 Cor 11, failing to discern the real presence of Christ, however liturgically correct its formulations might continue to be, once it had been left to "worship in peace."

writing carries a heightened somatic attention, capturing his embarrass-ment over and his reverence for the warmth of Stephen's embrace, while also reflecting his anguish over Stephen's exclusion.[9]

In a book written sixteen years later, John takes us to church again, this time with Loraine. Here his practical-theological method is not autoethnography but qualitative research done in collaboration with Elaine Powrie into the spiritual lives of people with intellectual dis-abilities (Swinton 2017, 90ff). "Loraine was a middle aged woman who loved Jesus very much. She also happened to have an intellectual disability" (Swinton 2017, 91). Reading this as a researcher and doc-toral supervisor, I was aware how (valuable) terms such as "qualitative research" and "research project" can sometimes obscure the searing, revelatory effect of moments when we realize that the most important thing our "project" has done is create a place of shared humanity, when someone who is vulnerable is finally seen and heard. Loraine loves going to chapel, but "struggled to find friends." In response to gentle inquiries, she reveals that though she received a friendly welcome in church, the relationships ended at the door. When Mass ended, she, too, seems to have been dismissed from the lives of the other worship-ers.[10] Reflecting on what they have heard from Loraine, is John doing liturgical theology or has it passed over into "pastoral theology" or could it in fact also be "political theology"? Whichever it is (probably all of them), it breaks me to read this sentence: "Loraine was included within the fellowship of the church, but she did not *belong*. No one visited her, no one *missed* her, because no one, I suspect, really loved her" (Swinton 2017, 92). As his reflection continues, it also becomes clear we are doing ecclesiology ("Loraine's loneliness pointed toward a subtle hidden brokenness within Jesus' body as it revealed itself within her experience of church") and also Christology ("I imagine that Jesus wept for her loneliness") (Swinton 2017, 92).

A few pages later in the same book, John takes us to church again. We are back in the mode of ethnography/autoethnography, or we might also call it by an older word, *testimony*. This time we go with two Johns, and the other John has "a profound intellectual disability and cerebral

[9] I am of course echoing the memorable phrase of Miroslav Volf (1996), "exclusion and embrace"—John engages with this book particularly in his 2007 work of practical-pastoral theodicy, *Raging with Compassion*; there is also an echo of it in the title of the 2018 collection he has edited with Brian Brock, *A Graceful Embrace: Theological Reflections on Adopting Children*.
[10] Ite, missa est?

palsy" requiring posture support and use of a wheelchair for much of his days. He loves the music of the worship band in this apparently charismatic evangelical or Pentecostal church (we are not told which), singing wordlessly and shouting joyously as they played. A good situation deteriorated when the church's introduction of a healing ministry revealed widely held convictions that disabilities were a consequence of "transgenerational sins" and related "curses." John Swinton reflects that this theological framing of "healing" showed the other John was "included" but was not seen as truly belonging to the congregation as a disciple in the way that the nonaccursed understood themselves to be: "John was *in* the Body, but not truly *of* it" (Swinton 2017, 97–8). Attentiveness to John's situation takes us into questions of soteriology, sanctification, and discipleship.

The above are deeply disturbing and troubling examples for all those who, like John Swinton, love the church; but John also bears witness to the inspirational witness of disciples who are living with disabilities. Sharing a story from *L'Arche* in Trosly, France, he introduces us to Danny, a man with Down syndrome who has had a heart scan with a specialist in Paris. Asked by a friend in *L'Arche* about what the doctor saw when looking into his heart, Danny replies, "He saw Jesus." "What was Jesus doing?" the friend asks. "He was resting," Danny says. For John, as I suspect for many of us, this is a profoundly moving testimony, but his response is also to receive Danny's witness as "the gentle bearer of deep revelation"; a pneumatological insight into the mystical indwelling of God within our lives (Swinton 2017, 80). It also leads John to break the fourth wall of academic theology and confront us, his readers, with a Jane Austen/Mark 13:14 inquiry into the state of our own souls: "I ask the readers of this book, is Jesus resting in your heart?" (Swinton 2017, 80). I know of very few academic theologians who could get away with that. But John does.

One final example, again from *Becoming Friends of Time*, is of Katie, "a very sociable, lively, thirteen year old . . . diagnosed with Sturge-Weber syndrome," who has very limited communication, mostly using Makaton alongside a few words. Katie loves to pray and to invite others to pray with her. In this testimony, based on the same research project mentioned before, we are asked to reflect on the fact that going to church with Katie, we might get healed if she prays (wordlessly) for us (Swinton 2017, 126). John's reflection takes us to Romans (an epistle he returns to often for insights on grace, baptism, adoption, the body of Christ . . .) where we read Katie's story in the light of Paul's teaching about the Holy Spirit "who prays for us with sighs too deep for words." His attention to

Katie's story leads John to reflect on pneumatology and the spirituality of prayer but also, once again, on discipleship and on divine and human agency (Swinton 2017, 124–26).

A CURRICULUM FOR DISCIPLESHIP IN FOUR WORDS

Slow

The theme of discipleship which we find in Katie's story is a resurgent theme within much of contemporary Christianity in the United Kingdom, as it responds to secularization and accelerating church decline with a "missional" refocusing of the church. When I come across it, very often the theme is presented in terms of an intensifying of Christian life and calling. There is a common rhetoric which goes something like this: "It's not enough to be retaining or recruiting members; we need to be *making* disciples." The grammar of these statements has an urgency to it, conveying a call to activist Christianity. The times are urgent, the waters outside are high and rising. We need to get on task and pray for the quickening of the Holy Spirit. My intention is not to disparage that. I have some real sympathies with the words of the remarkable twentieth-century Scottish church leader George MacLeod, who once said, "The Iona Community was founded so that the whole church would not always have to go at the pace of the slowest." Nevertheless, I am grateful to those like John, who start with the other pole of this dialectic. Like him, I too have been influenced by the Japanese theologian Kosuke Koyama. In 1985, fresh out of my undergraduate degree in politics, and with very little theological knowledge, I went to a gathering in Edinburgh marking the seventy-fifth anniversary of the 1910 World Mission Conference. I listened in amazement and fascination to Kosuke Koyama as he spoke to us of the "Three Mile an Hour God," who walked at the pace of the poor woman or man in Asia, as they followed their water buffalo in the fields. I heard him wonder aloud about whether God was hot or cold, about the difference between Mount Fuji and Mount Sinai. I heard him honor the Western lay missionary Herbert Brand, through whose preaching "in broken Japanese [a hard language] with a heavy English accent" his grandfather had been converted to Christianity.[11] Koyama's work is not so often cited in Scottish theology, but I felt the memories of his face and voice return when I read John's discussion of his work in the 2017 chapter "A Brief Theology of Time" (Swinton 2017, 68–69). Their two starting points are thousands of miles apart, in very different cultures and yet their affinity

[11] I heard him tell the story, but it is also written down in Koyama 1984, 22.

makes complete sense. They are both theologians of the slow liberation to be found in Jesus, the Word made three-mile-an-hour flesh. They are both attentive to the ways in which our attempts to *not* go at the pace of the slowest, if we are not careful, may blur into a speedy form of works righteousness. Swinton, like Koyama, though with a different starting point, reminds us of the prevenient grace of God, in which the race is not to the swift, nor the battle to the strong. In contrast to the anxious, tightly wound urgency of contemporary appeals to hurry up and make disciples, John attends to the discipleship of those who will never be able to move quickly or keep up with the rest. Turning aside to liturgical theology once again, we sense another layer of meaning waiting in Paul's injunction in 1 Corinthians 11:33 for those gathered at the Lord's Table to "wait for one another." John's work, we could say, complements MacLeod's with his reminder that the whole church cannot always go at the pace of the fastest.

Friendship

While we are talking of the whole church, another Swinton word for exploring discipleship is *friends*. It is a New Testament concept (John 15:15) not always given enough attention within theology. John reads it, like Stanley Hauerwas, through their shared appreciation for an Aristotelian account of virtue; but he also reads it as a critique of the professionalization of "care" into a paid-service relationship, in which there is a danger of the shared humanity of carer and cared-for being eclipsed. In an early published piece, coauthored with Andrew McKie, having affirmed the McIntyrean and Hauerwasian premise of the development of virtue being consequent on the existence of particular "moral communities," they ask the question, "What could bind mental health nurses together and enable them to become a therapeutic context for the development of the Virtues?" (McKie and Swinton 2000, 37). Drawing Jürgen Moltmann and Scottish philosopher John MacMurray into the conversation, they suggest that "care" requires genuine personal involvement with the other, in which an authentically human connection is established as a kind of "union" that extends our sense of ourselves (McKie and Swinton 2000, 38). Discipleship, within the church, is discipleship into being in relationship with the others whom Jesus has called "friends." So, writing about Stephen in 2001, John says "the greatest pastoral gift that the church community can offer to Stephen is the gift of friendship" (Swinton 2001, 48). This is no more intended to be based only on natural affinity than is Jesus' identification of himself in Matthew 11 as "a friend of sinners"—or do we somehow think within the church that we are called friends because we just happened to be Jesus' type! Bringing this term into play once again undercuts excessively activist definitions of discipleship, because the kind of schooling, learning, and discipling we need to become friends of Jesus and friends of Jesus' friends is not easily reduced to a program or course, nor dependent upon our capacity to absorb or reproduce scriptural or theological knowledge. A final note here is that, in looking at John's career and prominent influences and collaborators, the subject of friendship also raises the painful issue of friends who have behaved in abusive and unfriendly ways toward those who trusted them. His important reflections on the difficult work of forgiveness in *Raging with Compassion* (Swinton 2007) serve as a reminder that sometimes our friends also disappoint and let us down.[12]

With

I share John's admiration for the work of English theologian Sam Wells, and I hope someday someone will write a discipleship course for the church which draws heavily on both of their work. That curriculum, in line with Sam's 2017 Nazareth Manifesto, would do a lot with the preposition *with* and might take its bearings from the call of the twelve in Mark's Gospel, when we see these unlikely apostles being gathered before they are sent; the first thing we are told being that they are "to be with him."[13] Both John and Sam caution us against our presumptions about doing things *for*, without learning how to be *with*. Both of them are attentive to the way in which going to church is going to be *with* other people before God. They are also very aware of those who are often not with us in church, because it has been made physically, socially, economically, or culturally inaccessible for them. Where that is the case, our discipleship will involve us going as Jesus did, to welcome those who are marginalized and to eat with them (Luke 15:2). There is a Scottish term *outwith*, which is used to mean "outside." Sometimes, in the spirit of Hebrews 13:13, our calling to be with others may mean we have to be out, with them. I think if this discipleship course informed by the work of Wells and Swinton is ever produced, it will have to be called the "Immanuel course."

---

[12]   I remember here that among those who have been friends to John's theological development and to many of our learning are Karl Barth, John Howard Yoder, and Jean Vanier.
[13]   Mark 3:14; cf. Wells 2015; a striking earlier treatment of these themes can be found in Lohfink 1984.

Jesus

The final word I associate with John's work on discipleship is Jesus. Before anyone suggests that is pretty unremarkable, I want to make the point that it is less common than we might suppose. There is a certain tone which we learn to adopt as theologians writing within the academy, which makes our writing sound like proper scholarship as opposed to what we might fear could be taken for mere "devotional" or "pietistic" writing. Within that, we may often prefer to speak of "the incarnation," "the Logos," "Christ," or "the Second Person of the Trinity," or even God, the sacred, and the divine (though all these terms, of course, have their place). Reading back through two decades of John's writings, I kept hearing the name of Jesus, in a way that felt unabashed, unforced, and unapologetic. Perhaps it was going to church with Stephen, who had few words, one of which was "Jeeshuss," launched loudly and joyfully into the liturgical assembly at times others may not have felt appropriate. Or Danny's vision of gentle Jesus, resting. Discipleship starts from our being with Jesus and Jesus being with us. Our sole requirement for being a disciple is that we are someone Jesus is graciously willing to be with. Our mental or physical capacity, our vocabulary or lack of one, our intellect, or drive or fervor—God may also graciously meet us through these and use these in the service of the kingdom. But they are extras.

I am drawn, therefore, to the idea that one way to summarize a vision of discipleship informed by John Swinton's writing would be to speak of "slow friendship with Jesus." I hope he would smile and nod in recognition at that. I am one of those people who have urged a stronger missional focus on the church in recent years, but my missiology is richer for having reckoned with John's reflections on discipleship. One of the merits of the much-discussed focus on *missio Dei* is that it that it suggests a way of thinking about mission whose starting point is the triune God. David Bosch put it simply, that "there is mission because God loves people" (Bosch 1991, 392). It has continued to be a fruitful concept for me, because there is an order of mission within *missio Dei* in which we are always the objects of God's mission before we become subjects within it. In terms of grand narratives, this ensures a radical subversion of the history of Western missions and enables a postcolonial missiology. In relation to a theology of disability, it reminds us that "we love because he first loved us." Whatever loving agency in mission apostles or disciples are given through Jesus' breathing the Spirit on them and sending them out is born of their first having learned to rest in the heart of Jesus.

READING LAZARUS

I am a practical theologian, a regular preacher and small-time homiletician[14] who teaches preaching to ministry students. I want to end this essay with a brief theological reflection on practice, which takes the form of autoethnography or what my colleague and John's friend Heather Walton calls "spiritual life writing." It is a reflection on how we influence one another for good as theologians and for me, therefore, on what it is to prepare a sermon with John Swinton in the room alongside me.

We were each friends of friends and now we are friends. We bonded over a strange invitation to preach together, one after another, in a Christian Aid venue at Greenbelt Arts Festival. She is a charismatic Lutheran Priest from Colorado, whose sharp and tender books make the New York Times Best Seller Lists. *He is a wonderfully insightful and lyrical Irish poet and was about to become leader of the Corrymeela Community. Since we first met, the other two have become box office and I am the poor Presbyterian relation, but they have kept me on. Inexplicably the triple preach format is hugely popular and we are preaching this time to hundreds of preachers at a "festival of preaching" in Oxford. In the past we've done three Beatitudes and three parables and the other two have insisted that this time we do three Marys. I am assigned Mary of Bethany. I am in my study in Glasgow preparing. As I read and reread the gospel verses about this remarkable family, there's something I can't get my head around. So many biblical scholars have noted the prominence of these two sisters in John's Gospel. I have in my homiletical sights Martha's great confession, worthy of being placed alongside Peter's at Caesarea Philippi, but never historically having been given the same weight. I am also heading firmly toward Mary choosing the good place, the place of the active disciple. But I get distracted by Lazarus. Why have I never seen this before? The flip side of the prominence of these woman in a patriarchal text, of their visibility and, even more remarkably, their audibility as named women of faith—is the silence of Lazarus. Now I have noticed it, I am haunted by it. I check and check again. I even doubt myself to the point of checking with a New Testament scholar that I haven't missed some elusive verse where Lazarus speaks, but he confirms I'm right. And this becomes the knot in the text which will not come undone.*

I go back over what we know about Lazarus. The first thing we are told about him comes via his sisters, "Lord, the one who you love is ill." This is then reinforced by the narrative, "Although Jesus loved Martha and her

---

[14] Gay 2018 is my small book on preaching.

sister and Lazarus." The next reference is Jesus' reference to him as "our friend." After the remarkable dialog with Martha and the reproachful, regretful encounter with Mary, Jesus is encircled by grief. They weep, he weeps. "See how he loved him." Jesus, in distress, finally comes to the tomb. After the instruction to take away the stone, Jesus cries out with a loud voice. And Lazarus comes out. We might surely now expect some expression of thanks to Jesus or some shout of glory to God. But Lazarus says nothing. In the next chapter, the resurrected Lazarus is once again at dinner with them, when Mary anoints Jesus' feet. Crowds show up not only to see Jesus but also to see Lazarus. But they, like us, still hear nothing from him.

I am baffled by this. I can find little in the commentaries on Lazarus' silence. It is mostly passed over in silence. And then, because John Swinton was in the room (resting on a bookshelf) and I hope, because the Holy Spirit was also in the room, I had a thought. Perhaps Lazarus, the one over whom Jesus wept, the one Jesus loved, Jesus' friend—perhaps he was someone with an intellectual disability. Perhaps he was someone with Down syndrome. Perhaps he was someone with few or no words. Beloved. Always at table with his sisters and his friend Jesus. But the reason no words of his are recorded is because there were no words to record.

It's pure supposition, I thought to myself. I could call it midrash to make it more respectable . . . But once I had thought it I could not unthink it. Neither could I unthink the picture I was left with of who Jesus was weeping over; nor the extraordinarily beautiful image I was left with of what an affirmation of Lazarus was worth and life this was, as well as of the glory of God; nor the image of them all reunited around the table at dinner.

And so, uneasily, uncomfortably—while the focus on Mary stayed, this became part of the sermon. Mary's gutsiness became that of someone who loved her brother greatly and had been a fierce advocate for his life and his place in the world (no parents are mentioned, so the siblings seem to only have each other?). Her gratitude, poured out at Jesus' feet, a lavish response to what Jesus had done for her family. And for Lazarus.

So I preached it. And someone said afterward, at the passage on Lazarus, it was as if all the air was sucked out of the room for a moment.

It was a sermon that would never have happened without John Swinton in the room when I was reading John's Gospel. I've no idea what he will make of it. I hope, at the least, he might agree that if that had been how things were and if that had happened, it would have been such a Jesus-like thing to raise from the dead one of his friends who was slow in speech and slow in his walking. And given that just as before, he said nothing after being raised, it would have been just like Jesus to raise him, without feeling the need to change him.

What a difference it makes to our theology where our starting points are. What a gift John Swinton has given to us by over and over again starting in a place where he is waiting with, thinking with, resting with, or raging with people who have disabilities, or dementia, or who live with challenges to their mental health or who, like him, have been adopted. To return to that O'Donovan quotation, his starting point is not his stopping point, but it is also one he never abandons or loses sight of. So I write this in celebration of John's gifts and in gratitude for what he has given us. He is a skilled philosophical thinker and an able systematician. He is a serious, subtle, and original reader of Scripture. He is a mental-health professional with a developed understanding of disability, psychiatry, and neuropsychology. He is a Scottish theologian of color with a nuanced awareness of identity, ethnicity, and postcolonial context; a theologian both evangelical and political. He's actually not bad-looking, all things considered. And though I would like to know him better, I'm honored to call him my friend.

I know he appreciates the worship songs written by a remarkable collective in the United States called the Porter's Gate, who have given the church songs of justice and lament and work. Two of their songs come to mind as I finish this: the first an affirmation, "Your Labor Is Not in Vain"; the second a prayer, "Establish the Work of Our Hands."

WORKS CITED

Barth, Karl. 1975. *Church Dogmatics*. Edited by G. W. Bromiley and T. F. Torrance. Translated by G. T. Thomson. 2nd ed. Vol. 1, pt. 1, *The Doctrine of the Word of God*. Edinburgh: T&T Clark.

Bosch, David. 1991. *Transforming Mission*. New York: Orbis.

Deacon Blue. 1987. "Loaded." *Raintown*. CBS.

Dix, Gregory. 1945. *The Shape of the Liturgy*. Westminster, UK: Dacre.

Gay, Doug. 2018. *God Be in My Mouth: Forty Ways to Grow as a Preacher*. London: Saint Andrew.

Gutiérrez, Gustavo. 1990. *The Truth Shall Make You Free*. Translated by Matthew J. O'Connell. New York: Orbis.

Healy, N. 2000. *Church World and Christian Life: A Practical Prophetic Ecclesiology*. Cambridge: Cambridge University Press.

Jasper, R. C. D., ed. 1982. *Getting the Liturgy Right: Essays by the Joint Liturgical Group on Practical Liturgical Principles for Today*. London: SPCK.

Koyama, Kosuke. 1984. *Mount Fuji and Mount Sinai*. London: SCM Press.

Lohfink, Gerhard. 1984. *Jesus and Community: The Social Dimensions of Christian Faith*. Philadelphia: Fortress.

McKie, A., and John Swinton. 2000. "Community, Culture and Character: The Place of the Virtues in Psychiatric Nursing Practice." *Journal of Psychiatric and Mental Health Nursing* 7, no. 1: 35–42.

O'Donovan, Oliver. 1999. "Political Theology, Tradition and Modernity." In *The Cambridge Companion to Liberation Theology*, ed. Christopher Rowland, 235–47. Cambridge: Cambridge University Press.

Swinton, John. 2001. "Building a Church for Strangers." *Journal of Religion, Disability & Health* 4, no. 4: 25–63.

———. 2007. *Raging with Compassion: Pastoral Responses to the Problem of Evil*. Grand Rapids: Eerdmans.

———. 2017. *Becoming Friends of Time: Disability, Timefullness, and Gentle Discipleship*. London: SCM Press.

———. 2018. "Why Would I Look for My Parents? Living Peaceably with the Only Family I Have." In *A Graceful Embrace: Theological Reflections on Adopting Children*, by John Swinton and Brian Brock, 121–30. Leiden: Brill.

Swinton, John, and Brian Brock, eds. 2018. *A Graceful Embrace: Theological Reflections on Adopting Children*. Leiden: Brill.

Swinton, John, and Esther Mcintosh. 2000. "Persons in Relation: The Care of Persons with Learning Disabilities." *Theology Today* 57, no. 2: 175–84.

Volf, Miroslav. 1996. *Exclusion and Embrace: A Theological Exploration of Identity, Otherness and Reconciliation*. Nashville: Abingdon.

Wells, Samuel. 2015. *A Nazareth Manifesto: Being with God*. Oxford: Wiley.

II

Vulnerability Subverted

4

The Subversion of Strength and Weakness

Paul's Grammar of Salvation and Autism

Grant Macaskill

It has been a joy and a privilege for me to have been a colleague of John Swinton at the University of Aberdeen since 2015. Our collegial relationship has facilitated a genuine and sustained encounter between the two academic disciplines that we principally represent—practical theology and biblical studies—of a kind that is richer than what is often realized through attempts to achieve "interdisciplinarity." Much of this conversation has revolved around a shared investment in autism and the experiences it generates within Christian communities. Recognizing that Scripture continues to shape and define the thinking of most Christians, who will ask in various ways what it means to "think biblically" about the realities they encounter, I have sought to reflect on how the Bible might be read responsibly in relation to autism. Because autism was not known *as such* in the ancient world—it would have been a reality but not named or conceptualized in today's terms—reflecting upon how the ancient texts of Scripture might function normatively in relation to the contemporary experience of autism within the church requires us to press against the limits of much standard practice in biblical studies (Macaskill 2019).

This essay will pick up on one aspect of this, the subversion of the language of "strength" and "weakness" in the writings of Paul. Read through the lens of Swinton's theological "redescription" of disability and cognitive difference, this aspect of Paul's writing has the capacity to direct much of our effort to use Scripture responsibly in relation to autism and contemporary experience. What I seek to highlight is that Paul embraces a standard, socially powerful binary and shows how the gospel, both in its content and its constituency, revalorizes the elements within this binary, without evincing any naivete in relation to the functioning of those elements.[1] The binary is not dismissed or rejected, and neither is it destabilized through an attempt to make its elements fluid. But it is reframed in terms of the divine economy, and the language that pertains to the binary thus functions differently, altering fundamentally the *evaluation* of "strong" and "weak" without altering their *definition*.

LANGUAGE, GOD-TALK, AND CONCEPTUAL MODELS OF AUTISM

Swinton's work has been particularly attentive to the implications of theology for value systems, as these are embodied in language.[2] When we speak rightly of God, the way that we speak of other things is challenged and altered; the performance of grammatically careful God-talk modifies all other talk. Such an emphasis demands that we pay attention to our God-talk and ask seriously whether we have sought to squeeze our theology into our own native moral language-system, or have recognized the need to develop that language to accommodate a God who says, "My ways are not your ways." One strong but necessary development of this is the acknowledgment that the language of creatures will always reach a limit in its capacity to speak of God, a limit beyond which we must embrace both apophaticism and silence (Williams 2014). In complex ways, the biblical material both exemplifies this act of linguistic transformation through "redescription" of the

---

[1]   Cf. Tonstad 2016. As an advocate of queer theology, Tonstad offers an internal critique of approaches to this theology that neglect what she calls the "affective power" of binaries:

> The power of binaries lies in their affective, associative relationships, not in straightforward limitation of all humans to one or other position in a single, determined pair—especially on the level of representation. In other words, binary sexual differentiation lives via associative relationships between male or masculine and rational, reasonable, white, light, potent, active, and so on, and female or feminine and irrational, emotional, dark, receptive, passive, and so on. Any individual binary can be destabilized fairly easily, but the relations between binaries—where their power lies—are not easily undone thereby. Further, since binaries are not neutral with respect to value, fluidity alone is not enough to dismantle them. (5)

[2]   This is a characteristic of Swinton's work, rather than something articulated in specific locations, and it is hence difficult to provide a single reference to support the claim. Good representative examples, however, are found in Swinton 2012, particularly in chapter 1, where he defines the mode of practical theology as "redescription" (17–19) and in the practice of chapter 2 ("Redescribing Dementia") and chapter 4 ("Moving Beyond the Standard Paradigm: From Defectology to Relationships").

world and resources responsible God-talk far beyond its own linguistic acts, contextualized as they are historically.

This intentional commitment to the linguistic implications of theology has frequently intersected in Swinton's work with a sensitivity to the problems of modern individualism. The significance of that word for Swinton is not the one popularly identified—the problem of individuals seeking their own good without adequate attention to their responsibilities toward others—but the more fundamental problem that attends the concept of the "individual" itself. Within the modern period, the *individual* has been considered a self-subsistent thing, isolable as an identifiable entity from the communities and world in which it exists. This idea becomes entangled at a basic level with the way that we speak of persons. The individual person is the entity to which rights and significance are ascribed, and the person is conceived in individual terms. The capacity of the individual to function in certain ways becomes determinative of their status as a person, a point forcefully noted by Swinton in relation to dementia: as someone's ability to remember deteriorates, people feel that they are "losing" that person, and the person may feel they are losing themselves (Swinton 2012, in toto, but see esp. 212, 258–59). Once this move has been made, the question of the status and associated rights of any particular body will be decided (whether deliberatively or not) in ways determined by this identification: Does the individual in question satisfy the definition of a person or have all the requisite stuff to qualify for rights? Can they be considered eligible to enjoy a meaningful life within society? Individualism does not necessarily minimize the value of society but rather conceives it to be generated by the interplay of self-subsistent, productive individuals, who qualify as "persons."

For autism, this has been particularly problematic, since the dominant linguistic models[3] by which it is conceptualized typically involve the language of deficit, and the putative deficits in question have involved the capacity of the individual to participate in society. Whether framed in terms of "theory of mind" or "empathy-deficit," these approaches see the autistic individual as "lesser" or even as "other": they are "subpersons" or even "nonpersons." If that last statement seems excessive, it captures quite precisely the evaluation of autism advocated by Peter Hobson. He asks the question, "What does it mean to have the human form of social life?" (Hobson 1993, 227) and proceeds to represent personhood as necessarily relational, quoting John Macmurray's statement that "persons, therefore, are constituted by their mutual relationship to one another"

---

[3] On models in relation to disability, in general, see Haegele and Hodge 2016.

(Macmurray 1961, 24). In further exploring the kinds of relationship that might constitute persons, he cites Daniel Dennett's language of the "conditions of personhood" (Dennett 1976) and discusses those characteristics that persons recognize in other persons. Hobson then discusses various pieces of evidence which indicate, in his words, that "autistic individuals are deficient in their understanding of other persons as persons" (Hobson 1993, 240). The logic of his argument is that autistic individuals participate deficiently in "the human form of social life." Deborah Barnbaum comments: "For Hobson, the autistic person is outside the moral community, biologically human but not a person in the moral sense" (Barnbaum 2008, 92).

This way of thinking about autism has actually been taken up in theological discourse (e.g., Stump 2010) that uses the perceived deficits as a means to highlight "normal" relational capacities and their oft-overlooked significance. The perception of autism here is intrinsically negative, and the word itself comes to be used in fundamentally pejorative ways: the lack of proper relationship to God is described as "spiritual autism" by some who take this approach (McFall 2016). Proponents of this approach might claim that they are using autism metaphorically, but all metaphors work by building upon the literal meaning of the images they deploy. Only by assuming a fundamentally negative understanding of autism as *deficiency* can this approach do what it does.[4]

This deficit-based approach to autism reflects the dominance of the medical model and its conceptualizing of the phenomena at work. It is important to stress that models are not the same as theories: a theory is an attempt to explain phenomena, while a model is an attempt to conceptualize the phenomena and describe their relationships. Consequently, while explanatory theories will vie with each other or will demand to be refined until a truly satisfactory explanation is reached for *why* phenomena occur, it is possible to maintain the simultaneous validity of multiple models, specific to different contexts. We might allow the validity of a medical model for any given condition within a specific set of contexts, while refusing to allow it to totalize discourse about that condition to the exclusion of other models. The medical model will analyze and evaluate the data retrievable from the range of scientific disciplines that fall under the umbrella of the "medical sciences," using the standard terminology operative within them. These data are not the sum total of reality, however, and some aspects of reality may not be quantifiable or conceivable as data at all; social models and experience models, examined through

---

4   On this, see Leidenhag 2021.

qualitative and not merely quantitative approaches, are necessary to the proper understanding of any condition of being. Further, responsible reflection will allow these models to frame each other, so that the interpretation of data in any one does not become distortive.

In practice, however, discourse about autism has been governed disproportionately (and, in many circles, exclusively) by the medical model, which in turn has caused research to reinforce many of its characteristic representations of the autistic experience and to perpetuate the hegemony of its linguistic culture.

If we are sensitive to the issue of language, a conversation about models invites reflection on the model-specific use of terminology. In all medical models, for example, the word "normal" has a very specific significance in relation to the distribution of data associated with populations. If the data associated with an individual fall outside certain ranges, they "deviate" from "normality." This is not necessarily a negative thing: athletes, for example, might present with physiological markers that fall outside the ranges of normality. When the language of normality is utilized outside a medical model, however, it typically has different associations; to speak of any individual as "deviant," or "deficient," or "abnormal" is to speak of them pejoratively, to label them as *lesser* or *other*.

Crucially, one of the themes running through Swinton's work is that modernity has allowed the hard sciences to totalize discourse about human experience, naively fusing reductionism and individualism, so that the medical model governs discourse well beyond its limits. What happens then is precisely what we see in Hobson (and in the theological equivalents to his work): the autistic individual is considered to fall short of the conditions of personhood or the embodiment of the image of God.

Simply invoking a different model is not necessarily enough, however. Alternative models often have their own intrinsic or conceptual limits, articulating particular levels or fields of relationships. And the categories operative within those models may not easily accommodate some of the aspects of genuine experience addressed by others. In practice, we can challenge the totalizing effects of one model by advocating that another is used totally.

The value of Swinton's work is that it allows the positive reidentification of the thing represented negatively in one model without ducking the difficult realities that the thing might present, as it is experienced in the context of the divine economy. It does not merely advocate a different model in which the difficult thing is no longer difficult, or is glibly affirmed as an unqualified good. We might say that it "leans in" to those difficulties but so entirely reidentifies them within the divine economy that it inverts their standard value.

THE WISDOM OF GOD: A STRANGE (TO US) VALUE SYSTEM

Set within their canonical context, Paul's writings offer resources for thinking about difference and disability that are sometimes overlooked. Many will look to the gospel stories for narratives of inclusion but without recognizing the complex problems that attend such an appropriation of their content (including a common tendency toward interpretations of Jesus and his contemporaries that fundamentally misrepresent ancient Judaism, to the point of constituting a form of anti-Semitism. Cf. Tonstad 2016, 2). Paul, meanwhile, is often neglected because of certain interpretative cultures that have represented his teaching as being in opposition to that of Jesus, constituting a kind of conservative corruption of the message of Christ. This is unfortunate, because his writings contain much that can speak in nuanced ways to the experience of difference and disability and the obligations that obtain for the body of Christ toward its members. The Corinthian correspondence, in particular, involves extended reflection on the values that must be seen as corollaries of the gospel as these speak to the standard social values practiced within the city.

The subversion or queering of values in Paul's writings is driven by three things. First, the identification of the cross, or the crucifixion of Jesus, with the wisdom of God and his victory over the reality of sin challenges all natural human notions of power and success. It is important to note that the death in question is not a heroic one but a shameful and tragic one.

> For the message about the cross [lit: the word of the cross] is foolishness to those who are perishing, but to us who are being saved it is the power of God. For it is written, "I will destroy the wisdom of the wise, and the discernment of the discerning I will thwart" . . . We proclaim Christ crucified, a stumbling block to Jews and foolishness to Gentiles, but to those who are the called, both Jews and Greeks, Christ the power of God and the wisdom of God. (1 Cor 1:18–19, 23–24)[5]

The force of this idea is attenuated when we locate the cross too quickly within a theory of atonement, thus shifting it into a heroic register, and do not dwell on its essential or natural significance as an event of senseless injustice (so, famously, Moltmann 1973).

---

[5]   Unless otherwise indicated, all quotations are from NRSV.

In natural and political terms, the power of the cross was precisely wielded by those who crucified him. Crucifixion was a declaration of Roman power, an act of state and soldier, a termination and denigration of resistance. The observation that Rome might have acted in expedience rather than in justice was simply swallowed up by the power that acted powerfully and publicly.

By presenting the cross as something to be *proclaimed*—not from the standpoint of the authorities who crucified but from that of the one put to death—and precisely as an embodiment of power, Paul articulates a radical reevaluation of the event in its natural and social significance. That evaluation in turn negates the power structures that naturally, socially, and politically legitimate claims to worth and status within polite society. By this, it also negates the value systems aligned with these: the wisdom of the wise and the discernment of the discerning are no longer presumed to be fit for purpose in the passing of judgments. The wisdom of the cross holds these to account.

Second, Paul affirms the surprising character of divine choosing (election): God has chosen the weak and the foolish things to nullify the strong and the wise, the "things that are not" (*ta mē onta*) to nullify the things that are. We need to recognize the extent to which these expressions align and disalign respectively with the concepts of social or symbolic capital. Strong people and smart people have a certain social currency: people want them to be in their group because they bring something *evident* to the group. They enhance the group's status in relation to other groups and provide the group with resources that can be used to pursue its collective good. The landscape of how individual and group identity related to each other in antiquity was probably more complicated and variegated than some tend to assume: individualism may have been conceptually radicalized in the modern period, but it existed in the past (MacIntyre 1981), as did prosocial concepts of group responsibility (Williams 2020). But even if oriented to the good of a group and not an individual, the perceived value of those with seemingly high stocks of "strength" and "smartness," as well as those with material commodities, would be greater than that of those perceived to lack these. Further, there is no separation of the value of the person from the value of their commodities, something illustrated vividly in Paul's expression *ta mē onta*: "the things that are not." Those that "have not" *are* not. They are nothings. In societal terms, their entire significance is negated by their lack of capital. Yet it is these who are chosen by God, and not those whom a power would be expected to select to enhance his collection.

Third, Paul recognizes the cognitive and volitional significance of idolatrousness. I use this particular form of the word to stress the subjective origin of the idol: things become idols because we make them so, and their power is one that they have because we have given it (cf. Macaskill 2022). The classic statement about idolatry in Romans is important because of the active voice that it uses: "they exchanged the truth about God for a lie and worshiped and served the creature rather than the Creator" (Rom 1:25; cf. 1:23). *They* did it; it was not done *to* them. The cognitive aspect of this is also important to Paul: "They did not honor him as God or give thanks to him, but they became futile in their thinking, and their senseless minds were darkened. Claiming to be wise, they became fools" (Rom 1:21–22). The darkening of the mind here is again not a passive thing: "in wickedness, they suppress the truth" (1:18). Paul represents idolatry, then, as something that originates within the idolater, rather than inhering in the idol. As it turns the object of its desires into an idol, it actualizes the sin that inhabits and rules us (cf. Rom 3:9, 7:17), distorting our perceptions of world and worth.

This idolatrous instinct, further, is constitutional. It is part of our "flesh," a word that is typically, though not invariably, used by Paul in ways synonymous with the sinful nature. For Paul, it is "natural" to think wrongly, and this becomes bound up in the narrative of rejection and reception of the truth embodied in Jesus: "From now on, therefore, we regard no one according to the flesh. Even though we once knew Christ according to the flesh, we know him no longer [in that way]" (2 Cor 5:16; my translation).

The theme of idolatry is also quite widely found in 1 Corinthians, often considered using scriptural resources that map the ongoing reality of idolatry among Spirit-filled followers of Jesus onto the narratives of Israel's past failures. Notably, in 1 Corinthians 10, Paul warns his readers about idolatry, representing this as an outworking of the desire for evil things (10:6–7). It is basic to his rhetoric that the generation of the Exodus enjoyed a salvation that *corresponds* to that now experienced by Christians: "All were baptized into Moses in the cloud and in the sea, and all ate the same spiritual food, and all drank the same spiritual drink. For they drank from the spiritual rock that followed them, and the rock was Christ" (1 Cor 10:2–4). The corollary of this is that a corresponding vulnerability to the instinct for idolatry remains even among those in the church who have drunk of the Spirit and turned to Christ. Commitment to the One God and his One Mediator (1 Cor 8:6) summons believers to a pure service, but the desire to worship wrongly will continue to be present and must be resisted.

It is especially striking that while this concern is focused on participation in idol feasts—which would have been part of the civic operation of the city, a ritual glue for its social identity—the passage very quickly turns to consider the true significance of the Eucharist (10:16–22). While this might initially seem to be about the contrast between one worship and another, between the good and the bad, the rhetorical approach that Paul develops is principally concerned with *participation* and its implications. Participation in the Eucharist entails a participation in Christ himself, which is incompatible with participation in demons.

> The cup of blessing that we bless, is it not a sharing (*koinonia*) in the blood of Christ? The bread that we break, is it not a sharing (*koinonia*) in the body of Christ?

> . . . I do not want you to be partners (*koinōnous*) with demons. You cannot drink the cup of the Lord and the cup of demons. You cannot partake (*metechein*) of the table of the Lord and the table of demons. Or are we provoking the Lord to jealousy? Are we stronger than he? (1 Cor 10:16, 20–2)

Participation in Christ, however, also entails participation in his body, the community unified and identified through its members, common union with him. So, in the ellipsis between the two verses quoted above, we find Paul considering the body and its oneness: "Because there is one bread, we who are many are one body, for we all partake of the one bread." (1 Cor 10:17). The image of the one body with its many members will become central in 1 Corinthians 12, following an extended discussion of the Eucharist in 1 Corinthians 11, and we will consider these passages in a moment. Here, the key point of note is that Paul's analysis of idolatry as a bad kind of participation entails identifying it as incompatible with participation in Christ *and* his body. Its distortive power compromises the life of the *ekklēsia*.

These three moves are basic to Paul's consideration of the gospel and its subversion of "normal" and "acceptable" ethical standards. That this is basic to Paul's ethical thought needs to be stressed: its ramifications for how we think about disability and difference are simply particularizations of this. We are not, in other words, identifying otherwise irrelevant parts of the apostle's thought that have a capacity to create new ways of thinking about disability and difference. It is the basics and the universals of strength and weakness that are reframed through the gospel.

The instinct to retain the old valorizations, to prize a socially acknowledged strength over weakness or to maintain the economy of symbolic capital manifests the residual instinct for idolatry. The content of the New Testament leads us to expect that the conflict of worldly and heavenly values will be played out within the church, as the true worship of God through the appointed *eikon*, Christ, collides with the instincts of idolatry. Interestingly, Paul's rhetorical strategies for challenging worldly values do not represent the state of being in Christ as something that will be attained once the moral order has been rectified; rather, the state of being in Christ is presently real and this is precisely why the enactment of worldly values within the church is so monstrous.

THE BODY OF CHRIST AND ITS COMPLEX MEMBERSHIP

These reevaluative threads run through two interlinked sections of Paul's ethical teaching. The first is the description of the Eucharist/Lord's Supper in 1 Corinthians 11 and the second is the subsequent description of the body of Christ in 1 Corinthians 12.

Paul's discussion of the Supper initially highlights two problems in its practice. First, there are "divisions" (*schismata*) and "factions" (*aireseis*) that rupture the unity of the body (11:19). Earlier in the epistle (1:10–16), he has referred to the existence of factions at Corinth that appear to have grown up around individuals with the natural symbolic capital that he is so concerned to disavow: "Each of you says, 'I belong to Paul,' or 'I belong to Apollos,' or 'I belong to Cephas,' or 'I belong to Christ.' Has Christ been divided? Was Paul crucified for you? Or were you baptized in the name of Paul?" (1 Cor 1:12–13). It is the very existence of these factions and their association with individuals that leads to his statements on the gospel's negation of human wisdom and power. Second, there is a certain individualism, by which "each goes ahead with their own meal" (11:21), functionally noncognizant of the other members of the body of Christ. So fundamentally incompatible are these with the significance of the Supper that they negate its very status: "When you come together it is not [really] the Lord's Supper that you eat" (11:20).

As Paul continues, he draws in further language that resonates with his programmatic comments in 1 Corinthians 1:18–31. Those who rush ahead to eat, perhaps because their social status ensures that they are served first, "humiliate those who have nothing." This group—the "have nothings"—is actually labeled with a participle (*mē echontas*) that parallels the one used in 1 Corinthians 1:28 of those who "are nothing" (*mē onta*). That term, as we have seen, was connected to Paul's distinctive emphasis on God's surprising standards of election and there is good reason, even beyond the parallel structure, to conclude that this account is also shaped by that emphasis. The shaming of the "have nothings" corresponds to the showing of hatred toward "the church of God" (*tēs ekklēsias tou theou*), a term Paul also uses in 1:2 where it is explicated by the definer, "those who are sanctified in Christ Jesus, called to be saints." There, in other words, it combines the common status of being "in Christ" with the language of "calling," closely associated with election (cf. Rom 8:28–30): this is the church of God, and it is defined by God's standards of election, not ours. The shaming of the "have nothings" is an act of contempt toward this, an effective scorning of God's election of *ta mē onta*.

Paul's response to the social standards enacted in the Supper focuses on the full significance of the body of Christ. By invoking the words of the Lord at the Last Supper—words that identify *broken* bread with the body that is "for you"—he reminds his readers of the sacrifice by which they are saved and identified: "Whoever, therefore, eats the bread or drinks the cup of the Lord in an unworthy manner will be answerable for the body and blood of the Lord" (1 Cor 11:27). A personal self-examination is demanded concerning the recognition of this (1:28), entailing an examination of the personal values embodied in table practice, sacrificial or selfish. When we appreciate the participatory significance attached to the meal, as noted above in our discussion of 1 Corinthians 10:16, we can begin to recognize that what is at stake here is not simply a following or emulation of Jesus' example, but a sharing in his identity. Those who eat selfishly embody something contrary to what is rendered to them in the Supper. And when Paul goes on to say that all who eat or drink without discerning the body (*mē diakrinōn to sōma*), that participatory emphasis means that we must see something more than the symbolism of Christ's sacrifice; we must also see that of the body that participates in him through its members' shared union. This is anticipated by the coordination of these concepts by Paul in 1 Corinthians 10:16–17: "And is not the bread that we break a participation in the body of Christ? Because there is one loaf, we, who are many, are one body, for we all partake of the one loaf." Recognizing this allows us to see the connections between the teaching on the Supper and the subsequent teaching in 1 Corinthians 12 on the body of Christ. Famously here, Paul develops the image of the body with many members, a picture of unity and diversity that extends the discussion of the Spirit's diverse operations within the community. Within this image of diversity, though, there is a particular emphasis placed on the perceptions of importance or status attached to *kinds* of members.

> The eye cannot say to the hand, "I have no need of you," nor again the head to the feet, "I have no need of you." On the contrary, the members of the body that seem to be weaker are indispensable, and those members of the body that we think less honorable we clothe with greater honor, and our less respectable members are treated with greater respect; whereas our more respectable members do not need this. But God has so arranged the body, giving the greater honor to the inferior member, that there may be no dissension within the body, but the members may have the same care for one another. If one member suffers, all suffer together with it; if one member is honored, all rejoice together with it. (1 Cor 12:21–6)

We should note here the particular combinations of language: the "weaker" parts of the body are indispensable, the parts with less "honor" and "respect" are clothed with "greater honor." This is value language and Paul's strategy is not to reject it but to recast it. Once again, the elective sovereignty of God is asserted as crucial to this: it is God who has "so arranged" (12:24) the body. But crucial, too, is the identification of the one body as the decisive factor in the evaluation of its members: they must not consider themselves apart from this context. Further, the basis for this mutuality is not voluntary collaboration, and its evaluative significance is not simply that of collaborative advantage, obtained through the parts coming together to form a collective. The basis for the mutuality is the common union with Christ and the sharing of the one Spirit: "For just as the body is one and has many members, and all the members of the body, though many, are one body, so it is with Christ. For in the one Spirit we were all baptized into one body—Jews or Greeks, slaves or free—and we were all made to drink of one Spirit" (1 Cor 12:12–13). Paul does not say, "so it is with the church"; such language might indeed suggest that the significance lies in the social collectivity of the community or organization. His language, instead, identifies the one Lord as the basis for the value of each of its members.

This is important, for while Paul stresses the dependency of the parts of the body upon each other and their mutual need, his logic resists the approach that might reduce this to a kind of utilitarianism. It is all too easy to map the mutuality of the church onto a model of productivity that is still essentially capitalistic, in which the value of the "weak" and "inferior" is celebrated in terms of an overlooked contribution, much as a low-paid workforce might be applauded as the real cogs of an economy, the "real heroes." Socially, this is still accompanied by a diminished value in real terms, and it reaches its limit when someone is deemed to be incapable of making a contribution to society. As I have noted elsewhere, this is precisely why there is a danger of using such language of "productivity" and "contribution" as a basis for defending the continued existence of the disabled (Macaskill 2019, 191–94). Paul's language, instead, represents the mutual need of the parts of the body for each other as a simple function of their shared union with Christ. We have not come together to derive mutual benefit; we have been arranged together in him by God.

The connection of this image to the earlier part of the chapter (12:1–11), in which Paul discusses the same themes in terms of the ministry of the Spirit, can now be appreciated. The mutuality of need and blessing in Christ is not reducible simply to the natural properties of any members but must be considered in terms of the divine economy. This section of the epistle is often mistakenly considered simply as an account of the diversity of spiritual gifts (*charismata*), but the setting of these alongside "services" (*diakoniai*) and "operations" (*energēmata*) indicates something more comprehensive. What unifies them is precisely that it is the "same God who works (*ho de autos theos ho energōn*) all in all (*ta panta en pasin*)." This is the language of divine operation or economy, used of the providential and the miraculous. It shifts the significance of mutuality away from any expectation that the members of the body might need each other for what they can naturally provide, out of their native resources, and frames it instead in terms of the working of God through his creatures. As with providence in general, it *may* involve the natural properties of those creatures, but it can never be limited to these. Indeed, in this section of the epistle, such natural properties are not the primary or conspicuous concern; rather, it is the dynamic of God working through those united to Christ. Human "weakness" and "strength," like "honor" and "shame," are in the end simply not material to this. They remain as natural or social categories and Paul does not stop using them or try to argue that they have been attached to the wrong things, as if the key is simply to change some details. Rather, he reframes them within a new context: he moves their value basis from one economy to another.

THE SUBVERSION OF STRENGTH AND WEAKNESS AND THE AUTISTIC EXPERIENCE OF THE CHURCH

We turn now, finally, to consider how this might be particularized in relation to autism and the autistic experience of the church. This part of the essay will be fairly brief and will conclude the essay. Its brevity relative to the body of the discussion should not be seen as minimizing the significance of autism, but rather as a reflection of our key observation: the reevaluation of autism that should be a corollary of the gospel is a particularization of the theological evaluation of *all* things. What considering autism does is force us to recognize that the moral reality embodied within the church is typically an unreconstructed one, still governed by the standards of exclusion and symbolic capital.

As we have seen, autism is widely conceived in the terms provided by medical models of deficit or disorder. While *some* of the language used in these models may have a validity within the specific definitions of medicine, the pervasiveness of such language through public discourse around autism results in a generally negative perception of the condition, with any positives represented as limited or as partially offsetting the problems. In extreme cases, autism is explicitly dehumanized or demonized, with autistic people failing to meet "the conditions of personhood." But even general discourse effectively presumes that the status of the autistic is "pitiable." Those who thrive have "overcome" their autism, and whatever applause they receive, they are still seen in essentially negative terms.

The alternative models that center on social and sensory difference, rather than disorder, have had limited traction outside the autism community itself for two reasons. First, science continues to be regarded as the proper means by which to consider "objective truth." The scientific and medical models are considered the proper and precise descriptions of what autism objectively is, with other accounts dismissed as more subjective. Second, this is enabled because it fits with the values of society, built as they are on the expectations of the neurotypical. The perception of "deficit" or "disorder" is based on its measurement against what neurotypicals consider "normal." Autistic people are often socially undervalued because they cannot perform this "normality" and are consequently perceived to be unimpressive. These ascribed deficits constitute a social "weakness" and diminish the "honor" that autistic people can be expected to attain within society, unless those weaknesses can be offset in some ways. The tendency to cherish autistic savants, even though they are statistically a minority within the autistic community, reflects this. Under all of this lies an economic account of society by which competent individuals contribute out of their own resources to a collaborative social good that is benefited or limited by the scale of the resource they bring to the table.

Paul's theological subversion of strength and weakness challenges and resources reflection upon the autistic experience within God's church, which must be understood in terms of a different economic model, the divine economy. The value of any thing within this economy is not the resource that it might represent in itself but rather its significance as one of the "all things" through which and in which God works. Natural properties and abilities participate in this, but they do not define the terms of the economy, constituted by the limitless good of God's being working all in all. Properly, then, the value and capacity of any thing is determined by grace, without its natural qualities thereby being effaced. The tendency to judge things according to an accepted human perception of their intrinsic capital value is vicious and involves a genuine misprision of the thing because it seeks to apprehend the thing itself, where—theologically speaking—the thing's value can never be considered in isolation from God's economy (Griffiths 2009, *in toto*). God's economic operations, moreover, manifestly disdain such ascriptions of worth, choosing the things that are not to nullify the things that are. The values of stronger or weaker, greater or lesser, and full or deficient are human values. They are the embodied judgments of the idolatrous.

On one level, Paul's application of this economic principle to the body of Christ affirms a theological model of diversity rather than a deficit for autism. To consider autistic difference in terms of deficit and to withhold the status of "person" from those marked by such difference is to decide on their comparative value dislocated from the economy of grace embodied in union with Christ. When this kind of evaluative decision is further recognized to manifest the sinful normalcy of the "flesh," with its own intuitions about value, then we can press further in our critique of the deficit model: it idolizes a particular way of being human, of being a person, and excludes all who differ from it. Its idolatry lies in its exaltation of one standardized embodiment of the image of God to the status of the principal *eikon*. For Paul, Christ is the image of God (2 Cor 4:4); we participate in that image through our union with him, our membership of his body. The assumption that the neurotypical conforms most closely to the image is made because concepts of participation have largely vanished from our consciousness in modernity and the concept has become attached to the individual. Even the development of "relational" models of the image can often be compromised by a basic tendency to think about the capacity of the individual to relate, which becomes problematic when autistic people are seen as deficient in this regard. A truly Christomorphic account of the image is a participatory one: Christ alone is the image of God, and we share in it through our union with him, a relationship that requires no cognition on our part for it to be real.

Beyond this affirmation of diversity, however, Paul's language also creates space for the realities named with words such as *strength* and *weakness* to be accepted and affirmed, but with new significance because they are now understood within the divine economy. Paul has no need to argue that the weak are actually strong, just differently so; he can affirm the reality of weakness and acknowledge its implications. Precisely because the revalorizing is a consequence of framing human experience within a divine economy that centers on the incarnational reality, the reality of weakness and suffering can be affirmed as locations of divine working. This is why Paul can say, without deceit, "If I must boast, I will boast of the things that show my weakness" (2 Cor 11:30). God's power is perfected—it reaches its telos—in weakness (2 Cor 12:9).

Together with the concept of diversity, this creates an important space for reflection on autism. It allows us to affirm autism as difference, and to acknowledge the real problems that are created by the idolatrous assumption of what "normality" must look like; it allows us to identify the marginalization and undervaluing of autistic people as a genuine evil, a work of the flesh. This way of thinking is, if anything, a radicalizing of the neurodiversity model, because it is committed to naming normalcy as an evil. But it also allows us to acknowledge that autism might manifest with genuinely difficult realities as a disabling condition and to sustain that acknowledgment hand in hand with an affirmation of the autistic condition as a gift. There is an autistic gain for the church that is realized through the presence of diversity within the body of Christ, as God works all in all. But some autistic people who constitute this gain may also bring suffering and anxiety that need to be cared for by the body of Christ (1 Cor 12:26). Some of that suffering might be generated by the expectations of a neurotypical world, but perhaps not all. Some may simply be the result of living with an autistic sensorium in a world of stimuli.

I am autistic. Mostly, that generates good experiences for me and has enabled me to have the career and ministry I have had. But sometimes it leaves me disabled and distressed, and that is not always because of social expectations and the marginalizing of the autistic; often (perhaps, for me, most often) it is because my brain loops over scenarios until I am crippled with anxiety or fragments because of sensory overload. Paul's theology of weakness allows me to name that for what it is and to ask the body to care for me.

WORKS CITED

Barnbaum, D. 2008. *The Ethics of Autism: Among Them but Not One of Them*. Bloomington: Indiana University Press.

Dennett, D. C. 1976. "Conditions of Personhood." In *The Identities of Persons*, edited by A. Rorty, 175–96. Berkeley: University of California Press.

Haegele, Justin Anthony, and Samuel Hodge. 2016. "Disability Discourse: Overview and Critiques of the Medical and Social Models." *Quest* 68, no. 2: 193–206.

Hobson, R. Peter. 1993. "The Emotional Origins of Social Understanding." *Philosophical Psychology* 6, no. 3: 227–49.

Leidenhag, Joanna. 2021. "The Challenge of Autism for Relational Approaches to Theological Anthropology." *International Journal of Systematic Theology* 23, no. 1: 109–34.

Macaskill, Grant. 2019. *Autism and the Church: Bible, Theology, and Community*. Waco, Tex: Baylor University Press.

———. 2022. "The Idolatrous Self and the Eikon: The Possibility of True Worship." In *The Finality of the Gospel: Karl Barth and the Tasks of Eschatology*, edited by Philip G. Ziegler and Kait Dugan. Leiden: Brill.

MacIntyre, Alasdair C. 1981. *After Virtue: A Study in Moral Theory*. Notre Dame, Ind.: University of Notre Dame Press.

McFall, Michael T. 2016. "Divine Hiddenness and Spiritual Autism." *Heythrop Journal*. 10.1111/heyj.12324.

Moltmann, Jürgen. 1973. *Der gekreuzigte Gott*. Munich: Christian Kaiser Verlag.

Stump, Eleanore. 2010. *Walking in Darkness: Narrative and the Problem of Suffering*. Oxford: Oxford University Press.

Swinton, John. 2012. *Dementia: Living in the Memories of God*. Grand Rapids: Eerdmans.

Tonstad, Linn Marie. 2015. "The Limits of Inclusion: Queer Theology and Its Others." *Theology and Sexuality* 21, no. 1: 1–19.

Williams, Logan Alexander. 2020. "Love, Self-Gift, and the Incarnation: Christology and Ethics in Galatians, in the Context of Pauline Theology and Greco-Roman Philosophy." PhD thesis, Durham University.

Williams, Rowan. 2014. *The Edge of Words: God and the Habits of Language*. London: Bloomsbury.

5

On Disability and the Dread of Vulnerability

Marcia Webb

As I walked across my university's campus one afternoon, a brief flutter of darkness crossed my field of vision. A crow was struggling on the concrete path some twenty feet in front of me. Had it accidentally stepped on a stone? Had it wounded itself? I hardly had time to consider these possibilities before a large, loud, pulsating shadow of black feathers descended upon it. Several other crows, shrieking and flapping their wings, landed near the downed bird and began stabbing it with their beaks as it floundered beneath them.

I walked quickly toward the birds, hoping the attackers would fly away at the sound of my approach. Instead, they simply stopped momentarily in their assault, lifting their heads and cocking them to one side—as if attempting to listen and discern the cause of my footsteps. In that moment, the harassed bird in their center managed to gather its strength and fly to safety. The others then dispersed, cawing obnoxiously as they went.

For a few moments, I stood, staring into the sky and watching as the birds settled into the high branches of surrounding trees. I wondered still what had caused the first bird to flounder briefly as it had, and I felt troubled by the naked aggression of its peers.

I have often remembered this image of the flailing crow when I have considered the problem of vulnerability in a fallen world. Too often, it seems, nature rejects vulnerability. Not that all responses to the perception of weakness are as harsh as that of the crows I observed that day, but there are tendencies in the animal kingdom toward abandonment of, and at times outright aggression against, those among them who are weaker and more vulnerable. And tragically, even with our greater cognitive capacity—including our potential for deeper reflection on the value of all life—this tendency to reject those perceived as weak seems at times to seep also into human attitudes and behavior. One of the most challenging issues for health care is an age-old, and perhaps instinctual, aversion to human vulnerability of all sorts, including both physical and mental disability.

John Swinton has devoted much of his scholarship to theological concepts of human persons in light of disability. His insights have forged the path toward greater understanding of cognitive and mental-health impairments, facilitating awareness of the essential personhood of individuals who are too often among society's most "forgotten" members (Swinton 2000, 127). In this chapter, I reflect upon psychological research regarding human responses to vulnerability and various underlying factors that may be driving these responses. Theological implications of this research are considered, focusing on what I describe as our nonconscious dread, including our dread of vulnerability. This dread will then be discussed in light of Swinton's call both to the "re-membrance" (127–28) of persons with mental-health impairments and to the "reforming" of our understanding of personhood itself (Swinton 2019, 5).

VULNERABILITY AND THE JUST-WORLD ASSUMPTION

Where, then, might social scientists find evidence for humanity's seemingly natural aversion to vulnerability? This aversion may be detected in various circumstances. For example, social psychologists have long observed a troubling tendency for humans to "blame the victim," that is, to assume that persons who suffer a range of afflictions are somehow deserving of their problems. Although research demonstrates individual differences in this general tendency, evidence does suggest the presence of an underlying motive in persons across cultures to understand the universe as orderly, predictable, and just. Given this understanding, we may then assume that individuals are blessed or cursed according to their relative merit. Rather than alter presuppositions about the justice of the world or "fate," blaming the victim allows us to justify implicit tendencies toward rejection of those experiencing adversity and thus perceived as vulnerable or weak (Gangloff, Soudain, and Auzoult 2014; Ellard, Harvey, and Callan 2016).

From a theological standpoint, these assumptions are not only illogical, as demonstrated in scriptural portrayals of innocent sufferers (such as Job and Jesus), but they are also destructive. From time to time, we are all that struggling crow I observed one afternoon, thrashing about, trying to find our balance. Any pervasive rejection of vulnerability or weakness in persons, including inclinations to blame persons for their hardships, has the potential ultimately to harm us all. Yet the tendency to believe in a "just" and predictable world in which individuals are the source of their misfortune is not the only theory proposed by social scientists to describe our aversion to vulnerability.

STIGMA: DIFFERENCE, DEVIANCE, AND DEATH

In addition to the just-world assumption, psychologists have considered the role of stigma in the rejection of various people, including those who experience adversities, impairments, or other challenges that create vulnerability for them. John Swinton has written extensively regarding the devastating problem of stigma against persons with various physical, cognitive, and mental-health disabilities. He has portrayed stigma as "a malignant mode of social description that is very often aimed at some of the most vulnerable people within society" (Swinton 2020, 16).

A wealth of psychological research supports Swinton's depiction. Evidence suggests that humans tend to seek resources and safety and to accomplish personal and social goals through identification with a perceived "in-group," just as we may also attempt to distinguish ourselves from an assumed "out-group." That is, persons who differ in noticeable ways from one's in-group may be stigmatized and then rejected, allowing for the firmer establishment of the in-group and one's security within it (Greenwald and Pettigrew 2014; Heatherton et al. 2000). The potential threat of out-group members to the in-group may be a critical factor in their rejection, and this threat may include perceptions of deviance or vulnerability that are viewed as undesirable (Dovidio, Major, and Crocker 2000). Stigma, then, functions as a potent and pernicious social force for marginalization.

Research further suggests the existence of a cognitive link between our perception of vulnerability and our nonconscious awareness of our physical mortality. While stigma may be driven at least in part by the preservation of one's place within the secure confines of the in-group, theorists have also considered the particular motivations potentially underlying this drive. These motivations may include, for example, existential concerns surrounding the fear of death, which are elicited by exposure to others' vulnerability.

> Stigmas may also arouse a particular type of existential anxiety in others—an existential anxiety originating from awareness of their own mortality. . . . Perceptions of difference and deviance are often sufficient to arouse existential anxiety; however, it is especially likely to occur

when these differences generate concerns in people about their own vulnerability, such as when these stigmas involve physical disability or disfigurement. (Dovidio, Major, and Crocker 2000, 8)

In his 1973 book, *The Denial of Death*, Ernest Becker argues that humans are instinctually repulsed by the reality of personal mortality. We are, he claimed, gripped by a perpetual, underlying "terror of death" (11). So overwhelmed are we by this terror that we expend enormous, lifelong efforts first to deny our ultimate demise, and then to create various cultural edifices affirming our imagined immortality. These edifices may include our worldview convictions and our understanding of ourselves within that worldview. As Becker describes it, "Society itself is a codified hero system, which means that society everywhere is a living myth of the significance of human life, a defiant creation of meaning" (7). Becker paid little attention to the possibility that individuals may contribute to society from motives other than to defy death. Of course, he wrote from his own worldview perspective, one which was perhaps antithetical to a religious framework. Even so, as I will discuss, his emphasis on an innate terror of death underlying much of human activity may still be relevant for both religious and nonreligious worldviews and may thus inform our understanding of stigma and vulnerability.

Since the mid-1980s, researchers investigating "terror-management theory" have grounded their work in Becker's theory and provided empirical support for at least some of his more modest claims. It appears, for example, that humans from cultures around the world do exhibit nonconscious tendencies to seek protection from reminders of mortality. Evidence suggests that when we are exposed to explicit reminders of death (such as news reports of mortality rates for various disorders), we are likely first to engage in *vulnerability-denying defensive distortions* (Koslof et al. 2019). This form of rationalization is perhaps more easily recognized by Steve Chaplin's alternate title, the "not-me, not now" response, as described in his 2000 text, *The Psychology of Time and Death* (quoted in Koslef et al., 37). In other words, immediately following an explicit death cue, we may consider why this particular sort of death is unlikely to happen to us at this particular point in time. After all, we take care of ourselves; we eat vegetables regularly; we are still relatively young; no one in our family ever had this disorder; and so on. Alternatively, and especially in situations when it is more difficult to support these arguments consciously, we may attempt to dismiss thoughts of death altogether by means of avoidance or distraction (37–38).

Regardless of our ability to guard ourselves against the terror of death immediately following an explicit death cue, we may demonstrate other cognitive processes following a period of delay. In numerous studies conducted in multiple nations, participants have been presented with an explicit reminder of mortality, after which there is a specific time interval during which researchers engage them in a distracting activity. Later, when compared with control participants, those persons exposed to the death cue tended to make greater efforts to reaffirm their cultural worldviews and to bolster their self-esteem. Researchers have suggested these increased efforts signal nonconscious attempts to reaffirm a sense of *symbolic immortality* in response to a prior death threat (Schimel, Hayes, and Sharp 2019).

Beyond the research laboratory, our daily experience presents us with a myriad of reminders of our mortality. And while some of these reminders, such as mortality data or news reports, provide us with explicit, even graphic, cues for death, others we encounter routinely may be less obvious. Research indicates that cues for death may be as broad-ranging and implicit as regular health exams, insurance advertisements (Bultmann and Arndt 2019), physical proximity to a funeral home, reflections about atheism (for religious persons; Koslef et al. 2019), pictures of senior adults (for younger persons; Martens, Goldenberg, and Greenberg 2005), and decision-making about retirement funding (Koslef et al).

Preliminary evidence further indicates that physical disabilities may remind people of mortality. Researchers have suggested that these impairments provide visual displays "of the human body and its fragility and vulnerability" (Hirschberger, Florian, and Mikulincer 2005, 247) and thus signal the reality of our ultimate demise. Others have remarked, "From the perspective of terror-management theory, if human beings cope with the existential threat associated with the awareness of death through symbolic constructions of meaning (worldview) and value (self esteem), then reminders of the sheer physicality of human beings should threaten the efficacy of these symbolic defenses" (Martens, Goldenberg, and Greenberg 2005, 226).

Fortunately, there is also early research suggesting it is possible to mitigate these terror-management responses by encouraging interpersonal contact with persons with disabilities. Even brief interactions can alter how persons with disabilities are perceived, and thus minimize others' reactive tendencies toward enhancement of symbolic immortality. That is, the experience of the person in relationship can override initial terror-based responses to disability (Ben-Naim, Aviv, and Hirschberger 2008, 464–70).

Yet physical disabilities are likely only one category of human vulnerability that potentially elicits terror-management reactions. Other theorists have indicated that reminders of death may be remarkably subtle and pervasive. Some have suggested that "consciously encountered threats, the contents of which may bear no overt connection to mortality, function to elicit unconscious thoughts of death" (Lawrence, Kisely, and Pais 2010, 752–60). Vulnerability in its multitudinous forms may perhaps be numbered among these "consciously encountered threats," in that the perception of weakness may reflect an unwanted, and yet possible, fate, and this fate may then be linked in some indirect way to one's eventual demise. The word *vulnerability* itself is from the Latin *vulnerabilis*, meaning "wounding." Perhaps, embedded within the assortment of wounds—or vulnerabilities—common to humanity, we detect latent signals of our mortality.

Mental disabilities, for example, reflect profound human vulnerability. While these conditions may remain hidden from outside observers, they are, in fact, predictive of increased mortality from a variety of health concerns, including cardiac disease (Lawrence, Kisely, and Pais 2010). Epidemiological studies also indicate that 90 percent of all persons committing suicide suffer with some form of mental disorder. For example, conditions such as anxiety, depression, and schizophrenia are associated with greater potential for suicide (Perna and Schatzberg 2014; Harvey and Espaillat 2014). Anorexia nervosa is also linked to suicide risk, and to multiple health concerns resulting from prolonged starvation, including hormonal changes and damage to the heart, which may then lead to death (Hewitt, Coren, and Steel 2001; Smith, Witte, and Crow 2014). Persons with substance-use disorders may sustain serious physical harm to their bodily systems over time. They may experience an overdose, which on a single occasion can result in permanent physical impairment (e.g., brain damage) or death.

It is also true that persons with more severe mental disability, regardless of diagnosis, have greater difficulty completing the responsibilities typically necessary to maintain an income and to foster meaningful, enduring relationships. Isolation and homelessness may result, both of which again are evidence for marked vulnerability. In general, then, the multiple symptoms of mental disorders of all types suggest the potential for psychological, biological, social, occupational, and economic challenges, and thus may be linked—perhaps on a nonconscious level—to vulnerability and even death.

ABOUT TERMINOLOGY: FEAR, ANXIETY, TERROR, AND FINALLY DREAD

I have described thus far terror-based responses to vulnerability, yet I wish to suggest we also have reactions to human weakness that include, but extend further than, the factor of "terror." For this additional experience, I use the term *dread*.

A word about terminology might prove helpful here. *Terror*, as it is employed by researchers of terror-management theory, is to be distinguished from social science's use of terms describing emotional responses such as "fear" or "anxiety." Debate and discussion regarding the precise nature of these latter two phenomena are ongoing. Even so, psychologists generally understand fear as one of the most basic of human emotions, evident even in infancy, and thus believed to be a universal, conscious reaction to a perceived (and perhaps actual) threat. As such, it may be an appropriate response. Both our survival as a species, and as individual persons, depends in part on healthy fear reactions to those circumstances which may in fact endanger us (Jong and Halberstadt 2016). In addition, fear—because it tends to emerge in specific circumstances—tends to be temporary, enduring only as long as the particular danger is present. It is further characterized by an unpleasant, highly aroused state, often accompanied by specific physiological responses, such as a rapid pulse or increased sweating, and these responses diminish as the threat passes.

While anxiety may be associated with physiological reactions similar to those seen in fear, theorists suggest that anxiety is accompanied by more complex cognitive activity. It requires more than a general assessment of one's circumstances and any immediate threat associated with those circumstances. Some theorists suggest that while fear tends to focus on concrete forms of threat (e.g., physical attack), anxiety may also concern those threats that are abstract or symbolic in nature (e.g., loss of status). Furthermore, anxiety can include the higher-order cognitive ability to form expectations for experiences viewed as negative occurring in a comparatively distant future (Jong and Halberstadt 2016). In anxiety, people may imagine various unwanted events, as well as perhaps a series of cascading, future outcomes emerging from those events. They may further ruminate over and ultimately reimagine memories of previous incidents. A neutral or seemingly positive memory may over time be deemed problematic due to anxious preoccupation. Because of the fixated, highly cognitive nature of anxiety, it is more enduring than fear. For some persons, anxiety becomes so powerful that it interferes significantly and consistently with their relationships and daily responsibilities. Anxiety at this level of severity may be indicative of psychological disorder.

While some anxiety at certain times is universal among persons and at least some animals, anxiety as a psychological disorder is less common.

Terror, on the other hand, as described in terror-management research, is not necessarily, nor even commonly, experienced on a conscious level. Research has consistently indicated that while persons react to reminders of death in such a way to reaffirm a sense of symbolic immortality—reinforcing their worldview convictions or self-esteem—they do not typically describe any emotional correlate to these efforts. That is, they do not report fear or anxiety. Nor do they indicate any particular "terror of death" at the time of the study. Researchers instead infer that nonconscious processes, including nonconscious emotions, are responsible for our tendencies to react to mortality reminders in specific ways. A wide range of research evidence indicates that we do experience emotions on a nonconscious level, that is, apart from our self-awareness and therefore our ability to recognize and express them verbally (Badgaiyan 2019).

Despite the array of emotion suggested by these three terms, fear, anxiety, and terror, none encapsulates all that I think relevant to a discussion about our human reaction to vulnerability or weakness. When I use the term *dread*, I mean to refer to a sentient response on the opposite end of the spectrum, which begins at one point with fear, moves through anxiety and terror, and then reaches finally, and most fundamentally, toward dread. Dread may incorporate physical, emotional, and cognitive components, but I would argue also that it involves the person at the most foundational level of the will, or the essential direction and intent of the self. I am speaking here, of course, not of psychological variables studied through research—as with fear, anxiety, or even terror—but more of phenomena occurring at the spiritual core of the person, involving the relation of the self to God.[1]

These differences in response might be explained this way. We have a particular type of emotional reaction—fear—when we happen upon

[1] I should perhaps acknowledge here that I understand the term *dread* has been used in other contexts for theological purposes. In recent years, it has been associated with a form of Black Pentecostalism. Historically, it was also used by existential philosophers such as Hegel and Kierkegaard. My reference to the term is not meant to elicit either of these uses, nor the potentially nuanced understanding of the word in these larger philosophical or theological systems. Instead, I thought merely that the current use of the word across various segments of the English-speaking world suggested an emotion perhaps more profound, negative, and enduring than terror, as described by terror-management theorists. I wanted a contemporary reader to grasp the sense of this experience; *dread* seemed the best word for that purpose.

a wasps' nest, accidentally disturbing it, and realize we are the object of its inhabitants' sudden wrath. We have another sort of emotional reaction—anxiety—when we ruminate about the likelihood that we will not be able to pay our rent or mortgage as a result of new, unexpected expenses. And, as research increasingly demonstrates, it seems we have a third reaction—terror—when confronted by the inescapable reality of our eventual death.

But each of these emotional responses, fear, anxiety, and terror, differ from dread. Dread may be similar to terror, in that I imagine it is largely nonconscious, and it includes issues of ultimate meaning for us, involving our very existence. But dread moves beyond terror. Dread involves the mysterious or that which is unknown, and which we also sense—perhaps with some apprehension—cannot be fully known by us. It assumes the presence of spiritual significance or power apart from us; it points to the possibility of a force, something distinctly other, of a transcendent nature.

Dread may initially involve elements that are arguably elements of terror. As currently outlined by researchers, terror includes awareness not just of our mortality, but of what that mortality may signify for the self. From our earthly vantage point, death robs us of everything and everyone we have ever known, including ourselves, as impossible as it may be for us to understand that latter reality. It might be argued that we cannot genuinely comprehend death—how can consciousness imagine its potential non-existence, if one conceives of death this way? Death as non-existence in the self-aware creature is the unthinkable thought. Still, amid humanity's general ignorance about death, we do not have the comfort that mere ignorance of our mortality might provide. Instead, we know with indisputable certainty that we are continuously within death's grasp and will eventually succumb to its influence at an unknown time in an unknown way.

While dread may involve many of these "terrifying" components of death for us, I imagine dread traverses beyond the reality of our death or our potential non-existence and insignificance, as discussed in contemporary terror-management research. That is, dread includes more than our demise may signify and involves the possibility (I would argue, the reality) of a greater spiritual power beyond the frail limits of our personhood.

Dread is a response to that which death ultimately implies, including, first of all, not only that we may perhaps lack significance but also that we absolutely do lack self-determination. After all, we do not choose the reality of death, just as we did not choose life. And while we can imagine the possibility of self-determination, we recognize by the inevitability of death that we do not have it; we cannot sustain ourselves freely and consistently. In this, death unveils the simple fact that we are not God. This realization alone may alarm us—depending perhaps on our particular sense of personal influence and authority over our lives—but on the heels of this understanding lurks another, potentially more disturbing, revelation, and the source of dread itself. There may be (perhaps, logically, there must be) an elusive, indefinable other upon whom we are continuously and intricately reliant—some self-originating, self-sustaining, death-transcendent, self-conscious Being—in a word, God, from whom all creation has its life. And, with only the hint of an acknowledgment of such a Being, there comes then the automatic understanding that this Being, to whom we owe our moment-by-moment existence, also deserves our moment-by-moment allegiance. We are not our own.

With this awareness, whether conscious or nonconscious, we may experience dread. Our recognition of our death, and any terror we may have about that reality, becomes then an overture to greater, and perhaps more troubling, considerations. To the extent that we are in conflict with our creatureliness, that is, with our dependent, nonsubsistent nature, and its relation to an all-powerful other who is God, we are in dread. The more powerfully we resist this reality, the more entrenched is our dread, and the more rigid our conscious rejection of that which evokes dread in us.

I should perhaps clarify here that I do not imagine a neat cleft in the experience of dread between those who consciously report belief in God and those who do not. Just as research indicates persons have nonconscious emotions which can and do influence their attitudes and behavior, I am suggesting that we may have nonconscious responses to any internal sense we have of God, regardless of our conscious report regarding belief in a particular faith system. (And I suppose there are any number of reasons why individuals consciously report religious belief or the lack thereof.)

With the use of the term *dread*, then, I mean to evoke a universal human experience in our fallen nature that is both immediate and primal, similar perhaps to fear; but also advanced and enduring, that is, requiring greater cognitive ability, as evident in anxiety; and yet still subtle, convoluted, and typically nonconscious, as demonstrated by terror. However, in dread, I imagine the necessary nonconscious machinations are even more elaborate and enigmatic than in terror (perhaps especially so in those circumstances where one's conscious report regarding belief in God and one's nonconscious experience of God lack congruence).

Decades ago, as a graduate student, I listened in class as my Jungian psychology professor described the psychoanalytic concept of the shadow. It is sometimes assumed that the Jungian shadow refers to those morally depraved impulses within us. My professor expressed his view that the Jungian shadow was the nonconscious mind, or elements of the nonconscious mind, which may contain immoral impulses, yet may also hold positive qualities which we still consciously reject. His main point, it seemed, was that the shadow was the repository for all that we deny about ourselves or life experience more broadly. My professor continued then by wondering aloud whether God was in the shadow for some persons.[2] In the years since, I have often thought of this strange notion—God in the shadow—not just for some persons but instead for all persons, to the extent that we struggle with God's power and authority, or God's absolute, utter *Godship*, and our own lack of self-determination, our fundamental nature as *creature*.

Thus I am describing dread as a confrontation not merely with ourselves and our finitude, as might be the case in terror alone, but also as a confrontation with God. While terror may be said to be focused on the self, and the potential obliteration of the self in death—a reality which is indeed "terrible"—dread involves more than this. It is about self and other. In this sense, dread is relational—or perhaps dread might be understood as the inverse of all relationality, as it is based in rejection of the first, most essential relationship between each self and God, from which all other relationship emerges. It might be said, then, that dread's counter is not merely acceptance of our creaturehood and thus peace, but acceptance and peace with intimacy, as created self finds rest in Creator God.

And while the phenomenon of dread may typically remain bound within the protected confines of the nonconscious (barring those comparatively rare moments of unsettling insight), this does not mean that there are no conscious indicators of dread, just as there are conscious indicators of terror. One such indicator of dread may be disdain or contempt for that which reminds us of our lack of self-determination. The accompanying behavioral impulse, then, is to avoid, reject, ostracize, or even harm those objects, ideas, events, or persons that evoke this sense of dread. These emotions and behavioral impulses, while unpleasant in themselves, may be more palatable to the conscious mind than dread itself.

As an implicit reminder of our eventual mortality, human weakness itself may evoke the reality of our creatureliness, our dependent nature,

---

[2]   Unfortunately, I do not recall the name of this insightful professor to give him credit for this idea.

and of the God to whom we owe allegiance, and thus, hypothetically, it may evoke our nonconscious dread. The conscious correlate to this dread may then be an aversion to vulnerability in all its many forms, even when we encounter that vulnerability in those beloved of God. As Hauerwas notes, "We do not like to be reminded of the limits of our power, and we do not like those who remind us" (Hauerwas 2004, 103).

It perhaps goes without saying that the ideas I present here regarding dread extend beyond what social science researchers have theorized or attempted to support with empirical evidence. This does not in itself negate their merit. My intent here is to integrate psychological science and theological insight, and thus I have considered these possibilities.

VULNERABILITY AND THE MYTHIC IDEAL OF THE INVULNERABLE NORMAL

Now, if dread as portrayed here is a key component of human experience, and if the perception of human weakness can evoke dread, then it follows intuitively that at least some social conceptions of vulnerability may be skewed. After all, a reluctance to admit to personal weakness—given that this admission perhaps signals dread to various degrees within the human spirit—will likely taint social understandings of vulnerability as a whole.

Perhaps not surprisingly, then, we find social constructions, certain cultural illusions, that seem at times to suggest that only some persons are vulnerable some of the time. The unspoken imperative, then, is to entrench oneself firmly in the camp of the invulnerable (possibly the most desirable of all in-groups). As portrayed in these social constructions, vulnerability is not assumed to be part of the "normal" human experience.

But vulnerability *is* normal. It is, in fact, everywhere in the created world. Like death itself, it is inescapable reality because it is the very nature of human experience. While vulnerability includes a vast range of physical and mental disabilities, it is not limited to these phenomena. Instead, our weakness includes all the apparently limitless forms of "wounding"—psychological, physical, social, political, economic, and environmental—with which we as imperfect beings must daily live in a fallen world.

Yet vulnerability is not just a characteristic resulting from our fallenness. While there may be forms of vulnerability due inherently to the fallenness of this world (and disabilities of multiple kinds may qualify among these forms), our vulnerability is actually embedded in our creaturehood. It is the essence of the creature's dependent and trusting relationship with the Creator. Thus, it is also the path to intimacy between creature and Creator, and between all members of the created world. It is only through vulnerability, through the acceptance of our creaturehood, and not any pretense of invulnerability, that we may genuinely give of ourselves and receive from others in relationship. It is also in our weakness that we receive grace from God and exchange forgiveness with one another. In contrast, pretense of invulnerability hides the self, even from the self; it also obscures others. It is a mask behind which we are unseen, and behind which we cannot see one another.

DREAD AND THE MISUNDERSTANDING OF PERSONS

When we do not understand our vulnerability, then, we limit our understanding of our humanity. The failure to accept our weakness circumscribes our perception of others, perhaps particularly those whose vulnerability is more readily apparent, whose vulnerability cannot hide behind psychological or cultural walls of denial. Unfortunately, in the denial of human weakness, that is, in the experience of dread, we may understand persons with vulnerabilities as little more than reflections of what we fear or reject in ourselves. We may not see these persons holistically; we may not perceive their essential humanity and relation to us in our shared creaturehood.

John Swinton has reflected on this tendency not to recognize the personhood of individuals with disabilities, including those with mental-health problems. He has noted, in a statement rich with both comedy and tragedy, "It is quite possible to look at things and not to see them" (2019, 5). According to Swinton, media representations, social stereotypes, and even the diagnostic labels of mental-health professionals can work to obscure the essentially human nature of persons with these health concerns (Swinton 2000; 2020). This obscurity may then alter social reactions to persons with mental-health conditions. As Swinton has observed, "People do not respond to the *person as person*, but to the *person as illness*" (2000, 102; italics his). In his research with persons with mental-health impairments, he has found that "understanding lay at the heart of their perceptions of what they would want in terms of 'spiritual care'" (Swinton 2001, 125). Understanding requires, at the very least, an ability to see more than disorder, an ability to acknowledge the presence of a multifaceted self that exists both within and beyond the reach of impairment.

According to Swinton, the misperception of persons as illness is also integral to their status as "forgotten" among society (2000, 127). To be forgotten must rank among the least desirable of all out-groups; this status alone may carry with it the perception of weakness and thus also the terror of death. In accordance with this, Swinton has commented that forgotten persons do not exist in the social consciousness. They are without substance, without influence or power, without life in the minds of those around them. If physical death involves at the very least the loss of physical life, one's status as forgotten also suggests loss—the loss of presence among others, the loss of self in relationship, the loss of belonging. And as relationship is central to the experience of personhood, Swinton has suggested that the process of reestablishing the personhood of those with mental-health problems involves a commitment to their remembrance, but this remembrance carries a deeper significance in a Christian context. Swinton has stated,

> it is easy to forget that the word "remember" means re-member, that is, to put back together that which has been broken. The opposite of remember is not to forget, but to dismember; to take something apart. We have already seen the ways in which people with mental health problems are forgotten and dismembered by assumptions, images, and attitudes that reduce them from persons to illnesses, seeking to identify their whole being by only one aspect of their experience. Rather than being seen as whole persons with holistic needs and expectations, they are seen as nonpersons whose needs are rarely taken seriously. Thus, their identities are fragmented. . . . By drawing them together in our understanding, thinking, and caring, "the person behind the illness" will be re-membered and the Christian community enabled to take a crucial initial step in the process of resurrecting and liberating those whom society considers to be "dead." (2000, 127–28)

From a theological perspective, Swinton's allusions to the "resurrection" of persons with mental-health conditions from social death is more than figurative. This is true in part because Christian thought portrays death as more than the cessation of physical life; instead, death saturates every aspect of our earthly existence. Thus, Swinton has associated the destructive social impact of stigma with Christian concepts of the insidious and multidimensional impact of death, commenting that this death may include "the marginalization and oppression of a very vulnerable section of the population" through stigma (2000, 144).

Yet Swinton's allusion to resurrection is also more than figurative because of our psychological response to reminders of our ultimate demise. Perceiving persons merely as disabilities, and forgetting their personhood, serves the dread-based purpose of avoidance of the acknowledgment of our common mortality. Paradoxically, then, in our attempts to deny mortality by avoidance of weakness in others (and thus in ourselves), we unwittingly foster the social death to which Swinton has referred.

And, to follow Swinton's reasoning further, we discover a curious parallel: dread-based impulses to fleeting *reminders* of our vulnerability, and thus mortality, may be countered with holistic *re-membrance* of persons. It is in our memories that we have inscribed our assumptions—our understanding of what is true about ourselves and others, and about the God we worship and the creation that surrounds us; thus, it is in re-membrance that we may find transformation.

Yet this re-membrance process will ultimately involve an encounter not only with the vulnerability of others but also with our own vulnerability. Where do we find the courage to look honestly at our weakness?

THE REORIENTING VISION

I wonder if we ever do see ourselves truthfully in this life. While we may sometimes catch sight of fleeting traces of our nature, I suspect what T. S. Eliot wrote about us remains the case, "Human kind cannot bear very much reality" (1971, 20). Perhaps this is especially true regarding our vulnerability. We do not have the strength within ourselves to face our weakness. We cannot stare directly into the vulnerability of our position, as frail creatures in an unimaginably vast and mystifying universe, subject to the whims of both the physical world and our own mysterious nature, and inexorably positioned toward the seeming black hole of death.

Instead, I wonder if we must start by looking elsewhere, not toward our weakness but toward the power of God, revealed throughout creation and most perfectly in Christ. Yet, to access and then to endure this bright vision, we need the Spirit to illumine our minds and encourage our hearts. And through the Spirit, much to our surprise, we begin to discover that God's power is often unexpectedly shrouded in weakness—as it once appeared in our own time-sphere in the person of Christ.

If we observe closely, we may detect even in creation this puzzling reflection of the power of God. We encounter there an inextricable intertwining of weakness and strength. Even the single, delicate petal of a flower reflects the majestic beauty of God's handiwork. And snowflakes, each one intricate and fragile, have the ability together to halt the entire, rushing, frenzied modern world, and to compel us to stillness before their awesome silence. We recognize, too, that it is amid profound weakness and need, and in great physical agony, that a woman's body offers a holy and miraculous gift, the birth of a child. The human infant itself, while equipped with potential for the most advanced brain in creation, and a divine commission eventually to lead and care for that creation, starts life as the most dependent of all creatures, requiring more years of nurturing and parental investment than any other life-form on earth. And while we may fear the presence of vulnerability in persons (including ourselves), if we learn not to look away from this reality but instead consider this vulnerability over time, the power of God can reveal itself there in a myriad of new and surprising ways.

Yet perhaps the most explicit presentation of God's power in weakness is found in Scripture through the person of Christ. We read the apostle Paul's enigmatic description of the incarnation as Christ "taking the form of a slave" (Phil 2:7), signifying the shocking, dramatic nature of his self-emptying. The gospels also do not shy away from the humbling nature of the incarnation, offering stories surrounding the birth of the infant Christ, not of a Messianic King initially emerging on the scene as a commanding adult. No, we are introduced to our Savior as a dependent baby, still "craving for the love of his mother" (Le Pichon 2010, 95). Even as an adult, in his earthly ministry, Christ did not attain great social status or physical power, but openly aligned himself with "the least of these" (Matt 25:40), the most devalued members of society. Yet it is through the paradoxical and glorious shame of the crucifixion that the immeasurable strength of God is most terribly manifest—a shame that became the astonishing precursor to all our hope, Christ's resurrection.

How do we comprehend God's choice to swathe his power in such earthly powerlessness? God's strength in weakness is ineffable mystery, and yet as we meditate upon what we cannot grasp, we may begin to experience this vulnerable Savior upending our entire understanding of the structure of power and thus of fear about ourselves. Christ forged the way for a new resurrected humanity through obedience to God (not resistance in dread), a path leading to that most "terrible" event, his death. While we in terror may deny death, and then in dread reject our weakness, Christ did not shrink from his mortality but in confronting death miraculously overpowered it. In Christ, human weakness is transformed. The black hole of death is suddenly, for all eternity, alight with resurrection life. As the apostle Paul proclaims, "Where, O death, is your sting?" (Rom 15:55).

Christ, then, is the antidote to every death-denying, dread-based impulse toward self-protection and self-assertion, and potential other-rejection, that exists within the human heart. Nestled securely in the person of Christ, we may find courage also not to shrink from death, and all those reminders of death that pervade daily life. As continued communion with the Spirit gradually penetrates our experience (both conscious and nonconscious), we may increasingly recognize Christ standing in resurrected glory in the very center of all that terrifies us. We begin then to see our own reflection, and over time, to understand ourselves more truthfully, as we receive grace and move "from glory to glory" (2 Cor 3:18) away from immediate impulses toward fear and dread. It is thus first in encountering God's power in weakness and in seeing Christ that we can ultimately "re-member" also ourselves, discarding distorted and shallow self-images, and embracing our created selves with the vulnerability in us that God first embraced. We develop new awareness both of the creaturely powers God has genuinely given to us and of the creaturely need we must continually entrust to God, neither neglecting the one nor abhorring the other. Thus, for all of Christ's followers, our boast with Paul is in Christ crucified (Gal 6:14), as we increasingly discover within us God's power "made perfect in weakness" (2 Cor 12:9).

Thus, the re-membrance to which Swinton alludes involves not turning back to former stigmatized perceptions but moving forward to holistic visions of personhood (2000). It involves a reorientation of our focus or, as Swinton has described it, "a deep re-forming of how we go about looking at things and how we discern and assess our perceptions" (2019, 5). We must learn to see

> the truth of who we are [which is] not to be found in who we might think or remember ourselves to be. Rather, the truth of who we are is found only in Jesus. We are who we are "in Christ." Importantly, in Colossians 3:3 Paul states: "For you died, and your life is now hidden with Christ in God." This is a truly mysterious passage. Paul urges us to realise that as Christians, we discover that we are not who we may have thought we were. Our identity is not comprised of *our* memory, knowledge about ourselves, or the state of our current capacities. We are who we are *in Christ*, and importantly, even that is hidden from us. (Swinton 2019, 11)

This new awareness, and the inner perceptual transformation that results, may then alter our outward perceptions. Just as we do not own ourselves, we do not even know ourselves, and yet, having begun to see Christ and then to see ourselves, we are empowered to learn to see others, including—but also beyond—the presence of their vulnerabilities. We can begin to acknowledge the whole person who shares with us the weakness common to humanity, and with whom we may celebrate the gift of God's all-sufficient grace. In this, we engage in re-membering the person, just as we also are re-membered in the light of Christ's reflection.

WORKS CITED

Badgaiyan, Rajendra D. 2019. *Neuroscience of the Nonconscious Mind*. San Diego: Academic Press.

Becker, Ernest. 1973. *The Denial of Death*. New York: Free Press.

Ben-Naim, Shiri, Gali Aviv, and Gilad Hirschberger. 2008. "Strained Interaction: Evidence that Interpersonal Contact Moderates the Death-Disability Rejection Link." *Rehabilitation Psychology* 53, no. 4: 464–70.

Bultmann, Michael N., and Jamie Arndt. 2019. "Physical Health under the Shadow of Mortality: The Terror Management Health Model." In *The Handbook of Terror Management Theory*, edited by Clay Routledge and Matthew Vess, 369–90. San Diego: Academic Press.

Chaplin, Steve. 2000. *The Psychology of Time and Death*. Ashland, Ohio: Sonnet.

Dovidio, John F., Brenda Major, and Jennifer Crocker. 2000. "Stigma: An Introduction and Review." In *The Social Psychology of Stigma*, edited by Todd F. Heatherton, Robert E. Kleck, Michelle R. Hebl, and Jay G. Hull, 1–28. New York: Guilford.

Eliot, T. S. 1971. *Four Quartets*. New York: Houghton Mifflin Harcourt.

Ellard, John H., Annelie Harvey, and Mitchell J. Callan. 2016. "The Justice Motive: History, Theory, and Research." In *The Handbook of Social Justice Theory and Research*, edited by Manfred Schmitt and Clara Sabbagh, 127–44. New York: Springer.

Gangloff, Bernard, Coralie Soudain, and Laurent Auzoult. 2014. "Normative Characteristics of the Just World Belief: A Review with Four Scales." *Cognition, Brain, Behavior: An Interdisciplinary Journal* 28, no. 2: 163–74.

Greenwald, Anthony G., and Thomas F. Pettigrew. 2014. "With Malice toward None and Charity for Some: Ingroup Favoritism Enables Discrimination." *American Psychologist* 69, no. 7: 669–84.

Harvey, Philip D., and Stacey Espaillat. 2014. "Suicide in Schizophrenia." In *A Concise Guide to Understanding Suicide*, edited by Stephen H. Koslow, Pedro Ruiz, and Charles B. Nemeroff, 101–8. Cambridge: Cambridge University Press.

Hauerwas, Stanley. 2004. "Suffering the Retarded: Should We Prevent Retardation?" In *Critical Reflections on Stanley Hauerwas' Theology of Disability: Disabling Society, Enabling Theology*, edited by John Swinton, 87–106. New York: Routledge.

Heatherton, Todd F., Robert E. Kleck, Michelle R. Hebl, and Jay G. Hull, eds. 2000. *The Social Psychology of Stigma*. New York: Guilford.

Hewitt, P. L., S. Coren, and G. D. Steel. 2001. "Death from Anorexia Nervosa: Age Span and Sex Differences." *Aging & Mental Health* 5, no. 1: 41–46.

Hirschberger, Gilad, Victor Florian, and Mario Mikulincer. 2005. "Fear and Compassion: A Terror Management Analysis of Emotional Reactions to Physical Disability." *Rehabilitation Psychology* 50, no. 3: 246–57.

Jong, Jonathan, and Jamin Halberstadt. 2016. *Death Anxiety and Religious Belief*. New York: Bloomsbury Academic.

Koslof, Spee, Gabrial Anderson, Alexandra Nottbohm, and Brandon Hoshiko. 2019. "Proximal and Distal Terror Management Defenses: A Systematic Review and Analysis." In *The Handbook of Terror Management Theory*, edited by Clay Routledge and Matthew Vess, 31–64. San Diego: Academic Press.

Lawrence, David, Stephen Kisely, and Joanne Pais. 2010. "The Epidemiology of Excess Mortality in People with Mental Illness." *Canadian Journal of Psychiatry* 55, no. 12: 752–60.

Le Pichon, Xavier. 2010. "The Sign of Contradiction." In *The Paradox of Disability*, edited by Hans S. Reinders, 94–100. Grand Rapids: Eerdmans.

Martens, Andy, Jamie L. Goldenberg, and Jeff Greenberg. 2005. "A Terror Management Perspective on Ageism." *Journal of Social Issues* 61, no. 2: 223–39.

Perna, Giampaolo, and Alan F. Schatzberg. 2014. "Anxiety, Depression, and Suicide: Epidemiology, Pathophysiology, and Prevention." In *A Concise Guide to Understanding Suicide*, edited by Stephen H. Koslow, Pedro Ruiz, and Charles B. Nemeroff, 93–100. Cambridge: Cambridge University Press.

Schimel, Jeff, Joseph Hayes, and Michael Sharp. 2019. "A Consideration of Three Critical Hypotheses." In *Handbook of Terror Management Theory*, edited by Clay Routledge and Matthew Vess, 1–19. San Diego: Academic Press.

Smith, April R., Tracy K. Witte, and Scott J. Crow. 2014. "Eating Disorders and Suicide." In *A Concise Guide to Understanding Suicide*, edited by Stephen H. Koslow, Pedro Ruiz, and Charles B. Nemeroff, 123–29. Cambridge: Cambridge University Press.

Swinton, John. 2000. *Resurrecting the Person: Friendship and the Care of People with Mental Health Problems*. Nashville: Abingdon.

———. 2001. *Spirituality and Mental Health Care*. Philadelphia: Jessica Kingsley.

———. 2019. "Reforming, Revisionist, Refounding: Practical Theology as Disciplined Seeing." In *Reforming Practical Theology: The Politics of Body and Space*, edited by Auli Vähäkangas, Sivert Angel, and Kirstine Helboe Johansen, 5–12. Oslo: International Academy of Practical Theology.

———. 2020. *Finding Jesus in the Storm: The Spiritual Lives of Christians with Mental Health Challenges*. Grand Rapids: Eerdmans.

6

Does L'Arche Need Another Saint?

Hans S. Reinders and Cristina Gangemi

For more than a decade, John Swinton has been a friend and inspiring colleague whose work has contributed much to theology and disability, a growing field of academic research in the last decade. His spiritually informed authorship has led many of us to look beyond the typical and into the possible. Swinton has enabled a liberating trajectory to ripple out into the work and lives of many individuals. His work has been important for students and researchers who are thinking and theorizing about disability, learning disability in particular, as well as for practitioners working in support of persons who experience disabilities and their families. A genuine achievement for a prominent scholar in practical theology who constantly pushes contemporary reflection on disability and theology beyond its own limits.

In a field with so many different voices and positions, the presence of a beacon of certainty will appear as a blessing. For many of our colleagues, including John himself, such a beacon has been provided by the communities of L'Arche, exemplified by the towering figure of its founder and leader Jean Vanier. Vanier's life and work was a banner. As such, it has been an unquestionable guide in the last decade. "Has been" because, as is probably familiar to the readers of this volume, the banner has fallen. Vanier's reputation is tainted. Even more so, it has been broken, proved to be disguised in a mire of betrayal. After the appalling news about decades of sexual misconduct, any expectation of Vanier's unparalleled rise to sainthood in the Roman Catholic Church came to ruins. The official report published by L'Arche International caused a sense of devastation such that, henceforth, thinking about Vanier will be associated with "*After the fall*" (L'Arche International 2020).

The time has come that silence is not an option, not really, if only because a necessary critical assessment will also invoke the quest for a constructive account. At any rate, the communities of L'Arche will move on. That much is certain. But what to say about the valued role ascribed to Jean Vanier and his work in the many pages devoted to theological reflections on disability in the last decade or so?

The authors of this essay have chosen to respond to this question by dividing responsibilities. Being one of several Protestant theologians who have given much attention to Vanier's life and work, Hans Reinders is well qualified to write a reassessment. He visited Vanier more than once, devoted a number of publications, including a work of fiction, to him, sat together with his wife at Vanier's dinner table, and thus experienced his friendship. He worked with Vanier in Trosly-Breuil together with John Swinton, and their friend in common and mentor Stanley Hauerwas. He also visited Vanier with younger colleagues such as Brian Brock and Miguel Romero, and he discussed his life and work with students such as Benjamin Wall and Jason Greig.

Overseeing this *tableau de la troupe*, however, the reader will not fail to notice the listing of male colleagues and friends here. What about the female voice? In her contribution to the essay, Cristina Gangemi will present the voice of several female theologians and refer to the writings of Medi Ann Volpe, Pia Matthews, Anne Masters, Talitha Cooreman-Guittin, as well as to her own.

Furthermore, the fact is that not only male voices in praise of Vanier have tended to be Protestant but also that the female theologians listed have always kept a distance toward Vanier, and they happen to be Roman Catholic. As a matter of fact, these women share an important criticism in rejecting one very fundamental claim in Vanier's thinking.

Finally, to heighten the reader's curiosity, in fleshing out a constructive argument Cristina suggests that much can be gained from turning to the work of Edith Stein, a true Saint in the Roman Catholic Church and towering female voice in Roman Catholic thought from about a century ago.

In short, our contribution to this volume presents a two-staged argument, in which Hans describes how vulnerability occupies a fundamental place in Vanier's thought and shows how his thought is reflected in the work of Hauerwas and Swinton, as well as in his own. Then, Cristina argues why Vanier's overemphasis on vulnerability is a mistake that may be overcome by turning to the thought of Edith Stein.

VULNERABILITY

In an interesting essay on the philosophy and practice of L'Arche from the perspective of disability studies, Madeline Burghardt has suggested recently that scholars in disability studies (DS scholars) have often expressed their concern, and rightly so, about the language used to characterize persons with intellectual disabilities. Of particular concern is the language of vulnerability and "brokenness" in L'Arche and in Vanier's work (Burghardt 2016).

Herself a trained DS scholar, Burghardt is also experienced as a member of L'Arche communities, which explains her interest in a fair exchange between the two. As someone living in both worlds, she is committed to what they can learn from each other. This means she does not buy into the subordination of theology ("religion") to a critical social theory, as has been advocated by other DS scholars.

Take as an example David Pfeiffer's account of DS as a "*fundamental paradigm*" (Pfeiffer 2003) that enables the understanding of what it is to live with a disability. Anything that is important to know about disability, according to Pfeiffer, will be discovered within this paradigm. Thus it provides us with a perspective from which to criticize other accounts of disability. Pfeiffer demonstrates the hierarchical ordering of knowledge implied here by looking at religious claims about disability as rooted in sin. The DS paradigm enables us to see the falsehood of such claims, in Pfeiffer's view, in that they are exposed as expressions of "a deep-seated fear of difference" (Pfeiffer 2003). While I have no stake whatsoever in defending such fraudulent claims, I do have a stake in arguing that only theological discourse can show why these claims are fraudulent. The DS paradigm that Pfeiffer advocates can overrule such religious views, denounce and marginalize them, but it cannot, in truth, produce arguments rebutting them without presenting itself implicitly as a rival version of theological reflection (Reinders 2014).

Burghardt is well aware of this, apparently, and does not presuppose any hierarchical ordering of knowledge grounded in a fundamental paradigm. This is shown by her suggestion of a "potential for mutual and worthwhile exchange from theoretical and practical perspectives" between the two disciplines (Burghardt 2016). In light of this much more modest epistemic claim, it is striking, however, that she abandons her interest in an even-handed and mutual exchange as soon as the language of vulnerability—or "brokenness"—is introduced. As a matter of fact, the critique of such language is introduced as a primordially contestable issue. Apparently, from a DS perspective, the critique of "vulnerability" is key.

Burghardt contends that the language of vulnerability has always been used to justify treating persons with disabilities as second-rate citizens and has foreclosed acknowledgment of their full potential (Burghardt 2016). Addressing people's vulnerability and brokenness is misleading in that it blocks acknowledging their capacities as human beings. At the same time, however, the author concedes as commendable the theological recognition of vulnerability and brokenness in *every* human being. It renders vulnerability as "that which belongs to all people," in which connection Burghardt refers to Hauerwas' claim that vulnerability is one of the "ontological characteristics" of our lives (Hauerwas 1998).[1] While she is not entirely averse to that description, she nonetheless insists on DS' critique because it "can facilitate a semantic slide into the dangerous ontological position of being unwhole or incomplete, a notion against which most disability activists have struggled for decades" (Burghardt 2016). So, while there is a point in seeing vulnerability as a shared characteristic in all of human existence, it is nonetheless dangerous to use that language, particularly for persons with intellectual disability who do not have the opportunity to tell their own story. "The ontological naming on behalf of one assumed incapable of doing so, even when that ontology includes a shared human condition, remains contestable" (Burghardt 2016).

Vanier On Vulnerability

Surely Jean Vanier was "guilty" of characterizing the persons with intellectual disability he lived with throughout his life and work as "vulnerable" and "broken." He preferred to speak about them as "the poor" in the sense in which that term is used in the Beatitudes, the passage in Jesus' Sermon on the Mount in the Gospels of Matthew and Luke. Anyone who ever read a few pages written by Vanier will see that the charges of DS scholars laid against the language of vulnerability apply to his work.

Looking at his texts, however, it appears that Burghardt and others in DS gloss over the difference between two perspectives on vulnerability. Vulnerability may be seen as part of a language to represent human beings and therefore also representative of persons with disabilities. It

---

[1]   As a matter of fact, Hauerwas posits "dependency, not autonomy" as one of the ontological characteristics of our lives, instead of "vulnerability," but I will gloss over this difference as I assume he would readily accept Burghardt's version of this claim.

may also be seen as the result of the kind of life that such persons often-times have been forced to live. While there may be a legitimate question about the former, it does not follow that also the latter must rest on a mistake. If true, the question is this: did Vanier actually think that vulnerability was an ontological *datum*, characterizing human being as such, or did he consider it a fact of life given the rejection that persons with disabilities often have been facing in the course of their lives?

Vanier frequently emphasized this particular experience when speaking of the brokenness of his friends in L'Arche, which suggests he saw this primarily as a consequence of the social conditions of their existence. They are often excluded from common social arrangements like school and work, but the deep source of their suffering is rejection, particularly if this is caused by their family. So when Vanier talks about the "broken-ness" of "the poor," he essentially talks about something that *happened to them*. Beaten up, kicked around, expelled from their homes, living in the gutter—images that Vanier recounts when talking about people he met during his travels to other continents—they never lost the longing for community and love. This is what Vanier has discovered in L'Arche and what he wanted to communicate as a profound religious experience. "We have all seen the dead rise," he says at one point (Vanier 1982).

The longing for community is what brings people together in L'Arche, then, at least according to Vanier, and this holds true for persons with disabilities as well. "Community" marks the possibility of overcoming the devastating consequences of being rejected. But Vanier didn't talk about community in endearing terms. *Community* means coming together with people one does not necessarily like, let alone like in terms of them living together and sharing a home. In Vanier's view community is the hard work of learning to love people not of one's own choosing as companions, to receive them as a gift from God (Reinders 2010). If it is true that Vanier argued about vulnerability of "the poor" predominantly in the context of theological argument, this notion was grounded in recognizing that the suffering they had endured had not annihilated their longing for community. In this regard the lived experience of persons with disabilities, particularly intellectual disabilities, reflects the Janus head of human existence, the recognition of which was very important to Vanier. "As long as we refuse to accept that we are a mixture of light and darkness," claims Vanier, "we will divide the world into enemies and friends" (Vanier 1989). Curiously, then, denying the two-faced nature of human being with regard to persons with intellectual disabilities would indeed result in what DS scholars rightly criticize. Had their rejection and marginalization eradicated the desire of being loved and accepted, then *that* would have shown their brokenness as an undeniable charac- teristic of their being. In other words, 'vulnerability' as *hypostasis* made community impossible.[2]

As a matter of fact, he had founded L'Arche on the contrary experi- ence of his friends. Notwithstanding the pain and suffering in their lives, their desire to be loved and accepted had not withered away. This was where Vanier saw the presence of God's spirit. God made him see that no human being, however mistreated by society, is cast outside God's love. Only when it is recognized that being loved and accepted can save people from being confined to vulnerability is there a chance for com- munity to become real. But if so, it must also be clear, in Vanier's view, that "community" will not survive the tendency of many nondisabled people—assistants, volunteers, people like Vanier himself—to hide their weakness in strength. This is, I think, the crux of his theological argu- ment (Reinders 2012). The possibility of community resides in the bro- ken body, in communion, which for Vanier is what the story of Jesus' life and death reveal.

It became the cornerstone of Vanier's theology. The tendency of peo- ple to come to L'Arche to do good by serving "the poor" was uncovered as a self-serving display of disguised superiority. "Doing for" turned out to be a recipe for condescension toward persons with intellectual disabili- ties, as if they were waiting to be acted upon from a surplus of "giving." In contrast, Vanier and his colleagues in L'Arche had to learn that receiving the gift of friendship was the hardest thing to do precisely because their friends with disabilities refused to be treated as vulnerable and broken (Reinders 2008).

Perhaps the most convincing case for this argument is made by pointing out how Vanier discovered the attitude of disguised superiority also in himself, even though he had already been the leader of L'Arche for almost a decade. Having taken a sabbatical from his leadership, he went to live in one of their houses as an assistant, and so came to be looking after a severely disabled young man completely without verbal communication. He especially needed help with bathing and dressing. They became Vanier's task. At first it was a mess, and Jean didn't succeed in doing what he needed to do. To his own dismay, Vanier found violent

---

[2]   In an odd sense, then, what DS scholars object to in Vanier is what he him- self saw as the one true obstacle to making L'Arche the kind of community it tried to be. This observation warrants the mediating position that Burghardt and others have attempted to flesh out regarding the exchange between the two.

tendencies in himself toward this young man when he failed to comply with what Vanier wanted from him. It was at that time that Vanier, despite all his talk about community, had to face his own bad samaritanism. In reflecting upon this deeply unsettling experience, he noticed that operating from the position of strength was inevitable as long as he did not recognize his own brokenness. This insight was the moment of his "second calling," as narrated in my novel on Vanier's life and work (Reinders 2016). Violence is what remains when hiding one's own history of brokenness dictates "serving" a person with disabilities from a position of strength. This was the time, in my view, that Vanier came to truly understand what in his own mind L'Arche was about.

Responses From Hauerwas, Swinton, and Reinders

Hauerwas

It appears that Stanley Hauerwas would be a key witness in support of the claim that vulnerability is fundamental to Vanier's thinking on intellectual disability. At least that is how Burghardt read him when he coined the term *ontological characteristics* to refer to this aspect of the human condition (with the reservation noted before). But Burghardt misread Hauerwas in not seeing that ontology is not a basic category in his thinking in that he always frames it theologically. In the present case, the framing notion is "creation." As human beings we are creatures. We do not live on our own account, nor are we meant to live alone. That is what Christians know. Understanding peoples' existence is embedded in a narrative that makes possible the sharing of their lives with one another. It teaches them the two-faced nature of human existence. "Our need for one another means that we will suffer as well as know joy" (Hauerwas 1998). He finds himself on the same page here with Vanier. We are mixtures of light and darkness.

Hauerwas confesses, however, not to be at ease when writing on people with intellectual disabilities because he always felt that he was using them for his own theological project (Hauerwas 1998, also Reinders 2005). That project critiques modernity's exaltation of individual freedom and autonomy, which cannot but render "the disabled" as human beings of a lesser kind. Also, in this regard, Vanier appears to have Hauerwas at his side.

But there is reason to pause here. The charge of using people with intellectual disabilities is typically connected with the position of an outsider, a position that Hauerwas has always been keenly aware of as being his own. It is quite significant that the essay referred to here was originally published in a collection that carried "*Holiness Exemplified*" as its subtitle. The life and work of Vanier in L'Arche exemplified holiness. Hauerwas never saw—sees—holiness reflected in his own life, nor in that of most of his fellow Christians, so it may seem that he was in awe, full of admiration for what he saw happening in L'Arche: Vanier's life with his friends appearing as an outstanding example of the Christian moral life, as it has indeed been looked at by many commentators.

Such reading, however, would be a mistake because it overlooks the crucial difference that the notion of exemplification makes for Hauerwas. The key point about L'Arche is not that was an outstanding example but that it embodied a moral epistemology without which Hauerwas' critique of modernity would be impossible. For Hauerwas, Vanier and L'Arche embody truth, which is what makes their example indispensable. In a recent essay titled "Why Jean Vanier Matters," he writes, "I have contended that exemplification is not just an example that illuminates a more basic principle, but rather is constitutive of moral reason" (Hauerwas 2016). Given the historical nature of human understanding, and the embodiment of human reason, there is no moral argument than can be justified independently from the narrative that produces it. "Exemplification is the form of the argument itself" (Hauerwas 2016). Christian moral reasoning, like any other kind, is embedded in the practices of the community that brings it to life. There is no other option—other than moral idealism—than accounting for the truth of moral reason by exemplification through the story that produces it.

Understanding why Vanier matters to Hauerwas, therefore, is to see that arguing what the life of "following Jesus" looks like cannot succeed unless it builds upon a lived reality. As I ventured to express the same notion somewhere else, "L'Arche had to be lived before it could be thought of" (Reinders 2012). Or, as Hauerwas noted in a private conversation, "You and I would not have a leg to stand on if Vanier did not exist."

Now, all of this was in the past, and we have to come to terms with what we have learned the year after Jean Vanier's death and downfall. One thing, however, can be said without reference to this terrible aspect of his history and it regards the point I am trying to make here. Hauerwas' Wittgensteinian moral epistemology indicates why Vanier, or Henri Nouwen for that matter, could not be charged with using L'Arche to find *their own* spiritual needs fulfilled. This charge presupposes an idealist conception of their moral reasoning, as if they were following the logic of the precept, If you want to come closer to God, go and spend time with the disabled and you will see that in spite of their brokenness they remain open to sharing their life with you; that will teach you something important about yourself. As a precept for moral instruction this is the exact opposite of moral reasoning as exemplification. As if they believed they were setting an example that was for other Christians to follow. Their story is a story of what has been witnessed in the course of a life shared together. It was a discovery, not a pursuit. The story provides the argument, not the other way around. Misrepresenting what they thought they were doing originates from seeing L'Arche as something it wasn't, a strategy, a planned endeavor, a project. Instead, it was a way of responding to what came their way, and it turned out to be a journey into the unknown. A journey that in their view was guided by the light of a single experience: however broken a person might be, the longing of the human heart for being received with loving kindness is never extinct.

Swinton

In his book *Becoming Friends of Time*, John Swinton investigates the temporal dimension of current perceptions of disability (Swinton 2017).[3] Particularly with regard to persons with profound intellectual disabilities, Swinton shows how their lives are fraught with difficulties stemming from the way modern capitalist societies exploit time. Their advanced economies and technological innovations make life better, Swinton acknowledges, but only at the expense of producing their own "misfits." Living in a society where "time is money," people with intellectual disabilities are subject to being regarded as unfit and condemned to marginal existence: "Not to be able to move one's body or one's mind in such a temporal rhythm is to live in a way that pushes the boundaries of acceptable humanness" (1, 8). In other words, the modern conception of time ("clock time") creates its own victims, foremost among which are persons with profound intellectual disabilities. These persons are "essentially vulnerable and dependent" in that they appear as "slow" in every respect of their lives and are therefore excluded from participating in "hypercognitive Western societies" (5, 2).

Swinton contrasts the temporal rhythm of capitalist society with the slow pace of biblical time, exemplified by the story of Jesus Christ as the "God who walks at three miles per hour, a God who waits for us if we cannot keep up and sits with us if we cannot walk" (4, 11).

Being called to become followers of Jesus, Christians face the question of what it takes to respond to that calling. Swinton answers the question in a way that comes close to naming intellectually disabled

---

[3] Page numbers in what follows refer to this publication.

persons as "teachers," as they are named in Vanier's work. He argues that because of their diminished intellectual capacity they are more likely to be open to God without the preconceptions and expectations that are usually brought into thinking about human-divine relationships: "It may be that our brothers and sisters living with profound intellectual disabilities are in a stronger position before God than are those of us who in many ways held back by our intellect and the desire for life to be reasonable" (5, 12). Like Hauerwas, Swinton refers to Vanier and L'Arche for their witness: "Vanier and L'Arche communities bear witness to a different kind of time" (4, 6). The tribute paid to Vanier is telling. In his acknowledgments Swinton writes, "Jean's gentle footsteps provide the basic cadence and the enduring rhythm that guide the movements of this book" (Swinton 2017). The inference here cannot be missed: if it comes to knowing what it is to follow in the footsteps of Jesus, Jean Vanier is as close as you can get.

Once again, we face the notion of acknowledging vulnerability as key. Vanier reminds us, according to Swinton, "that in God's good time those people whom the world refuses to spend time with become the very focus of God's attention" (5, 2). From the perspective of living in God's time, persons with disabilities, profound intellectual disabilities in particular, are pointed to as living exemplary lives: "It is a vital and most beautiful fact that some members of Jesus' body may simply be called to bear witness to the powerful truth of *being*. In a world that has been seduced by the idolatrous power of speed, clocks, and business, bearing witness to the divine significance of simply being is indeed a noble vocation" (6, 7). Clearly Swinton's argument on "God's time" as opposed to "clock time" follows Vanier's reflections on the experience of living in L'Arche. In the surrounding society, many approach those with intellectual disabilities with honorable intentions for improving their lives. In doing so, however, they mostly act from the wisdom of the present day and run the risk of missing the most important point. Despite being rejected, people with disabilities exemplify a desire for community and friendship, which for Vanier marks the presence of God in their lives. This he expressed (as noted before) by reference to the very essence of Christian belief: "We all have seen the dead rise." To see their disability predominantly as something that needs to be overcome is our loss, not theirs. Swinton affirms Vanier's understanding of vulnerability and brokenness. We are not only called to welcome the weak and marginalized but also to welcome the weak and broken person within us and discover the presence of God in the very places of our own weakness (11, 5).

Reinders

Coming originally from the field of contemporary bioethics, Hans Reinders has pursued different avenues but in the end presents much of the same reflections on theology and disability one finds in Hauerwas and Swinton (see, e.g., Reinders 2000, 2008, 2014; also Brock 2016). In his *Receiving the Gift of Friendship*, he investigates the question of why people with profound intellectual disabilities are cared for, when the dominant account in DS claims them as citizens with equal rights. In a culture attuned to the values of individual choice and self-determination, Reinders wants to argue, caring for persons with profound disabilities is a practice without a convincing story to support it. In framing disability discourse as a discourse on equal rights, DS has in fact replaced ethics with political philosophy. Having the rights of persons with disabilities enacted is crucially important, but it is a limited concern. It is a move that has deferred moral concern for sharing these persons' lives to public services rather than leave the question in our own hands as morally responsible human beings. Persons with disabilities are human beings before they are citizens, Reinders wants to say. Consequently, they need friendship before they need citizenship (Reinders 2008).

The quest for an alternative account to what liberal society has on offer takes him toward the story of L'Arche. The first thing Reinders discovers is the strength-weakness dynamic that governs reflections on the experience of Vanier and his friends. Only someone who is aware of their own weakness can approach the person with a disability without a (mostly unaware) sense of superiority. Assistants coming to L'Arche often want to prove themselves and show that they are capable of doing good deeds, thereby ignoring the division of roles presupposed by this attitude: some are here to give and others are there to receive. Acting out of a posture of strength, people fail to understand that a truly human community is characterized by a giving and receiving that goes both ways. The "mixture of light and darkness" means that sometimes we are in need of receiving and sometimes we are capable of giving. The need of receiving signals our incompleteness, which, when accepted, creates the possibility of giving. "If we come into community without knowing that the reason we come is to learn to forgive and be forgiven seven times seventy-seven times, we will soon be disappointed" (Vanier 1989). L'Arche is ultimately based on the discovery that learning to receive is the precondition of giving (Reinders 2008).

The strength-weakness dynamic, in Reinders' account, is key to his understanding of Vanier's theology. Because we are all a mixture of light and darkness, there is no creature without the desire for true companionship and love, notwithstanding the irreducible marks of their own vulnerability. Whenever we approach the other in search of this light, we will be open to receive the presence of God in that person. This is the new vision that Vanier proclaimed to have discovered in L'Arche (Reinders 2008). In Vanier's own terms: hope for the communities of L'Arche is founded "on the acceptance and love of ourselves and others as we really are" (Vanier 1989). This holds true for any human being, persons with profound intellectual disability as good as any other.

Betrayal

As noted, perceptions have changed. That is to say, Vanier could have distinguished himself, hypothetically, in a number of ways and left these three authors—and many others—without the problem they now face. There is, after all, a distinction between something produced, a "product," and the one who "produced" it, the producer. In the present case that avenue is foreclosed, however. Jean Vanier did not produce anything, but he narrated a life he had discovered in living his desire to follow Jesus. The truth about the Christian moral life was exemplified by Vanier because he lived it. That is what exemplification means. As a matter of fact, exemplification accounts for "truth" in terms of "truthfulness." In the beginning was the deed (to borrow a phrase from Bernard Williams; Williams 2005). In view of these considerations, it must be said that any argument in the field of theology and disability built on the presupposition of Vanier's truthfulness is seriously undermined by the history of sexual misconduct that came to light after his death. That is to say, it is hard to reread what he wrote and not think that he knew he was fraudulent. Christians have every reason to understand that self-deception is a given, Hauerwas assures us (Hauerwas, unpublished paper). True, but self-deception in a man who knew how easily people are deceiving themselves by hiding their own brokenness and by keeping up false pretenses, that is another matter.

REACHING OUT TO EDITH STEIN

There are quite a few Roman Catholic voices which have questioned Vanier's emphasis on vulnerability and brokenness as a universal and unifying description of the human condition, and many of them are female. In this second part of this chapter, Cristina takes stock of these criticisms. Drawing from the writings of Edith Stein, she suggests "empathy" as an alternative starting point for thinking on theology and disability. Stein rethinks "the humanity of all humans" by displacing vulnerability as an anthropological starting point with "value-ability" (or "valuability"). By unveiling her account of the phenomenological structure of the human person, Cristina intends to show how Stein's thinking might enable us to reach out beyond vulnerability into the infinite and unrepeatable potential that exists at the core of every human person.

Beyond Vulnerability

I do not believe that pointing toward vulnerability and brokenness is the predominant way to find value in the person who experiences disability. As Reinders suggests above, Vanier's writings, lectures, and prayerful meditations are full of the language of brokenness, poverty, and value as predominantly discovered through acknowledging vulnerability. While recognizing the importance of careful attention to the rejection and abusive treatment of persons with disabilities (rightly identified by Vanier as a common experience), there are also dangers in habitually stereotyping people's experiences into a single story. Vanier's work as a whole does not argue that persons with intellectual disabilities are only vulnerable, poor, broken, and rejected, but I have found that the emphasis on this aspect of their being is most limiting in practice. Let us zoom in on this aspect of his work.

As Reinders has just outlined, Vanier's voice and witness have guided many voices in theological reflection on disability. It stands to reason, therefore, that his emphasis on vulnerability is reflected somehow in their work. What might be labeled the "Vanier mold" shapes many people's preconceptions of how to account for a life lived with an intellectual disability. Here we must ask, however, If Vanier's thinking consistently finds value in vulnerability, does it allow recognition of the fact that God enables us to be strong in His love? Not all people's stories are marked by rejection, nor are all people's stories subject to violence. To generalize disability experience into an anthropology of loss is fraught with danger. In my own ministry and practice of theology, and that of the many "creative communicators" (Raji and Gangemi 2021) with whom I minister, I have noticed how an even-handed, mutual exchange with persons with disabilities is inhibited by a narrative of global brokenness. As creative communication, they are overshadowed as soon as that language is introduced.

My own ministry was developed outside the witness of L'Arche, occurring in parishes, schools, and secular settings, where I have witnessed people living and working together in a genuine attempt of sharing with one another. I have met many people who in and through their body and creative ways of communicating expressed much about the presence of God in their lives. Creative communicative techniques have enabled us to receive their stories, as encapsulated in our motto, "EveryBody has a story" (Gangemi, Tobanelli, Vincenzi, and Swinton 2010). It emerged from a research project investigating the religious and spiritual practice of people who experience intellectual disabilities. Our research partners were persons who are often disabled in terms of inaccessible intellectual boundaries, yet they engaged in this project as "creative communicators." Their stories include experiences of all different kinds, including vulnerability, without being identified by it. For this reason, I have to agree with the concerns that Madeline Burghardt expressed. The danger of a narrative of vulnerability frequently destroys the power of individual stories. A similar concern is highlighted by Anne Masters in her doctoral thesis on the U.S. Roman Catholic Church and theology, disability, and pastoral practice: "Who Do You Say That I Am?" (Masters 2020). Masters investigates how the Catholic Church accounts for lived experience of persons with intellectual and developmental disabilities (IDD) in its parishes. She uncovers a string of promising documents issued by the American bishops since the 1970s, grounded in Catholic social teaching and based on theological frameworks derived from the Second Vatican Council. Yet these promises of inclusive ministry largely remained unfulfilled in practice. Looking for an explanation of this failure of practical enactment, Masters detects what she calls the "shadow narrative" (Masters 2000). This is a metanarrative which shadows and eclipses the light of the gospel and the light of the person. For Masters, *narrative* represents a particular perspective that promotes influential values and visions, which she distinguishes from *story* as the sequences of unfolding events in the lives of individual persons.

In view of this distinction, I would argue, where the story of the lives of persons with disabilities is framed in terms of vulnerability, there is the danger of blocking different and diverse personal stories from sight. The unique character of the subjects of these stories is placed in peril vis-à-vis stereotypes. Furthermore, I would like to suggest that we must take heed of the peril of the dynamics of a shadow narrative that places vulnerability before a Christian account of valuability. Moving beyond Vanier's mold will encourage a more balanced premise for the lives, faith, and discipleship of individual persons. My concern has always been that Vanier's insistence that walking with Jesus will take us to "the poor, the weak, the lonely, and the oppressed" betrays his adherence to an anthropology of vulnerability. It ends in a stifling embrace that ultimately, I would suggest, could indeed create a space where the inherent value of the women he abused can be overlooked. Beginning with value limits potential abuses.

Beyond Vanier: A Catholic Aggiornamento

What motivates theologians such as Anne Masters and me in resisting a theological trajectory that moves from vulnerability and brokenness to value is illuminated by our turning to Roman Catholic doctrine. At the core of all its doctrine the Catholic Church, in Canon Law Code 208, states and orders that "flowing from their rebirth in Christ, there is a genuine equality of dignity and action among all of Christ's faithful because of this equality they all contribute, each according to his or her own condition and office, to the building up of the body of Christ" (Code of Canon Law 208 1983). When Christian theology assures that the lives of persons with disabilities are always held in dignity, then surely a theology dominated by the language of vulnerability must be replaced by one that begins and ends with their valuability. Only such a theology can help us to live the active body of Christ, over and above the ability to be broken and find value in that.

Predominantly but not exclusively articulated by female voices within the Catholic tradition, such deliberations have led to reclaiming the foundational principle of human dignity to overcome the rupture between theology and practice identified by Masters' "shadow narrative." These voices move beyond Vanier, inviting an in-depth investigation of magisterial teaching, so that patronizing and sentimental stereotypes about individuals with intellectual disabilities do not reinforce low expectations of particular members of the church. The influence of this renewed orientation is deeply felt in the theological writings of Pope Francis, who encourages the church to note that the "presence of persons with disabilities among catechists according to their own gifts and talents" is a resource for the community (Francis 2020). Here the pope reflects what canon law calls the church to do.

A similar claim characterizes Medi Volpe's thinking in her *Rethinking Christian Identity: Doctrine and Discipleship* (Volpe 2013). Volpe engages theological accounts of Christian identity by noting the temptation to emphasize a certain type of intellectualism, which threatens to exclude those whose intellectual capacity requires creative and neurodiverse methods of formation. Doing so, she argues, allows one nuanced understandings of Christian doctrines such as the Trinity and incarnation.

Exploring Catholic theology, however, Volpe's argument shows that the role of Christian doctrine is to form those intellects that require it; its role is not to exclude those who cannot grasp it.

Pia Matthews' groundbreaking work on the experience of disability and writings of John Paul II further investigates the ontological premise of dignity (Matthews 2013). She demonstrates how Catholic social teaching holds that all human beings, whatever their capacity, are acting persons. The doctrine of the incarnation plays a pivotal role in her argument. It shows that human creatures in their very being "reflect an aspect of the mystery of Christ, united in a sense with every human being" (John Paul II quoted from Matthews 2013). It is in this state, Matthews tells us, that they are guaranteed human dignity. It is through Christ's redeeming act, according to Matthews, that "humankind is newly created and rediscovers the greatness, dignity and value that belong to our humanity" (Matthews 2013). Unfortunately, the exchange between disability experience and theology is usually more influenced by the Vanier mold than by Matthews' meticulous opening up of Catholic doctrine.

The magisterial teachings of the Roman Catholic Church have thus provided us with a rich resource for unfolding new methods in religious education that, as Talitha Cooreman-Guittin suggests, can enable catechesis and create pathways for friendships within the church that move beyond the barriers of disability prejudice (Cooreman-Guittin 2019). Her intuition is that friendship between persons of all abilities is a key way to build an inclusive society, rather than the other way around. Cooreman argues that the church has a responsibility in making this happen, as it can shape the perception young people have of themselves, which in turn shapes their perception of dignity that is shared in by persons with disabilities.

One of the most influential female voices in disability theology, at least in the Roman Catholic Church, is that of Sister Veronica Donatello. Taking office within the episcopal conference in Rome, she has become both adviser to Pope Francis and an influential voice in conciliar offices. Sister Veronica has advocated a growth in awareness and understanding of the foundational meaning of human dignity, in which the presence and inclusion of people with disabilities can be celebrated within the ecclesial community (Donatello 2020, 12–14). Working with her has enabled me to contribute to the development of practical guidelines directing the church to recognize and attend to the Christian formation of persons with intellectual disabilities (Fisichella 2020)

As I hope to have shown, "dignity" is a common starting point in working with and reflecting upon the everyday experience of being disabled. Theological deliberations in this connection are not exclusive to the Roman Catholic tradition. The attempt to open up Catholic doctrine to be explored and critiqued, however, suggests it can provide a different angle on the stories of all people who communicate, live, and act creatively. In an attempt to move beyond "brokenness and vulnerability" and into the foundational meaning of valuability, I now explore the work of another Catholic female voice, namely, that of Edith Stein. As I hope to show, her life story—as a brilliant Jewish phenomenologist in Nazi Germany and as a Carmelite nun—has much to bring to the project that I have outlined above. Further, Stein's anthropology highlights the value of life and emphasizes the unrepeatable nature of each and every person. I suggest that Stein's philosophy enables us to move beyond the field of disability theology as described by Reinders in the first part of this combined essay. My hope is to show that a journey into her copious spiritual writings invites the reader to follow her exploration of the innate dignity of human beings and their experience of God.[4]

The Phenomenology of Edith Stein

Stein's life was lived out in a constant search for truth. As Edmund Husserl's assistant, she became a brilliant phenomenologist who understood phenomenology as a science of the soul, the soul investigated as the "constitutive structure of the human person" (Stein 2013). This interest led her to an encounter with Theresa of Avila and eventually to conversion to Christianity. This transformational journey led Stein to recognize how every human being has "an essential openness towards a theological completion" (Jose, unpublished paper). Everybody has a capacity to know and express God and thus holds a "tension towards the transcendent, and an imprint of God, deep within their being" (Stein 2000). Her investigation into the human experience of being alive in the world opens all people up to potential. Indeed, in her reflections on human beings who experience disability she advocates that each person "has an ability to be educated so as to develop abilities for life" (Stein 2017).

Stein's much-acclaimed *Structure of the Human Person* provides an in-depth anthropology based on interdisciplinary studies of lived

---

[4]   In a philosophical introduction to Stein, Macintyre has noted a "general neglect of her philosophical work in the English-speaking world" (Macintyre 2006). In studying Stein's phenomenology for my doctoral thesis, I hope to contribute to address this neglect.

experiences. Stein's aim is to discover God in each person's creative and particular nature. Her metaphysics is built upon "encounter and uniqueness," which explains why empathy—the subject of her doctoral dissertation—is a central concept in her thought. Stein defines empathic acts as acts by which other human bodies are constituted as conscious persons, which renders empathy as a condition for all types and varieties of intelligible and sensory experience: "We need to be constantly guided by empathy through outer perception. The constitution of the foreign person is founded throughout on the constitution of the physical body. Thus the givenness in outer perception of a physical body of a certain nature is a presupposition for the givenness of a psycho-physical individual" (Stein 1989). Without a capacity to imagine oneself in the position of another consciousness, human beings would not understand themselves as persons in a world that exists independent of the subject. Stein deploys Husserl's threefold concept of the human being—as body (Leib), psyche (Anima) and spirit (Geist)—paying particular attention to the spiritual dimension of the person, their individual, singular, and so in this way universal, nature. For Stein, every person is both temporal and primordial, with an innate essence—*Wesen*—initiated by God in an unrepeatable way (Stein 2000). Nobody can be separated from this threefold way of existing. Animated by nature, the person is thrown into being by God's breath. Stein holds that "everybody is moved by their soul. As this movement occurs, they express states of affairs and states of being, and from within their tripartite existence they become animated" (Stein 2000; see also Gangemi 2020). As a spiritually animated body, no human being can be reduced to a case, or instance, or type, for they are "unrepeatable" (Stein 2000). In Stein's view this means that the physical exteriority of a person can never be measured against any restrictive "norm," or been seen merely as material body. Each person is individually moved by their own spiritual core, from where it holds a space for God and from where it draws its spiritual nourishment. Stein tells us:

> I have a person before me, singular in their own particularity. Their individual glance, movement and facial expressions gaze into my life and I know them as this person and no other. Their "I" is present to me and "I" am present to them as we share in the world. The human soul (anima), with its personal structure and individual qualities, is manifest in the psycho-physical person, it is the nucleus (kern) where all that they are finds its center and from where they are formed. And this is for all people, not only for some. (Stein 2013; see also Gangemi 2020)

For Stein this mutual presence leaves no room for any reductive or "measurable" characterizations of people according to a single stereotype. It is, instead, an invitation into the valuability and dignity of that person as they coexist with you, before God. Stein's anthropology asks us to recognize the gaze of God in the gaze of another being. In this way she avoids building her anthropological descriptions on the human conditions of vulnerability and limitation. For her, brokenness is one but only one of the many experiences that form and inform our lives, not the defining characteristic of the human person.

CONCLUSION

Stein's transformational account of human being raises important questions about Vanier's work, at least to the extent that it appears to hypostasize "vulnerability" as the main characteristic of the human person. While there is no reason to belittle, let alone deny, the many violations of persons with intellectual disabilities, there is no reason either—following Cristina's reading of Stein—to regard these as other than historically mediated, accidental experiences. In Stein's language, the "essence" of human being is irreducible in that the human person in each and every one cannot be separated from God's love.

As Reinders' account of Vanier suggests, however, it is not obvious that Vanier would disagree. It is likely that he would have appreciated Stein's personalist metaphysics, which suggests, further, that "metaphysics" or "philosophy" may not be the right level at which to object to his emphasis on vulnerability and brokenness. What is at stake is probably better seen when we shift our focus to the performativity of our language. In that case the question arises as to what Vanier was *doing* in his oft-repeated stories about "vulnerable" and "broken" people. The answer, presumably, is what motivates DS scholars in their critique of Vanier: the language he spoke seemed to feed upon the popular stereotypes of "the disabled" as weak and in need of protection from others, rather than as persons in their own right.

In support of this suggestion, we end this essay with a reflection by Cristina on what the language of vulnerability does in actual practice. She recalls sitting in class with one of her students, reading through his IQ scores. Noticing all the results that named him as being a below-average student, he asked her, "But Miss, am I really that bad?" She answered him that her friend Edith Stein would affirm that no test in the world could characterize who he was, and she told him that he was "unrepeatable" and valuable. "You have a unique valuability, which includes how you learn and how you express what you learn, together we can explore creative ways of doing that, together we can learn," she said. His response was to gaze right back at her once again, digging deep down into her soul. "Thanks Miss, for seeing me. That made me feel million dollars."

Even if little separates, perhaps, what Jean Vanier aimed to achieve in his life and work and what Edith Stein established in her philosophical writings, there is a clear difference in the ways they deployed the language of vulnerability and brokenness. Stein recognizes and includes it in her account of the human person without relying upon it as fundamental, as something that dominates all stories and needs to be repeated again and again. In actual practice, that language evokes the wrong kind of memories in persons with disabilities like Cristina's student. It makes them feel weak and ashamed of themselves. Vanier no doubt found his own journey motivated and oriented by excavating his own experiences of vulnerability and brokenness, which in its own way commendable. And yet the effect was to present himself and his friends in L'Arche in a manner that played to problematic popular stereotypes about people with intellectual disabilities. Stein's writings provide us with the phenomenology to counter these perceptions in positioning us to empathetically appreciate the dignity of all human persons over and above any projection or presumption regarding a person's life.

"*Does L'Arche need another saint?*" the admittedly playful title of this essay asked. When we strip the myth from the man, it is clear that the people of L'Arche do not need a founding saint at all. There is no doubt that Jean Vanier was a man with extraordinary gifts, but as Stein's anthropology suggests, so is each and every person in L'Arche. Each has been endowed with the greatest gift of all, which is being created in the love of God. To tell stories witnessing this extraordinary gift may be a better way to account for their valuability and dignity than to perpetuate the language of vulnerability.

WORKS CITED

Brock, Brian. 2016. "On the Transformation of Hans Reinders." In *Knowing, Being Known, and the Mystery of God: Essays in Honour of Professor Hans Reinders, Teacher, Friend, and Disciple*, edited by Bill Gaventa and Erik de Jongh, 193–208. Amsterdam: VU University Press.

Burghardt, Madeline. 2016. "Brokenness/Transformation: Reflections on Academic Critiques of L'Arche." *Disability Studies Quarterly* 36, no. 1: https://dsq-sds.org/article/view/3734/-4214.

Cooreman-Guittin, Talitha. 2019. "Growing in Humanity: On Vulnerability, Capacitation, and Encounter in Religious Education: A Christian Practical Theological Approach." *Religious Education* 114, no. 2: 143–54.

Donatello, Veronica. 2020. *Nessuno escluso! I riferimenti alle persone con disabilita' nel Magistero e nella atechesis ecclesiale.* Rome: Libreria Ateneo Salesiano.

Fisichella, Rino, ed. 2020. "General Directory of Catechesis." *Pontifical Council for the Promotion of a New Evangelisation.* Translated by C. Gangemi. Rome: Libreria Editrice Vaticana.

Francis. 2020. "The Message of the Holy Father Francis for the International Day of Persons with Disabilities." The Holy See. http://www.vatican.va/content/francesco/en/messages/pont-messages/2020/documents/papa-francesco_20201203_messaggio-disabilita.html.

John Paul II. 1983. *Code of Canon Law of the Roman Catholic Church.* The Vatican. London: HarperCollins Liturgical.

Jose, R. n.d. "The Unconditional Hospitality: The Human Being and the Host of the Eternal Being." Unpublished paper.

Gangemi, C., M. Tobanelli, G. Vincenzi, and J. Swinton. 2010. "EveryBody Has a Story." Unpublished paper, Aberdeen.

Gangemi, Cristina. 2020. "Ways of Knowing God, *Becoming Friends in Time*; A Timeless Conversation between Disability, Theology, Edith Stein and Professor John Swinton." *Journal of Disability & Religion* 24, no. 3: 332–47.

Hauerwas, Stanley. 1998. *Sanctify Them in the Truth: Holiness Exemplified.* Edinburgh: T&T Clark.

———. 2016. "Why Jean Vanier Matters: An Exemplary Exploration." In *Knowing, Being Known, and the Mystery of God: Essays in Honour of Professor Hans Reinders, Teacher, Friend, and Disciple*, edited by Bill Gaventa and Erik de Jongh. Amsterdam: VU University Press, 229–39.

———. "Remembering, Retractions, and Commentary: A Biography of Books." Unpublished paper.

L'Arche International. 2020. "Summary Report." www.larcheusa.org/news_article/summary-report-from-larche-international/.

Macintyre, Alasdair C. 2006. *Edith Stein: A Philosophical Prologue.* London: Continuum.

Masters, Anne Marie. 2020. "'Who Do You Say That I Am?' Overcoming the Marginalization of Individuals with Intellectual and Developmental Disabilities in the Church." PhD thesis, VU University Amsterdam.

Matthews, Pia. 2013. *Pope John Paul II and the Apparently Non-Acting Person.* London: Gracewings.

Pfeiffer, D. 2003. "The Disability Studies Paradigm." In *Rethinking Disability: The Emergence of New Definitions, Concepts, and Communities*, edited by Patrick Devlieger, Frank Rusch, and David Pfeiffer, 95–100. Antwerp: Garant.

Raji, Oyepeju, and Christina Gangemi. 2021. "Intellectual Disability." In *Spirituality and Psychiatry*, 2nd ed., edited by Chris Cook, Andrew Powell, and Andrew Sims. Cambridge: Cambridge University Press.

Reinders, Hans S. 2000. *The Future of the Disabled in Liberal Society: An Ethical Analysis.* Notre Dame, Ind.: University of Notre Dame Press.

———. 2005. "The Virtue of Writing Appropriately. Or: Is Stanley Hauerwas Right in Thinking He Should Not Write Anymore on the Mentally Handicapped?" In

God, Truth, and Witness: Engaging Stanley Hauerwas, edited by L.G. Jones, R. Hütter, and C.R. Velloso Ewell, 53–72. Grand Rapids: Brazos Press.

———. 2008. *Receiving the Gift of Friendship: Profound Disability, Theological Anthropology, and Ethics*. Grand Rapids: Eerdmans.

———. 2010. *The Paradox of Disability: Responses to Jean Vanier and L'Arche Communities from Theology and the Sciences*. Grand Rapids: Eerdmans.

———. 2012. "Being with the Disabled: Jean Vanier's Theological Realism." In *Disability in the Christian Tradition: A Reader*, edited by Brian Brock and John Swinton, 467–511. Grand Rapids: Eerdmans.

———. 2014. *Disability, Providence, and Ethics: Bridging Gaps, Transforming Lives*. Waco, Tex.: Baylor University Press.

———. 2016. *The Second Calling: A Novel Inspired by the Life and Work of Jean Vanier*. London: Darton, Longman & Todd.

Stein, Edith. 1989. *On the Problem of Empathy*. Translated by Waltraut Stein. CWES 3. Washington, D.C.: ICS Publications.

———. 2000. *Knowledge and Faith*. Translated by Walter Redmond. CWES 8. Washington, D.C.: ICS Publications.

———. 2013. *La Struttura della Persona Umana*. CWES 14. Translated by Michele D'Ambra and A. Ales Bello. Rome: Città Nuova Editrice.

———. 2015. *Gli Intellettuali di Edith Stein*. Translated by A. Togni. Rome: Lit Edizione SRL.

———. 2017. *Formazione e Sviluppo dell'individualità*, Translated by Anna Maria and Alice Togni. Rome: Città Nuova Editrice.

Swinton, John. 2017. *Becoming Friends of Time: Disability, Timefullness, and Gentle Discipleship*. London: SCM Press.

Vanier, Jean. 1982. *The Challenge of L'Arche*. London: Darton, Longman & Todd.

———. 1989. *Community and Growth*. New York: Paulist Press.

Volpe, Medi A. 2013. *Rethinking Christian Identity: Doctrine and Discipleship*. London: Wiley & Blackwell.

Williams, Bernard A. 2005. *In the Beginning Was the Deed: Realism and Moralism in Political Argument*. Edited by Geoffrey Hawthorne. Princeton, N.J.: Princeton University Press.

7

Being Remembered When We Forget

Finding God in Dementia and Suffering

Michael Mawson

Lost Time, a wearable artwork by the Australian artist Alexandra Banks, explores the nature of memory and identity. It consists of a cascading series of small, fragile origami cubes and shapes, made from translucent paper and connected to one another by wool. The artwork is worn around the neck, having been created for an exhibition on stoles in early 2020: *Stole: The Show*.[1] The brief that was provided to the artists had the form of a question: "What are the hopes and aspirations we carry on our shoulders as vulnerable and compassionate human beings?" (Banks 2020).

Banks has provided some commentary and reflection on her contribution: "The fragility of the sculpture indicates the vulnerability of our memories, and the act of wearing another's memories implies the responsibility and privilege it is to journey with someone who is navigating the emerging 'differently abled' person" (Banks 2020). In other words, the sculpture depicts a kind of externalization of vulnerable memories in the form of these origami shapes. *Lost Time* suggests how, especially in the case of persons with dementia, memory and identity might still be held and carried by others.

With this artwork, Banks therefore challenges a widespread assumption that identity and memory are simply something private and internal. She contests the sense in which identity is understood as exclusively located in internal, cognitive processes. Exemplifying this latter position, David Keck argues that "*we are our memories*, and without them we have but a physical resemblance to that person we each suppose ourselves to

---

[1] This exhibition in Newcastle was curated by Anne Kempton and Rod Pattenden. See "Stole: The Show Rod Pattenden," n.d.

Fig. 7.1 Alexandra
Banks, *Lost Time*, 2020.
Courtesy of the artist.

be" (Keck 1996, 32).[2] Against such a view, *Lost Time* draws attention to
the bodily and communal aspects of identity, to the more complex ways
in which we are and remain connected and present to one another.

In her comments, Banks also directly reflects on how such individualistic, cognitive understandings of memory and identity impact those
with dementia: "When one looks at the public perception of dementia it
is profoundly negative, it has become a highly stigmatized illness" (Banks
202). This fear of dementia results from an assumption that losing one's
memories means losing oneself. In light of this, *Lost Time* draws its view-
ers into a new way of thinking; it invites them to reconsider dementia
and to begin seeing and responding to persons with dementia in more
generous ways.

[2]   Quoted in Swinton 2012a, 191.

Many of the themes and concerns of *Lost Time* resonate deeply with John Swinton's theological work on dementia. (Banks refers to Swinton briefly in her comments). In his work, Swinton has provided rich and sustained reflection on this phenomenon, giving close attention to the relationship between memory and identity. In the first part of this chapter, I outline some key insights from Swinton's work, focusing on his central claim that our memories and identity are held and sustained by God. In the second part, I turn to the writings of the medieval theologian Julian of Norwich. While noting deep resonances between Swinton's and Julian's work, I draw attention to Julian's more direct and sustained focus on suffering. By way of conclusion, I suggest how Swinton and Julian both offer something important for those of us negotiating the complexities of dementia and trying to find a way forward.

JOHN SWINTON ON THE MEMORY OF GOD

John Swinton has provided his most detailed engagement with dementia in his 2012 book, *Dementia: Living in the Memories of God*.[3] In the early chapters of this book, Swinton presents and contests the standard story about dementia: namely, that it involves a progressive deterioration and loss of identity. He traces how such an understanding has emerged from a reductive scientific approach that focuses on the physiological effects of the disease, that is, on the disease's impact on areas of the brain that govern memory and higher cortical functions. In this widespread view, the neurological damage done to these areas is equated with losing what it means to be human.[4]

In addition, Swinton notes the high levels of fear and anxiety that typically accompany a diagnosis of dementia. He cites a survey indicating that "dementia is more feared than cancer" (187). For Swinton, this fear is closely related to the standard story. "At the heart of people's fear is the fear of losing their memory, and in so doing losing themselves" (188). Like Banks, he suggests that this fear can be attributed to wider cultural values and norms: "There is an explicit and implicit negative cultural bias towards diseases which involve deterioration in intellect, rationality, autonomy, and freedom, those facets of human beings that Western cultures have chosen to value over and above others" (81).

Swinton observes that there is also a fear of dementia that is particular to Christians: a fear of forgetting God. "Who are we before God when

---

[3]   In this section, all page numbers in brackets refer to this book

[4]   See also Swinton 2016, 138. Swinton provides rich reflections on dementia in two chapters of this more recent book, *Becoming Friends of Time*.

we have forgotten who God is?" (187). This fear is especially prevalent in forms of Christianity that emphasize cognitive knowledge and confession of God. "In an ecclesial culture where remembering the acts of God and proclaiming the name of Jesus are often assumed to be central to a person's salvation, a loss which prevents one from engaging in such intellectual orientated propositional spiritual activities creates dissonance and uncertainties" (188). The realities of dementia pose significant challenges for these ways of understanding what it means to be Christian.

This standard story about dementia has influenced Christian understandings and responses more broadly. Most Christians have simply accepted this story on its own terms. At one point Swinton provides the example of the theologian Glen Weaver, who spends "seventeen of the twenty-four pages of his chapter on embodied spirituality in dementia explaining the neurobiology of dementia." As Swinton asks, "Why would he assume that knowledge from the psychiatric community . . . is necessarily the best place to reflect theologically on dementia?" (43). More centrally, Swinton identifies this impact in the work of another theologian, David Keck. In his 1996 book, *Forgetting Whose We Are: Alzheimer's Disease and the Love of God*, Keck provides a rich meditation on dementia precisely as a deconstruction or loss of self: "The loss of memory [in dementia] entails a loss of self . . . Our entire sense of personhood and human purpose is challenged" (Keck 1996, 15). In Swinton's analysis, Weaver and Keck have too readily accepted the standard story about dementia by taking it as their point of departure.

Accordingly, in his own work, Swinton aims to present a *genuinely* theological alternative: a "counter-story" about dementia that properly begins with God and understands what it means to be human only in relation to God. With echoes of Karl Barth,[5] he suggests that for Christians it is theology, not science, that must provide our primary language for understanding and responding to dementia: "We do not do theological reflection on dementia within a medical, psychological, or neurobiological context. . . . These disciplines do not set the context in which theology speaks" (8). By beginning with God and God's story, Swinton intends to challenge many of our basic assumptions about what dementia is and what it means.

In particular, he suggests that beginning with God allows us to resist claims that dementia straightforwardly involves a loss of identity

On Barth's understanding of the relationship between theological anthropo- and scientific anthropology, see Barth 1960, 25–26. Also see Wood 2012, or selfhood.[6] This is because, from a theological standpoint, it is never our cognitive capacities or memories per se that make us who we are. Our identity or personhood comes from God alone. Put differently, what makes us human is simply that God knows us and remembers us. This is the central and organizing claim of Swinton's book: *those who experience dementia are and remain fully human, even when they forget themselves and others, because they are remembered by God.*[7]

Swinton develops a rich and complex account of what it means to be remembered by God. He draws on Scripture, especially passages such as Jeremiah 17:7–10 and Psalm 139:2–12, which testify to the constancy of God's knowledge of and intimate care for human beings. As he reflects, "God is mindful of human beings. To be human is to be held in the memory of God. God watches over human beings, knows them intimately, and remembers them" (211). God attends to and remembers all human beings; this alone is what secures our personhood.

Swinton acknowledges that this idea of being remembered by God resembles wider claims about the relationality of memory and identity. He is broadly supportive of these claims, undertaking a lengthy and appreciative review of Tom Kitwood's work. Kitwood has similarly contested the standard story about dementia, but specifically by developing an alternative understanding of human personhood. For Kitwood, "personhood is primarily a relational concept. Here, it is not capacities that count. The thing that makes a human being a person is his/her relationships" (140). While largely agreeing, Swinton notes that many of those with dementia quickly begin to lose their relationships (140). And this means that Kitwood's relational personhood by itself is insufficient. Unless relational personhood is more ultimately grounded in God, the full humanity and personhood of those with dementia remains in question.

In clarifying what it means to be remembered by God, Swinton takes care to point out the differences between God's memory and our own: "human memory is not the same as God's memory" (202). On the one hand, he draws attention to the many limits to human memory: "our past and our memories of that past are much more mysterious, fragile, and unclear and much less accurate that we often assume them to be" (209). Our memories by themselves are unable to provide us with accurate

[6] Swinton concludes: "There is no reason to think that God chooses to forget those with advanced dementia. Thus there is no reason to suggest that a person's identity has been lost when he/she encounters advanced dementia" (218).
[7] Or as Swinton himself puts this, "Memory is first and foremost something that is *done for us*, rather than something we achieve on our own" (198).

knowledge of who and what we are. This means that for all of us, not just those with dementia, our memories cannot provide a sufficient basis for personhood (210).

On the other hand, Swinton contrasts these limits with what it means to be remembered by God: "God's memory holds and remembers us as we *actually* are, not simply as we think we are or have been" (213). God's memory is deeper and more expansive than any human memory or self-knowledge. And this is why God's memory can "open up a whole new story about the nature of memory" and provide a "place where all other memories are held" (214).

That we are remembered and held by God has significant implications for pastoral care. If God remembers those with dementia, this not only allows us to affirm their full personhood, but it invites us to attend to such persons in new ways: "The idea of being remembered by God . . . has potential for helping us to understand some vital but often hidden aspects of memory loss in dementia" (196). Put differently, this idea invites us to closely attend to these persons and the complex ways they may be continuing to express who they are, whether through bodily practices, small gestures of response, or other forms of presence. If we "are prepared to give people with dementia the benefit of the doubt, dementia begins to look different" (109).

This new story of being remembered by God provides grounds for hope: "We can, and should, mourn our personal loss of memory. But if God remembers us, we are provided with a source of deep and enduring hope" (198). This theme of hope is integral to Swinton's work on dementia. The recognition that we are held in God's memory "is the promise and the basis for enduring hope" (221). In other words, recognizing that we are remembered by God means we need not fear dementia; we can have hope even in the midst of this disease and its effects.

One possible objection might be that this kind of hope is too otherworldly or "eschatological" (199). This objection has been forcefully made by Peter Kevern: "The proclamation of a God who always remembers . . . leaves us alone in our struggle with the terrifying contingency and flux of dementia, maintaining hope only in a God who will somehow be there at the end of it all" (Kevern 2010, 177).[8] According to Kevern, that God remembers may well allow for a hope of sorts, but at the expense of action in the here and now. In response, Swinton

---

[8] Also quoted by Swinton 2012a, 199–200.

insists that God's remembering is never just about hope for the future but also has direct import for the present: "God's memory has to do with *sustenance* and *action*" (214).

In developing this claim, Swinton draws attention to Old Testament texts in which God remembering his people entails acting and intervening on their behalf. When God remembers, "it is not purely eschatological action; it is something that occurs in the past and in the present as well as in the future" (216). Here Swinton points to examples of God remembering "Noah and delivering him from the flood" (Gen 8:1), God remembering Rachel and granting her children (Gen 30:22), and God remembering the "covenant that existed before creation had even begun" (Gen 1:26–29) (216). In every case God's memory is intimately bound up with God's action.

When God remembers persons with dementia today, this again means that God is actively present and working among such persons. Swinton suggests that God is directly present and working among such persons through the work of the Spirit. And that this is the case even when it is not clearly visible to us: "We trust that God is with and for the person even if we have no real idea of what this might mean" (222).

Furthermore, Swinton suggests God is active and at work among persons with dementia through the life of the church. The church is the concrete embodiment of God's memory: "If people act towards us in ways that remind us that we are remembered, then we see, feel and touch God's memories in action" (222). With echoes of Stanley Hauerwas,[9] he understands the church as a community of formation, "where people learn to see what God's memory looks like" (223). Through its narrative and practices, the church forms its members as a "contrast society," a community that embodies an alternative understanding of the world: "A church that remembers well and is attentive to the needs of people with dementia is a church that is remaining faithful" (226).[10]

[9]   Swinton has engaged Hauerwas in a number of places in his wider work (see Swinton 2012b; Swinton 2005).

[10]   Peter Kevern usefully summarizes Swinton's ecclesiology in *Dementia*: "If we exist as perpetually 're-membered' by God, then the church expresses and realizes that fact in the world as a community of attentive, shared remembering; as a community that values time as a gift to be redeemed and sanctified; and as a place of belonging and hospitality to friends, strangers, and friends-become strangers" (Kevern 2015, 248).

JULIAN OF NORWICH ON SEEING THROUGH THE CROSS

The medieval theologian Julian of Norwich wrote just two theological texts. The first, *A Vision Shown to a Devout Woman* (referred to as her "Short Text"), records and reflects on sixteen visions that she received in 1373, at around age thirty. Julian received her visions while experiencing an unknown illness and believing herself to be on her deathbed. The second text, *A Revelation of Divine Love* (her "Long Text"),[11] was carefully constructed over the next several decades. It contains much longer meditations on these visions and their meanings. In neither text does Julian say anything about dementia. Nonetheless, there are themes and insights running through her theology that resonate with Swinton's more recent work.

Like Swinton, Julian sets out to tell a different story about God and human beings to that of her prevailing culture. In a political and ecclesial context that emphasized hierarchy and order, Julian proclaims a God whose abundant love extends to and encompasses all human beings. She proclaims a God whose love crosses boundaries and knits people together in deep solidarity and community. And for Julian, we can only properly understand who and what we are in relation to this God: "we cannot know ourselves in this life except through faith and grace" (99).

In telling her story, Julian writes of a God who upholds all creation. Her visions consistently witness to a God who loves and sustains all things. In one of her most famous images, she recounts the Lord showing her "a little thing, the size of a hazelnut, lying in the palm of my hand." Upon inquiring, the Lord reveals to her that it is "all that is made." And then it is further revealed to Julian's understanding that "it lasts, and always will, because God loves it; and in the same way everything has its being through the love of God" (45). For Julian everything that exists has its being only due to God's love and providence. God's love and providence even extends to human beings in the midst of their sin and suffering. In another oft-quoted passage, Julian reflects: "He wants us to know that he takes heed not only of noble and great things, but also of the little and small, the humble and simple, both of the one and the other. And this is what he means when he says, 'All manner of things shall be well.' For he wants us to know that the smallest thing will not be forgotten" (80). God remembers the lowly and all those who find themselves in difficult and desperate situations. And this provides hope when we think we have been overlooked and forgotten. Elsewhere Julian writes of

[11]   Most of the quotations I use in this section are from Julian's Long Text. All numbers in brackets in this section refer to Windeatt's edition.

human beings as "mercifully enclosed in the compassion of God and in his gentleness, in his kindliness and in his favour" (104). God's love enfolds us, providing gentle comfort and reassurance.

As with Swinton, Julian is concerned with how knowledge of God's love can help us avoid fear and the temptation to despair.[12] Julian herself seems to be constantly wrestling with this temptation as she receives her visions: "At this time I began to experience a quiet fear, and to this the Lord replied, 'I am keeping you very safe.' This was said with more love and assurance of spiritual safekeeping than I can or may tell" (87). While Julian's fear is of sin (rather than of dementia and its effects), she continually returns to God to find hope.

Finally, Julian is also adamant that nothing can separate us from the love of God. In one of her more curious reflections, she suggests that there is a part of every human being that is and remains with God, which stands beyond the vicissitudes of life and sin: "In every soul that shall be saved there is a godly will that never assented to sin nor ever shall" (87). "This godly will," Julian later explains, is "so good that it can never intend evil, but always intends good constantly, and does good in the sight of God" (118). There is something in each of us that can never be separated from God, neither by "death nor life, neither angels nor demons, neither our fears for today nor our worries about tomorrow" (Rom 8:38).

Nonetheless, there are also points of divergence between Julian and Swinton.[13] Julian can more readily be described as a "theologian of the cross."[14] Her revelations of God's love are consistently focused on and grounded in Christ's suffering and death. Indeed, Julian received her sixteen visions while lying in her bed gazing at a crucifix that was held up before her by a parson (5).[15] And a number of her visions are directly of Christ's bodily suffering.[16]

[12]   In her theology Julian identifies and discusses different kinds of fear, labeling the fear that "draws us on to despair" as "doubting fear" (150).

[13]   The cross and suffering certainly feature in Swinton's work but tend be less constitutive than for Julian. Swinton at one point undertakes a rich discussion of the isolating effects of suffering and affliction (264–68), before suggesting that "love overcomes strangeness'" and advocating community and hospitality (268–79).

[14]   Bradley Holt has used Martin Luther's language to position and read Julian (Holt 2013).

[15]   Grace Jantzen writes, "The theology and spirituality that Julian develops in the Long Text ought not to be detached from the context of intense suffering in which the revelations occurs" (Jantzen 1987, 169).

[16]   Connecting this to medieval practices of reflecting on Christ's suffering, Donyelle McCray has suggested that "Jesus's body is Julian's text" (McCray 2019, 46).

Accordingly, Julian resists thinking and speculating about God otherwise than through the cross.[17] Rather than looking to or contemplating God directly, she keeps her gaze firmly fixed on this one place:

> I wanted to look up from the cross and I did dare, for I knew that while I contemplated the cross I was safe and secure . . . Then I thought my reason said to me, as if there had been said to me in a friendly way: "Look up to his Father . . ." I answered inwardly with all my soul's strength and said, "No, I cannot for you are my heaven." (65)

Even when Julian talks about God's love and care, as outlined above, this is always within the context of visions of Christ's suffering. For Julian, the cross is the one place of safety and security for all those who suffer. And she refrains from appealing to God's love and care in a way that steps away from the cross and all that it represents.[18]

What is at stake with this thoroughgoing emphasis on the cross? First and foremost, this leads Julian to give sustained attention to the depths and complexity of human suffering, both Christ's suffering and our own. With respect to Christ, several of her visions dwell on and draw out the "astonishing suffering" of the Passion (62). In true medieval fashion she imagines and vividly describes Christ's suffering in all its graphic detail: from his scourging with blood flowing from his wounds (56), to the "contempt, spitting and soiling, and blows" inflicted on his body (52), to the "discolouring of his face and drying of his flesh" when he finally passes (61). It is while Julian is having these graphic visions that she begins to discern and speak of God's love and care: "I saw in Christ what the Father is" (69).

In particular, Julian locates God's love and care in Christ's *willingness* to suffer and take on our sin: "Contemplating all of this through his grace, I saw that his love for our souls was so strong that he chose to suffer willingly . . . and meekly suffered with great satisfaction" (67). Indeed, there is a sense in which the very detail of Julian's visions of this suffering give emphasis to the extent of God's love; she goes into graphic detail to convey how much God in Christ loves and willingly embraces human beings.[19]

---

[17]   As Martin Luther famously insists in the Heidelberg Disputation, "None of us can talk adequately or profitably about God's glory and majesty unless we see God also in the lowliness and humiliation of the cross" (Luther 1957, 52)

[18]   See MacFarland 2020, 151.

[19]   And even this is not enough. Julian recounts Christ as saying to her, "If I could suffer more I would suffer more" (69).

For our part, because Christ suffered and died in this manner, we, too, should expect our share of suffering. "Just as Christ is only Christ as one who suffers and is rejected, so a disciple is a disciple only in suffering," as Dietrich Bonhoeffer has put it (Bonhoeffer 2001, 85). Like Bonhoeffer, Julian affirms that suffering places us into deep solidarity with Christ. "I understood that we are now—in our Lord's intention—dying on his cross with him in our pain and our sufferings" (68). Looking to the cross allows us to recognize and affirm Christ's presence in and embrace of our own bodily suffering.[20]

At the same time, this solidarity with Christ means that our suffering, too, no longer has the final word. Because in Christ God embraced and overcame human suffering, we in our place are able to hope that our suffering will similarly be redeemed. "If we remain willingly on the same cross with his help and his grace until the last moment, he will suddenly change his expression towards us, and we will be with him in heaven" (68). In other words, by looking to the cross we are able to see our own suffering in a new light. "And the harder our sufferings have been with him on his cross, the greater will be our glory in his kingdom" (68).

Pastorally, this means that Julian commends patience and trust whenever we encounter suffering and hardship. In the midst of distress, we are to cling to God's promise of a time when "all shall be well" (22). Julian herself yearns "to be released from this world and this life." This is because, she reflects, "I often considered the misery that is here, and the well-being and bliss that is to be there" (136). Yet she recognizes that God will bring about this desired release and redemption in God's own time.[21] She insists that "God rewards man for the patience he shows in awaiting God's will" (137).[22]

Finally, this indicates the central role of eschatology for Julian's theology. While she certainly wants us to act rightly and find healing in the here and now (93), she is more directly oriented (than Swinton) to the peace and joy of the life to come. "It is more blessed for man to be taken from suffering than for suffering to be taken from man; for if suffering be taken away from us it may come back again" (137). For Julian, it is

[20] Julian writes, "In our times of suffering and misery he shows us his face in his Passion and on his cross, helping us to endure by his own blessed strength" (146).
[21] Julian makes much of the fact that in the scheme of things this will seem like "no time." "Between one moment and the next there will be no time, and then everything will be turned to joy" (68).
[22] As Grace Jantzen summarizes, "Julian receives the Lord's assurance that sin and its afflictions are temporary and will come to an end" (Jantzen 1987, 183).

the recognition that God shall ultimately take away our suffering that gives us hope and helps us to endure. Any affliction we experience in the meantime will be taken up by God and redeemed.[23]

Stepping back, this also means Julian is less interested (than Swinton or Hauerwas) in how the church might form its members into virtue or right practices in the here and now. Arguably she is less confident that the church and its members will be able to get it right. In addition, she spends less time directly contesting or attempting to reform the wider culture's understanding of suffering and sin. Her theology is oriented to helping her readers and listeners align themselves to God's will; her concern is with helping us see ourselves and our suffering through God's love and presence on the cross.

For Julian, the main way that we begin to do this is through prayer. "Prayer is a true, gracious, lasting will of the soul united and joined to the will of our Lord by the precious and mysterious working of the Holy Spirit" (92). Through prayer we turn from ourselves and our own way of seeing things; we begin to open and orient ourselves to God's love.[24] And this means that in prayer we gain just a small foretaste of the peace that will be ours in the life to come: "We shall, by his precious grace, in our humble and continued prayers, come into him now in this life through many mysterious touches of precious spirituality revelations and feelings, apportioned to us as our simplicity can bear it." (96).

CONCLUSION

Soon after I began working on this chapter, in late 2020, I received news that my father in New Zealand was entering his final days. My father had received a diagnosis of Parkinson's disease around six years earlier, which was eventually updated to a diagnosis of Lewy body dementia. Since this initial diagnosis, the progression of his disease had proved rapid and unrelenting. By the time of his passing, he had limited mobility, his memory was highly impaired, and his speech and thinking were confused and often incoherent. He had been living in full-time residential care in a dementia unit of a local nursing home for about a year. Throughout much of the time that my father had been unwell, I had

---

[23]   Julian is not entirely clear how this will take place. And she acknowledges her inability to fully reconcile God's promise that "all shall be well" with her own experiences. "The reason why he allows sin [and suffering]" still remains a mystery that God "will make openly known to us in heaven" (75). In other words, the cross provides comfort and reassurance of God's love. But it does so without removing us from suffering and its complexities.

[24]   "Prayer unites the soul to God," as Julian elsewhere puts it (95).

lived at a distance, initially in Scotland and more recently in Australia. (Thankfully I was able to spend six months living close to home while on a research sabbatical in 2019.) Because of restrictions on international travel during the COVID-19 pandemic, I was unable to visit him during his final days or attend his funeral.

Over the last few years John Swinton and Julian have both proved faithful companions; they have helped me make sense of my father's situation and to find a way forward. John's work (and friendship) has helped me to actively affirm and attend to God's presence and work in the context of the many changes that my father underwent; his work has helped me to be less anxious and fearful in the face of such changes. In addition, his work has helped me better appreciate the role of relationships for sustaining and upholding my father's memory and identity. Even from a distance, it was clear that family members and caregivers were working to sustain and support his identity as his disease progressed. Finally, John's central claim that God always remembers, even as we forget, has provided safety and stability during the many challenges of this situation.

Julian's theology of the cross has provided me with hope and sustenance in a different way. Julian received her visions of God's abundant love while in the midst of her own bodily suffering. She continually focused on and returned to the suffering of Christ as the single place of safety and hope. And this means that Julian wrote and thought in ways that are close to the ground; she was willing to remain in the midst of the messiness and complexity of bodily suffering.[25] From within the context of suffering, her theology has helped me to cling to God's promise that "all shall be well," even when I have not been able to see how this will be the case. Julian has thus helped me to recognize the limits of what might be achieved this side of the eschaton. And finally, in the midst of the last few years, Julian has reminded me to continually turn to God in prayer.

John and Julian both proclaim a God who remembers and upholds human beings, even when this is not fully apparent to us. They both witness to a God who loves and cares for us in ways that continuously exceed our grasp and our expectations. And they both insist that God provides grounds for hope as and when we encounter suffering. To give John the final word, "even in the midst of the pain and affliction that can accompany dementia, there are hidden possibilities if we trust God and allow the challenge of our sadness to stimulate new ways of thinking and being with one another" (Swinton 2012, 285).

---

[25]   As I have argued elsewhere, this is also reflected in the style of Julian's theology and language (Mawson 2021).

WORKS CITED

Banks, Alexandra. 2020. "Lost Time: Dementia, Theology and the Arts." *The Cooperative Hub*. September 1, 2020. https://thecooperativehub.com/index.php/2020/09/01/lost-time-dementia-theology-and-the-arts/.

Barth, Karl. 1960. *Church Dogmatics*. Edited by G. W. Bromiley and T. F. Torrance. Vol. 3, pt. 2, *The Doctrine of Creation*. Edinburgh: T&T Clark.

Bonhoeffer, Dietrich. 2001. *Discipleship*. Edited by Geoffrey Kelly and John D. Godsey. Translated by Barbara Green and Reinhard Krauss. Minneapolis: Fortress.

Byron-Davies, Justin. 2020. *Revelation and the Apocalypse in Late Medieval Literature: Writings of Julian of Norwich and William Langland*. Cardiff: University of Wales Press.

Hall, Amy Laura. 2018. *Laughing at the Devil: Seeing the World with Julian of Norwich*. Durham, N.C.: Duke University Press.

Holt, Bradley. 2013. "Prayer and the Theologian of the Cross: Julian of Norwich and Martin Luther." *Dialog: A Journal of Theology* 52, no. 4: 321–31.

Jantzen, Grace. 1987. *Julian of Norwich: Mystic and Theologian*. London: SPCK.

Jenkins, Jacqueline, ed. 2007. *The Writings of Julian of Norwich: A Vision Showed to a Devout Woman and A Revelation of Love*. Translated by Nicholas Watson. University Park: Pennsylvania State University Press.

Julian of Norwich. 2015. *Revelations of Divine Love*. Translated by Barry Windeatt. Oxford: Oxford University Press.

Keck, David. 1996. *Forgetting Whose We Are: Alzheimer's Disease and the Love of God*. Nashville: Abingdon.

Kevern, Peter. 2010. "What Sort of a God Is to Be Found in Dementia? A Survey of Theological Responses and an Agenda for their Development." *Theology* 113: 174–82.

———. 2015. Review of *Dementia: Living in the Memories of God*, by John Swinton. *Theology Today* 72, no. 2: 247–48.

Kitwood, Tom. 1997. *Dementia Reconsidered: The Person Comes First*. Rethinking Ageing. Buckingham, UK: Open University Press.

Luther, Martin. 1957. "Heidelberg Disputation." In *The Career of a Reformer I*, edited by Harold J. Grimm and Helmut T. Lehmann, 37–70. Vol. 31 of *Luther's Works*. Minneapolis: Fortress.

McCray, Donyelle C. 2019. *The Censored Pulpit: Julian of Norwich as Preacher*. Lanham, Md.: Lexington/Fortress Academic.

McFarland, Ian A. 2020. "Sin and the Limits of Theology: A Reflection in Conversation with Julian of Norwich and Martin Luther." *International Journal of Systematic Theology* 22, no. 2: 147–68.

Mawson, Michael. 2021. "Speaking of God: Unruly God-Talk with Julian of Norwich." In *Doing Theology in the New Normal*, edited by Jione Havea, 196–208. London: SCM Press.

"Stole: The Show Rod Pattenden." n.d. *Timeless Textiles* (blog). Accessed December 4, 2020. https://timelesstextiles.com.au/events/stole-the-show-rod-pattenden/.

Swinton, John, ed. 2005. *Critical Reflections on Stanley Hauerwas' Theology of Disability: Disabling Society, Enabling Theology*. New York: Routledge.

———. 2012a. *Dementia: Living in the Memories of God*. Grand Rapids: Eerdmans.

———. 2012b. "The Importance of Being a Creature: Stanley Hauerwas on Disability." In *Disability in the Christian Tradition: A Reader*, edited by Brian Brock and John Swinton, 512–45. Grand Rapids: Eerdmans.

———. 2016. *Becoming Friends of Time: Disability, Timefullness, and Gentle Discipleship.* Waco, Tex.: Baylor University Press.

Turner, Denys. 2011. *Julian of Norwich, Theologian.* New Haven, Conn.: Yale University Press.

Weaver, Glen. 2004. "Embodied Spirituality: Experiences of Identity and Spiritual Suffering among Persons with Alzheimer's Dementia." In *From Cells to Souls—and Beyond: Changing Portraits of Human Nature*, edited by Malcolm Jeeves, 77–101. Grand Rapids: Eerdmans.

Wood, Donald. 2012. "*This* Ability: Barth on the Concrete Freedom of Human Life." In *Disability in the Christian Tradition: A Reader*, edited by Brian Brock and John Swinton, 391–426. Grand Rapids: Eerdmans.

III

Quests for Faithful Embodiment

8
Bearing the Reality of Dementia
Aileen Barclay

John and I have been close friends for more than twenty years and remain so. Both John and his wife Alison journeyed with me through my husband Peter's dementia until his death in 2014.

Not long after Peter's medical diagnosis, John asked if I would be willing to allow him to write on our experiences, to which I readily agreed, knowing that I could trust him and that his work on dementia would have worldwide influence, as the composition of this book clearly demonstrates. John and I have not always agreed, but as friends, most of the time we have been able to acknowledge to each other that our respective starting points are different. I believe this is a healthy stance that encourages more questions, thereby leading to deeper personal and professional understandings as well as facilitating further research on the subject.

So, with a great deal of prayer and thought, I will attempt to reflect broadly on a few of the familiar themes contained within John's vast treasure box of books and articles, as they relate to my lived experience of bearing the reality of dementia. First, I compare areas in John's theology with aspects of my own experience that seem to be at odds with it. But as I move on, I hope it will become clear to you, the reader, the enormous gift that John as my friend has been to me from the outset and as I began to heal from the devastation of dementia.

JOHN, THE THEOLOGIAN: BEING HUMAN AND BEARING REALITY

Stanley Hauerwas focuses on the question of how much reality we can bear and yet remain human (Hauerwas 2013). He also asserts that we live in a time when Christians and non-Christians alike truly do not know any longer what it means to be human. Regardless of our human perceptions, not everyone agrees, with many feeling the need to tell us the truth from their own respective standpoint. Yet no matter how we understand humanness, in my view it is certainly true that dementia strikes at the basis of our understanding of what it means to be human and be made in God's image.

John contends that it is our ideas about what humanness, the nature of the self, and self-fulfillment mean that will have to be dissolved and recreated if we are to understand and respond well to what dementia means (Swinton 2012). He argues that to be fully human as Christians is to know that we are embodied creatures who are wholly dependent and contingent on God. Our human value and identity are held and assured by God the Creator, who has inspired us with His breath, sustaining us in the power of the Holy Spirit who continues to offer all of us the gift of life and relationship (Swinton 2012, 182).

Now I cannot disagree with him at a theoretical level, but from my own perspective as the prime carer at that time, exasperated and broken with all I needed to attend to, such rarefied thoughts were far from my lived reality. John, however, does note that love and relationships do change for those of us practically living with a partner who has dementia. He speaks about willful love, fidelity, and determination as the key to maintaining a marital relationship through progressive dementia.

All I can truthfully say is that none of us is a saint all of the time or even, in my own case, none of the time. Instead, I propose that people deeply submerged in dementia are given too much reality that is hard to bear, exemplifying my point by imagining some of the questions Peter and I were asking to which there are no real answers.

> "What am I to do when no one understands me any longer and I get lost in conversation? What am I to do when Aileen wants me to read all the notes she's left for me before she goes to work? Does she even know I am struggling to understand the written word?" (Peter)

> "What do I do when I get home and find Peter has dismantled the gas boiler in an attempt to fix it, even though it was never broken in the first place. Where on earth has he hidden the kettle? How many things has he thrown out the window today? Why does he always destroy the sticky notes I leave to help him find things around the house?" (Aileen)

So, I welcome Hauerwas' view that at base, it is stories that make us human (Hauerwas 2001). He notes that rational, logical, and objective observations may have led to some wonderful breakthroughs in science and medicine. Yet even scientists tell stories, influenced as they are by the communities around them as they write up their research findings. For Hauerwas, metaphors and stories suggest how we should see and describe the world, asserting that this is how we should look on ourselves, others, and the world in ways that rules themselves do not. Stories and metaphors do this by providing the narrative accounts that give our lives a degree of coherence (Hauerwas 1974). Yet human life by its very nature is messy and includes unanswerable questions like the ones quoted above in our stories.

CARING

In relation to caring, it is a very difficult job to be the sole carer of a person who is dementing, even if that person is much loved. Both Peter and I lived in a world more determined by commodity than Christian love. Our social worker repeatedly told me about the cost of providing care to my husband and expressed her view that, as his wife, I should give up my job and care for him. Moreover, she was not in the least interested in the two terminal relatives for whom I was also trying to care. Still, I did reduce my hours at work to be home more for Peter, but that had significant financial implications for my final pension.

Acquiescing to the power of service providers and the professional frameworks within which they worked was not an easy task. The professional person-centered language of care is dehumanizing and liberally sprinkled with terms more familiar to business—service users, providers, human resources, placements, allocation of funds, and so on. The irritation aroused in me by what was well-enough intended turned out to be both demeaning and stigmatizing for both Peter and me. Our reality took the form of a complete and utter dislocation from what was being offered, and all it did to me as a Christian was to arouse my sense of inadequacy in my own inability to care well for my husband (Barclay 2012, 90).

John's counter-story as a firm foundation for dementia care may seem to be a far cry from my personal experience, though I think in his published writing he may be thinking more about professional caregiving (see Swinton 2012). In analyzing the various ways by which dementia is understood professionally, he sets out his own views on what it means to care. Clarifying the nature of care, he asserts that it lies at the heart of the vocation given to human beings by God. Neither cognitive nor reasoning ability has much to do with care, he contends, but rather the prerogative of love. Being human is to love like God and be loved by God. Being human is to act faithfully toward the creation that God has made and loves, suggesting that to be a recipient of care is a profound and vital aspect of that process. To give and receive care from others is fundamental to the Genesis story of dominion (Barclay 2015). Consequently, to be a person in the later stages of dementia should not mean any loss of dignity or a diminishment of humanity. At a conceptual level I agree, but I am also glad that David Deuel (n.d.), in a review of John's book, notes that John does not propose easy, feel-good solutions but rather real growth rooted in the truth about God's ways with his people and their illnesses. For having watched Peter, in all his humanness, struggling to control his bodily functions, it is hard for me to say that there is no loss of dignity. Little wonder many of us fear the onset of life-limiting diseases in our own lives. Moreover, as a carer watching her husband's decline, my heart was overwhelmed with compassion for him, even if I did not enjoy the task of keeping him safe and clean.

Once a gracious, capable, intelligent man, I knew my husband had dementia years before his medical/psychiatric diagnosis of Alzheimer's disease (Barclay 2012, 94). The deterioration was a slow, relentless destruction of his capacities as a competent adult. He became a frightened child, petulant and manipulative, dependent on me for what little order could be created around his disappearing capacities.

I began to notice the similarity between my experience as a teacher and the experience of caring for Peter. Having spent almost forty years working in schools with children who found learning difficult and their families, I recalled my own vocation spent promoting educational change for the children who had won my heart from my first day as a probationer teacher. Now Peter had become that child who was the victim of systems, attitudes, cultures, and practices controlled by notions of economic worthiness, achievement, and attainment. And the practices merely shone a light on his lack of competence. The main difference though, is that children are cute and likable, at least most of the time, but Peter—not so much! Within this world of dementia care, both of us had become commodities made to fit into the values or nonvalues of professional care.

Tom Kitwood, well known for his work on person-centered care for people with dementia, argues that paid caregivers do not know what they are doing most of the time (Kitwood 2007, 208). He contends that from a social-psychological perspective, professional services require a robust theory of care to alleviate the confusion around them. Responding to his view a few years ago, I argued that from a Christian perspective, not only is there a robust theory of care in the form of the gospel but also a spiritual imperative to care for each other (Barclay 2012, 91). Throughout John's writing on dementia and disability, he has gone a long way toward clarifying what the gospel means for us Christians, all of which is helpful, but like all our human musings does not tell the whole story. Our habitual vision is never fully correct but only ever provisional and one of an infinite number, which supports my view of the power of stories. Stories do not necessarily have hard and fast rules, nor prescribed beginnings and endings, which links now into John's theology on the fluidity and reinterpretation of time.

BECOMING FRIENDS OF TIME

Discussing contemporary perceptions of disability, John demonstrates that not being able to keep up with others has a particularly devasting effect on those who have cognitive difficulties (Swinton 2016). He asserts that this is strongly connected with how modern people understand the purpose of time. Looking through the eyes of God's love, however, he notes that prevailing concepts of time have made the Creator unseen. Tracing the historical development of clock time, from the industrial and technological revolution in Western cultures, through to the current dominance of the global market economy, he shows that the move from premodern society where most of us lived by Christian narratives of creation, redemption, and service to God, has highlighted a standard definition of time as a commodity. Such an emphasis produces its own strangers. For those of us unable to contribute to a commodity-weighted economy, our deficits are revealed, making us of little value and consequently endangering our humanity (Barclay 2012, 92).

John contends that when you hang around with people who see the world differently and perceive things in ways that are unconventional, you begin to see that there is a lot of truth to that way of seeing the world and that some of our established norms are always open to challenge (Swinton 2016).

As I watched Peter becoming frailer, I realized that I was beginning to experience time differently and was not particularly enamored by what I could see lying ahead of me in terms of my own career and preoccupations. Yet John asserts that time as commodity will eventually be exposed for the violence it causes. Our timeless Creator God is not affected or determined by time. God himself participates in time itself through the Son's incarnation. John believes that through Cross and Resurrection time is fulfilled. In the past, the present, and the future of every historical moment, God's time is expressed in the notion of God's timefullness. Timeful and timeless, God is a full inhabitant of creaturely time, a being whose timelessness is of a different order that has spilled over to create the time we know. God's presence is in every moment. As Christians, we receive time as a creaturely gift, which enables us to participate faithfully in Jesus' redemptive work in time. As we live there, it exposes the true nature of the times we live in, dominated by economic reason and violence. If time then is a gift, it changes our relationship to it, and so we ought not to try to master it, for when we do so, violence becomes inevitable (Swinton 2016). Thus, participating in Christ's redemptive work, we Christians learn to resist the terror of clock time and instead, learn to become friends of time, to which I add that John has certainly been a friend of time to me.

As Peter's Alzheimer's progressed, the psychiatric nurse who attended to us asserted that this time was the worst for caregivers, trying to assure me that it would not last forever. She later became a wonderful friend, who knew the services on offer were not in the least suited to Peter's needs. He refused to go the dementia-care center twice a week. He refused to have the carer who came to give him lunch while I was at work. And no one was able to persuade him differently. So I would return from work where he would say to me, "You're not Aileen Barclay! You're not my wife! Get out of my house!" (Peter). Plus, because he had a habit of throwing the mail out into the garden, I fitted a locked mailbox but would find him trying to take the letters from a slot on the top of the locked box using salad servers. On the days when I was working, there would be endless phone calls from him to the receptionist at university, demanding to speak to me. And the carpenter doing some work for us phoned me at university to tell me that Peter believed I had run off to Australia with another man that day and had taken all his money with me. But, if losing capacity means slowing down, then I am vexed. For at least three years, Peter's intellectual capacities simply changed, and they kept changing! He would go for a walk and not return for hours, telling me he had had an amazing time. I read this as meaning he got lost and could not find his way home, often being taken home by the police. On holiday in Ireland with my brother and sister-in-law, John (d. 2012) and Sandra, we bought him Coke instead of Guinness after he had had a couple of pints. Demanding Guinness and being refused led him to walking out of the pub and being brought back to our holiday flat by the Garda hours later where he next climbed into bed with John and Sandra. And on the flight home, he was violently sick, so that was the end of holidays. I laugh at his antics now, but at the time I was often at the end of my tether. In the introduction I spoke of John's notion of Christian vocation as being a central tenet of what it means to be a Christian. He recognizes that there are important aspects of the Christian life with which we all need help and nurturing throughout our lives (Swinton 2020).

VOCATION

John declares that the task of the church is to help people to hear the call of Jesus and to fulfill the calling that is gifted to them. He describes various aspects of vocation as missiological, liturgical, and ecclesiological, going on to suggest that vocation is perhaps best framed as an aspect of God's providence. The call to be with Jesus and to participate in God's work in the world is perceived as the embodiment of our calling that places us and the events of the world within a hopeful narrative that is bigger than ourselves. It is a place where we open up our hearts to the Spirit enabling us to participate faithfully within God's work in the world. But John argues that not everyone recognizes or chooses to respond to that calling. Culturally, reason and the emphasis on choice, free will, and autonomy have replaced vocation. However, John argues that this is a mode of false consciousness. Theologically, to have a vocation is to receive something from outside yourself, to have your life profoundly shaped and directed by forces beyond your own control and comprehension. Far from being simply a matter of personal choice, vocation very often contradicts the will of the person who is called (see for example, Moses, Abraham, and Paul). To be reasonable, John says, is to be able to think clearly, make good choices about yourself, and run and plan your own life. Reason asks us to personalize our talent and use it for whatever we desire. Vocation asks us to obey Jesus' command and use our talents for whatever God desires. But how does this apply in reality?

Certainly, the onset of Peter's dementia contradicted my own will and perhaps I did not recognize it as a vocation as it profoundly shaped and directed my life by forces beyond my control. Vocation it may or may not have been, but I did not like it, for there seemed to be no way out—at least not during the time of Peter's demise. Of course, I could have walked away, but that never crossed my mind. Maybe that is what John means when he speaks of willful love, but even willfully loving Peter, I still wrestled with the question of why God would have asked me to be a nurse to three seriously sick people at the same time, when anyone who truly knows me would laugh at the very thought of me as a nurse. Being on the receiving end of all that dementia for an extended period does change the nature of relationships not only with the person one loves and care for but also many others, even in church. In my view, John's notion of vocation as providence only has credence within a Christian context inasmuch there are Christian people willfully loving at one's back, and certainly John, not as a theologian but as a friend, is a prime example. Yet, for both Peter and me, those who mostly stepped up to the mark were not Christians. So how do I understand that one?

Instead, I am of the view that all life is endlessly relational, and I think my view would stand up to biblical scrutiny (Sittler 2000). For life exceeds the possibility of our capacity to ever know it entirely.

Timeful and timeless, life, death, and recreation roll on from one generation to another endlessly. The first human beings were placed in a garden, in a community of abounding life on which humans subsist. Without the abounding life, human beings simply would not be. Dominion in Genesis means to care for the Earth, which ultimately means caring for each other—Christian and non-Christian alike. Through the Spirit, made in God's image, and part of the body of Christ, it seems to me, that caring for each other is built into our very DNA.

Still, regardless of the efforts I made to learn to live in this strange world of dementia, I was not very successful. But I wondered if there is ever such a thing as success in bearing the reality of dementia. Remembering Dietrich Bonhoeffer, I thought a lot about his definition of success, which is to be on one's knees in that place of hopelessness and despair, where the Holy Spirit lifts us up to a new and different life (Bonhoeffer 2005). Of course, Bonhoeffer's understanding of success is worlds apart from worldly norms. Yet I was often on my knees pleading with the Lord, and this takes me to the place of lament!

DEMENTIA AROUSES LAMENT

Caring for Peter at home over the years, along with the death of two of my closest relatives, led to a great deal of time (not clock time) spent in the world of lament. I grew up knowing the word *lament* as music my father played on his bagpipes and something that sounded sore to my ears. So, when John as a friend first spoke to me about lament in a faith context, it opened up a whole new language of prayer and worship for me and I loved it! Walter Brueggemann became my favorite author, particularly his work on the psalms of lament (Brueggemann 1984). Drawing from Brueggemann, John contends that lament provides language and structure within which pain, suffering, grief, and despair can be ritualized, moving us from one way of seeing to another, from protest to hopefulness (Swinton 2012). Lament is like the silence of a friend who listens and accompanies us through the shadow of death. Lament is not an act of faithlessness but an act of faithfulness in situations where faith and hope are challenged, as they certainly were in my own situation. Like listening to bagpipe lament, it is in paying attention to the grace notes of the lament that we meet with the God of grace when our lives have fallen apart. And discovering the one person who "gets" what we think and feel as he journeys with us is painfully liberating. Holy Saturday, too, made a lot of sense to me. The practice of lament began to give me hope and the possibility of a future. I may not have found a new way of living with the unwelcome gift of Alzheimer's that had come my way, but I was beginning to learn how to live in the present (Caussade 2010). Psalm 88 became a favorite because it is entirely about living in the present—in Holy Saturday and cannot be understood through some glib theodicy (Barclay 2012). It speaks directly to the place of chaos and despair so familiar to many who do the caring as well as to those who are cared for. In its strangeness, the psalm does not seem to speak of resurrection where none exists, but rather speaks into the serious limitations of human abilities to care at an individual level and within our society. What a gift Psalm 88 is for those of us struggling alone with caring for people who are dementing. Yet I have never heard a sermon preached on the psalm.

JOHN, THE FRIEND

So now, having compared my lived experience with some of John's theoretical insights, I want to tell you about John, the friend. To begin, I make a distinction between what it means to be a friend as compared with friendship or being friendly (Reinders 2007, 20). There was never a clear reason aside from our shared faith why John and I became friends. I was lecturing in inclusive education at the University of Aberdeen where John was a lecturer in practical theology. We did, however, worship in the same congregation where John was a long-standing member and Peter and I were relatively new members. Suffering, also one of John's themes, came at me like a tempest on returning from church one Sunday to find a detective on my doorstep with the most devastating news for me. My twenty-three-year-old son had been found dead earlier in the day. To say that John became a friend of time in suffering with kindness, gentleness, and compassion is an understatement. Both he and his wife, Alison, were "there for me" from day one. Even at night when I was unable to sleep, my computer would ping as an email from John arrived in the mailbox wondering if I wanted to chat. A few months down the line, John suggested that I write about my son's death, further suggesting that I write him a monograph as a way of dealing with long-term grief. And out of that came my doctoral study (Barclay 2009). It was a long haul for John to remain a faithful friend, and I will never know how he managed the complexity of his role as supervisor and close friend, but he did through his encouragement and support to Peter and me. Completing my doctoral studies was the therapy I needed to learn to live with the pain of losing my son, but Peter's dementia remained an ongoing sorrow. So it was a very difficult decision to request full-time nursing care for him.

TOWARD HEALING

Peter was eventually received into full-time nursing care, and on that first day as both of us were wandering around the sadly neglected garden of the home, a new horizon opened up for me that over time caused me to begin to see dementia differently. Set on the banks of a river in an area known locally as a beauty spot, we both stopped to watch how swiftly the current flowed in an expansive turn as the water gushed over the remains of a water channel, where nineteenth-century paper mills used to provide labor for the community. Standing in silence together for a while, Peter put his arm around me, and I started praying my constant prayer, "Your will be done, on earth as it is in heaven" (Matt 6:10). Somehow, the beauty of natural environment on one side of the home met with the despair of dementia within the home, which began to change my understanding of God's story at a deeper level. The moment was a kind of spiritual purification where the barriers preventing me from truly sensing God's love began to be removed, possibly more akin to the story of the disciples on the road to Emmaus. This kairos moment, as Thomas Merton noted, "is an awakening, enlightenment[,] and the amazing intuitive grasp by which love gains certitude of God's creative and dynamic intervention in our daily life . . . It is a pure and virginal knowledge, poor in concepts, poorer still in reasoning, but able, by its very poverty and purity, to follow the Word 'wherever he may go'" (Merton 1999, 5).

And in this transformation, a new vocation took shape, to build a healing garden for Peter and the other residents of the home. John was largely instrumental in helping me get the project off the ground, pointing me in the direction of spiritual literature on the subject and helping me to apply for funding from our denomination. I came to realize that healing gardens are about eternal change and transformation, and like life itself, about uncertainty from which a sense of awe and wonder can spring. Going beyond human reason, gardens challenge our senses, bringing us to a sacred place filled with harmony and hope, where our notions of time end and spiritual truths are discerned. Our Christian story both begins and ends in a garden, with notions of heaven and paradise in Scripture liberally sprinkled with metaphors and images of gardens. From lament to transformation, the project was for both Peter and me together, a vocation for the good of others associated with the care-home community and set within the broader context of God's story and providence. And in the last couple of years of Peter's life, the healing garden project brought space for us to bring our human longings for life in all its fullness harmoniously together, as it also did for residents, staff, and relatives. In this garden, once neglected and forgotten, came joy, peace, and hope for a community usually more concerned with the fear of old aging and death. For death seems to be the last taboo in care homes and in our society, the thing over which none of us has any control. No more did it matter that in church Peter and I both had become pariahs from the time-honored married coupledom status that exists there. No more did it matter that invitations once eagerly accepted to our home were refused with lame excuses after Peter's diagnosis. With a sense of having been cast aside in a dung heap, here in the care home, the garden became church for us—a church living and moving in God's time where it did not matter about having the necessary intellectual capacities to fully participate in the normal services of a Presbyterian church. Contemplatively, and released from the burden of being the sole carer, instead of seeing the empty, blank stare in the faces of those with advanced dementia, I saw and sensed God's simple lingering look of love for all of us and realized that I loved them all. Still, the metaphor of a dung heap remains a challenge to the church. For as all gardeners know,

> out of the dung heap, the earth produces new riches, transforming dementia into a power of life and the possibility of creativeness. Open to storms and sunshine alike, the earth is always ready to receive any seed we sow with the capability of bringing thirtyfold, sixtyfold, a hundredfold out of every seed. Humility requires us to stay close to the earth, to let go of the false and to contemplate paradise. (Dementia Garden Project 2012, https://www.abdn.ac.uk/sdhp/documents/Persley_Garden_Project.pdf)

On the day Peter died, I felt I had been released and so had he. What an awful end—struggling for breath, with no more morphine available to him in the nursing home where he had lived for four years in case it would hasten his death. The law, I was told, forbade it, even though the doctor had said he would die that evening. Would a couple of hours have made that much difference, given his obvious distress? I did not cry. I did not grieve. I was not sad. But I was still angry that he had left me years before, unable as he was to believe that he did in fact have Alzheimer's disease.

I conducted his funeral because I did not think anyone else could tell his story better than me. Not even our friend John Swinton, who had a copy of the script in case I found it too emotional. How arrogant of me!

Shortly before Peter's death, I had moved to a new house twenty miles away from Aberdeen seeking solace on Deeside from where my own forebears had come. And there another kairos moment came my way. Time has no limits as our humanly understanding of linear time may suggest. Not that I can give you great theories of what I mean, but what I can give you is a sense of the eternal. Mountains rising from deep valleys, resplendent with mighty trees, fast-flowing rivers tumbling over massive granite boulders, their powerful energy drowning out the noise of contemporary life—endless, timeless, timeful, and somewhat frightening. Silent, still lochs glistening in the sunlight and shadowing the hills above them. Marshland thriving with life left alone to fulfill the purpose for which it was made in God's mysterious creation. A sense of presence from both the noise of nature and of its silence overcoming all else. Freezing cold winters; ice glinting among dark cloudy skies bringing welcome light. Ruined crofts on sparse, boggy grassland arousing thoughts of those who had scraped a meager living from the hard rough ground. Overgrown graveyards from generations ago, tucked in remote corners but still telling stories of people and their communities. Kairos moments that awaken us to the mystery of God's goodness, faithfulness, and compassion and the readiness to accept uncertainty without the need for more knowledge. Surely the mountains we climb in our lives exceed the possibility of our own capacity to ever know it entirely.

After the storm, I stumbled into Zion with a whole new life I could never have imagined. Falling on my knees one day, I was finally able to thank God for walking the long journey with me, and now I can say in all honesty that it has been a great blessing for me to have been asked to write this chapter around the theme of dementia and aging. I hope I have approached the task with humility in attempting to reflect on the very significant contribution John Swinton has made to the theology of dementia. But more important to me is that you are able to see in my writing just how wonderful it is to have a living embodied person in the form of John share the road with me.

"The command to care is gentle; the results of not caring are violent and fatal . . . If we believe that the judgements of the Lord are true and righteous altogether, dare we suppose that he will keep his anger forever? Or that he who marks the fall of the sparrow will forever withhold the fateful working out of the forces that created, sustained, and make rich and various the life of both created garden and created and loved children?" (Sittler 2000, 205).

Keep on with your heaven-appointed task to break down the barriers of limitation, John!

WORKS CITED

Baldwin, C., and A. Capstick, eds. 2007. *Tom Kitwood on Dementia*. Berkshire, UK: Open University Press.

Barclay, Aileen. 2009. "On Becoming Educators of the Cross: A Faithful Christian Response to Pupil Disaffection." PhD thesis, University of Aberdeen.

———. 2012. "Psalm 88: Living with Alzheimers." *Journal of Religion, Disability & Health* 16, no. 1: 88–101.

———. 2015. "Lost in Eden: Dementia from Paradise." *Journal of Religion, Spirituality & Aging* 28, nos. 1–2: 68–83.

Bonhoeffer, Dietrich. 2005. *Ethics*. 4th ed. Minneapolis: Fortress.

Brueggemann, Walter. 1984. *The Message of the Psalms*. Minneapolis: Fortress.

———. 1986. "The Costly Loss of Lament." *Journal for the Study of the Old Testament* 36: 55–71.

Caussade, J. P. 2010. *The Sacrament of the Present Moment: A Spiritual Manifesto Reminding Us That It Is Only in God That We Live and Have Our Being*. ReadaClassic.com.

Deuel, David C. 2013. Review of *Dementia: Living in the Memories of God*, by John Swinton. *Themelios* 38, no. 3: 547–49. Also available online at https://www.thegospelcoalition .org/themelios/review/dementia-Living-in-the-Memories-of-God/.

Hauerwas, Stanley. 1974. *Vision and Virtue: Essays in Christian Ethical Reflection*. Notre Dame, Ind.: Fides.

———. 2001. *With the Grain of the Universe: The Church's Witness and Natural Theology*. Grand Rapids: Brazos Press.

———. 2005. "The Gesture of a Truthful Story." In *Critical Reflections on Stanley Hauerwas' Theology of Disability: Disabling Society, Enabling Theology*, edited by John Swinton, 71–80. New York: Haworth Pastoral Press.

———. 2013. "Bearing Reality: A Christian Meditation." *Journal of the Society of Christian Ethics* 33, no. 1: 3–20.

Kitwood, Tom. 2007. *On Dementia*. New York: Open University Press.

Marcus, Clare Cooper, and Marni Barnes. 1999. *Healing Gardens, Therapeutic Benefits and Design Recommendations*. New York: Wiley.

Merton, Thomas. 1999. *New Seeds of Contemplation*. London: Burns & Oates.

Reinders, Hans S. 2008. *Receiving the Gift of Friendship: Profound Disability, Theological Anthropology, and Ethics*. Grand Rapids: Eerdmans.

Shepherd, Nan. 2011. *The Living Mountain*. 2nd ed. Edinburgh: Canongate.

Sittler, J. 2000. *Evocations of Grace*. 7th ed. Grand Rapids: Eerdmans.

Swinton, John. 2007. *Raging with Compassion: Pastoral Responses to the Problem of Evil*. Grand Rapids: Eerdmans.

———. 2012. *Dementia: Living in the Memories of God*. Grand Rapids: Eerdmans.

———. 2016. *Becoming Friends of Time: Disability, Timefullness, and Gentle Discipleship*. Waco, Tex.: Baylor University Press.

———. 2020. "Disability, Vocation, and Prophetic Witness." *Theology Today* 77, no. 2: 186–97.

Vanier, Jean. 2005. "The Needs of Strangers." In *Critical Reflections on Stanley Hauerwas' Theology of Disability: Disabling Society, Enabling Theology*, edited by John Swinton, 27–35. New York: Haworth Pastoral Press.

9
Navigating Mental Health

A Personal Narrative

Elahe Hessamfar

When God calls one through his irresistible grace, is there an escape? I think not. Our daughter Helia's calling came to her in spring 2000. Seemingly out of nowhere, our beautiful daughter was snatched into the grip of darkness. The Helia we knew was taken away from us. With that, life changed forever.

I have spent the past twenty-two years doing extensive scientific and theological research and prayerfully reflecting on the overarching phenomenon of psychosis. I have tried to make sense of this mysterious spectacle while caring for Helia, who carries the diagnosis of "schizophrenia" in her medical files. This has been a heart-wrenching journey, one that has thrown many of my beliefs about God, life, reality, humanity, and relationships out the window. The journey has forced me to change and see everything through a lens that magnifies God and makes me needy of his grace. The experience has emptied me of all my flair, pride, vain self-confidence, and attachment to worldly dreams. But don't feel sorry for me! I have never felt this free! I am free of much that held me in bondage, much vanity and falsehood that occupied all my capacity, time, and energy. No, I haven't "arrived" yet; I am still a broken sinner. But the journey has shaken me and has opened my eyes to much that I was not capable of seeing before.

Before going further, let me clarify how I use some common terminology. I may refer to mental challenges as an illness but never as a disease. My distinction is based on the work of Harvard psychiatrist and anthropologist Arthur Kleinman. Kleinman defines illness as the innate "human experience of symptoms and suffering." Illness, for him, points to "the principal difficulties that symptoms and disability create in our lives." For Kleinman, illness is "always culturally shaped" and may vary in different contexts. He views an "illness" as distinctly different from a "disease," which refers to "an alteration in biological structure or functioning" (1988, 3–5).

Although theories abound on the causes of "schizophrenia," many people of faith have been silenced, or their experiences reframed by those around them, preventing them from speaking candidly of their experiences for fear of being mocked. Indeed, many people label as psychotic those who speak of their "extreme" spiritual experiences. I realize that it is not in vogue to believe in God, sin, and the spiritual realm in our postmodern world. However, sooner or later we all encounter experiences that refuse to fit into the secular and reductionist categories we impose on them. If encountering intense psychotic phenomena does not humble us and force us to question our usually tacit assumptions about reality, then I don't know what will.

HOW IT ALL BEGAN

It was in the year 2000 that Helia was hit with severe mental anguish and began a dark journey of illness toward what psychiatry labels "schizophrenia." I will not debate the validity of psychiatric labels in this chapter. Simply for the sake of communication, I am using the term commonly understood in our culture. Helia was twenty-three years old when her descent into madness began. The journey that has lasted to some extent to this day has been dark, chaotic, confusing, and torturous. But here and there, it has also been filled with awe-inspiring mysteries and striking bursts of light.

Growing up, Helia was a very sensitive and creative child. She was perceptive beyond our understanding. She could see things that we never saw until she pointed them out. Both my husband and I had very demanding careers, and these occupied a lot of our time. Helia had a fragile soul and longed for love and tender care beyond what we could give her. She was stunningly beautiful and the center of attention in high school. School was not a high priority for her, and because boys were all over her, this led to many regrettable relationships and heartbreaks. Her lack of interest in school and her very active social life created tension between her and us, but she always surprised us with her resourcefulness. She finally graduated from high school and was accepted to a premier university in New York City. It was there in college that her life took a turn for the better.

She was tired of superficial relationships and was seeking answers to life's deeper questions. In her second year in college, she had a dramatic, Damascus-road kind of conversion experience and her life completely changed. She had regrets about some of her past mistakes, but for that reason, she experienced God's grace far more deeply and worshiped him far more intensely. She became very engaged not only at school but also at her local church, growing steadily in her faith and dedicating a good chunk of her time to ministries in her church. She attended an inner-city charismatic megachurch, a multiracial refuge for many homeless people, prostitutes, and drug addicts. Helia had such a heart for those who were broken and marginalized. Helping such people and mingling with them had become a good part of her church life.

Unlike Helia, whose life was centered on her Christian faith, in those days I was a marginal Christian and a high-flying corporate executive. My life was focused on my career, a career that I later gave up to care for Helia personally. At that time my main office was based in New Jersey. That granted Helia and me a lot of time together. I was so proud of who she had become, and I marveled at God's overwhelming grace and transforming power in her life.

It is an understatement to say that her illness "caught everyone by surprise." About a year after her graduation from college, the girl who was known to be fun, happy, and talkative, who lit up every room, abruptly became removed and self-reflective, spending enormous amounts of time on her knees praying and reading Scripture for hours. Something was stirring inside her, and she was not communicating much. During that period, she had had a couple of unusual experiences in her church. One Tuesday evening, during the service attended by more than a thousand congregants, the pastor, unbeknownst to anyone, started casting out demons in the church with a loud voice, commanding evil spirits to leave the worshiping people jumping up and down before him. During that service, Helia experienced extreme sensations in her body and soul. The whole thing was remarkable and caused her great anguish. The encounter that night left her feeling as if someone "had cut the wires in her brain." She had other extreme experiences in the following weeks, some lifting up her soul and some bringing back dark visions of her past mistakes before her conversion to Christianity. I believe these experiences led to her continual state of prayer and spiritual reflection.

Her extreme behavior was not "normal" for those around her with secular beliefs or superficial Christian faith; we interpreted her behavior as signs of illness. Instead of affirming her experiences and helping her to find meaningful answers to them, everyone was pushing her to see a psychiatrist and take medication. Sadly, as a culture we are strongly conditioned to see any deviation from conventional behavior as a sign of illness. She was feeling lonely, though friends and family were all over her to bend her will to accept she needed help. Finally, to quiet us down, she went to see a psychiatrist who prescribed her some antidepressants. She threw away the prescription because she was not impressed with how the psychiatrist had rejected what she had wanted to talk about and basically had told Helia that her experiences were irrelevant to how she was feeling. The psychiatrist told her that she was clinically depressed and that the medication would solve her problem.

This did not help the situation. Helia was spiraling down deeper and deeper and could no longer work. She lost her job though she had recently been promoted to a position of higher responsibility. Her life was changing fast. Her friends did not know how to interact with her, and she was no longer interested in social gatherings that previously attracted her. In response to my barrage of questions, she kept telling me, "You would not understand. Please trust God and give me space." I felt so unequipped and helpless. I wanted so badly to reduce her pain but did not know where to turn.

IN SEARCH OF A DIAGNOSIS

Helia's illness forced our family to question everything and search for what might have caused this. Before all this, our family life had seemed nearly idyllic. We had everything that everyone else dreamed of: a beautiful family, wonderful kids, successful careers, influential friends, health, wealth, and the like. No wonder Helia's illness was absolutely incomprehensible to us.

But we were blind to our own flaws. My husband and I were highschool sweethearts who married when we were both twenty-one years old. We were young, immature, ambitious, and spoiled by our families. While our relationship was romantic and passionate, and our love deep, the competitiveness between the two of us often reared its ugly head. The battle for authority, power, and who would have the last word was continually present in our relationship. I in particular was consumed by my career. I was overambitious and driven by worldly success and power. My husband and I loved each other deeply and thought we had a great marriage. Like *all* other families, it took us a crisis and some sobering self-assessment to realize our pervasive dysfunction. We were all living for ourselves and could see no wrong with our lifestyle—a lifestyle that by God's providential plan was ultimately turned upside down.

"How could something like this happen to us?" we asked. Foolishly, we thought that we could easily overcome this problem with all the resources at our disposal and all the important people we knew. We assumed there was no treatment that we could not buy with our money, no famous doctor that we could not hire. I even knew people in the executive ranks of large pharmaceutical companies. We imagined solving Helia's problem would be as easy as talking to them.

We finally persuaded Helia to take her medications, but the promise of recovery never materialized. In fact, doubling and tripling her medication only made things worse. We had embarked on the darkest journey of our lives, one for which neither my husband nor I were prepared. God was about to shake us out of our stupor.

I soon found out that no one could help us. The psychiatrists, even the more sympathetic ones, were not making sense to me. I was coming from the business world, and I was not used to accepting superficial answers. They could not tell me what was wrong with Helia and why this had happened to her. They could not answer my challenging questions about the scientific research in the field. The best doctors, the honest ones, would tell me, "We really don't know what this is, but we are sure that something is wrong with her brain." "But why? Why are you so sure that it is her brain?" I asked. Their response was, "Because it cannot be anything else."

Without an accurate worldview about human nature, one that recognizes the human spirit with all its complexity, formulating correct treatment strategies is impossible. I believe psychiatric anthropology is reductionist and flawed.[1] According to psychiatrist Thomas Szasz, we have accepted the secularization of everyday life, which leads to "the medicalization of the soul and of suffering of all kinds" (2010, xiv). This leaves no room in biological psychiatry for concepts of evil and redemption, for it suffers from a materialist bias where anything that isn't physical is nonsense. In physicalism, human beings are nothing but a collection of atoms and molecules.

Since psychiatry believes that all thoughts, feelings, and emotions can be reduced to electrochemical events in brain cells, then mental problems must be brain problems, and the "broken brain" must be fixed. John Swinton cautions that this makes the illness ontological and

[1]   See the formulation of "A Theological Anthropology of Suffering" I have developed elsewhere (Hessamfar 2014).

definitive of the person: "People no longer *have* an illness; now they *are* an illness" (2020, 30). This intractable commitment to the biological model precludes any search for a deeper meaning for or cause of the illness' "symptoms." When we reduce human mental suffering with all its inherent mystery and fragility to mere pathology, we end up treating the person as "diseased," and seek the solution primarily in medicine. Swinton, who cautions against labeling people, notes the significance of how we describe their experiences: "Descriptions are thus identity form- ing, action oriented, and action determining. . . . What we think we see determines how we respond to what we see" (2020, 12–13).

In my opinion, this is where the problem lies. This is why, after decades of research and billions of dollars of investment, psychiatry is nowhere closer to finding the cause of mental illness. That is also why full recovery is out of reach. We are blaming brains, when these brains are acting exactly as God created them to act in the face of environmental experiences and unique traumatic circumstances. Sharon Dirckx, a brain scientist, explains the brain's plasticity, in the sense that the brain is con- stantly changing as we go through life. Dirckx argues, "Changes to the brain affect our thinking, but our thinking, our lifestyle, and our habits also shape the way our brains grow and develop" (2019, 15).

The brain is always involved in the expression of our thoughts and emotions. But is the brain the source of all our thoughts? Is the brain the same as the mind? This has profound implications not only for psychiatry but also for religion. Our experiences are far more than brain irritations. "Since it has come to light that the brain is highly involved in religious belief and experiences, can neuroscience now explain religion away?" asks Dirckx (2019, 109). She rejects that premise and explains that this simply helps us understand brain regions and mechanisms as mediating certain religious experiences. British psychiatrist Andrew Sims explains that if looking at a cherry tree generates electrical activity in his occipi- tal cortex, this precise localization in the brain does not mean that that cherry tree never existed and that Sims never saw it (2009, 111). This concept applies to any mental experience.

It was as one who suffered from a broken brain that multiple psy- chiatrists treated Helia. She was discredited entirely by the people who treated her. They rejected as "crazy" everything she believed about her spiritual experiences. Over the next few years, Helia was given many diagnoses, among them "psychotic depression," "anxiety disorder," "bipo- lar disorder," "obsessive compulsive disorder," "schizoaffective disorder," and finally "schizophrenia." She was put on all kinds of medications and was hospitalized forcibly several times.

It was the most heart-wrenching and traumatic experience to hospitalize Helia forcibly. Although today there is plenty of research showing the long-term adverse effects of compulsory treatment, not knowing better at the time, my husband and I played our part in those hospitalizations. In taking Helia to the hospital, we needed help from several adults to hold her tightly, drag her into the car, and drive to the hospital as she kicked and cursed and screamed for her freedom. In the hospital, things were no better. A few large men took her by force and strapped her to a bed, pulled her pants down against her will, and gave her a shot to knock her out. Marc Rufer, MD compares the experience of involuntary treatment and its traumatic effect to "rape, torture, and sexual abuse" (2007, 386). Peter Breggin, a psychiatrist, explains, "Involuntary treatment humiliates and demoralizes people, reinforcing their feelings of being worthless, powerless, and helpless. It leads to outrage, which is then crushed by psychiatric drugs" (2016).

A meta-analysis published in *JAMA Psychiatry*, looking over fifty years of research into postdischarge suicide rates, is alarming.

> The suicide rate of studies that followed up patients for no more than 3 months was 100 times the global suicide rate. Studies with follow-up periods of 3 to 12 months had almost 60 times the global suicide rates, and the suicide rate among discharged patients was more than 30 times that in the general population even for periods of follow-up of 5 to 10 years. (Chung et al. 2017)

Helia was presumed to be incompetent and lacking "insight"—merely based on her resistance to treatment. This was a blow to the dignity of her suffering and her humanity. She always begged me, "Mom, please get me out of this place . . . there is nothing wrong with me . . . please trust God . . . Please don't let them touch me." But I failed her over and over again! I trusted the psychiatric system, not her. I thought, "they must know what they are doing." But they failed my trust over and over, and sent us away empty-handed.

None of the treatments was helping Helia. She was drugged so heavily that she could not think. She was like a zombie who had lost contact with our world, spiraling deeper into darkness. The drugs were not reaching the depth of her spirit from where her pain was swallowing her. Days were becoming weeks, weeks months, and months years.

HOW LONG, O LORD?

There is not enough space here to recount the mistakes that both the mental-healthcare professionals and our family made in dealing with this enormous challenge. With Helia's illness our lives had changed completely. Our house had become a somber place. There were no sounds of laughter, no music, no gathering of friends and family—only heavy clouds of gloom and darkness.

At times like this, everyone feels guilty and wonders how they may have contributed to the situation. I was on my knees crying to God day and night, begging for wisdom, light, and a glimpse of mercy. But God was silent, as if he had completely abandoned us. I was not sure if my prayers were going anywhere. But I was determined to cling to God and not let him go until he would reveal himself to me. I knew that my only hope was in him. And he did not disappoint.

We did not know how to stop Helia's deteriorating condition. Life was confusing and nothing made sense. I had lost control entirely, and my precious daughter no longer looked like herself. She started showing signs of catatonia. With her twisted body, frozen in the strangest poses, it was hard to recognize her. Engulfed in darkness, I was losing her—and I did not know to whom or to what! That is when she started refusing to take any more medication. She threatened us that she would run away from our home if we forced her to take drugs. We decided to support her.

In the West, we do not even understand the true substance and natural progression of these illnesses because by medicating the person we never allow the illness to reveal itself naturally. I certainly understand that many people's lives are more functional because of these medications' calming effects. My problem is not so much with taking medication, if someone chooses to do so, understanding both its benefits and side effects. That is a personal choice. My concern is that we diagnose people with broken brains in the absence of any conclusive scientific research. This is misleading to the person and their families. They think that this is the end of their personal struggle, that if the person takes her medication she will be fine over time. Every experienced psychiatrist knows that this is simply not true. Yet such a diagnosis releases persons from any need to change their lifestyle, because after all, they are told that this is just a biological disease like any other.

I found no hope anywhere I turned. The church was of no help either. The best it could do was to offer some prayers. Most people at our church were no longer comfortable around us. They did not know how to interact with Helia. In those days, many thought she was demon-possessed. Many thought we must have committed some major sins and that our daughter was being punished for that. This made us even more isolated. In his important research, Swinton has interviewed people who had spiritual encounters while suffering from mental challenges. He notes that even some chaplains, though well-intended, are not well equipped to deal with extreme spiritual experiences without rushing to judgment and calling people "demon-possessed." The outcome can be truly detrimental and send the person deeper into despair (2020, 189).

Helia's condition was declining, and her expressions were becoming more puzzling and scary. She did not eat or drink for days at a time and was becoming less mobile. She would freeze in bizarre postures for hours and sometimes for days at a time, keeping her mouth and eyes wide open without the slightest movement. She did not even seem to blink! Fixed in one location with her body twisted and her fingers twisted, her head held strangely, she was petrified staring at something through the wall. Her contorted body was a projection of her contorted soul. She was being driven mad by the sight of what she was seeing. Helia was speechless, motionless, and seemingly lifeless. She had become uncommunicative.

I often wondered what it was that she was looking at. I wondered whether it was painful to keep such a pose for hours or days at a time. Sometimes I poured some juice into her wide-open mouth, hoping that she would swallow it. But to no avail. She would keep the juice in her open mouth for hours, then finally spit it out and get a cup of water or milk, without talking or responding to us, then return to another frozen state. The psychiatrists could not convince me that this was due to bio-logical brain dysfunction and that it was her brain that made her freeze that way—only for her to break out of it suddenly and start walking nor-mally around the house as if nothing had happened! It seemed to me that there was an order to her chaotic behavior, a narrative at work. Her seemingly random behavior appeared to me to be orchestrated.

A spirit of rebellion was at work against us. It appeared everything was intent on driving us to our limits and provoking us to anger. We had become the enemy in Helia's eyes. She would not look us in the eye or talk to us. Sometimes, she would take some food from the refrigerator, warm it up in the microwave oven, stare at it for hours trying to take a bite, then move it to another plate, and another one, and finally throw it in the trash. She would pick up the fork to put food in her mouth and then set it down. This process would go on for a few hours. She would make several plates and many items of cutlery dirty in the process, and perhaps consume a single bite. She seemed to be seeing things on the plate that prevented her from eating.

As she became more catatonic and less mobile, her hygiene became a serious challenge. She would fight me aggressively if I tried to clean her body. Yet given her lack of nutrition and lack of hygiene, her physical health in all those years was truly beyond comprehension. She never suffered from so much as a cold. Even though she brushed her teeth only a few times over the course of several years, her teeth were healthy and white, and her body rarely smelled. Her psychiatrist's explanation was that she had trained her body that way, or that her teeth were clean and her body never smelled because she rarely ate!

The days and weeks and months and years were passing. Helia was regressing. If left alone, she would have spent all her time in her bed. She rarely moved, staying in one position for days. She also rarely closed her eyes, staring attentively at something far away. I wish I knew what it was that consumed her attention.

Our lives were completely changed. I was at home all the time caring for her, there being no room left in my life for anything else. My emotional capacity was so stretched by responding to the incessant demand this was putting on me. The strain was killing me from the inside. God had sustained me by his grace and had become my best friend. Besides caring for Helia, I spent all my time studying, researching, praying, reflecting on my readings and on what the Spirit was showing me. I had cried so much that I had no tears left. By observing Helia day after day, I had become convinced that God was doing something in her and through her.

THE ROLE OF EVIL

Could it be that Helia was demon-possessed? The more I looked at her, the more I was convinced of the presence of evil. But "possession" was too much of a stretch. In my view, those who deny the presence of evil in "schizophrenia" have not stared long enough into one's natural madness without the aid of antipsychotics.[2] Many people recommended that we try "deliverance ministry," or exorcism, and in our desperation we did. Today I am of the opinion that the act of exorcism cannot be trusted to just anyone who claims to be a good Christian or believes themselves to have the gift of exorcism. Many people have been damaged by these processes. It takes such a strong spiritual discernment, purity of soul, humility, solid holiness, pure faith, selfless love, and deep devotion to

[2]   I have written about the relationship between "schizophrenia" and demoniacs in great detail in Hessamfar 2014.

Christ to enter into such spiritual battles that I venture to say not many will qualify for it. Exorcism is a risky process that itself can cause one's spirit to fracture. When the idea of possession is entertained, says German psychologist and philosopher T. K. Oesterreich, the act of exorcism itself affects the person, and through autosuggestion, it occasions the possibility of demonic influences (1930, 4–5).

Andrew Sims, a Christian psychiatrist who has worked on diocesan teams for deliverance ministry in the Church of England, stresses how important it is that psychiatrists take seriously how the person explains her experience of illness. Helia herself considered her struggles to be a spiritual battle with the devil to overcome her negative conscience. Sims believes that the possibility of "possession" is not as widespread as some make it. However, he believes to be real the possibility of demonic temptations: desiring destructive things; or demonic obsession: where normal life begins to become impossible because of ideas planted in mind; or demonic oppression: where the spirit is oppressed, enslaved, and severely persecuted (2009, 168, 175).

In the latter cases, which I believe to be more like what Helia was suffering from, a malign spiritual influence is at work. The most helpful approach to such cases is offering unconditional love, compassion, patience, and care for the person, while working to help her gain agency. While actual possession might be rare, demonic attacks and oppression are very common in mental illness. In most cases, spiritual care should not be about exorcism but about high-quality relationships that affirm a person, reminding them of God's love and protection over their soul. They need to know that for a child of God these attacks are not ontological, that their soul remains intact in the hand of God.

While it is perilous to keep throwing the label of "demon-possessed" at people, it is also naive for caregivers to ignore the presence of evil. In my experience with hundreds of people who have been diagnosed with "schizophrenia," evil is rarely the fault of the person who is suffering. It is often very vulnerable souls, the most sensitive and broken among us, who will be used by evil powers as an instrument to expose the sins of a community in stark ways. The voice of madness manifests in a prophetic fashion, similar to how prophets in Scripture, such as Ezekiel, Micah, and Jeremiah, symbolized Israel's rebellion against God with their strange behaviors. If we close our ears to the mysterious yet loud voice of madness, then sufferers have suffered in vain. Finnish psychiatrist and philosopher Martti Siirala explains the encounter with a person suffering from "schizophrenia" as follows:

[W]e see the sick person as a man in whose sickness and in whose total situation our inhumanity, our unlived life, our idolatry, and our blindness become crystallized; in the encounter this total situation is brought under judgment. The sick person is manifestly a prisoner under suspicion, hate, unfaith, and hopelessness, which qualities to a great extent remain hidden in us. He is as a stone crying out. . . . if only we have ears to hear . . . Not only the original cause of the anguish but also the continuation of it, and his increasing aloneness, are connected with our withholding our association with him. We protect ourselves from becoming entangled in his skein because what is revealed in him exposes our common guilt . . . We try to protect ourselves even against the anticipation that what we encounter here perhaps calls into question our whole reality, our faith, our conduct, our self-understanding. Here is perhaps the deepest reason for our strong need to isolate the anguish of illness and to keep it at a distance, beyond the reach of our ears. (Siirala [1964] 1981, 94–95)

It is difficult for us to believe in the spiritual realm's existence and entities such as angels and demons, not only because that takes away our sense of control but also because it severely challenges our conception of reality and renders us powerless.[3] There is evil all around us. The devil is a deceiver and the father of lies (John 8:44). He prowls around like a roaring lion, seeking someone to devour (1 Pet 5:8). Many of us are under influences of evil with our temptations and ways of life. Many of us carry a deep sense of guilt and shame, knowing we have not yet fully reconciled with God. That sense of guilt and shame makes us a target for the devil's accusations and persecutions.

In a brilliant article, Wilfred M. McClay, director of the Center for the History of Liberty at the University of Oklahoma, writes about the persistence of guilt as a psychological force in advanced Western societies, a force which makes us vulnerable. It is not easy to identify and understand this sense of guilt, since it is often hidden in our subconscious, and could easily be mistaken for something else. It often appears to us, as Freud argued, as a kind of dissatisfaction, forcing us to chase its roots. McClay contends, "Guilt is crafty, a trickster and chameleon, capable of disguising itself, hiding out, changing its size and appearance, even its location, all the while managing to persist and deepen" (2017). As McClay suggests, as participants of families, communities, and wider

[3]   McGruder shows in her research that common acceptance of spiritual influences in other cultures makes the course of illness much more tolerable than the medical model (1999, 2002).

cultures, we suffer from "a mounting tide of unassuaged guilt, ever in search of novel and ineffective, and ultimately bizarre ways to discharge itself." We zealously refrain from rendering any judgment as to whether the guilty feelings burdening our conscience have any moral justification. As Freud advocated, we have robbed guilt of any moral significance "by treating it as a strictly subjective and emotional matter," a barrier to one's pleasure-seeking life (2017).

McClay says our secular life "requires us to be silent about, and forcibly repress, the very religious frameworks and vocabularies within which the dynamics of sin and guilt and atonement have hitherto been rendered intelligible." Indeed, this destroys our souls since we find ourselves least able to name the root of our pain, let alone find moral release from the weight of what burdens us (2017).

We later realized that Helia was deeply conflicted about Rob (not his real name), the man to whom she was about to become engaged. Rob was Helia's supervisor during one of her summer internships while she was still in college. They had been dating for a few years and were deeply in love. Rob had started attending church and was going through all the motions to please Helia. But Helia was feeling very guilty about that relationship. She was unwilling to let Rob go, and yet she knew inside that Rob was not devoted to Christ in the way she was. She felt she was about to enter into a marriage that was against God's will: "Do not be mismatched with unbelievers. For what partnership is there between righteousness and lawlessness? Or what fellowship is there between light and darkness?" (2 Cor 6:14). To what extent her sense of guilt and inner struggles about Rob and some of her past mistakes made her a target for spiritual attacks, we do not know.

We do wonder, How could a God of love allow such suffering in one's life? We forget that God of the Bible is not the tame god we hear preached in many churches. He is mighty and a consuming fire, and he hates sin and disciplines his children (Rom 6:3; Heb 12:8, 29; Hab 1:13). And we all have different callings in life. Those who desire to live a holier life of devotion to Christ and are far more effective in leading others to the Light are greater targets for spiritual attacks. "Indeed, all who want to live a godly life in Christ Jesus will be persecuted" (2 Tim 3:12). Jesus himself became a target of the devil's temptations right after his baptism before his ministry began (Luke 4). Jesus predicting Peter's denial forewarned him: "Simon, Simon, listen! Satan has demanded to sift all of you like wheat, but I have prayed for you that your own faith may not fail; and you, when once you have turned back, strengthen your brothers" (Luke

22:31–32). Notably, Jesus did not assure Peter that Satan's request was denied because God so loved Peter; instead, he encouraged him to stay resolute and unwavering in his faith.

As I cared for Helia every day for years in the most awful and frightening conditions, as I cried out to God on my knees, praying for a miracle, God sustained me, revealed himself to me, and guided me through the journey that saved my family. Caring for Helia taught me much about the human condition, our fragility, and the depth of our depravity. I learned about how demanding selfless love is, the violence we unleash on each other, and our insatiable longing for God's grace in times of genuine need. I learned about Helia's illness, way beyond what I could find in scientific papers and the wooden categories of the *Diagnostic and Statistical Manual of Mental Disorders*. Amid unrelenting pain, I lost patience for simplistic explanations about what we were experiencing. Our experience was nothing short of pure evil.

Andrew Delbanco puts it quite well in his perceptive book *The Death of Satan*, and in fact the below quotation was used on the back cover:

> We live in the most brutal century in human history, but instead of stepping forward to take the credit, the devil has rendered himself invisible. The very notion of evil seems to be incompatible with modern life, from which the ideas of transgression and the accountable self are fast receding. Yet despite the loss of old words and moral concepts—Satan, sin, evil—we cannot do without some conceptual means for thinking about the universal human experience of cruelty and pain. . . . If evil, with all its insidious complexity, escapes the reach of our imagination, it will have established dominion over us all. (1995, 9ff.)

If the influences of evil are hastily dismissed in the church, how can we expect psychiatrists to take it seriously in clinical practice? William James, in his seminal work, *Varieties of Religious Experience*, writes about the horrors of madness, its "rational significance," and how all intellectual arguments disappear in its presence.

> Not the conception or intellectual perception of evil, but the grisly blood-freezing heart-palsying sensation of it close upon one, and no other conception or sensation able to live for a moment in its presence. How irrelevantly remote seem all our usual refined optimisms and intellectual and moral consolations in presence of a need of help like this! Here is the core of the religious problem: Help! Help! No prophet [or a physician, or a therapist] can claim to bring a final message unless he says things that will have a sound of reality in the ears of victims such as these. But the

deliverance must come in as strong a form as the complaint, if it is to take effect; . . . [in] religions of deliverance: the man must die to an unreal life before he can be born into the real life. (2007, 151, 154)

DIVINE PROVIDENCE AT WORK

After many years of agony, watching Helia become unrecognizable, one day my prayers were answered. Helia finally came out of her catatonic state, and what a blessed day that was! Helia is not back to her former self yet, and she may never be, but by God's grace, she is alive today and participating in our family life without any medication. Her return to life humbled us deeply and taught us that this was not a mere coincidence or as a result of anything we had done, but our God was showing us his sovereign power (Rom 11:33). He showed us that he rules and controls the situation. This was a display of his lordship (Frame 2013, 178). Not only was God working in Helia's spirit, he was also using her as an instrument to awaken the rest of us. There was a purpose in what we were going through. He gave us a sign and hope to hang on to and to remember his sovereignty as we faced further challenges in the years that followed. He showed us that Christ was alive, present, and involved in our lives. He graced us to taste his goodness to gain strength for the rest of the journey.

Helia has a very tender and fragile spirit that is not prepared to face this world yet. There is an innocence and simplicity about her. She rejoices in the small pleasures of life, such as eating. She refuses to talk about her experience in fear of retaliation from her voices. She spends all her time among the family members who adore her. Because of her, we moved to the countryside, where there are lots of horses and other animals. She spends a lot of time in nature, hiking, walking, and swimming. Most of the time she listens to worship music. She attends sessions of art therapy and music therapy every week. She plays drums and organ to release some of her emotions. We have traveled around the country, and even on a few long international trips with our extended family. She is very much an active participant in our lives. But the voices are still there. They still try to torment her, at times quite severely, though she is trying hard to fight back.

Helia is my hero! What she has endured is incomprehensible to most of us. She inspires me to go on and to cling to our God who has sustained her against all odds. Helia has carried her cross every day for the past twenty-two years, and she has fought her battle in fellowship with Christ's suffering.

Swinton stresses that Jesus experienced a sense of abandonment from God and inner alienation, similar to what all victims of evil endure: "In the passion of Christ we discover such genuine identification with human suffering that Jesus undergoes precisely the abandonment and inability to feel the presence of God that is a primary mark of the human experience of evil. Jesus felt abandoned . . . and yet, ultimately he was not" (2007, 163). The Cross of Christ is an affirmation for those who suffer evil, reframing their experience as a significant spiritual encounter, and not a sign of rejection from God. Recall that it was amid immense evil and darkness that crucifixion led to resurrection.

In the phenomenon of "schizophrenia," one loses all human filters. The person becomes a naked image of the human condition, of human fallenness—an intense picture of our true selves (Sugerman 2008). This usually happens to those who are naturally sensitive to the pain around them. They become empty vessels in the hand of God to awaken a world that is spiritually blind and deaf. Michel Foucault wrote about how in Western cultures pathologizing madness brands those suffering as strangers to human nature, when in reality they are the ones who expose true human nature fully and vividly (Foucault 1988). Scientific research has shown that people experiencing "schizophrenia" take on the external stimuli from their environment, internalize it, and manifest it in the forms of "symptoms" (Whitfield-Gabrieli 2009).

Helia had become the manifestation of all that was wrong in our family. In her madness, we were afforded a mirror to gaze at our true selves long enough to be shaken out of our comfort zones. And in doing so, our family encountered our own sickness in hers. Madness lays bare a family's frailty. Helia was revealing right before our eyes our wretchedness and ugliness, which were covered by our masks of civility. She had, as it were, taken on all our sins and was acting them out in physical forms. The pain of our depravity had transcended the theoretical realm and stared us in the face with vivid clarity; no longer could help be found in our "sense of acumen," or "elegance," or "wealth," or "eminence," or "connections" to rescue us from despair. Her illness was prophetically pointing to our destiny. Encountering her madness, I was forced to look at my own insanity; the veil was pulled back, and I was impelled to confront my naked existence. Through her I saw who I was—and I did not like what I saw (Hessamfar 2014, 198, 202–3).

I don't suggest that all people should interpret their encounter with madness as I did, or as Helia did. Psychosis is not a monolithic phenomenon. But I can say with certainty that this is a deeply human experience, one painted by the finger of none but God himself, for no purpose but healing and redemption—not only of the sufferer but of her immediate community as well. Madness has a voice that speaks deeply into our soul, exposing our depravity and our need for God. It demands a discerning spirit to pay attention. Jesus says, "The Spirit of the Lord is upon me, because he has anointed me to bring good news to the poor. He has sent me to proclaim release to the captives and recovery of sight to the blind, to let the oppressed go free, to proclaim the year of the Lord's favor" (Luke 4: 18–19).

I know that our family's numerous mistakes and the approaches applied by mental-healthcare professionals had a lot to do with worsening Helia's condition. There is well-documented research on how the person's cultural contexts shape the illness' "symptoms." (Luhrmann 2016). Nev Jones, one of the most effective voices in the recovery movement, has profiled the journey of her own madness, and how the reaction of people around her sent her deeper into madness, and likewise, how a couple of people's willingness to give her second chances and take her seriously brought her out of it (Dobbs 2018). The popular NPR podcast, *Invisibilia*, looked at the problem of mental illness and communities that have been successful in caring for such individuals. Their researchers concluded, "Crazy as it sounds, [when dealing with people with mental illness] our private thoughts about a person, our disappointment in them, or even our wishes for them to get better, shoot out of us like lasers and can change their very insides" (2016).

Anyone who has had the opportunity to spend an extended time with an *unmedicated* person suffering from psychosis is bound to have encountered this phenomenon. It is an inescapable fact that in psychosis the person embodies representations of the collective consciousness of the immediate community and reverberates them back as signs and "symptoms." In light of this it is not surprising that when Shekhar Saxena, the director of the World Health Organization's mental-health unit, was asked where he would prefer to experience "schizophrenia" as a potential patient, he said without hesitation, "[F]or big cities he'd prefer a city in Ethiopia or Sri Lanka, like Colombo or Addis Ababa, rather than New York or London, because in the former he could expect to be seen as a productive if eccentric citizen rather than a reject and an outcast" (Dobbs 2018).

The good news is that today thousands of people who were formerly diagnosed with "schizophrenia" have recovered, either outside the medical system, or with the help of an enlightened psychiatrist who has looked at their problem more holistically. Swinton says:

> Mental illnesses are not biological entities any more than they are social, psychological, theological, or spiritual entities. They are occurrences that happen within the life narratives of real individuals who require to be recognized as whole persons within whom each of these aspects—biological, psychological, theological, spiritual—need to be recognized as fundamental building blocks that are necessary in order that we can truly discover what mental illness is. (2014)

Many people who have recovered from "schizophrenia" are loud and active. Their persistent efforts have forced the field of psychiatry to pay attention and change to some extent. Although most psychiatrists today admit that environmental factors are essential in understanding the experience of mental illness, rarely is one willing to accept that the same applies to severe psychosis. They usually believe that "schizophrenia," especially an extreme case like Helia's, is purely biological, and feel handicapped to address it in any way but through strong antipsychotics.

Yet there is hope. Hearing Voices Network (https://www.hearing -voices.org/) is one of the strongest advocacy groups to reject the "broken brain" hypothesis, even in the most severe cases. This group understands the phenomenon of madness as a natural outcome of a traumatic life, requiring love, care, patience, and personal attention.[4] It is very inspiring to go to their conferences where hundreds of people from around the world show up to share their experiences of voice-hearing, and how they have found a way to live a functional life despite their voices.

John Foskett, a former chaplain of Bethlem Royal and Maudsley Hospitals, writes about the profundity of madness and how one ought to "incarnate like" enter into it to grasp its deep meaning (1984, xi). Caring for Helia, I was pulled into her madness. What I witnessed there crushed me and changed me forever. It humbled me like nothing else could and opened my eyes to the majesty and glory of our God. We have advanced in science and technology to such an extent that our lives are enslaved to the progress we have made. We have lost sight of the mightiness of God. Our Western culture has distorted our view of who God is. It is now the nuclear bomb, chemical and biological weapons, and cybercrimes that frighten us. The enemy has become human-made. Yet the cosmic battle continues; our God is still on his throne!

---

[4]   For an inspiring story of recovery, see the TED Talk, Longden 2013.

Before Helia's illness, nothing could break into my prideful nature; I was proud of my family, my achievements in life, and who I was. And then, we lost so much; we lost life as we knew it. I came to experience the reality of the cross and see life through that lens. I was swallowed by despair. I experienced what Scripture preaches: "In the morning you shall say, 'If only it were evening!' and at evening you shall say, 'If only it were morning!' because of the dread that your heart shall feel and the sights that your eyes shall see" (Deut 28:67). I experienced the "valley of the shadow of death," overtaken by darkness, rising in the morning hopeless, and going to bed at night with such anguish, wishing I would never have to open my eyes again.

Helia's madness made me see. It was through Helia's journey that I learned the meaning of true love. I learned how difficult it was to love the unlovable, as God had loved us. Sometimes God whispers his love into our ears. But when we are so distracted that we cannot hear him or give him any attention, he raises his voice. It is only through his love that we are enabled to love each other unconditionally. If we turn our face away from him and close our hearts to his way of shaping and forming us, we can never truly love as God intended: the unconditional love that can heal is selfless, patient, and kind, not arrogant, and never takes into account the wrongdoing of the other. God knocks at our door and keeps knocking until we open the door. At some point, he may have to remove the door by force to come in. That is what happened to our family.

WORKS CITED

Breggin, Peter. 2016. "Forced 'Treatment' Is Torture." *Mad in America*. June 19, 2016. https://www.madinamerica.com/2016/06/forced-treatment-is-torture/.

Chung, D. T., C. J. Ryan, D. Hadzi-Pavlovic, S. P. Singh, C. Stanton, and M. M. Large. 2017. "Suicide Rates after Discharge from Psychiatric Facilities: A Systematic Review and Meta-analysis." *JAMA Psychiatry* 74, no. 7: 694–702.

Delbanco, Andrew. 1995. *The Death of Satan: How Americans Have Lost the Sense of Evil.* New York: Farrar, Straus & Giroux.

Dirckx, Sharon. 2019. *Am I Just My Brain?* UK: Good Book.

Dobbs, David. 2018. "The Touch of Madness." *Pacific Standard*. November 26, 2018. https://psmag.com/magazine/the-touch-of-madness-mental-health-schizophrenia.

Foskett, John. 1984. *Meaning in Madness: The Pastor and the Mentally Ill.* New Library of Pastoral Care. London: SPCK.

Foucault, Michel. 1988. *Madness and Civilization: A History of Insanity in the Age of Reason.* Translated by Richard Howard. New York: Vintage.

Frame, John. 2013. *Systematic Theology: An Introduction to Christian Belief.* Phillipsburg, N.J.: P&R Publishing.

Hessamfar, Elahe. 2014. *In the Fellowship of His Suffering: A Theological Interpretation of Mental Illness—A Focus on "Schizophrenia."* Eugene, Ore.: Cascade.

James, William. 2007. *The Varieties of Religious Experience: A Study in Human Nature.* Charleston, S.C.: BiblioBazaar.

Kleinman, Arthur. 1988. *The Illness Narratives: Suffering, Healing, and the Human Condition.* New York: Basic.

Longden, Eleanor. 2013. "The Voices in My Head." TED Talks video, 14:04. https://www.ted .com/talks/eleanor_longden_the_voices_in_my_head.

Luhrmann, T. M., and Jocelyn Marrow, eds. 2016. *Our Most Troubling Madness: Case Studies in Schizophrenia across Cultures.* Berkeley: University of California Press.

McClay, Wilfred M. 2017. "The Strange Persistence of Guilt." *The Hedgehog Review: Critical Reflections on Contemporary Culture* 19, no. 1: 40–55.

McGruder, Juli. 1999. "Madness in Zanzibar: 'Schizophrenia' in Three Families in the 'Developing' World." PhD diss., University of Washington.

———. 2002. "Life Experience Is Not a Disease, Or Why Medicalizing Madness is Counterproductive to Recovery." In *Recovery and Wellness: Models of Hope and Empowerment for People with Mental Illness,* edited by Catana Brown, 59–80. New York: Haworth Pastoral Press.

Miller, Lulu. 2016. "The Problem with the Solution." *Invisibilia.* Released July 1, 2016. Podcast, 59:30. https://www.npr.org/2016/07/01/483856025/read-the-transcript.

Oesterreich, Traugott Constantin, and Dora Ibberson. 1930. *Possession, Demoniacal and Other, among Primitive Races, in Antiquity, the Middle Ages, and Modern Times.* Translated by D. Ibberson. London: Kegan Paul.

Rufer, Marc. 2007. "Psychiatry: Its Diagnostic Methods, Its Therapies, Its Power." In *Alternatives Beyond Psychiatry,* edited by Peter Stastny and Peter Lehmann, 382–99. Berlin: Peter Lehmann Publishing.

Siirala, Aarne. (1964) 1981. *The Voice of Illness: A Study in Therapy and Prophecy.* 2nd ed. New York: E. Mellen Press.

Sims, Andrew C. P. 2009. *Is Faith Delusion? Why Religion is Good for Your Health.* London: Continuum.

Sugerman, Shirley. 2008. *Sin and Madness: Studies in Narcissism.* 2nd ed. San Rafael, Calif.: Barfield.

Swinton, John. 2007. *Raging with Compassion: Pastoral Responses to the Problem of Evil.* Grand Rapids: Eerdmans.

———. 2014. Foreword to *In the Fellowship of His Suffering: A Theological Interpretation of Mental Illness—A Focus on "Schizophrenia,"* by Elahe Hessamfar. Eugene, Ore.: Cascade.

———. 2020. *Finding Jesus in the Storm: The Spiritual Lives of Christians with Mental Health Challenges.* Grand Rapids: Eerdmans.

Szasz, Thomas S. 2010. *The Myth of Mental Illness: Foundations of a Theory of Personal Conduct.* New York: Harper Perennial.

10

"I Could Not for the Life of Me Remember His Name!"

Dementia Care in Australia

Stephen Judd

I first met John when he came to Sydney, Australia, to speak at HammondCare's International Dementia Conference in 2014. HammondCare is a Christian health- and aged-care charity that is the recognized Australian leader in dementia care. For over twenty years HammondCare has led the industry in dementia design and best-practice care, particularly for people with severe behavioral and psychological symptoms of dementia. HammondCare's biennial conference started in the mid-1990s to encourage a focus on practical issues associated with supporting people with dementia. The conference grew over two decades to include thousands of attendees and headlining international and Australian speakers and delegates.

John flew into Sydney on a brilliantly sunny midwinter's day. I picked him up at the foyer of his city hotel, from which we walked down to Sydney Harbour together and caught one of the iconic ferries across the Harbour to Manly Beach. We enjoyed refreshments there, all the while interrupting the sightseeing commentary with discussions about the subject that united us: dementia.

Years later, in 2020, as I stepped down from my role as CEO of HammondCare, John recalled that first meeting and confessed with self-deprecating humor that he could not remember my name for the whole day! Those of us who know and love the absentminded Aberdeen professor are not sure jet lag was to blame for the memory loss.

John had come to my attention through the publication of his 2012 book, *Dementia: Living in the Memories of God*. I was troubled that at HammondCare there was dissonance between the hypercognitive theological statements that described our Christian beliefs and the practical reality of people with dementia. HammondCare was avowedly Christian, yet there was a concomitant, unstated discomfort that accepting Jesus and the ongoing appreciation and celebration of the gospel required cognitive abilities that most of the residents and clients for whom we cared simply did not have. I wondered if our "best-practice" care and compassion was based on naked self-interest—doing unto others—and merely received passing theological endorsement from the promise that comes in the fifth commandment.

Perhaps unconsciously, as an organization, we had unhappily assimilated to the prevailing perspective of society that human value is reliant on an individual's capacity and contribution. As the arguments for euthanasia intensified, an increasing number of our clients—or rather their families—believed "self-interest" was expressed not in treasuring life with dementia but in choosing death. For HammondCare the question was what was the philosophical and theological framework that informed our efforts and commitment to care for those with dementia? Or were we merely motivated by outdated sentimentality?

Swinton's book bridged the gap. In a powerful corrective to the hypercognitive and individualistic narratives of our age, *Dementia: Living in the Memories of God* reminded me that I was looking at assurance the wrong way round. Right relationship with God, John reminded me, is not dependent on us being able to remember God but on the assurance that God remembers us. God's promise of "I will not fail you or forsake you" (Josh 1:5) means he is faithful, even when we are faithless. He remembers us even when we have forgotten him. He has engraved us on the palm of his hand (Isa 49:15–16; Deut 31:6; 2 Tim 2:13).

For me, this issue was personal as well as professional. My father-in-law, Donald Robinson, was a Greek New Testament scholar and theological savant who influenced generations of seminarians. He worked as a code-breaker in signals intelligence in the Pacific during the Second World War and later served as Anglican Archbishop of Sydney from 1982 to 1993 (Robinson 1981). His dementia was severe by age ninety-one. One of his lifelong friends lamented to me how terrible it was that Don's "Rolls-Royce mind" should be so diminished. This Christian elder saw Don's worth as inextricably linked to his theological contributions which were now in the mists of time. This attitude saddened and disappointed me then, but Swinton's work was an important corrective and challenge to this perspective. Don's dementia years were ones of inestimable worth and value. God had not given up on Don, but rather he was living wonderfully in the arms and memories of the Savior.

GOD IS MORE RELIABLE THAN YOUTUBE

At first my enthusiasm for John's work was not universally shared at HammondCare. While I extolled the virtues of this Aberdeen academic to anyone who would listen, others were uncertain whether he should be a keynote speaker at our conference. Head of HammondCare's Dementia Centre, Professor Colm Cunningham, wanted above all a captivating speaker. Yet his research with the impeccable assistance of YouTube had only uncovered a somewhat obscure and uninspiring lecture John had done at a midwestern U.S. university. Cunningham was skeptical: maybe this Scottish academic could write but could he inspire an audience?

Colm undertook a visit to Scotland to interview John and settle the matter for himself. John—somewhat bemused by the visit as he was, in truth, a recognized international speaker—remembers it as the first time he ever auditioned for a speaking gig. Good-humored as he was, he passed the interview with distinction.

Like his book, Swinton's visit to Sydney was a triumph. His keynote address received rave reviews from a critical audience. Importantly, Swinton sweetly deconstructed Tom Kitwood's view of personhood in dementia. Kitwood—a pioneer in dementia care based at the University of Bradford until his untimely death in 1998—rightly challenged the medical and institutional approach to dementia, which looked at the disease and ignored the person. Kitwood argued that people with dementia were first and foremost *persons* and that their personhood comes first. From the 1990s Kitwood's perspective dominated any discussion on dementia care and the term *person-centered* became ubiquitous (Kitwood 1997).

The problem with Kitwood's definition of personhood is the suggestion that it is "a status or standing that is *bestowed upon one human being by others*, in the context of relationship and social being" (Kitwood 1997; emphasis added). Swinton affirmed Kitwood's rejection of a Cartesian framework for understanding dementia, which separated mind and body, and shared his holistic view of persons in which body and mind cannot not be separated (Swinton 2012). Further, Swinton affirmed that humans are also shaped by their societal environment and interactions.

Yet Swinton queried the underlying premise of Kitwood's definition of personhood. If the definition of one's humanity is dependent upon a status that others dispense, then it is possible for others to choose to withdraw that status of personhood. Swinton exposed this vulnerability in Kitwood's relational framework: who are you when society decides you are without capacity because of your diminished cognition? While it was almost certainly not Kitwood's intention, his paradigm places the most vulnerable squarely at risk. Kitwood's definition ironically advances the cause of those who would euthanize individuals with dementia employing this utilitarian ethic.

AN AUSTRALIAN RELATIONSHIP IS BORN

Too often, keynote speakers are like "fly-in fly-out" workers on an oil rig. They arrive, dispense their pearls of wisdom to the assembled throng, and after their presentation is complete they fly out. It is debatable whether their influence persists after the conference concludes.

Yet Swinton's 2014 keynote for HammondCare outlasted the churn of the conference season and stage personalities. In fact, it was the beginning of his minor celebrity status in Australia, though I suspect he would quibble with the term *minor*. He has returned for encores at all of HammondCare's subsequent international dementia conferences and speaks prolifically at other venues throughout Australia and New Zealand. Importantly, it was the start of an immensely rewarding relationship between an Aberdeen academic and an Australian charity that has furthered the purpose of showing God's love for his creation.

The thing about practical theologians is that they often don't get an opportunity to *practice*. True to their academic nature, their stock-in-trade is contributing to learned publications and delivering incisive lectures. The result is words in search of deeds. Conversely, Christian social-service organizations suffer from the opposite excess. Deeds, not words, become their trade, and too often motivation is weakly expressed in phrases like "Christian founding principles and values." And, if people can act Christian by simply adhering to certain values and principles, Jesus is soon unnecessary and an inconvenient historical impediment.

From that initial encounter in 2014, HammondCare became Swinton's laboratory to test and develop concepts in the field of dementia care. In short, the HammondCare team became Swinton's willing collaborators. By 2020 three projects illustrate the impact Swinton has practically made to support HammondCare and other social-service organizations in their respective missions: *Faith for Life: The Bible and Dementia*, the Presence Project, and Organizational Faithfulness.

I now turn to a discussion of each of these.

THE BIBLE AND DEMENTIA: LIVING WELL AND FAITHFULLY WITH DEMENTIA

The Bible is central to Christianity and to the Christian experience. Evangelicals believe that the Bible is trustworthy and the divinely inspired Word of God and the ultimate authority in all matters of faith and conduct. Other Christian traditions may be less emphatic than evangelicals and ascribe authority not simply to the Bible but also to developed church tradition and personal experience. But regardless of their approach, for all Christians the Bible is core to understanding God's relationship to humankind, how God is known, what the Bible says about being human, and how we should conduct ourselves both with God and each other. It is core to the Christian's identity and well-being.

But the Bible is also usually presented as a collection of books that require cognition to access, read, understand, and appreciate. Even people with full cognition who are unfamiliar with the Bible find it challenging to interpret. So how can a person with dementia possibly expect to access, appreciate, and enjoy it? While there are many children's Bibles and other resources that make access achievable for the young, people with dementia are often excluded from the Bible because of their diminished cognition.

Swinton and HammondCare wanted to make the messages of the Bible accessible to people with dementia. If the Bible is central to the identity and well-being of Christians, then enabling people to remain connected to the gospel messages regardless of their dementia was fundamental at a spiritual and psychological level. The communal aspect was also vital. The Bible is a book that belongs to the Christian community writ large. Sharing in the Bible is a part of sharing in that community. Not to make that possible is a form of social exclusion. But what to do about it? In 2015, the Bible Project was born. Swinton wrote a concept paper, which explained the project's intention.

> The intention of the Bible Project is to create a set of resources that can enable people at various stages of their dementia journey to have access to the Bible in ways that are enabling, encouraging and appropriate to their particular needs. In this way, we hope to assist people in their process of recovery, understood not in terms of neurological functioning, but in terms of the attainment of satisfying life goals. The project will contribute to:
>
> 1. The spiritual support and well-being of Christians who are in danger of being alienated from a fundamental source of hope and comfort.

2. The pastoral and evangelical mission of the church. The gospel is proclaimed and re-proclaimed as people with dementia are enabled to meet Jesus in and through the scriptures.

3. Spiritual Capital within broader society, by helping to meet the particular needs of a vulnerable and growing people group. (Swinton unpublished paper 2015)

Previous publications on dementia and the Bible tended to focus on carers and support workers (Van Nordstrand and Charles 2005). By contrast, this project's ambitious primary focus was on the experiences of people with dementia, directly involving people with dementia at every stage. Over two years, the Bible Project team, led by Linda Barclay and Rebecca Forbes from HammondCare, developed, researched, and produced the *Faith for Life* series, a series that consists of ten A5 color books first published in March 2018. Various books in the series include *He Restores My Soul*, based on the Psalms with pictures; *Joy to the World*, covering the Christmas message; *Textures of God's Love*, which is a resource that invites a tactile response with textures, objects, prayers, and photos; and *Words of Hope*, pairing Bible verses with well-known hymns and images.

Swinton provided editorial oversight and coupled critical analysis with encouragement for this project. He helped to refine the products and give confidence to the team's development. In several conference talks John has jokingly suggested that theologians like himself practice "complexification"—making the simple complex. *Faith for Life* shows that is demonstrably untrue. His conception, shape, and guidance of the Bible Project resulted in a remarkable and practical *Faith for Life* resource series. It is a testament to how a practical theologian, humbly working in the field, can enable others to bring the gospel of Jesus to people with dementia in simple and imaginative ways. The *Faith for Life* series was not authored by him, but John's fingerprints are all over it. It may not have won him any academic or literary awards, but in terms of impact for the kingdom, his contribution is inestimable.

TO BE HUMAN IS TO BE PRESENT

The Presence Project (also known as the Being Present project) developed in 2018 in conversations between Swinton and senior Hammond-Care executives. HammondCare's residential care homes focused on supporting people with dementia in small domestic care homes of eight to fifteen residents. Its model of care emphasized social engagement, where the rhythms of life were determined by the individual rather than the organization. Above all, there was a strong emphasis that staff should relate to the person rather than the execution of tasks.

But HammondCare executives knew how this philosophy or model of care too often did not translate into daily staff practice. As is commonplace in the health- and aged-care space, a culture of *absence* develops. This is where the nurse or carer, while physically present, is focused on completing tasks. There is neither engagement nor relationship with the person.

This especially happens when staff are with residents who have advanced cases of dementia. Some residents who have behavioral and psychological symptoms of dementia will have difficulty in expressing themselves verbally. So the temptation for the carer is to dis-engage or withdraw from the person and get on with the tasks of the day as if the individual person didn't really matter. Basic care quality, while still achieved, will lack an attentiveness. The result is invariably a poorer quality of life because of the absence of relationship.

Carer presence—or lack of it—is a critical ongoing success factor for HammondCare's model of care. Presence defines the quality of being there for others and the ability to understand what kinds of caring practices most enhance them as human beings. Presence is both a quality and an intervention in professional care.

> It is a quality in that it is a way of being with others that recognizes the fullness of their humanness and seeks to be present in ways that respect that recognition . . . Presence is also an intervention insofar as it is carried out in a structured and intentional way by professionals who, whilst recognizing presence as a basic way of being with others, realize that this needs to be carried out with integrity, competence and intentionality. You need to consciously notice what you are doing and why you are doing it. People have actively to think about what they are doing when they are present and also when they are not present. (Swinton, Patton, and Robinson 2018)

The Presence Project explored some of the reasons why an absence of presence may occur within HammondCare, and it developed insights, understandings, new initiatives, and interventions to enable carers to practice presence well. The first part of the project looked at service development, working with staff to improve outcomes for staff and residents alike. The second part was a formal research project that looked at the issues from an empirical perspective. As of now the research dimension is still in progress.

The service development component of the Presence Project is immensely practical. Swinton, who led the project, recognized a difficult tension between therapeutic relationships that focus on the tasks of care and the enhancement of well-being and holistic relationships, which champion the uniqueness of individuals. He sought to resolve these tensions not in isolation but by involving staff from a care home displaying the greatest dissonance between the desired model and the practice of care.

HammondCare's residential care home in the southern Sydney suburb of Miranda has dedicated eight cottages for ninety-two residents with dementia. Swinton selected it as the site for the Presence Project because, unlike other HammondCare residential care homes, its staff attrition rate was high and the care home had experienced management instability, which had caused staff unrest and dissatisfaction. Within this environment, Swinton and his project team established two focus groups of care workers to bring clarity to the significance of presence for effective dementia care, explore issues germane to the HammondCare cottages, and gather baseline data suggestions for practice improvement.

Through these focus groups, the project team developed recommendations to improve staff and organizational practices for carer presence. None of the recommendations was revolutionary. Rather some simply aimed to help carers appreciate that being present and completing a task need not be mutually exclusive. Daily functional encounters with residents could present meaningful and relational opportunities for the staff member. The Project also proposed some basic operational changes which would reduce staff frustrations and feelings of being overwhelmed, recognizing that if carers are burned out they are less likely to emotionally connect with the residents.

There are two reasons why the Presence Project is noteworthy. First, its genesis. Too often, academics develop their thoughts and research projects in splendid isolation, perhaps only engaging with industry to affirm their theses. By contrast, the Presence Project was industry-led: HammondCare had a problem, and Swinton worked with the organization to find a solution. The Jesus of the gospels met people where they were. The Presence Project is but one example of how John as a practical theologian modeled this posture, giving priority to answering the questions and issues of real people in immediate settings (Martin and Swinton 2019).

The second reason is related to the first. While it is tempting to dismiss the findings of the Presence Project as mundane or unexceptional, it is actually an excellent example of Swinton's practical theology at work. The Trinitarian God is one who dwells in a rich fabric of relationships. This God is a God of Relationships and being a human is about being loved and cared for in relationship to others. To this end, if being coworkers with God means being in caring relationship to others, we should then expect a practical theologian like Swinton to apply a theological framework to the very smallest of life challenges in a dementia care home. As Kevin Vanhoozer says, "Theological competence is ultimately a matter of being able to make judgments that display the mind of Christ" (Vanhoozer 2015).

ORGANIZATIONAL FAITHFULNESS: A FUTURE FOCUS

The *Faith for Life* and Being Present projects were products of Swinton's existing thinking about dementia and time (Swinton 2016 and Swinton 2012). Swinton's third project sought to answer the new question, What makes and keeps an organization Christian?

As HammondCare's then–Chief Executive, my keen interest in this question stemmed from both research and experience. So many charities and social-service organizations that had been founded as unashamedly Christian in character were now secular and even antagonistic to the gospel. Others rebranded with the apparent purpose of distancing the organization from their founding Christian identity and purpose (Judd, Robinson, and Errington 2014). This secularization of formerly Christian organizations is a worldwide phenomenon: "It's the exception that an organization stays true to its mission. The natural course—the unfortunate natural evolution of many originally Christ-centered missions—is to drift" (Greer and Horst 2014).

This issue has especial relevance in Australia. Whereas in the United States, only five of the top twenty-five nonprofit charitable organizations by income were Christian—and in Britain only three of the top twenty-five were Christian—in Australia twenty-three of the top twenty-five were Christian. Church and faith-based charities remain a strong, even dominant, presence in the delivery of health and social services in Australia (Piggin 2006). Therefore, the consequence of actual and potential "mission drift" in Australia in the twenty-first century is both profound and urgent.

The Christian motivation for charitable work has a clear theological base. The Christian message is indeed "Your kingdom come, on earth as it is in heaven," a powerful and revolutionary prayer (Matt 6:10). As citizens of the kingdom of God, we bring real and effective signs of God's renewed creation, here and now. This means incarnating a physical reality in which forgiveness and justice reign, where the hungry are fed, the orphaned, the widowed, and the weak are served, and the lonely are placed in families.

Christians model themselves on Jesus, who healed the sick and called people to repentance and faith. As Jim Wallis says, "If your Gospel is not good news for the poor, it is not the gospel of Jesus" (Wallis 2015).

Furthermore, as Tom Wright claims, "To hope for a better future in this world—for the poor, the sick . . . for the slaves, the refugees, the hungry and homeless . . . the downtrodden and despairing . . . is not something else, something extra, something tacked on to the gospel as an afterthought" (Wright 2007). What Jesus was doing and promising, in his preaching and his healing, "was not saving souls for a disembodied eternity but rescuing people from the corruption and decay of the way of the world presently . . . so they could enjoy, already in the present, that renewal of creation which is God's ultimate purpose" (Wright 2007). So for organizations whose mission is motivated by the life and deeds of Jesus, the question of how to retain that Christian identity and purpose is paramount. Swinton addressed this question with enthusiasm. His first response was, not surprisingly, a theological one.

> Whilst the term "Christian organization" has been used with frequency, working out precisely what such a term actually means is difficult. At one level the answer to the question of whether an organization can be Christian is a simple "No." Nowhere in the Bible or within Christian tradition do we find organizations being described as Christian in the way that human beings are described as Christians. Organizations can certainly be in the service of God, but does that make them Christian? Perhaps, but we would have to think of the term "Christian" in a quite different way from the norm. To be a Christian is to become a follower of Jesus; a disciple who has chosen to follow Jesus and has been given a vocation and a calling to participate within the mission of God. (Swinton 2019)

Warming to his task, Swinton then challenged the view that an organization is Christian because it insists on the primacy of Christian values. Values such as respect and dignity and the inestimable worth of each human can be affirmed by believer and unbeliever alike, which for an organization will have operational advantages. These values might even be derived from the theological truth of the *imago Dei*.

However, there is a significant theological problem with that way of determining that an organization is Christian. If it is possible to extrapolate *values* from the gospel to which a broad range of people with varying beliefs can adhere, and that values adherence is what makes the organization worthy of the label Christian, there is no real need for Jesus. Christianity has then been reduced to a set of moral values to which any decent person can give their assent.

The theological difficulty is that Jesus is not a system of moral values. Rather he is a God made flesh, a God of relationships. Relating to a person is quite different from adhering or relating to a principle or a value. Rules and values may ensure that God is to an extent glorified, but that does not imbue the organization with a Christian ethos. Rules and values may be necessary, but they are not sufficient.

An interesting creative tension arises from this dilemma. On the one hand, being a Christian is a personal rather than an organizational experience, requiring a commitment to Jesus. On the other hand, earthly institutions do have a role to participate in God's redemption of the world, even if their staff members are not all Christian. So how do we resolve this conundrum?

Together with Swinton, we decided that the best determinant for what makes an organization Christian is best found in the idea of faithfulness. The concept of faithfulness means that it is not the values that the organization claims to hold but the way it lives out the vision it has been given. This outcome-based approach is as much theological as it is practical: "Not everyone who says to me, 'Lord, Lord,' will enter the kingdom of heaven, but only the one who does the will of my Father who is in heaven" (Matt 7:21).

The meaning behind the term *organizational faithfulness* is still evolving but it will encompass three key elements: a) the characteristic spirit or ethos of the organization, b) the identity that is not simply conceptual but empowered by the Holy Spirit, and c) the impact that the organization has externally on those it serves and internally with staff and other stakeholders.

Christian organizations exist in all sectors: in aid and development, in schools, in health and aged care, in social service and welfare, and many other areas. The Organizational Faithfulness project will address questions that need to be confronted by those who work in these organizations such as:

- What are the characteristics of an organizational culture that is demonstrably faithful? Or unfaithful?
- Is a faithful organization one that has a board of directors and executive whose members are all believers?

- Can believers and unbelievers serve within a faithful organization and, if so, how?
- What active measures can be taken to protect an organization against "mission drift"?

The real strength of the HammondCare-Swinton partnership will find expression in the answering of such questions. Case studies will address all aspects of an organization's faithfulness in areas of governance, strategy, human-resource management, finances, evangelism, communication, and much more. This exciting future promises lasting value for the international Christian community.

CONCLUSION

John Swinton's special devotion to the idea of personhood and what it means to be truly human has helped HammondCare make great strides in aligning *what* it does as an organization with the more fundamental *why*. I trust God's love is evident through the Faith for Life and Being Present projects already undertaken as a result of this partnership. I look forward to seeing how the Organizational Faithfulness project will challenge organizations, sometimes uncomfortably, for the sake of maintaining or perhaps even reclaiming their Christian identity. The HammondCare-Swinton relationship has been founded on mutuality and respect. While Swinton has actually been able to practice as well as preach, HammondCare has had its theological roots deepened and its practices challenged.

But these activities are overshadowed by Swinton's quiet modeling of relationship within HammondCare. As one staffer observed, "John grew quickly on HammondCare not unlike someone you might meet for the first time and hours later you depart having a new friend, without realizing how it happened."

It was John's complete inability to be offensive, awkward, or off-point that meant wherever he went within HammondCare, people seemed to want to listen carefully to what he said. Even when appearing in a corridor or a lift—seemingly briefly lost and a long way from his Scottish home—there was a calmness and availability and evident compassion that drew people. He knew how to challenge HammondCare's beliefs even while remaining disarming and approachable. For a theologian, he was remarkably well received by those who might have considered themselves not particularly interested in God.

Books, lectures, and projects aside: that is the supreme mark of a practical theologian. It does not really matter that he cannot remember your name.

WORKS CITED

Barclay, Linda, Rebecca Forbes, and Ben Boland. 2018. *Faith for Life*. Sydney: HammondPress.

Greer, Peter, and Chris Horst. 2014. *Mission Drift: The Unspoken Crisis Facing Leaders, Charities, and Churches*. Bloomington, Minn.: Bethany House.

Judd, Stephen, Anne Robinson, and Felicity Errington. 2014. *Driven by Purpose: Charities That Make the Difference*. Sydney: HammondPress.

Kitwood, Tom. 1997. *Dementia Reconsidered: The Person Comes First*. Rethinking Ageing. Buckingham, UK: Open University Press.

Martin, David, and John Swinton. 2019. *Love in the Time of Dementia: Is Care without Love Enough?* Melbourne: Ethos Centre for Christianity and Society.

Piggin, Stuart. 2006. *Shaping the Good Society in Australia*. Sydney: Australia's Christian Heritage National Forum.

Piggin, Stuart, and Robert D. Linder. 2020. *Attending to the National Soul: Evangelical Christians in Australian History, 1914–2014*. Melbourne: Monash University.

Robinson, Donald. 1981. *Faith's Framework: The Structure of New Testament Theology*. Sydney: Albatross.

Swinton, John. 2012. *Dementia: Living in the Memories of God*. Grand Rapids: Eerdmans.

———. 2015. "The Bible and Dementia: Living Well and Faithfully with Dementia." Unpublished paper.

———. 2016. *Becoming Friends of Time: Disability, Timefullness, and Gentle Discipleship*. Waco, Tex.: Baylor University Press.

———. 2019. "Organizational Faithfulness." Unpublished concept paper for Stephen Judd.

Swinton, John, Julia Patton, and Joy Robinson. 2018. "Being Present: What is Required to Ensure Carers Remain Present with People Living with Advanced Dementia in HammondCare Homes." Unpublished paper, Sydney.

Vanhoozer, Kevin. 2005. *The Drama of Doctrine*. Louisville: Westminster John Knox.

Van Norstrand, Robert Charles. 2005. *Reaching the Unreachable: Devotions for Alzheimer's Patients and Their Caregivers*. Duluth, Minn.: Christian Life Resources.

Wallis, Jim. 2010. "Personal but Never Private." *Christianity Today*. September 13, 2020.

Wright, Tom. 2007. *Surprised by Hope: Rethinking Heaven, the Resurrection, and the Mission of the Church*. London: SPCK.

11

All God's Children Got a Place in the Choir

Discipleship, Disability, and Dementia

Bill Gaventa

> Likewise, when a person is caught up in a familiar prayer or hymn, or
> when they simply clap their hands to the rhythm of a song, they may
> well be remembering, cognitively or bodily, experiences they have had
> with God—or they may be having an experience with God at that very
> moment. (Swinton 2012, 251)

One of the most significant contributions of John Swinton's work has been
the way he has illuminated a pastoral theology that undergirds a pastoral
and congregational response to people with disabilities of all types and
their caregivers as well as to people with dementia and their caregivers.
Both dementia and disability in general are arenas of theology and practice that were, like the people they involved, mostly hidden until half a
century ago. Inclusive ministries to people with disabilities in modern
times first began with children through specialized religious education
programs, while pastoral theology and ministry to the elderly grew along
with the significant growth in life expectancy in modern times. Finding
common ground in our theological and pastoral response to both the
young and the old, as well as all in between, is no small accomplishment.

But as ministries with people with disabilities and dementia have
grown alongside theological explorations of those intersections, neither
John nor the movement has stopped there. To call followers of Christ,
or Christian disciples, to more inclusive ministry involving people who
have been hidden in institutions or nursing homes is only the first step.
It also means discovering that the majority of people with disabilities
(including mental illness) and dementia had been in our homes and
communities all along.

The second step has been the recognition that people with disabilities or dementia are also disciples, people who can and have responded to the person of Jesus, the movement of the Holy Spirit, and the desire to praise God. How do we know that? Because they kept saying so until their voices were heard. Moreover, if we are honest, many people who have felt called (like this author) to be in those arenas of ministry also began to talk about the ways we have both received and grown, by serving as witness and by the lives of people with disabilities and dementia. Gifts and call have been rediscovered as contributions given and received, no matter one's level of ability or label. As an American folk song goes:

> All God's critters got a place in the choir
> Some sing low and some sing higher.
> Some sing out loud on the telephone wire,
> And some just clap their hands or paws or anything they got.
> (Staines 1978)

The goal of this chapter is to talk about the evolution of understandings of inclusive discipleship, mostly by reflecting on my own journey, the moments and lights that have illumined it, and how we might come to see this shared discipleship across a full range of ages and capacities. John Swinton and many others have been treasured companions on that journey, both in their writings and, more so, in a variety of gatherings in which people of many faith backgrounds and abilities have come together to learn from one another. I will do so by using a thread and theme that represents another of John's gifts, but is very clearly not one of mine. We fellow travelers don't usually get to see it, but he is a musician and singer. Part of my premise is that those skills and passions are ones that have imbued his voice with the underlying tones and tunes of pastoral work and a theological harmony. I invite you along.

CLAIMING DISCIPLESHIP: ALL GOD'S CRITTERS GOT A PLACE IN THE CHOIR

In "Building a Church for Strangers," John Swinton focuses on Stephen, his friend and institutional resident of the facility he served in as chaplain.

> He simply knows it is a place where he can go to sing and be with his friends. He knows the word "Jeeshuss," and takes great pleasure in shouting it out, often during the quietest part of the service. However, this 'disruption' is not a problem. Within the small hospital fellowship that is his spiritual home, there is a sense of acceptance and community that I have rarely experienced elsewhere; a feeling that we are "church" in a very real and meaningful sense. Within the confines of that tiny

sanctuary there is "neither Jew nor Greek, slave nor free, male or female . . . black nor white, able bodied and handicapped," only friends dancing and singing with "Jeeshuss" their friend. (Swinton 2001, 28)

Four decades ago, at the first conference I ever organized on ministries with people with disabilities, our closing speaker was a young woman named Cathy. As a young girl with cerebral palsy, she had been sent to the Newark State School, thirty miles outside Rochester, New York, but had left in the first wave of deinstitutionalization before my first real job as Protestant chaplain at that developmental center. She had moved into a group home in Rochester and then into one of the early supported independent living apartments.

Her job in the conference was to tell her story, for a premise of the conference was that many more people were "coming home" in what New York State called "repatriation." Her raspy voice was shaky, as were her hands. She surprised me by the matter-of-fact manner of her story.

She noted the institutional school "wasn't too bad" and then talked about her move to Rochester and getting involved in a nearby church. She talked about attitudes. Then, using the language of the 1970s, she closed with, "You know, it is really important for you to be nice to handicapped people, but it is more important for you to let them be nice to you."

"To let them be nice to you." To serve you, to help, to contribute. I along with many others have spent decades calling clergy and laity to open the hearts and doors of congregations to be more welcoming and inclusive of people with disabilities and their families. Our message echoed the calls of Jesus to his disciples and followers to "let the children come unto me" (Matt 19:14) and God's wish that "my house will be called a house of prayer for all peoples" (Isa 57:7). It was part of a broader call to seek out those on the margins of our communities and crowds; to stop, touch, and break bread with people who may be poor, lame, blind, or marginalized for other reasons. Discipleship meant accepting, welcoming, and including people with disabilities in Jesus' church.

But to "let people with disabilities be nice to you" means that we are not the only ones who seek to be Jesus' disciples, or his hands, feet, and heart in the world in which we live. Jesus' call to discipleship is meant for everyone, not just the able-bodied, the strong, the powerful, or the so-called normal. Using the word *we* assumes too often that *we* means the able-bodied and "normal" people. For Jesus, *we* and *us* means everyone. Everyone is called to follow. Everyone is called to serve. Everyone is called to give. Everyone, whether or not all you have is five loaves, one or ten talents, or a widow's mite.

A Catholic chaplain and friend of mine at another institution in upstate New York in those years was Fr. John Aiello, later renowned for his writing and storytelling. He once told me that in his experience "people go from fear to pity to anger to love" as they get to know people with intellectual and developmental disabilities.

That progression became one early framework for me to talk about the journey to shared discipleship on the part of people considered "typical." When disability was seen as demonic or evil, we excluded them from society because we were afraid. Then, as people began to say, "No, they are also children of God," the feeling and attitude became more of pity or charity for God's "special children." But as relationships form, one learns about the multiple kinds of problems they have faced as people with disabilities, and far too often by the church, including stereotypes, prejudice, inaccessibility, discrimination, and rejection. That can and should produce anger, anger at what they have had to endure, and a desire to help change that part of our world. However, in anger, we sometimes jump too quickly to do things for others, to fight their battles for them. As we continue that journey together, we may hear them say, "Don't do things for me. Walk with me." Then we begin to realize that "we," as disciples and fellow human beings, may be doing something for people with disabilities but also that "they" are doing something for us. The relationship becomes one of giving and receiving, one of love and mutuality, rather than serving and helping in one direction.

I once used Aiello's progression at a workshop in Richmond, Virginia. A young woman with cerebral palsy who used a wheelchair said, "You know, that's my journey as well. I used to hate myself, thought I was bad or evil. Then I felt sorry for myself. Then I got angry. But now, thanks to God's help, I see my own gifts and my own worth as one of God's children."

Each of us, with whatever level of cognitive disability we may have, faces three core spiritual questions and tasks.

1. The question of identity. "Who am I?" What do I really believe? What is most important to me? What are my passions? What makes me unique? As each of us created in the image of God, what is that image in each of us? What do we put our faith in?

2. The question of purpose. "Why am I?" What am I called to do with my life? What kind of contribution do I want to make to my community, my church, and the world with the gifts I have been given? Where do we find our hope?

3.   The question of community. "Whose am I?" To whom do I be-
     long? Where is my community, the place where I give and receive
     support and friendship? In America, we sometimes say "Who are
     your people?" (Gaventa 2018, 70–84)

Just because people labeled with intellectual disabilities or dementia
may not be able to respond in "typical" ways to those questions does not
mean that they cannot express their preferences and feelings around each
of them, especially with support. People who are close to people with significant cognitive disabilities, whatever the cause, can tell you what their
preferences are, what they love or dislike, and name what they consider
to be unique personal qualities. People with intellectual disabilities need
opportunities to explore multiple dimensions of life and relationships
(i.e., community) as they grow in order to shape those preferences and
qualities. As John Swinton argues in *Dementia: Living in the Memories
of God*, people need community to shape who they are as well as to hold
their identity in ways that honor each person's uniqueness even when
(or perhaps especially when) dementia seems to be taking it away. What
gives and has given each person a sense of meaning and purpose goes
far beyond what Swinton terms the "malignant social psychology" that
holds sway in the assessment and treatment of people with intellectual
and developmental disabilities and dementia alike (Swinton 2012, 80).

This journey toward a recognition of the universality of discipleship
counts several secular movements as allies. One is the rebellion against
assessment and treatment that focused only on deficits that came in
the form of person-centered, rather than professional-centered, planning. Person-centered planning comes in a variety of forms (one might
say, somewhat tongue in cheek, "denominations"), but at their core it
is the philosophy that everyone has strengths and gifts as well as deficits. Essential Lifestyle Planning, one version with origins in both Scotland and the United States, asserts that the usual question in planning
supports for someone, What's important for that person? needs to be
balanced with another, What's important to that person? (Smull and
Sanderson et al. 2009). Thus, person-centered planning, done well, is a
form of extensive listening rather than prescribing a treatment process.
It is easily applicable to faith communities. It is still a process, but one
that calls for the kind of patient, attentive, and loving ("being with" or
"I-Thou") relationship with a person with an intellectual disability or
dementia that John Swinton calls for. It is the classic paradox of ministry:
the best thing to "do" is to "be" there, to be "a community of attention"

(Swinton 2012, 222) aware of the "sacredness of the present," practicing "soulful companionship" that watchfully waits in the face of helplessness, all coming out of a theology of visitation (Swinton 2012, 254). In that form of discipleship with anyone, ministry is staying hopeful that there will be moments when God visits and "things happen" (Swinton 2012, 280), moments similar to ones that Brian Brock describes with his "non-verbal" son Adam as an "assault of grace" (Brock 2019, 235).

Anything close to that form of listening is also a way of supporting and hearing the voice of a person, however they speak, through gestures, bodies, words, or actions, all of which can reflect agency. The second public movement and framework that recognizes the centrality of voice is self-advocacy, a movement encouraging and empowering people with intellectual disabilities to speak up and out, especially about matters related to their own personal welfare. Like most new words and concepts, its origin reflects a history in which advocacy by parents, families, caregivers, and other advocates often overrides the voices of people with intellectual and developmental disabilities themselves. "Self-advocacy" usually refers to people with intellectual and developmental disabilities claiming their own voice in systems of support. But self-advocates will also tell you that they sometimes have to do that within the broader disability advocacy movement where value judgments are sometimes made about the power of voice being dependent on cognitive capacity. Related frameworks include "supported decision making," now a legal recognition in some parts of the world. This recognition acknowledges that people with intellectual disabilities and limited communication skills still have the right to have their voices heard with the help of those who are closest to them and know how such individuals express themselves and respond to others (National Resource Center on Supported Decision Making 2021).

A third variation on this theme of listening closely is through the strategies of positive behavior supports, built on the principles that treatments should not compel or force a person to change behavior, but rather, that all behavior should be interpreted as communication. Thus, it is up to the circle of support and care around a person whose behavior is deemed problematic (or "noncompliant") to understand what is being said through behavior and help such individuals find new and more helpful ways to express feelings, attain something they need or want, and avoid things they dislike (Gaventa 2018, 231–45).

Moving back into the Christian world, the word "vocation" is often used to talk about not only the call that comes to ordained persons but also the call that comes to everyone: How does God want us to use our gifts and our life in service to God and the community in which we live? Who does God call each of us to be? What is it that God calls each of us to do? How do we make a difference in caring for all of God's creation? Call and response is a fundamental biblical theme for God's people as well as a liturgical standby in Christian worship in various forms, including the African American form of preaching and singing, the storied "call and response" (so named). For a profound example, read and see the wonderful story of Luke McCarty, a young man with cerebral palsy and very limited speech who finds his congregational home and community in the choir of a small African American congregation in Mississippi (Pearson and Clay 2011).

In the second institution in which I was a chaplain, my mind's eye goes to Kim, a young woman born too early (or in the wrong place) to get the commonplace insertion of a stent to help with hydrocephaly, thus forcing her to live her life in a custom-designed adjustable rolling stretcher/bed because of the size of her head. Kim understood everything you said, sometimes pretending that she did not, and loved being in worship especially when the singing was going on. The body of Christ, for her, in those moments, meant having someone else stand next to her, encourage her voice, and provide a hand against which she could clap, because she could not get her two hands together. More recently, my son as the new pastor at his church in Austin, visited Gene Alice, the beloved wife of Max, a member of his new church. Gene Alice, a woman of many gifts, had also been an accomplished organist and pianist. She is now in the "memory unit" of the retirement facility where Max also lives independently. One day, our son visited them in Max's apartment. The major connection that happened between them was her sitting at the piano and playing hymns, to which Max and Matthew sang along.

Thus, the role for people of faith is to help discover what "place in the choir" people with intellectual and developmental disabilities wish to have. For people with dementia and their families, the task is to help them stay connected to the people, experiences, rituals, and music that have always been important to them. In doing so, together, we are opening ourselves to the moments when "the works of God might be manifest" (John 9:3) in surprising ways, which can teach, inspire, and break open any facile presumptions about intellectual and learning disabilities we may harbor. As Dan Lunney argues (quoting Don and Emily Saliers):

> Music is central to many spiritual practices. Don and Emily Saliers describe the spiritual nature of music whether it is secular or sacred music: Coming alive to music is coming alive to deep memory, as

music recreates our sense of the world and who we are in it, right in the midst of the terrors and beauties, the pain and deep pleasures of human existence. Coming alive to music, we are led on a double journey: into the mystery of God and into the depths of our humanity. (Lunney 2017)

First, though, a crucial caveat. People of faith often end up talking about the role that people with disabilities or dementia play by teaching "the rest of us" about our own limitations, vulnerabilities, and weaknesses. They will talk about the rediscovery of the most important things in life: the power of interdependent relationships and communities, and then, deeper lessons about the power of the powerless, the strength that may emerge from suffering, and the God who lives and reveals the Holy Spirit in those relationships.

That is true for me, and it may be the same for many of you. Indeed, I found my own sense of call and vocation in listening to the stories of people with disabilities and their families over forty years ago. I felt both drawn and compelled to that area of ministry. Sometimes I even say, "I did not find my vocation, my vocation found me, and profoundly shaped the journey of my identity."

Yet—and this requires underscoring—many of my friends with disabilities and family members claim that they do not see their calling as one of teaching nondisabled people about what is most important. That may happen, but they have said, "My calling is simply to be a good parent." Or, "I feel called to be a baker." Or a cook. A computer programmer. A secretary. You name it. They want the opportunity and support to do what they love and feel called to, and, like the rest of us, be able to make a living out of it while contributing to our community. "I don't want to be special. I just want to do my part." Some have said it more bluntly to me, "I don't think my calling is to help you work through your own issues about disability, vulnerability, or limitations." They cannot stop people from projecting deeply personal and spiritual questions on to them, but they would rather spend their time focusing on their own dreams or the things they love to do with the support of others as needed.

Thus, if the church wants to help people with disabilities and dementia to be disciples, and to discover and follow their own calling, we have some work to do.

First, it means starting very early to recognize the gifts and strengths in each child or adult with a disability, and to celebrate those gifts and strengths. Everyone has them. Talk to people who support people with profound disabilities or dementia, and they can name some strengths and gifts they see, even if the person cannot voice them. The first major step in affirming or discovering someone's gifts is to have them be recognized, or even named, by others. Brian Brock says it more clearly in his profound theological exploration of Paul's use of the metaphor of the "body of Christ" in 1 Corinthians 12. There, he notes that a gift is not a gift until it is received by others as such; someone's qualities can be named and received as gift without necessarily performing any utilitarian purpose. They are gifts of *being* as well as of *doing* (Brock 2019, 201–24). I think here of Theresa, a young Catholic woman with very severe cerebral palsy at the facility where I served as chaplain in Rochester, New York. She could smile, but she could not speak or use any augmented communication device available at that time. Yet others besides her family saw and found in her a sense of holiness and gift. The same was true for Henri Nouwen's relationship with Adam when he first moved to the L'Arche community, Daybreak, described so movingly in his book *Adam: God's Beloved* (Nouwen 1998; see also Nouwen 1994).

But many gifts can be used. We are called to use them as a way of responding to the call to discipleship, by finding ways to help others, to do things that help sustain the church and the body of Christ. If we cannot find a way for someone to help, even with the smallest of mites and talents, then it says more about our lack of imagination than it does their ability. Help persons with disabilities to find a way to contribute, to be needed, to be seen acting and living out of their faith and talents, rather than being designated as the "disabled person" who has to receive all the time. Find ways to invite them to be givers. Think of all the things that need to be done to help a parish flourish. Break a given task into smaller components. Carve out a place for someone to help. The quickest way to help people feel really included, and like they really belong, is to deeply listen to the voice of who they are and want to be. "I am not me until my song is free."[1] Help them figure out, and grow into, their "place in the choir."

When others see people with disabilities living out their faith and calling in those ways, attitudes change, and barriers fall even more quickly. You, the reader, likely know stories of where this is happening. I know of people being ushers or members of the choir, or serving in a host of capacities, including as those who fold bulletins, serve coffee or parish meals, set up and clean up, or read Scripture. You can also serve

---

[1]   This is a quotation from this author's notes from a sermon or presentation by James Forbes Jr. in the 1990s, but I did not write down the title of the presentation, date, place, or event. But see his poem, "Release Your Song," quoted in Akinade 2016.

as a religious education teacher, a teacher's aide, aide or visitor to those confined to home or hospital. One man made it his mission to send a birthday card to every other man in the church. Emily Colson, mother of Max, her autistic son who happens to love vacuum cleaners, found a way back into the church when she came with Max toward the end of a service. The guys responsible for putting up the chairs afterward invited him to help. All of a sudden, he had a job to do. Buddies at the church. And they became his champions in that congregation (Colson 2010).

Chris was a teenager with Down syndrome and altar boy in a Catholic parish in New Jersey. After Mass, his mother could not find him (which sounds like a Bible story about a mother who could not find her son in the temple). She finally did, and Chris was talking to an older couple. They had come to Mass that day with pain, grief, and uncertainty, asking God why their new grandchild had been born with Down syndrome. Then they met this young man, in a revered role in his parish, and felt compelled to meet him after Mass. Think of the pastoral care he did that day.

Likewise, if people have been in the metaphorical choir for a long time, how does the community of disciples help them remember who they are even when dementia seems to be stripping identity away? The faithful continuity of a community that enables someone with dementia to see long-familiar faces is another part of surrounding someone with possessions that have been treasured, or enabling preferred routines to happen. Those are acts of "re-membering," helping people not to be forgotten but also to participate in the traditions and rituals of any given community by saying, essentially, "You are still part of this fellowship of disciples, this body of Christ." It is another reminder that a gift can simply be the presence and welcoming of a person loved in the eyes of God and others. A community of faith should not wait till a person dies to "remember" them as "saints who from their labors rest." They may be missing from their usual "place in the choir," but they are not gone.

NO MOVEMENT WITHOUT A SONG: WE SHALL OVERCOME

> The places in the brain that process art and music are close to the places where memories are stored, so the fact that such things might stimulate memory would seem to make some neurological sense. Think of it this way. When we listen to music, or at least when we're doing so in a more concentrated and intentional manner, we don't simply hum and sing along in a neutral way. Certain songs contain our memories. As soon as we hear them, we're whisked backward in time to

situations, events and people that were deeply meaningful to us and that remind us of things we have done and people we have loved. Such memories are laden with feelings and emotions. Music is a vehicle that we use as we travel through time; it brings us back to often-forgotten destinations, some of which we remember with joy, others with sadness. Understood in this way, we can see that things such as songs, music, art, dance and ritual actually function as modes of extended memory—that is, places where memory is stored external to its normal location in the brain. They act as keys that can unlock emotions, feelings, and recollection that would otherwise be inaccessible. People may not be able to access certain memories via the normal processes. But it may that music, art, prayer and so forth act as keys which allow aspects to memory to be unlocked and accessed even if that access is only temporary and sporadic. When we watch people with dementia move to the rhythm of music, when we see them dance without words, they may well be remembering cognitively or bodily something profound and deep about themselves and their pasts. (Swinton 2012, 250–51)

Following the 1979 conference in Rochester, my chaplaincy work on connecting people with developmental disabilities to congregations continued, and, in 1986, our Advisory Board hosted another conference, this one at the Jewish Community Center called "Merging Two Worlds." The goal was to reflect on what we were learning as communities and congregations became more inclusive. Two moments at that conference made indelible impressions on me.

The first was a keynote address by Parker Palmer. He was invited because of his early book, *The Company of Strangers*, which, among other things, was about hospitality and community (Palmer 1983). He had never spoken at an event related to ministry and disability. What we did not know was that he received the invitation as he was emerging from one of his journeys into depression, and, as he said in the talk, "I felt I needed to be here." His talk focused first on the role of the stranger in modern life, the importance of hospitality and welcome, and then on a number of typical human illusions "punctured" by relationships with people with intellectual and developmental disabilities and other disabilities, including lessons from his own depression. As discussed in the previous section, such relationships involve lessons of identity in discipleship with and through people with disabilities as we try to support persons with disabilities in their own faith journeys (Palmer 1986).

The second was a presentation by Bob Perske, one of the first chaplains in an institutional setting to write about the spiritual needs and gifts of people with intellectual disabilities and their families (Gaventa and Coulter 2003), who then went on to become the chronicler of the deinstitutionalization movement (from institutions to communities) with books such as *Circles of Friends* (Perske 1988) and *New Life in the Neighborhood: How People with Mental Retardation and Other Disabilities Can Make a Good Community Better* (Perske 1980). His wife, Martha, an illustrator who became famous for her pen and pencil drawings of children and adults with intellectual and developmental disabilities, illustrated those books, capturing individual character and beauty in ways that had not been done before (Perske 1998). In his talk, Bob explored the movement toward community. He told us that he had just been to the first statewide self-advocacy conference in New Jersey, and, while riding in a van with a number of self-advocates, listened and participated as they sang along to John Denver's chorus, "Country roads, take me home / To the place I belong / West Virginia, Mountain Mama / Take me home, country roads." He then cryptically noted, "We say there is a disability movement in this country. If so, we are the only movement without a song."

"The only movement without a song." I and many others already knew the power of music in worship services that included people with intellectual and developmental disabilities in institutional settings. I am not a musician, nor much of a singer, but my congregation did not care. They wanted to sing along with the taped songs, or when I was lucky, with the guitarist or piano player who accompanied me in leading the services. Responses and participation could be nonverbal, but the language of music was universal. At Newark State School, the old state institution where I had my first full-time professional job, I lugged around an old cassette recorder to do services on units where people could not come to the chapel. One of my biggest challenges, yet also memorable experiences, came when the staff and foster grandparents who led the "Disney Unit," the ward for children with severe multiple disabilities, asked me, "When are you going to come do something here?" Together with a recreation therapist who could play the guitar, we gathered the children and their most important community, the foster grandmothers who spent hours with them, for what we called "A Time for Joy." It was simply music, shared concerns, and prayer. At Monroe Developmental Center in Rochester where I began the religious services program, we recruited many groups of church or synagogue members to come to the center to help lead services (we wanted the people there to feel that they were part of a larger body of faith). No amount of verbal preparation would take away the anxiety that some of them felt on the first visit.

Then, with the first song, such as "This Is the Day that the Lord Hath Made," I could see their attitudes change in a moment, almost like "Now I know what to do, sing with them."

Similarly, those who have supported, ministered, and cared for people with dementia also know the power of music. Clergy and musicians in memory-care settings report that time and time again, people with dementia who seem unresponsive will come to life with a familiar song or prayer that has been part of their lives for decades. Those moments are sometimes termed MEAMs (Music-Evoked Autobiographical Memories). A number of those moments have been caught on video, including a very powerful video of Naomi Feil, the Jewish founder of Validation Therapy, using touch, eye contact, movement, and songs like "Jesus Loves Me" and "He's Got the Whole World in His Hands" to connect with Gladys, an eighty-seven-year-old African American woman with severe dementia (Feil 2015). Another more recent video shows a hundred-year-old ballerina begin to move her hands and body to the music of Swan Lake (González 2020). Remember also the earlier story about my son's pastoral visit with Gene Alice and her husband, Max. As Dan Lunney says, "Music that is familiar and evokes strong emotions has more potential of sparking memories which is essential in helping a person living with dementia to reclaim fragments of their story in order to affirm their identity" (Lunney 2017, 85).

That singing and music also usually meant movement and motion. Songs with appropriate hand motions were standbys. But music is not just heard and sung; it is both a body and soul language. It moves people spiritually, emotionally, and physically. It can calm, excite, inspire, lament, pray, inflame, protest, and praise. Name an emotion, and music can both reflect it and induce it. The civil rights movement, on which the newer disability-rights movement was modeled and built, depended on songs, as had labor movements, antiwar movements, and other civic, political, and religious movements.

We were "the only movement without a song." That stuck in my imagination as fact and metaphor. Some possible reasons began to emerge, the simplest of them being that I could not find any songwriters or singers with intellectual or other developmental disabilities. But that did not keep the self-advocates Bob Perske rode with from adopting some. Karl Williams has been involved in the self-advocacy movement since its inception, and he comes closest to being a songwriter closely aligned with that movement (Williams 1998). There have been a number of songwriters in the years since that have written songs about disabilities for kids (Tom Hunter 2002),[2] songs reflecting the experiences of parents (Joanie Calem 2018), and songs out of the lives of direct care professionals (Peter Leidy 2021). There have been people with autism known for their innate musical abilities, and, in recent years, more people with disabilities recognized as singers and musicians. But there have not been songs coming out of the world of disability that have become well-known anthems for the movement, as "We Shall Overcome" and "This Land is Your Land" have done for other movements.

One prime reason is that most of the language used in the world of intellectual and developmental disabilities (as well as in the world of dementia) comes, first, out of the medical and human sciences, or disciplines that purport to be objective, descriptive, and reflective of realities that can be measured and quantified, and, second, out of the world of civil liberties and rights. As John Swinton describes so accurately in his book on dementia, these are, on the one hand, languages that focus on defects and limits, and on the other, treatment plans and processes that sometimes reflect an assumption that healing is more of a technology that can be controlled (and fixed) by science than a process nurtured by emotion, spirit, mind, relationship, and environment. What's "good" in the world of science is what's observable, what's "true" is measurable, and what's "beautiful" is that which can be replicated. The languages of the sciences are far more languages of the head rather than the heart. This does not mean that the languages of the sciences cannot inspire, but the love, passion, beliefs, and curiosity which have fueled discovery are far too often seen as something that may bias scientific language rather than enhance it. This is yet another reason for the rise of the social model of disability, as well as assessments and plans that are more personal and context-centered. The real irony here is that the Latin root of *assessment* is "to sit next to" (Hilsman 1997, 8–9). Assessment in the medical and disability worlds usually assumes an objective description (at arm's length), a placing in categories, rather than the kind of attentive and deep listening explored in John Swinton's book on dementia and in many of his other writings. Indeed, *A Space to Listen* is the title of a project and resource on the spirituality of people with intellectual and developmental disabilities (Swinton 2001).

Meanwhile, the disability-rights movement has been based on the language of rights, laws, and participation as full citizens. Again, this has been crucially important, and the laws, policies, and rulings that have

[2] See songs such as "Seeing with My Ears" and "You're Not So Different Than Me."

emerged from these movements have broken down many physical and legal barriers to inclusion and participation. Rights, as John Swinton and many others of us have argued, can get one in the door, into a place, and into a school or a community setting. But they do not guarantee that friendships and relationships will form that lead to a real sense of belonging, one where, as John notes, "you will be missed if you are not there" (Swinton 2012, 279). There are certainly multitudes of songs about freedom and rights, but few, if any, have come out of the disability movement. There have been "movements" in the health sciences and legal worlds, but not ones inspired by, or reflected in, music and song.

In a number of presentations and keynotes in the 1990s and early 2000s, I took Bob Perske's observation and played with it by asking the question, What's our song? It meant learning to listen to rhythms and tunes underlying social, legal, and support systems of care. Somewhat tongue in cheek, I proposed that tunes played by the various roles in our systems had one verse for families ("Where do you go, where do we go, We've got to fight, write, bitch . . .") and one for professionals ("This is the way, this is the way, if you do as I say, if you do as I say"), both of which usually drowned out the voices of people with intellectual and developmental disabilities ("When all else fails, will you listen to me? Will you listen to me?"). In other words, both lament and the blues spoke that language, with far too few tunes of praise and celebration.

We needed to break out of prescribed roles by using and listening to other forms of language, languages that "regular" people use in community settings. Those are languages of story, poetry, art, music, symbols, shared meals, festivals, and shared passions. Many of them involve touch and physical movement, such as dance and ritual. In recent years, there has been a growing awareness of the artistic skills of people with intellectual and developmental disabilities in many different mediums. What inspires teams working together, as music and songs often do in a sports arena? John McKnight once noted that "it is only in community where you hear singing" (McKnight 1997). A Scottish philosopher (no, not John Swinton but . . .), Andrew Fletcher, was noted to have said, "Let anyone who wishes write a country's laws, let me write the country's songs" (Fletcher 1703).

This is an argument more of correlation rather than causality, an appreciation for the ways that music, song, and other languages of communities transcend intellectual capacity, and do, indeed, become parts of individual and communal identity and purpose in ways we often do not comprehend. The fact is, music and song can empower, connect, bind, and remind us of our journeys as disciples. And they have the power to help people with intellectual and developmental disabilities as well as those with dementia to remember who and whose they are, if only others of us not yet so categorized are willing to use that same power to walk, sit, pray, and sing with them.

FROM OUTSIDE TO INSIDE TO OUTSIDE? SINGING THE LORD'S SONG IN A FOREIGN LAND

> In the music, in the dance, in the bread and in the wine he (Stephen) encounters a joy and evokes a sense of celebration that surpasses rational understanding and deeply challenges a church that equates faith and knowledge of God solely with intellectual comprehension. (Swinton 2001, 55)

In the community of faith, music is a key language of community that grows out of the center of individual and communal relationships with God and with one another. It also moves believers and disciples in emotional, spiritual, intellectual, and physical ways. Music also attracts, invites, and welcomes, much like light in the darkness draws all sorts of living creatures. So many people will say, "I go to church (or synagogue, or other forms of communal worship) because of the singing, the chanting, praying, and the other ritual movements of the body and spirit." There, in what we call sanctuaries, we learn the music and songs of our spiritual community and home. Once embedded, thoughts, questions, and experiences outside the faith community will bring songs out of our body memories as a reference point. Once embedded, we cannot imagine certain times of the year, occasions, or rites of passage without the music we have come to expect, whether or not we are actually in the song's community at the time.[3]

Thus, music and songs serve multiple roles: first, as key "languages" of any given community of disciples and their identity; second, as things that move people in holistic ways; and third, as modes and means of

---

[3]   It is obvious that the impact of music and songs extends far beyond communities of faith. They are the language of many other kinds of communities, which flow out of them but also attract people to them. They both become key parts of identity, such as sports songs ("Take Me Out to the Ball Game!"), or patriotic songs ("God Bless the Queen"), or work songs. They also involve regional or ethnic music styles, or fans of particular singers. One thinks, for example, of the "Dead-Heads," or Bruce Springsteen followers, which connotates a community of shared interests but also, sometimes, literally those who follow a singer around or get to as many public appearances as they can.

sending people forth in the name of that community. "God is a Movement, an Embrace, a Flow . . . God is not even static within Godself as such. God in God's deepest identity is a relationship, a communion . . . God is Mission. This is what God is in God's deepest self: self-diffusive love, freely creating, redeeming, healing, challenging that creation" (Lunney 2017, 168). Or, said another way, many of us who grew up in Protestant Christian traditions know that music and songs were an act and symbol of the commitment to evangelism, to going out into the world, beyond the sanctuary of the "inside" to all the parts of the earth. In the Southern Baptist tradition in which I was raised, one committed one's life to Christ by walking forward during the last hymn, which usually focused on going forth to serve and save. So, in one act, you made a "profession" of identity, belonging, and service. But within all the Christian traditions, there are rituals, which include music and song, that send people forth to serve others, whether those be the people in need in our own communities or people in the "uttermost parts of the earth."

Going outside to serve in Christ's name, being led or sent, has also been an individual or communal act. While not stated explicitly, it is hard to imagine the cacophony of disciples speaking in different voices after Pentecost as not sounding, as some said, a group of drunken men. Most of them did indeed "go forth" into the Roman world, while others remained at "home base," that is, Jerusalem. One could choose to go forth to serve or be sent forth by a community. A disciple could feel led into a life of solitude and prayer, such as had early Christian hermits, and also profess a vow to a community of solitude and service in the hundreds of religious orders that emerged over time. Notably, for many of the early disciples, they were sent out, or felt led, into communities and countries where both they and Jesus were strangers to their inhabitants, the very people the disciples had to rely on for hospitality and welcome. Discipleship has always had a tradition of being sent forth into a "foreign" land, with a connotation of it being a somewhat risky endeavor.

The biblical prophets, Jesus, and the apostles all practiced and called others to follow them outside the boundaries of the familiar and "normal" to the communities of people who lived on or outside the margins, even if those boundaries existed only within one's head and habits. John Swinton has noted ways in which the "worlds" of intellectual and developmental disability, mental illness, and dementia are so often stigmatized as foreign lands, "worlds apart" from what is assumed to be typical human life. One also hears the language of departure to a foreign land by people writing about their own journeys, for example, when they acquired a disability (Frank 1992) or entered the land of mental illness (Styron 1989; Sullivan 2001; Jamieson 1996). Others have felt, along with their loved ones, that the person they have been was disappearing into the mists of dementia (Harper 2020; Sherman 2020). You hear it in the language of caregivers, both professional and personal, who talk about having to enter disability-worlds where the languages are foreign and the customs are mysterious, with feelings of powerlessness and helplessness about being able to do anything. One of my early sermons as a chaplain working in a state institution with people with intellectual and developmental disabilities was called "So Near Yet So Far: A Report from a Foreign Land," that is, a land right in our community which felt to many as far away as the mission fields in Africa where I grew up. The form was based somewhat on the innumerable times I heard "reports" by my parents speaking at churches here in the United States when our family was on "furlough."

One paradox of the call to discipleship that leads to those intimidating places is that while we may discover the limits of our assumed powers, we also discover the humanity, gifts, and strengths of the people who live and work there, and the irony of realizing our assumed strengths and limitations put us on an even plane in a world where everyone is vulnerable and limited. Thus, we get called back, so to speak, to re-explore our notions of autonomy, disability, omnipotence, control, and invulnerability. The great wonder is that those marginalized and foreign communities are often the ones where we may feel most welcomed by people who are eager to know who we are, why we are there, and what can we learn together.

Notably, those sent forth on the energy of call and song also carry their music and songs with them. Think of what we call "marching songs," including the one I sang almost more than any other in my Baptist upbringing, "Onward Christian Soldiers." Songs "embed" in us and can continue to provide comfort, strength, and inspiration. One sign of welcome and hospitality, at least in Nigeria where I grew up as the stranger, was a community's desire to share their music and dance. Missionaries and disciples have also wanted to share their own songs, which sometimes became evangelistic imperialism when they insisted that the songs of faith for a new Christian community had to be translations of the songs they had brought with them. But music and songs are often ways of seeing more quickly into the hearts of others, and discovering more connections and commonality than assumed, such as mentioned earlier in discussing what happened when people came into the "world" of the institution to help with a worship service. Or remember the varied forms of retelling the story of the First World War German and Allied troops whose shared songs led to a brief Yuletide truce.[4]

CONCLUSION: COME AND GO WITH SONG

To be a disciple, then, has much to do with personal and community identity, but it also has to do with *movement* (in multiple registers). It has to do with *doing* as well as with *being*. Disciples move and act in response to call, and out of faith, hope, and love.[5] Movement in response to God's call is a constant theme of the Torah, or the Old Testament. The disciples in the gospels were called, often unexpectedly, to move and follow this very different rabbi. After the resurrection, the disciples acted on the call to go forth. Church history is replete with the movement of disciples and missionaries into new countries and relationships with others once considered beyond God's pale. People with intellectual and developmental disabilities have often been some of those people, people outside the assumed embrace of God, and certainly outside our experience. However, in the Christian imagery of Paul's First Letter to the Corinthians, so beautifully explored by Brian Brock in his book *Wondrously Wounded*, all parts of the body have functions. They not only need to be connected to share their gifts, but the other parts need the gifts which they bring to help the functioning of the whole. It is more than a Western sense

---

[4]   See in particular *All Is Calm: The Christmas Truce of 1914*, a musical by Peter Rothstein.

[5]   Dan Lunney also describes the core sense of feeling led in spiritual practices.

Based on my experience, I propose seven characteristics of spiritual practices:

• Leads to/reflects integration of the person (identity, memory, narrative)
• Leads to/reflects connection with others (relational, communal, common narrative)
• Leads to/reflects connection with one's environment (heighten sensual/intuitive awareness)
• Leads to/reflects one's connection to God, the divine, the sacred
• Often uses ordinary materials, stimuli (bread, water, music, images)
• Is repeated regularly (habit of the heart)
• Has a transcendent quality through symbols, sounds, visuals, smells, tastes which are accessible through time.

Spiritual practices have a dynamic quality and that is why I included "leads to" which includes agency and "reflects" which recognizes that there is an element of being led. (Lunney, 119)

of an individual being part of a whole; it is that the whole lives, moves, and works its way through the lives of all its individual members (Brock 2019, 201–24).

This discussion could go in many directions, but let this inept musician (yet lover of music and song) make some final reflections about the movement of discipleship of being sent out, and the role of music and song.

First, the call to leave, to go forth, was always *accompanied* with a promise, "I will be with you." That promise speaks to the critical role of *companionship* in going forth into new places, whether it being the Acts' wisdom of sending disciples out two by two, the belief and awareness of the companionship of Jesus, the Holy Spirit, or God, or the promise of one's sending community to support you on the journey. The role of music and song, which can reflect all aspects just listed, needs to be further explored in theory and practice. The scene which comes to mind for me is the beautiful classical-guitar music being played by a volunteer professional musician, giving her services one morning a week in early 2019 to the people in the oncology center who were receiving several hours of chemotherapy. Those people included my wife in treatment, and me, simply being with her. The healing arts have a growing awareness of the role of music in recovery and in palliative care.

Second, in that journey of going forth, music and song have the capacity to transport one back to what is familiar and known, sometimes in an instant, to remembered places and times in one's life, for example: "That's what we sang in Sunday School." "That was our wedding song." "This is my favorite love song." Thus, the creative use of music and song by people who are companions to those with dementia and its power to help people remember part of who they are while forming a profound short connection with one's identity and community is a wonder to behold and experience. The creative invitation into song for people with intellectual and developmental disabilities is also, like for everyone else, an invitation into the heart of a community.

Third, in communities of faith, we are always called upon to honor and remember our elders who have come before us and gone before us as either part of the "saints who from their labors rest" or those elders who go before us toward the ends of their own lives. If that means they have to move out of their own personal homes and faith communities into residential care or into "memory care," our call as disciples is to ask, Who and what is going with them? For years, some of us have wondered if the people we call "shut-ins" are not more accurately called "shut-outs." How can visitation, as John Swinton closes his book on dementia, be recovered as such a powerful opportunity for the grace of God to be made known (Swinton 2012, 279–283)? The visit by a friend, a congregational member, a child, or an adult can bring a whole unseen community with them into the act of helping someone remember who and whose they are. Bringing the community's music with them is yet another gift.

If disciples are called to visit the sick, the lonely, the outcast, and all others, that can feel like an act of moving and going out into what may be a frightening land, where one does not know what to do, but where your being there is all that really matters (as well as remembering that they very well may become, may have been, and still are disciples as well). But taking music with you is a way to communicate presence and build connection, especially when usual conversation is difficult. Then and there we may learn that we can indeed sing the Lord's songs in a foreign land, be amazed that some people already know them, and maybe even learn some new ones . . . together.

WORKS CITED

Akinade, Akintunde E. 2016. "No Time for Foolishness: On the Prophetic and Progressive Projects of James A. Forbes Jr." *CrossCurrents* 66, no. 1: 108–22.

Brock, Brian. 2019. *Wondrously Wounded: Theology, Disability, and the Body of Christ.* Waco, Tex.: Baylor University Press.

Calem, Joanie. 2018. "Unsolicited Parent Advice." YouTube video, 3:07. https://www.youtube.com/watch?v=ejm6HzIbjLA.

Colson, Emily. 2010. *Dancing with Max.* Grand Rapids: Zondervan.

Feil, Naomi. 2015. "This Is Love! Lady Touches Soul of Alzheimer's Sufferer with Christian Hymns." YouTube video, 5:43. https://www.youtube.com/watch?v=CCRDzRd8kgQ.

"Fletcher, Andrew." 1703. Last modified August 5, 2021. https://en.wikiquote.org/wiki/Andrew_Fletcher.

Frank, Arthur. 1992. *At the Will of the Body.* New York: Houghton Mifflin.

Gaventa, William C. 2018. *Disability and Spirituality: Recovering Wholeness.* Studies in Religion, Theology, and Disability. Waco, Tex.: Baylor University Press.

Gaventa, William C., and David L. Coulter, eds. 2003. *The Pastoral Voice of Robert Perske.* Binghamton, N.Y.: Haworth Pastoral Press.

González, Marta C. 2020. "Prima Ballerina with Alzheimer's listens to *Swan Lake* and Starts to Remember." YouTube video, 3:16. https://www.youtube.com/watch?v=6-j5yeRDBaU.

Harper, Lynn Casteel. 2020. *On Vanishing: Mortality, Dementia and What It Means to Disappear.* New York: Catapult.

Hilsman, Gordon. 1997. "Spiritual Pathways: One Response to the Current Standards Challenge." *Vision: Newsletter of the National Association of Catholic Chaplains* (June): 8–9.

Hunter, Tom. 2002. *Still Growing.* The Song Growing Company.

Jamison, Kate. 1996. *An Unquiet Mind.* New York: Vintage.

Leidy, Peter. 2021. "[Homepage]." https://peterleidy.com. Accessed January 6, 2021.

Lunney, Dan. 2017. *"Personalized Music as a Spiritual Intervention for People Living with Dementia."* DMin thesis. Catholic Theological Union of Chicago. https://www.academia .edu/32534669/Personalized_Music_as_a_Spiritual_Intervention_with_People_Living _with_Dementia_D_Min_Thesis_Project_?email_work_card=view-paper.

McKnight, John L. 1987. "Regenerating Community." *Social Policy* (Winter): 54–58. Available at Minnesota Developmental Disabilities Council, https://mn.gov/mnddc/ parallels2/pdf/80s/87/87-RC-JLM.pdf.

National Resource Center on Supported Decision Making. 2021. http://www .supporteddecisionmaking.org. Accessed January 7, 2021.

Nouwen, Henri. 1994. "Response to Receipt of the COMISS Award for Pastoral Care: Reflections on His Life in L'Arche." Video, 38:11. https://faithanddisability.org/videos/.

———. 1998. *Adam: God's Beloved*. Maryknoll, N.Y.: Orbis.

Palmer, Parker. 1983. *The Company of Strangers: Christians and the Renewal of America's Public Life*. New York: Crossroad.

———. 1986. "Keynote Address on Hospitality and Community from Merging Two Worlds Conference." Video, 55:14, Rochester, New York. https://faithanddisability .org/videos/.

Pearson, T. R., and Langdon Clay. 2011. "Year of Our Lord: Faith, Hope and Harmony in the Mississippi." Fairhope, Alabama. YouTube video, 6:00. https://www.youtube.com/ watch?v=jYajZS4QZhU.

Perske, Martha. 1998. *Perske Pencil Portraits 1971–1990*. Nashville: Abingdon.

Perske, Robert. 1980. *New Life in the Neighborhood: How People with Mental Retardation and Other Disabilities Can Make a Good Community Better*. Nashville: Abingdon.

———. 1988. *Circles of Friends*. Nashville: Abingdon.

Rothstein, Peter. 2018. *All Is Calm: The Christmas Truce of 1914*.

Sherman, Max. 2020. *Releasing the Butterfly: A Love Affair in Four Acts*. Max Sherman.

Smull, Michael W., Helen Sanderson, Charlotte Sweeney, et al. 2005. *Essential Lifestyle Planning for Everyone*. Annapolis, Md. and Stockport, UK: Learning Community—Essential Lifestyle Planning.

Staines, Bill. 1979. "All God's Critters Got a Place in the Choir." *The Whistle of the Jay*. Folk Legacy Records FS1–70.

Styron, William. 1989. *Darkness Visible: A Memoir of Madness*. New York: Penguin Random House.

Sullivan, Andrew. 2001. *The Noonday Demon: An Atlas of Depression*. New York: Simon & Schuster.

Swinton, John. 2001. "Building a Church for Strangers." *Journal of Religion, Disability & Health* 4, no. 4: 25–63. https://doi.org/10.1300/J095v04n04_03.

———. 2001. "Spirituality and the Lives of People with Learning Disabilities." Foundation for People with Learning Disabilities. *The Mental Health Foundation Updates* 3, no. 6. https://www.learningdisabilities.org.uk/learning-disabilities/publications/spirituality -and-lives-people-learning-disabilities.

———. 2012. *Dementia: Living in the Memories of God*. Grand Rapids: Eerdmans.

Williams, Karl. 1998. "Respect: Songs of the Self-Advocacy Movement." http://www .karlwilliams.com/respect.htm. Accessed January 4, 2021.

IV

Gently Living in a Violent World

12

Belonging

Benjamin Conner

I joined a new gym. Actually, my wife joined the gym and can take guests without limit, so I joined a new gym. The atmosphere is not what I typically look for in a fitness center: Its ambiance is a cross between a McDonalds PlayPlace and middle-school guidance counselor's office. It is brightly colored with every machine matching the theme colors; it has a virtual mezzanine of televisions extending the length of the expansive interior; the walls are covered with some mirrors but equally with notifications of "pizza night" and "bagel morning" mixed with inspirational signs and slogans. The most prominent and consistent message being communicated through the signs and literature is the following: "you belong!" You are "respected" and "accepted" and have entered a "judgement-free zone."[1]

As a new pseudomember of this community, such affirmations were encouraging to read. However, I soon learned that belonging has its limits. One poster explained that there is a dress code for this inclusive community. The sign indicated that jeans, boots, and bandannas are among those items that are "subject to our judgement" in this judgment-free zone. Directly beneath some stenciling that announced that this gym "= no critics" was a warning sign—a "LUNK ALARM" warning which defined a *lunk* as one who "grunts," "drop weights," wears a "body building tank top," or drinks water from a "gallon water jug." Most of my previous gyms would have been filled with *lunks* who would not be accepted at this gym—despite the gospel of inclusivity and acceptance being proclaimed

---

[1] All the language quoted in this paragraph and the following paragraph is taken directly from signage in the establishment.

229

on the walls, they simply do not belong there. At the same time, the absence of such intimidating *lunks* would make others, particularly those who are exercise novices or who are otherwise self-conscious about their presence in a gym, more comfortable. What does it mean to belong? And how might we create spaces of belonging?

BELONGING AS A FUNDAMENTAL HUMAN NEED

Roy Baumeister (1995), a prominent social psychologist, and Mark Leary, a professor of psychology and neuroscience at Duke University, drawing upon years of empirical studies, summarize, "The need to belong, that is, a need to form and maintain at least a minimum quantity of inter-personal relationships, is innately prepared (and hence nearly universal) among human beings" (499). From the standpoint of the social sciences and evolutionary theory, the authors suggest many motivations for the drive to belong: the protection offered by being a member of a group, access to resources, and the possibility of reproduction (499). Whatever the drive to belong, the authors indicate that socially disconnected persons may have a compromised immune system, higher stress, a higher incidence of mental-health challenges, higher rates of death by suicide, higher rates of physical illness, and a greater likelihood to exhibit behavioral problems. They conclude, therefore, that these facts should lead us to understand belonging as a fundamental human need rather than merely a human preference or desire (511).

Other researchers confirm that the desire to connect to others and for belonging is so strong that if the connection is threatened an individual may experience physical or psychological consequences and, in fact, even *the fear* of rejection causes the body to respond with neural reactions that are similar to those associated with experiencing physical pain. The need for relatedness, to feel connected, or to belong is a "basic universal psychological need" and "innate in humans and thus universal" (Lavigne, Vallerand, and Crevier-Braud 2011, 1185).

A THEOLOGY OF BELONGING

> "Belonging" is not the same thing as "being included." To be included, one simply needs to be present "somewhere," wherever "somewhere" might be. Belonging is different. In order to belong, one needs to be missed if one isn't there. In order to belong to the community of strangers, people . . . need to be missed when they're absent. If they're not missed, they don't belong and if they don't belong, there is no true community—for anyone. (Swinton 2000b, 279)

John Swinton has invested his career in reflecting on belonging from the perspective of those persons who find themselves cast as strangers: people with dementia, people with intellectual or developmental disabilities, people who face mental-health challenges, refugees, and people seeking asylum. According to Swinton, strangers are intimidating because they "intrude on our security and raise issues that we might not want to address," and strangers do not "share our environment, values, and assumptions about the world" (227). Western culture is organized such that people who are "slow in thought" or who aren't attuned to society's "tempos, rhythms, cadences, and timings," are strangers and are not able to experience belonging (Swinton 2016, 11). Policies of inclusion designed to secure rights and access for marginalized peoples have been effective and important, but they are limited in that it is not possible to legislate love or spaces where meaningful friendships blossom. Swinton argues that is it this ability to love (signified by a heart that notices and longs for people when they are missing), and not to merely include others, that marks Christian community and is an indicator of authentic discipleship (93).

Swinton adds an important theological intonation to this discussion about belonging by expanding Jean Vanier's insight. Vanier (1998) was animated by the notion of belonging, writing, "My vision is that belonging should be at the heart of a fundamental discovery: that we all belong to a common humanity, the human race" (36). Swinton (2012b) follows Vanier that all people "belong to the same species and share a common humanity," but then anchors that claim more explicitly in the scriptural narrative of creation, suggesting that in the "general ethos of the doctrine of creation" humans are not merely included in creation: they belong, and creation wouldn't be the same without them (183). He also draws on the doctrine of the *imago Dei* and Paul's conception of the body of Christ in Corinthians and his notion of unity in Christ in Galatians, to contend that in Christ our status, ethnic diversity, variances in ability, and sex and gender are all relativized in light of the truth of our unity or fundamental belongingness in Christ. Referencing 1 Corinthians, "Don't you realize that all of you together are the temple of God and that the Spirit of God lives in you" (1 Cor 3:16, NLT), Swinton suggests that "this is truly the beginning point for a genuine theology of community and belonging that holds all of us together in the same way that Jesus holds us" (Swinton 2016, 205). And this beginning point for a theology of belonging is enacted through the ecclesial practice of baptism. When one is baptized into the body of Christ by the grace of God and the gift of the Spirit, that person is marked as belonging to Christ, his new creation, and is called to a unique place of belonging "within God's hospitable community" (110).

In baptism, and in Christ, human diversity is not a problem to be solved but a gift to be received. The waters of baptism remind us of God's redeeming work in the world and calls us—*all* of us—to our participation in that redeeming work. Whatever our capacity or giftedness, we are each called to foster one another's growth in faith and service. As Swinton explains, "As people are baptized into the body of Christ, so they enter into a space of deep and radical belonging. Within the body of Christ, every body has a place, and every body is recognized as a disciple with a call from Jesus and a vocation that the church needs if it is truly to be the body of Jesus" (208). The baptismal gift of belonging is contrasted by Swinton to concepts and strategies of inclusion. He, therefore, casts belonging as a "gift of the Spirit" to be lived into and not the consequence of agreement to an ideal of equity, nor contingent on the possession of an inherent common property or capacity, and not the result of policies of inclusion or any human effort to overcome differences related to human diversity.

The reality of our belonging in Christ is expressed and experienced through concrete Christian practices, whether liturgical and ecclesial (e.g., baptism and the Lord's Supper), devotional practices (e.g., practices of prayer and Scripture engagement), or everyday practices that find resonance in worship, are forged in devotion, and connect us to God's work in the world (e.g., practices of hospitality, friendship, or forgiveness). In what follows, I offer a definition and description of Christian practices, derived from Swinton's work and in conversation with others, as gestures that create spaces for people to live into belonging. Next, I examine two practices for which Swinton advocates in his work that address the human need to belong: friendship and hospitality. Finally, I draw upon Swinton's theology of belonging to point toward some ways in which practices that foster belonging can direct the White[2] U.S. church in embracing the "stranger" during an important season of protest against systemic racism.

CHRISTIAN PRACTICES

The concept of Christian practices provides a way of naming and describing the concrete ways in which people and communities participate in God's ongoing mission and the means by which individuals

[2] For more on the concept of whiteness, see DiAngelo 2011; Jennings 2018, or his longer treatment in Jennings 2011. I explain my understanding of *White* and *whiteness* below.

and communities are shaped and formed for such participation. According to Dorothy Bass and Miroslav Volf, "Christian practices are patterns of cooperative human activity in and through which life together takes shape over time in response to and in the light of God as known in Jesus Christ" (Volf and Bass 2001, 3). These gestures include ecclesial practices such as the Lord's Supper and baptism, practices that are paradigmatic for other everyday practices such as discernment, sabbath (living as creatures in the gift of time), testimony (speaking truth), friendship, honoring the body, healing and care, or hospitality. Through these complex social activities, or "gestures of love" (Swinton 2012a, 283)—engaged in corporately and individually, received from others and shaped by histories and narratives, catered to present circumstances for the sake of God's future—Christians have access to the goods or graces that can only be experienced through participating in Christ.

In focusing his attention on practices rather than doctrine, while valuing both and highlighting the interplay between them, Swinton calls the theologian to take embodiment seriously for comprehending epistemology and the life of discipleship, for informing theological reflection, and even as a means for bodily remembering when our minds are not able to serve that function. Practices help us to establish ways of living that lead to flourishing (both our flourishing and that of others) and they are a way that we connect our activity at work, home, and play within our larger society to the redemptive work of God in the world so we can live more integrated and faithful lives.

One of the most compelling ways of speaking about practices, introduced by Craig Dykstra and influential on Swinton, is as "habitations of the Spirit" (Dykstra 2005, 66; see also xv, 64, and 78) or "arenas" where knowledge of God is felt and tested (56).[3] Practices, rather than simply providing a means for social reinforcement, are instead a means of grace though which the Holy Spirit transforms people, shaping them for their witness in the world. Practices are the means by which the body of Christ embodies its witness to the reality of the reign and rule of God (Conner 2011, 99). Of course, as human social activities, our performance of Christian practices is not always faithful—our practices can be selfish, instrumental, technical, and sinful. And while God's redemptive work in the world is not contingent upon the church successfully proclaiming the gospel through it (Healy 2012, 198), Swinton (2012c) insists that "the

---

[3]   "I have been arguing that the practices of the life of faith have power to place us where we can receive a sense of the presence of God" (Dykstra 2005, 63).

practices of the empirical church are not inconsequential to the proclamation of the gospel" (72).

Christian practices differ from cultural practices in that they acknowledge and proclaim the need for redemption and are guided by an eschatological horizon of the coming kingdom of God. Christian practices create spaces for recognizing our encounter with the divine and for being transformed. Dykstra (2005) has summarized well, "After a time, the primary point about the practices is no longer that they are something we do. Instead, *they become arenas* in which something is done to us, in us, and through us that we could not of ourselves do, that is beyond what we do" (56).[4] Dykstra is arguing that our Christian practices are not so much our practices as they are "habitations of the Spirit, in the midst of which we are invited to participate in the practices of God" (78). The language of practices creating space for something to happen to us is found throughout Swinton's work. Yet, for Swinton, practices push beyond personal or communal spiritual formation to address the question, For what are we being formed?

According to Swinton, Christian practices are missional and boundary-crossing and are the way Christians create spaces or communities of belonging that signal something about the kingdom of God. He describes practices as "a reflection of the Church's attempts to participate faithfully in the continuing practices of the triune God's redemptive mission to the world" (Swinton and Mowat 2006, 24). While practices address fundamental human needs, their faithfulness is not evaluated pragmatically in terms of their effectiveness in addressing a need, but "by whether or not it participates faithfully in the divine redemptive mission" (22). While many practical theologians have been engaging and developing a notion of practices to speak about the life of discipleship or a way of life in the world, Swinton is among the few who promote an understanding of Christian practices as fundamentally and explicitly missional.[5] He explains, "The important thing is that the practice bears faithful witness to the God from who the practice emerges, and whom it reflects, and that it enables individuals and communities to participate faithfully in Christ's redemptive mission" (22). With respect to Christian witness, practices are "habitations of the spirit" and not human works—not technical "best practices" whereby a procedure, pattern of action, or technique is prescribed to

---

[4]   Dykstra explains further, "I have been arguing that the practices of the life of faith *have power to place* us where we can receive a sense of the presence of God" (Dykstra 2005, 63).

[5]   The only other text to address practices this way is my book, Conner 2011.

produce a desired result or impact. Christian practices are oriented toward the fitness of Christian witness (Conner 2019) and participation in God's ongoing work by becoming "the pivot point for the redemption of the world" (Swinton 2012b, 183–4).

This missionary trajectory of Christian practices is one of the most significant and unique contributions he makes to the discussion. One of his other contributions is his consistent grounding of Christian practices in the action of Jesus Christ, as we will see below. Perhaps it is the Aberdeen Barthian influence on Swinton that causes him to believe that peril lurks in generalities; to know what friendship or what hospitality really is, he must not begin with a general concept of hospitality or friendship but with the concrete action of God in Christ. Christians are called to the same practices as Jesus:

> I use the term *practices* here as a way of stressing the embodiedness of Christian theology. The gospel is proclaimed not only in words, but in the gestures and gesticulations that make up the life of the Kingdom as it works itself out on earth as in heaven. The practice of belonging is an embodied theology that embraces the excluded and offers hopeful modes of living to all human beings. (Swinton 2012b, 188, n. 3)

In truth, there isn't a *practice* of belonging; belonging is a fundamental human need. We can espouse or develop a theology of belonging and practices that create spaces of belonging. Swinton focuses on two practices of belonging in his writing: hospitality and friendship, and it is to these two practices that we turn.

HOSPITALITY

According to Swinton, hospitality is "an important Christian practice that relates, in essence, to the Spirit-enabled ability to show kindness, acceptance and warmth when welcoming guests or strangers" (Swinton and Mowat, 91). While hospitality does address physical needs such as the need for shelter and food (things we often associate with the so-called hospitality industry), hospitality as a Christian practice attends to deep interpersonal needs such as the need to be recognized and feel valued. At the heart of Swinton's understanding of the practice of hospitality is a biblically normed call for the church to reorient her attitude toward the stranger. He makes the case that people with dementia, people with intellectual and developmental disabilities, people with mental-health challenges, refugees, and asylum seekers could be understood as "strangers" in Western culture because their "status as citizens and indeed as fully human is always in question" (244–45).[6] Many of the people protesting racial injustices at Lafayette Square in Washington, D.C., brought with them painful histories in which their humanity and status as citizens was not affirmed by their government. Many feel as though they are strangers to the White church because they have received the same treatment from the White church as they have from their government. Strangers rarely experience belonging.

When the church imagines "strangers," Swinton argues, it needs to do so according to God's understanding of the stranger: "When a stranger sojourns with you in your land, you shall not do [that person] wrong. The stranger who sojourns with you shall be to you as the native among you, and you shall love [that person] as yourself; for you were strangers in the land of Egypt: I am the Lord your God" (Lev 19:33–34). Christians, as "aliens and exiles" (1 Pet 2:11) in the world whose true "citizenship is in heaven" (Phil 3:20), are always called to provide a place of belonging for the stranger.

Swinton develops his understanding of the stranger in conversation with Ian Cohen's (1997) contribution to Frances Young's edited volume, *Encounter with Mystery*, in which Cohen writes of the "strange vocation" of people with intellectual disabilities. Cohen notes that the *ger* or stranger played an important role in the Old Testament narrative by reminding the Israelites who they were—"strangers in the land of Egypt." The Israelite narrative is continued in Matthew's Gospel when Jesus is cast as the *ger*—he is not of this world but is living in it according to a kingdom way of life. While all Christians are aliens and strangers in the world, Cohen suggests that those with intellectual disabilities are more effective demonstrations of the otherness and the "true soul of God's people" as strangers (157). Brian Volck (2018), a medical doctor and theologian, similarly casts people with profound disabilities as strangers. Volck identifies the church as a countercultural community with a powerful witness to the world's values to the extent that it welcomes the strangers and offers a "dramatically expanded imagination of what it means to be human" (217). Hospitality is a practice that creates a place where people can bring their whole selves: laments, challenges, joys, and possibilities and belong as "no longer strangers and aliens" (Eph 2:19).

---

[6]   In this text Swinton is speaking primarily of people with profound intellectual disabilities, but he develops a similar case for the others in *Resurrecting the Person* (people with mental-health challenges as a kind of stranger); *Dementia: Living in the Memories of God* (dementia); *Becoming Friends of Time* (profound disability); and *Raging with Compassion* (the refugee).

The Christian practice of hospitality incorporates offering welcome and, more importantly, involves creating a space in which strangers are no longer perceived as strangers and become friends. The move from stranger to friend will require a mutual relationship in which the host learns how to be a guest and to receive the gifts the stranger brings. The church must learn to recognize strangers and listen to them, and, instead of trying to minister to them by welcoming them into "our" space, the church needs to open herself up to being the guest (Swinton 2015a, 178). As Henri Nouwen (1975) has phrased it, "We will never believe that we have anything to give unless there is someone who is able to receive. Indeed, we discover our gifts in the eyes of the receiver" (71). Christian hospitality acknowledges that the true host and guest, no matter who is playing the role of guest and host, is Jesus Christ. Christians extend the hospitality of Christ to the other and, at the same time, expect to encounter him in the guest. Additionally, according to the writer of Hebrews, it is possible that when we have shown hospitality to strangers we may have "entertained angels without knowing it" (Heb 13:2). Swinton would agree with Christine Pohl's (1999) characterization of hospitality as sacramental, central to the meaning of the gospel, a "closer alignment with the basic values of the Kingdom," a "lens through which we can read and understand much of the gospel, and a practice by which we can welcome Jesus himself" (8).

What does it look like for the church to make room for belonging through the practice of hospitality?

It involves creating space by listening well and by boundary crossing. It involves a shift in regarding marginalized people as potential friends rather than as dangerous strangers. For people with intellectual and developmental disabilities, it might mean creating a space in the middle of the theological and liturgical tradition where one's access and contribution is not dependent upon one's capacity for abstract reasoning and cogitation (Swinton 2000a, 103). With regard to engaging people with dementia, it means not accepting uncritically the biomedical and psychiatric understanding of mental-health challenges or assuming that people's experiences are "the product of misfiring neurons, chemical imbalances, or genetic defects." Swinton encourages congregations to slow down, attend to people's experiences and the meaning they have for them, and to respect those meanings as "important aspects of a person's life story that require understanding and respect rather than simply control and eradication" (Swinton 2015a, 178). Taking the time to enter into another's life and experiences and sharing space and time with another is an expression of hospitality. By getting to know people at a deep level, we avoid thin understandings of them and appreciate them in their complexity.[7] In fact, in Swinton's (2007) phrasing, "the practice of Christian friendship" can be "understood as a type of hospitality" (216).

FRIENDSHIP

Swinton grounds his vision for friendship as a missional Christian practice in the action of Jesus who was a friend to tax collectors and sinners, a friend of the marginalized and rejected with the hopes that this vision will inform the church's mindset and practices. One can explore Swinton's understanding of friendship by engaging his doctoral dissertation, later developed into two books, *Resurrecting the Person* and *From Bedlam to Shalom*, both books being about friendship as a legitimate model of care for people with mental-health challenges. He casts friendship as a practice not because it is an instrumental technique that addresses a problem along the lines of "best practices," but because it is a sacramental encounter grounded in the actions of Jesus and the redemptive work of God.

Friendship offers a way of care beyond the limitations of the medical approach to or model of disability—that is, an approach to disability that comprehends it in terms of etiology, signs and symptoms, technical solutions, and illness as a specific, definable pathology and individual problem to be eliminated. The medical model, while beneficial in some respects, does not always address the human as a person. Neither does the medical approach to disability account for the social setting of the problem or society's complicity in larger problems (stigmatization, alienation, oppression, exclusion). The medical approach to mental-health challenges, while often providing clarity and relief from symptoms, does not consider the person or the need to belong. Friendship does. *"The priority of friends is the personhood of the other and not the illness"* (Swinton 2000c, 37; emphasis in original).

---

[7] Drawing on Clifford Gertz, Swinton identifies challenges inherent in thin descriptions of people with mental health challenges in Swinton 2020. Elizabeth Newman argues against thin understandings of hospitality, which Swinton would argue issue from thin understanding of people. Newman identifies four distortions of hospitality: sentimental hospitality, which involves "superficial niceness" devoid of truth or hard realities; privatized hospitality, which involves a kind of entertaining invested in appearances and relegated to the home sphere; hospitality as a marketing tool connected to the "hospitality industry" and grounded in consumerism; and, finally, and most significantly for this discourse, "hospitality as inclusivity," in which diversity becomes the end of hospitality rather that "a certain kind of life, a life that reflects and extends the tradition in which the practice is embedded"; see Newman 2007, 30–33.

Swinton (2000b) claims that the practice of Christian friendship reveals something of God's shalom within our relationships, that friendships can participate in the restoration of the image of God in people, and, further, for his specific purposes, that friendship can be the foundation for the development of "an authentic, creative and effective model of mental health care for the contemporary church" (77). In terms of creating spaces of belonging, Christian friendship "creates an environment, or better, a space, within which individuals can experience themselves as unique, whole-persons and learn to understand what it means to relate to others as unique, whole-persons" (79). Friendship creates such spaces that allow people to enter into relationships of commitment and mutuality where they are both with each other and for each other (79).

Friendship is voluntary (involving the freedom to be rejected); friendship is marked by mutuality and reciprocity, care and concern; and, following the example of Jesus, friendship is not exclusive. In the language of Lesslie Newbigin's missiology, friendship is a sign, instrument, and foretaste of the coming kingdom and, as Swinton translates, allows people to experience themselves as "relational beings loved by a relational God and fundamentally connected to an open and accepting community which manifests that love in a tangible form within its own relationships" (82). Friendship is a practice that creates the relational space necessary for connections to be formed between people, that shifts the margins and challenges notions of insider and outsider, and that demonstrates the values and power of the kingdom of God by transcending relational boundaries of likeness (like attracts like), instrumentality, or social exchange.

Swinton (2015a) contrasts dominant cultural understandings of friendship with the Christian practice of friendship which he terms "shalomic friendship." As Swinton explains, "Jesus offered no 'technique' or 'expertise.'" Instead, he "simply gifted time, presence, space, patience, and friendship" (180). At the risk of overstating the point, practices are not techniques; they are ways Christians participate in God's creative and redemptive work. Swinton (2000b) explains:

> Shalomic friendship (that is a form of friendship which finds its roots in God's shalomic movement within human history), is an open relationship which is offered not only to those with who one has a natural affinity, but also towards that *outsider*; those with who one cannot "naturally" identify; those with whom one struggles to relate; those whom the 'principle of likeness' would ordinarily exclude from full relational participation in our society. (86)

Friendships that are shalomic are also sacramental in that they reveal something about the true nature of God (86). Jesus is not merely with the poor and oppressed; he identifies himself with them. How we act toward the marginalized is an act of worship, and receiving them is a sacrament because in receiving them we receive Christ (Matt 25).

Belonging is created when the practices of friendship and hospitality shift the margins. Churches that do not engage those who are marginalized in society in friendship might find themselves marginalized from Jesus (Swinton 2015b, 240). By extending the gift of friendship that Christians receive from Jesus, they "build a space for love; a space in the midst of the complexities of theology and tradition" (Swinton 2000a, 103). Missiologist Dana Robert (2019) writes, similarly, on the missional impact of boundary-crossing friendship, noting "To make friends witnesses to Christian community in all its promise and vulnerability. In their love for others, including people unlike themselves, Christians show what it means to follow Jesus Christ together. The practice of Christian friendship, therefore, creates Christian community" (4).

CONCLUSION

Swinton, through his writing and research, promotes the kind of belonging he is pursuing. He consistently moves the conversation into the human and into the concrete, rescuing the person from being defined by a diagnosis or pathology or being viewed as a problem to be solved. Therefore, he writes not about the dilemma of dementia, intellectual disability, refugees, asylum seekers, or mental health—he writes about people. He writes out of his own encounters and relationships about how people with dementia, mental-health challenges, intellectual disabilities, and who are displaced inhabit the world, move through time, express themselves spiritually, demonstrate longings or hopes, and require connection. He writes as a practical theologian, and practical theologians are invested in critically reflecting on the practices of the church, always observing, interpreting, and explaining Christian practice with the goal of calling congregations to more faithful ways of participating in God's creative and redemptive kingdom work in the world.

Consider how Swinton validates the call to discipleship and vocation of people with profound disabilities (*Becoming Friends of Time*), affirms the meaningful experiences and theological insights of people with mental-health challenges (*Resurrecting the Person* and "Time, Hospitality, and Belonging: Towards a Practical Theology of Mental Health"), reimagines what love "looks like" for people on the autism spectrum

("Reflections on Autistic Love"), affirms the personhood and capacity of people with dementia to know God when memory and cognition are failing (*Dementia: Living in the Memories of God*), and calls congregations to recognize and rehumanize refugees and asylum seekers (*Raging with Compassion*).

I began this chapter with a playful illustration about belonging. On a much more serious note, many minoritized or nonmajority culture people feel like strangers in the United States. When they rise up to contest the social, economic, and physical consequences of their strangeness, they are cast by those in power as not merely strangers but dangerous strangers. They are linguistically dehumanized as domestic terrorists, criminals, rioters, and thugs—an important step in communicating that "they" are not part of "us" and do not belong here. Religious symbols and language are often co-opted in an effort to baptize such marginalization as consistent with Christian traditions and resonant with American heritage. The protester is to be feared, because if we succumb to their agenda then *they* will "wipe out our history, defame our heroes, erase our values, and indoctrinate our children" (Trump 2020). This is an unacceptable loss, because "our founders boldly declared that we are all endowed with the same divine rights, given us by our Creator in Heaven, and that which God has given us, we will allow no one ever to take away ever" (Trump 2020).

Consider the St. John's Episcopal Church incident in Washington, D.C. The historic church had been damaged the previous evening during the largely peaceful protests with the unfortunate result of the nursery and basement having been burned by a few people who were not representative of the majority. On June 1, 2020, a group of people, many of whom felt marginalized or even terrorized by the U.S. government and by policies and practices related to policing and incarceration, along with their allies, were staging a peaceful protest at Lafayette Square. While many of the protesters had lived in the United States for their entire lives, they still experienced it as strangers due largely to systemic racial bias. On the authority of federal officials, law enforcement was commanded to extend the margins of the protest fence. In the spirit of "law and order," President's Park Police reinforced by National Guard troops used physical force, shields, batons, smoke canisters, and pepper balls to "dominate" people who already felt marginalized in society, pushing them physically further to the margins of Lafayette Square. It was a demonstrative way of communicating—"You don't belong here." Moments later, the President, accompanied by his aides and a security team, initiated a liturgical procession across Pennsylvania Avenue to exhibit the government's control over the chaos of protest by enacting a reclamation of St. John's, the President posing in front of the church before the media while brandishing a Bible.

Significant religious symbols meant to testify to a faith that announces *in Christ all belong* were manipulated in a way that attempted to set the strangeness of the protesters on one side and God and the government on the other. But, of course, God is with the marginalized, the oppressed, those crying out in pain and for justice, and Jesus had shifted the margins long ago when he sat with strangers and not with the religious and political elite. We can have possession of all the symbols of the faith and set ourselves firmly in the middle of a religious landscape, but if we are excluding the stranger, we are not standing with God.

A richer theology and practices of belonging is one place that the church, especially the White or majority culture church, can look to gain insight for how to provide comfort and support for minoritized, marginalized, and disenfranchised people who together with them make up the church. What insight might John Swinton's theology of belonging have to offer the White US church in engaging the protester of racial injustice? Drawing on Robin DiAngelo, Ruth Frankenburg, and Willie Jennings, I use the terms *White* or *whiteness* to designate a culturally produced sociopolitical position of privilege. In Frankenburg's (1993) terms, it is a structural advantage, a standpoint, and a set of practices that tend to be unnamed yet are essential to the dominion and flourishing of white people (European descent) over people of color in the United States (1). The White church holds to what DiAngelo (2011) describes as processes and practices that "include basic rights, values, beliefs, perspectives and experiences purported to be commonly shared by all but which are actually only consistently afforded to white people" (56).

While I believe there are several points at which Swinton can speak to this dilemma, I highlight two imperatives developed in this chapter: create spaces through hospitality where the stranger is no longer a stranger; and engage in boundary-crossing friendships as a form of resistance to evil. I recognize that the issue of structural racism is a systemic problem and these practices seem to address this with a personal solution. Jemar Tisby (2019), in his important book *The Color of Compromise*, emphasizes, "To be clear, friendships and conversations are necessary, but they are not sufficient to change the racial status quo. Christians must alter how impersonal systems operate so that they might create and extend racial equity" (193). At the same time, Christian practices are communal and shape our life together and the way we engage the world of which we are a part.

The incident at Lafayette Square and St. John's was cast as a response to a riot. There seemed to be little curiosity from either the administration or the White church about why a group of people was so obviously frustrated and angry, nor was there an acknowledgment of the complexity of the issues that separated people from each other. From the standpoint of the church, and in the service of creating spaces of belonging, this kind of curiosity and acknowledgment of complexity is necessary to avoid engaging "thin" people in "thin" ways. When people choose not to listen to or get to know the protesters in their depth and pain, then they can be painted broadly as rioters and dismissed. The rioters are frightening strangers. Sadly, what Martin Luther King Jr. explained over fifty years ago, March 14, 1968, in his oft-quoted speech "The Other America" could be delivered today.

> And I must say tonight that a riot is the language of the unheard. And what is it America has failed to hear? It has failed to hear that the plight of the negro poor has worsened over the last twelve or fifteen years. It has failed to hear that the promises of freedom and justice have not been met. And it has failed to hear that large segments of white society are more concerned about tranquility and the status quo than about justice and humanity (King 1968).

Both America and America's White church have failed to hear from protesters that racism and racist systems have been deadly to black bodies.

The hospitable church must welcome the gifts, critiques, and challenges of minoritized people as her own. How might admitting complicity in systemic racial inequality, repentance, and preparing parishioners for trauma-informed engagement with protesters create space for belonging?[8] Recognizing the mutuality involved in hospitality, how might belonging be fostered if the White church were to be hosted by minoritized Christians? If the minoritized protesters are strangers to the White church, the church must remember that "strangers are gifts given to us so that they can become friends" (Swinton 2000b, 237). What missiologist Lesslie Newbigin (1989) has stated about cross-cultural mission applies to boundary-crossing hospitality: "new treasures are brought into the life of the church and Christianity itself grows and changes until it becomes more credible as a foretaste of the unity of all humankind" (123–24). For the White church to become a hospitable place of belonging for all people, it must grow and change until it ceases to be the "White" church. In this way, the church will begin to resist evil or racism and move toward becoming a place of

---

8   I have been influenced recently by Rowe 2019 and DeGruy 2005.

belonging for all people. In Swinton's phrasing: "By examining the critical role of hospitality-in-friendship as a mode of resistance to evil, we will discover ways of creating communities-of-friends that care for strangers, resist evil, and absorb suffering" (Swinton 2007, 216).

White Christians will need to practice friendship by heeding the Spirit-led initiative to cross boundaries of likeness and comfort, identify with the struggles and challenges of minoritized others, and amplify their concerns as their own. At the same time, White Christians must be honest about the social conditions under which these friendships are being forged. Willie Jennings (2020) offers some perspective that both resonates with and deepens Swinton's understanding of friendship.

> Friendship is a real thing where people open their living to one another, allowing the paths of life to crisscross in journeys imagined as in some sense shared . . . But friendships form on a social fabric before they create a fabric, and it is that social fabric that deserves much more attention and reflection first for the ways it has been deformed—creating the illusion that we are only actually connected by choice—and second for ways it may be remade, making possible a reality of intimacy, communication, reciprocity, and mutuality that builds from a deepening sense of connection. (147)

Hospitality-in-friendship, which discerns and addresses the social fabric that shapes our practices in malformative ways and calls for them to be remade by the Spirit, will create the kinds of spaces for belonging that allow congregations to reimagine protesters as friends—they who belong as part of us and are missed if they are not there.

WORKS CITED

Baumeister, Roy F., and Mark R. Leary. 1995. "The Need to Belong: Desire for Interpersonal Attachments as Fundamental Human Motivation." *Psychological Bulletin* 117, no. 3: 497–529.

Cohen, Ian. 1997. "A 'Strange' Vocation." In *Encounter with Mystery: Reflections on L'Arche and Living with Disability*, edited by Frances M. Young, 152–66. London: Darton, Longman & Todd.

Conner, Benjamin T. 2011. *Practicing Witness: A Missional Vision of Christian Practices*. Grand Rapids: Eerdmans.

———. 2019. "For the Fitness of Their Witness: Missional Christian Practices." In *Converting Witness: The Future of Christian Mission in the New Millennium*, edited by David W. Congdon and John G. Flett, 123–38. Lanham, Md.: Lexington/Fortress Academic.

DeGruy, Joy. 2005. *Post Traumatic Slave Syndrome: America's Legacy of Enduring Injury and Healing*. Milwaukie, Ore.: Uptone Press.

DiAngelo, Robin. 2011. "White Fragility." *International Journal of Critical Pedagogy* 3, no. 3: 54–70.

Dykstra, Craig. 2005. *Growing in the Life of Faith: Education and Christian Practices.* 2nd ed. Louisville: Westminster John Knox.

Frankenburg, Ruth. 1993. *The Social Construction of Whiteness: White Women, Race Matters.* Minneapolis: University of Minnesota Press.

Healy, Nicholas M. 2012. "Ecclesiology, Ethnography, and God: An Interplay of Reality Descriptions." In *Perspectives on Ecclesiology and Ethnography,* edited by Pete Ward, 182–99. Grand Rapids: Eerdmans.

Jennings, Willie James. 2010. *The Christian Imagination: Theology and the Origins of Race.* New Haven, Conn.: Yale University Press.

———. 2018. "Whiteness Isn't Progress: How the Missionary Movement Went Horrifically Wrong." *Christian Century,* November 7, 28–31.

———. 2020. *After Whiteness: An Education in Belonging.* Grand Rapids: Eerdmans.

King, Martin Luther, Jr. 1968. "The Other America." Grosse Pointe Historical Society. Delivered at Grosse Point High School, March 14, 1968. http://www.gphistorical.org/mlk/mlkspeech/.

Lavigne, Genevieve L., Robert J. Vallerand, and Laurence Crevier-Braud. 2011. "The Fundamental Need to Belong: On the Distinction Between Growth and Deficit-Reduction Orientations." *Personality and Social Psychology Bulletin* 37, no. 9: 1185–201.

Newbigin, Lesslie. 1989. *The Gospel in a Pluralist Society.* Grand Rapids: Eerdmans.

Newman, Elizabeth. 2007. *Untamed Hospitality: Welcoming God and Other Strangers.* Grand Rapids: Brazos Press.

Nouwen, Henri J. M. 1975. *Reaching Out: The Three Movements of the Spiritual Life.* New York: Doubleday.

Pohl, Christine. 1999. *Making Room: Recovering Hospitality as a Christian Tradition.* Grand Rapids: Eerdmans.

Robert, Dana L. 2019. *Faithful Friendships: Embracing Diversity in Christian Community.* Grand Rapids: Eerdmans.

Rowe, Sheila Wise. 2019. *Healing Racial Trauma: The Road to Resilience.* Downers Grove, Ill.: IVP.

Swinton, John. 2000a. "Friendship in Community: Creating a Space for Love." In *Spiritual Dimensions of Pastoral Care,* edited by David Willows and John Swinton, 102–6. London: Jessica Kingsley.

———. 2000b. *From Bedlam to Shalom: Towards a Practical Theology of Human Nature, Interpersonal Relationships, and Mental Health Care.* New York: Peter Lang.

———. 2000c. *Resurrecting the Person: Friendship and the Care of People with Mental Health Problems.* Nashville: Abingdon.

———. 2007. *Raging with Compassion: Pastoral Responses to the Problem of Evil.* Grand Rapids: Eerdmans.

———. 2012a. *Dementia: Living in the Memories of God.* Grand Rapids: Eerdmans.

———. 2012b. "From Inclusion to Belonging: A Practical Theology of Community, Disability and Humanness." *Journal of Religion, Disability & Health* 16, no. 2: 172–90.

———. 2012c. "'Where is Your Church?' Moving towards a Hospitable and Sanctified Ethnography." In *Perspectives on Ecclesiology and Ethnography,* edited by Pete Ward, 71–92. Grand Rapids: Eerdmans.

———. 2015a. "Time, Hospitality, and Belonging: Towards a Practical Theology of Mental Health." *Word & World* 35, no. 2: 171–81.

———. 2015b. "Using Our Bodies Faithfully: Christian Friendship and the Life of Worship." *Journal of Disability & Religion* 19, no. 3: 228–42.

———. 2016. *Becoming Friends of Time: Disability, Timefullness, and Gentle Discipleship.* Waco, Tex.: Baylor University Press.

———. 2020. *Finding Jesus in the Storm: The Spiritual Lives of Christians with Mental Health Challenges.* Grand Rapids: Eerdmans.

Swinton, John, and Harriet Mowat. 2006. *Practical Theology and Qualitative Research.* London: SCM Press.

Tisby, Jemar. 2020. *The Color of Compromise: The Truth about the American Church's Complicity in Racism.* Grand Rapids: Zondervan Academic.

Trump, Donald J. 2020. "Mount Rushmore Speech Transcript at 4th of July Event." Edited by Ryan Taylor. *Rev,* July 3, 2020. https://www.rev.com/blog/transcripts/donald-trump-speech-transcript-at-mount-rushmore-4th-of-july-event.

Vanier, Jean. 1998. *Becoming Human.* Mahwah, N.J.: Paulist Press.

Volck, Brian. 2018. "Silent Communion: The Prophetic Witness of the Profoundly Disabled." *Journal of Disability & Religion* 22, no. 2: 211–18.

Volf, Miroslav, and Dorothy C. Bass, eds. 2001. *Practicing Theology: Beliefs and Practices in Christian Life.* Grand Rapids: Eerdmans.

13

The Being of Friendship

An Essay in Honor of the Tired John Swinton

Andrew Root

My first personal encounter with John Swinton was at a preconference event at King's College London.[1] I'd just arrived at Heathrow hours earlier from the United States. The plan was to go straight from the plane to the preconference session at King's before taking the train to the University of Oxford for the conference proper. I arrived jet-lagged and found myself, by chance, next to John. He was kind and welcoming. He, too, looked tired. I figured he had an early morning trip but since then have come to discover that's just how he *always* looks.

If this were a roast (which I think John would enjoy more!) and not a Festschrift, that's how I would have started my thoughts about John, because our friendship has been built through jokes and passing time in equal measure. From that preconference gathering, a small group of us headed to Oxford. We were delayed on a packed commuter train. John and I happened to be sitting together, both fatigued (though I had an excuse). Our waiting together made us friends. Since that conference John and I have escaped from multiple sessions at other conferences, waiting out lectures we were uninterested in with a drink and many laughs. And at every one of them John always looks tired.

Friendship has been a core theological motif of Swinton's field-defining work in disability theology and practical theology. For Swinton, friendship is a form of human action that draws us into divine action.

---

[1] Note: Parts of this chapter have been adapted from *Churches and the Crisis of Decline* by Andrew Root, copyright 2022. Used by permission of Baker Academic, a division of Baker Publishing Group.

To honor all of John's tireless (see what I did there?) work in disability theology and practical theology, this chapter discusses friendship as a distinct form of human action that opens us to divine reality. My objective here is to honor John's own work by building off it. Or maybe there's a better analogy. Like a musician who so admires another's song or style, I'll take a few of John's riffs on friendship and write my own melody. The careful reader will see how my melody is inspired by Swinton's practical theology of friendship, but my overall hope is to laud John's work by allowing it to inspire my own construction.

To build off from John and take it in my own direction, I'll draw from the work of two Frankfurt School thinkers from two different generations, Erich Fromm and Hartmut Rosa. This chapter then articulates what kind of human action friendship actually is. It then explores how friendship is a form of human action that can take the agents (in this case, friends) into a resonant experience of life. We look particularly at how *resonance* is a form of longed-for action that modernity often works against. Finally, the chapter shows that in actions of resonant friendship the most faithful way to theologically and pastorally *be* is in waiting. It is in waiting as friends together that we encounter the living God who is God.

TO HAVE OR TO BE

After immigrating to the United States to escape Nazi Germany, Erich Fromm wrote his most famous book, *To Have or to Be?* (Fromm 2018). One of the most insightful discussions in this now-classic text comes under the heading, "Activity and Passivity." Fromm explains that something odd has happened inside modernity. Activity, or what it means to be active, has been radically redefined. In the modern sense, *activity* means "a quality of behavior that brings about a visible effect by expenditure of energy" (Fromm 2018, 77). In this sense, modernity makes all human activity equal. It's *all just* behavior, which expends energy.

Modernity can only perform this "equalizing" of activity, per Fromm's understanding, because it picks up where the Reformation left off but twists things. The Reformation brought forth a revolution in activity, upending and ending both the classical and medieval sense of activity. In these earlier periods activity was fused with *what* you did. And what you did was determined greatly by *who* you were. Whether a priest or peasant, your activity was determined and even revealed your being. This led to a hierarchy of activity. The activity of the priest was believed to be higher than the peasant's because the priest was a consecrated *being* whose "activities" (exemplified in the Mass) crossed the line between the profane and the sacred.

Yet, once it became clear that those with consecrated being were misusing their activities, the revolution began. The Reformers shifted the focus from *what* you did to *how* you did it. This had the effect of making all activity—whether giving the Mass or giving a baby a diaper change—equal before God. Hence the Reformers didn't see all activity as "equal" in a profane sense but a holy one. All activity then, in one way or another, played out the drama of redemption. And all activity was equal, yet it still revealed being because all activity was done by sinners needing justification.

Modernity was happy to pick up and continue the commitment to the equalizing of activity. But this equalizing needed a very different purpose and objective. Modernity wanted to continue with all activities being equal, but now not for the sake of being in the world but to have the world itself. Activity or action was determined as a good by what it could possess.

What Fromm lucidly showed is that this kind of equalizing meant all activity is the *same*. Fromm showed that activity is not as much equal as it is *samed*. When this happens, then, an activity like mundane data entry is made the same as painting a landscape. Organizing your sock drawer is ultimately the same as teaching a class of eager fifth graders to write a poem. Waiting in a queue is the same as talking with a friend. They're not the same because any of this is done before God, but because action is only the expenditure of energy. If organizing your sock drawer and teaching fifth-graders poetry is shown as equal in energy expenditure, than these activities are the same.

Of course, even to us late-moderns, something feels wrong about equating such activities like this. We find more resonance with the second in the pair; we want those activities to mean more. But we have no reason for why. It's difficult to justify why these second activities are substantially *different* than those listed first. In late modernity, these activities are all the same because they are all reduced to behaviors that expend energy. And an activity can have no greater referent.

Fromm's point is that when activity is allowed free rein to have the world, we lose a sense of being, we lose an encounter with the world in friendship. We make all actions finally and completely behaviors, becoming blind "to the person behind the behavior" (Fromm 2018, 77)

Fromm thinks this is important because when activity takes no account of being, and seeks only having, there is then "no distinction between activity and busyness" (Fromm 2018, 78). This is very important and relevant for our time! When action is busyness, there is little time for friendship. Friendship is a mode of action that seeks not to rush to have the world but to share in the world with another. In *Resurrecting the Person*, Swinton highlights how friendship transcends the "having" mode and moves into being. He claims, "A concentration on friendship releases us from an overdependence on technology [an excessive having mode] and allows us to explore issues of human relationships, personhood, spirituality, value, and community, all of which can easily be overlooked or seen as of secondary importance within standard definitions and treatment models of mental health care" (2000, 37).

Fromm's point is when all activity is the *same* and for the sake of having, activity and busyness are made synonymous. Because of the loss of being, the only measure of activity is the expenditure of energy. The more energy expended for the greater gain, the more the activity has value. Inside this logic, busyness becomes a kind of nobility, because busyness witnesses to the actors' reach toward all sorts of having. It becomes a perverted kind of logic when people state proudly that they are too busy to have friends.[2]

In late modernity there is a push for all forms of action to be seen as busy activities used for the sake of possessing and having something. Activity is ultimately for *having* money, experiences, or even *having* a unique identity.[3] The late-modern life is fundamentally well lived when it is a busy life and therefore the best actors are the ablest actors who are the busiest.

WELCOME TO WAITING

What does it actually look like, then, to be in friendship and stand in opposition to this "having" mode? It means to *wait*. We love the world as God commands, allowing our action to take the shape of friendship in the world, by waiting with the world for God's act to come to the world. While waiting at first blush seems hollow, which may be why we resist it, a deeper look reveals that it's bursting with dynamism.

Waiting is dynamic when it comes to seeking God because this kind of waiting is *attentiveness*. It's no surprise that late modernity and its opposition to waiting has made attention the new staple of its economy. We are now living in an attention economy. The most sacred commodity in our digital age is no longer oil or some other raw material but attention

---

[2]   See Hochschild 1997 for more on busyness.

[3]   I explore this cultural phenomenon much more deeply in Root 2021, chaps. 1 and 2.

itself. Companies such as Facebook and Amazon are worth billions of dollars because they own and command our attention. And they own our attention by keeping us from ever waiting, promising us that inside the speed of digital information we can have the world. Yet, as most of us would testify, having our attention always grabbed and the world always have-able doesn't seem to make us more alive or even more connected to the world. For instance, Facebook gives us friends who aren't really our friends. Despite what Facebook executives might claim, always directing our attention to our so-called friends' posts makes us not more connected to them and life in general but less. Their digital tools are now weapons used, maybe over and against their desire, to breed hate and anti-friendship in the world.

To learn to wait is to be catechized; it is to enter a school that forms us to see the action of a living God, to see that friendship is a richer form of action than the expenditure of energy to have. Waiting is a school that teaches us to pray for our friends in the world, pleading for God to act for the world's salvation. Prayer itself is waiting in friendship, like Jesus asked of his disciples in Gethsemane (Matt 26).

WAITING AND APATHY

Inside late modernity and its drive to have, we're tempted to assume all waiting is apathy. But this can only be true if all action is for having. Apathy itself is a byproduct of *having*, never *being*. Apathy is more rightly understood as a hastening that has no place for waiting. When the energy for hastened action is spent and yet the need to *have* and *do more* remains, apathy is born. Apathy is a condition that arrives when you can't find the energy to keep acting. When the energy tanks are on empty and the spirit is fatigued from all the rushed action to have, it's then that despondency takes a hold.

Modernity hates waiting, because, for legitimate reasons, it fears it. This fear is legitimate because waiting unveils that the drive for having is misdirected in the first place. Waiting reveals that action cannot be understood as only, or in totality, the expending of energy. Waiting offers a very different understanding of action that includes every form of ability. Waiting sees the energy for action not coming from within what we can produce to have, but from a hope that is outside us. Waiting attentively seeks, as it waits for, the arrival of an all-new action that can save us. Waiting then rests squarely on hope coming from a horizon outside us. To go into the world in friendship and wait with the world is to actively embody hope for the world. It is to be present before the world as the one who hopes. Apathy, on the other hand, involves lost hope. Apathy ultimately means that we are trapped with no other way of acting.

Waiting, then, is always *for* something. Waiting is only truly waiting when we recognize that waiting cannot stand alone. It is not an independent activity. Waiting without being for something is a contradiction. Waiting needs to be *for* something. No one just waits. We always wait *for* something. And what we're waiting for often unveils what goods we believe give our life meaning and purpose. All waiting is for something, even if that is not defined. As contingent historical beings, it's not really possible to wait without waiting *for* something. Even when someone is asked, "What are you waiting for?" and she responds "nothing," she doesn't really mean "nothing." She means nothing *specific* or nothing *worth mentioning*, or her response leads to a recognition that she's not actually waiting but should get going. If she is waiting, she's waiting *for something*—like the restoration of her energy, or the bus to arrive, or the new episode of *Better Call Saul*. So even in these kinds of waiting there is a *for*. Waiting always needs a corresponding direction. To wait without the *for something* is a prison.

As Andy says to Red in *Shawshank Redemption*, when planning his escape from the prison, "You get busy living or you get busy dying."[4] But "get busy" is the key. This is one of the classic lines of cinematic history because it reveals a normative commitment of late modernity. Getting busy, as opposed to waiting, is now the sign of living. All people have to wait sometimes, of course; but, supposedly, the freer you are, the less you're forced to wait. Those who *have* more wait less.

This contrast between "getting busy" or "waiting" in relation to prison life mirrors another cultural touchstone, Regina Spektor's song "You've Got Time."[5] It was the theme song of the Netflix show *Orange Is the New Black*, and it offers haunting insights on the necessity of getting busy in late modernity. This is particularly poignant in Spektor's line, "taking steps is easy / standing still is hard." Standing still is very hard, even crippling to the human spirit, because waiting is cut off from some end. When there is nothing significant to wait for, and yet you're kept from getting busy, as in prison life (or a global pandemic), you're tortured. Spektor's lyric is directed toward those in prison, but just like the line from *Shawshank*, it says something important about the whole of late modernity.

---

4   *Shawshank Redemption*, dir. Frank Darabont, Warner Bros., 1994.
5   Regina Spektor, "You've Got Time," music from *Orange Is the New Black*, 2013.

We stay busy because it keeps us from having to face that what we're waiting for is cold and lifeless or thin and vapid. Better to face the risks of exhaustion from all the busy steps than to stand still and have to face the emptiness of late modernity's mode of action. Standing still too long means waiting, and not as just as a pause in action, but as a disposition of being in the world itself. Waiting makes us realize that what we long for most is friendship, but we must wait to receive it.

TWO KINDS OF WAITING

Late modernity may hate waiting but it can never completely escape it. So it *uses* waiting for the advantage of getting busy or "having the world," as Fromm would say. Late modernity uses waiting to build hype for the release of the next iPhone or next year's Coachella. Waiting then isn't a way of being in the world but a building of the momentum to race into the world and *have* more of the world. Ultimately, modernity refuses to make waiting a way of being itself in the world. Waiting is only a pause to make the busyness of *having* more eclectic (or to give a quick breather to soon get back to busyness). So, again, to follow Fromm, all waiting has a *for*. The question is, Is waiting an annoyed pause (or a hyped-engine rev) *for having* the world? Or is it a way *for being* in the world?

Late modernity struggles with this second way. We have a very hard time with the thought of waiting as a way of being, because such waiting demands we give ourselves to something outside ourselves, to friendship, for example. Waiting as a way of *being*, as opposed to a pause in *having*, means to release control. To wait as a way of being is to be dependent on something that is not you. To get busy, to always be busy, is to give ourselves a sense of control, which we often equate with freedom. Standing still and waiting for the arrival of something outside us, on the other hand, is to surrender our freedom to take hurried steps to have what we want in the world.

This difference in waiting naturally holds to different senses of time, as John's own work, particularly *Becoming Friends of Time*, has beautifully pointed out. In the first way of waiting, time is vacuous and vacant. In the second, time is full and replete. When Silicon Valley tries to innovate beyond waiting, understanding waiting to be a problem to be solved, it assumes that all waiting (because it's a delay in *having* something new or novel) is unnecessary. This is because of the view that time itself is empty of any sacred significance. So it's best to make the time of waiting as short as possible.

So then there is a kind of waiting that connects us to the world, a waiting that is for being in the world. And there is also a type of waiting that does not connect us to the world. The best way to name this kind of waiting that connects us to the world, pushing us into friendship, is to explore the thought of Fromm's protégé, Hartmut Rosa.

BUILDING TO RESONANCE

Following Fromm, Hartmut Rosa sees busyness, or what he calls "acceleration," as *the* problematic of late modernity. Rosa shows that acceleration, getting busy, stretches into all parts of modernity, both culturally and structurally. We feel the pace of our lives increasing, just as the economy functions and stabilizes itself by acceleration, seeking constant growth. Rosa's early contributions were to lucidly articulate this acceleration, showing in detail what Fromm hinted at: that in modernity activity has been made into busyness, and this accelerating activity breeds a form of action that disconnects us from the world.

Rosa's early work made an indelible impact both within academic thought and in the larger public conversations about European society. Rosa was dubbed the "Slowdown Guru" in the German media. But Rosa was uncomfortable with the label. Not because he was against slowing down. But because it was clear to him that the alienation that was inherent in modernity couldn't simply be mitigated by getting a little (or even exponentially) less busy. The conundrums and contradictions of modernity were too systemic to assume so.

Rosa resisted being called the "Slowdown Guru" because he didn't think a simple slowdown could help. He recognized he'd need to get more constructive. Just because modernity's problematic was accelerating speed, that didn't necessarily mean the answer was slowing down. A slowdown without a shift in aims would be counterproductive. We need a kind of waiting, but unless it were aimed outside wanting to have the world, it would make little difference. It wasn't really a slowdown, then, that we needed but a different conception of action, a very different way of experiencing the world itself: a way of learning to be in friendship again with the world. Rosa's next project picked up on Fromm's "being" mode of acting, turning those few paragraphs into four hundred field-defining pages (see his book *Resonance*).

Those pages showed that our understanding of action needed to shift, from an expenditure of energy to *have* the world to a hastened waiting that allows for the action of *being* in relationship/friendship with the world. All relationships that give life aren't for having but are for being together, which produces (rather than depletes) energy. And the energy it produces we call *life*. Being in relationships of friendship, bound in the *being* form as opposed to the *having* form, is experienced as being alive. *Rosa explains that a relationship that is for being together, which produces the energy of life, is best described as resonance.*

CONNECTING RESONANCE AND WAITING

Resonance is a kind of waiting filled with action. It's a waiting that *isn't* a desert but is teeming with life. The kind of action, this waiting, is filled with—or full of—relationships of friendship. The church waits by actively being in relationship with the world, by being a community of resonance. The church then doesn't so much *do* something as *be* something. You don't *do* friends (that has a very different meaning!); you *be* friends. Friendship is a being mode of action.

When the human act is assumed to be the expenditure of energy, we've moved into the "having" mode. This having mode turns both God and the world into objects to possess. Yet God cannot be possessed, and therefore in this having mode we seek *not* a God who is God but only, and pathetically, a religious object. When pastoral practice and congregational life is linked to action as energy expenditure, the best the church can offer the world is religion.

In turn, while parts of the world may be able to be had, the more we're in the world, in the logic of possessing it, ironically, the less we feel like we're in it. The having mode alienates us from life by telling us to possess the world, burning us out in the process. The more we seek the world, the more we're alienated from living, from being fully in the world as we wait. Then the form of human action that seeks to have the world loses the world. In the having mode, we forget that we are creatures in relationship with the world. We are creatures who need a relationship/friendship with the world to be. We forget that it is in the world—while living and finding life in the world—that we encounter God, who so loves the world as Creator of the world. We then can only seek the living God by waiting for this God to act. Waiting is pained when it's a barrier to expending energy. But when it is a way to just *be* in the world, it is a gift.

This being mode of action is resonance. Resonance is waiting action. By this I mean, resonance is always for the sake of *being* put in, or participating further in, relationships of friendship. Waiting is opening a space for encounter. And a description from the inside of what it's like to be encountered—to be found inside the gift of a relationship of friendship—is resonance. We then wait not in a state of inertia but in a state of resonance.

DON'T GET IT TWISTED

To name resonance as the quality of faithful waiting, however, risks misunderstanding. *Resonance*, particularly in English, insinuates a kind of effervescent state of high emotion. Some, then, may misunderstand resonance as bound up in an unduly emotive experientialism. In this sense a Hillsong service or night four of a middle-school camp-crying-worship-gathering would be the height of church life. But this is to misunderstand what resonance actually is and what Rosa is developing. Resonance isn't absent the emotive. Nor would I want to disparage a Hillsong sing-along or a good camp cryfest. There can be a quality of resonance in these. Yet resonance cannot be reduced to emotive experience. We need to remember that Rosa is a sociologist; his concern is not as much with emotion as with action. For him resonance isn't simply emotive expressivism but, more interestingly, both critique and constructive proposal for understanding human action itself.

Instead of seeing resonance as emotive experientialism, it's better to understand it as a mode of relations, even as a word-event (which moves us very close to the kind of friendship that is at the center of Swinton's work). Of course, resonance is felt. You feel connected and therefore alive. There is emotion to resonance but also affection. It's not just feeling something that matters. Rather, because this is a form of action, we must be drawn out to something. This being drawn out is engendered by affection. Resonance is a form of action that is moved by affection. Like a parent with a child, we wait with our child, finding our affection grow for the child. Our affection never fails to call us into all kinds of action for the child. Resonance is a form of action that waits by seeking affection for another. God's own action, even in its ultimate act of sending the Son, is prompted by affection. God so loves the world that God acts in the world by sending the Son (John 3:16) to be in the world to wait. The Son waits ("I do only what the Father tells me" [John 5:19]), attentive, seeking affection for the Father and the world the Father loves. From this waiting-attentiveness, affection produces action, an action of friendship (John 15).

Rosa, then, gives us a form of action—even from a sociological and philosophical perspective—that is built on a love for the world. Affection has emotion within it, but more so, affection is being drawn out into participation in life itself.

All forms of human action have some kind of feeling attached to them. Human action is never absent emotion, but it is affection that draws out action, while never destroying the necessity to wait and be with and for. In resonance the emotive experience is a sense of connection engendered at some level by affection. This affection moves you outside your self to recognize your relation to the world. The source, then, of this sense of connection is not your own self-enclosed affect, but is the *encounter* itself. It's the sense that your action moves you, out from affection, to share in the being of the world. Your action moves you into *being* in friendship. Resonance is a relationship with something outside you that you now find yourself related to, and therefore feel connected to. Resonance, then, is felt, yet not as a confined emotional state but as an atmosphere of affection that frames a mode of relations. This makes waiting anything but a boring escapist waste.

RESONANCE AND SUFFERING

Yet even if we're clear that resonance is not an emotive expressivism but a mode of relations engendered by affection, it still seems open to another critique. And this critique must be addressed, or resonance can be of little help to a practical ecclesiology and the practice of ministry. And in turn it can undercut our sense of friendship.

Consider this second critique: even as a mode of relations, resonance seems utopian and naively optimistic. As a form of action that is a mode of relations-with-the-world, at first blush, resonance seems unable to see the world as it is. Particularly, it can't seem to recognize suffering, loss, and pain. Resonance seems to be a form of action (a form of relations) that has little room or tolerance for suffering. It's a form of action that attends to connections and union, after all. Therefore, it is logical—though wrong, as we'll see—to assume resonance cannot tolerate suffering. Resonance may not be emotive expressivism, but feelings of sadness and loneliness would seem to short-circuit resonance. Practically, then, a congregation or individual Christian acting as a friend would need to guard against any carrier of negative emotions, eliminating them from the community (which unfortunately does happen but not because of the action of resonance).

This, too, is a deep misunderstanding of resonance. And it follows from the first critique that wrongly reduces resonance to an enclosed emotional state. Concrete suffering and the "negative" emotions that surround it don't destroy resonance, but they *can* create it. Resonance is a form of action that can directly accompany suffering and bear "negative" emotion. When action is assumed to be the expenditure of energy, rather than a being for resonance, the space—or even tolerance—for suffering and "negative" emotion is obliterated. When the church or friend sees action in the having mode of expenditure of energy, all "negative" emotion is a direct drain on the precious reserves of energy. The goal of this kind of action is not necessarily relations but the possession of resources (even relationships/friendships are turned into resources). Energy spent on negative emotion, which witnesses to concrete events of suffering, is energy regrettably diverted and wasted from being spent on having. Only action in the being mode, as opposed to the having mode, can make a place for suffering. And without a place for suffering, there is no way to find the crucified God.

When we're clear that resonance is *not* an enclosed emotional state but a mode of relations, then, as Rosa says, "'negative' emotions such as sadness or loneliness can lead to positive resonant experience" (2019, 168). But here, too, we should be careful. Rosa doesn't mean that these "negative" emotions are positive. Rosa isn't glorifying suffering. What Rosa means is that experiences of suffering, and the "negative" emotions associated with them, can produce a mode of relation, a ground for friendship. They are "positive" not in the sense of being good in themselves but in the sense of mathematics (e.g., a positive number). In resonance, relationship can be generated in and through suffering. "Negative" emotions such as sadness and loneliness *can* be the locale of resonance.

Rosa adds, how else would you explain "statements such as, 'The film was so good, I was bawling' . . . [These statements] are not semantically nonsensical but rather express a common fact of experience" (2019, 168). They express the fact that shared suffering can produce a deep sense of relational connection we call friendship. There is a fullness in the sadness that comes upon us as we listen to a beautiful piece of music and grieve love lost. The sadness of hearing those notes somehow takes us deeper, through sad affection relating us more fully with life. To be made sad through art doesn't take life away from us; it opens us up to higher dimensions of living. Our sadness somehow connects us more deeply to life itself. Sharing a sad moment with a friend can deepen the friendship. This kind of action is resonance.

Yet when action is understood as an expenditure of energy to have the world, suffering and negative emotions possess *no* possibility of yielding relationship. Suffering and negative emotions are then insatiable and lifeless. And there is no possibility of beauty even in the ugliness of the breakdown. Suffering in the having mode has no positive quality at all (it is only a negative number). Resonance as a being mode of action can relate to the world, binding itself to the world in and through the world's suffering because it's a waiting moved by affection. Resonance, then, can forge connection out of suffering. Theologically, we've often called this reality of relations born through suffering "ministry" or "to be minister to," believing it to be the heart of God's own action in the world.

This sense that suffering can host a deeper connection to one another and the world, making us friends. This phenomenon is something Martin Luther saw long ago. Attending to suffering, waiting for God in suffering, doesn't produce disgust for the world or and hatred for life; it produces love for the world and its beauty that comes even in its ugliness. Sharing in suffering produces a resonant relation to the world that can deliver a shocking paradox of joy in being alive in the world. The eyes of faith see beauty and joy in the suffering of the cross. From the cross comes an all-new relation to the world. From the suffering of the cross comes the freedom to be in and love the world for itself. Freely justified, Luther would assert, means we are free from the having mode (having to do works to save ourselves) to enter the joy of the being mode (being in Christ), embracing our neighbor in friendship. There is nothing to do but be in and with the world in friendship, waiting for God who is God to come to the world. There is nothing to do, no *having* action needed to save ourselves. We are now free to *be* in the world, and love the world, acting for the world as our way of waiting for a God who is God to come to the world. Resonance is a form of action that moves us into the being mode and therefore, paradoxically, resonance is a form of hastened action born from affection that is at the same time waiting.

RESONANCE AS CONVERSATION

Against this backdrop, we can say that resonance is best understood as a form of action that comes in the shape of a word-event. Across its many shapes, resonance is a form of friendship in conversation. It seeks not to possess (have) the world but to act in the world in a way that both addresses and is addressed by the world. In resonance, then, we feel spoken to by something outside us. Like a good conversation, action as resonance doesn't deplete our energy but produces more of it. At the same time, it actually makes us unconcerned for energy by drawing us far beyond worry for resources. We may feel tired after a long conversation but also full, not depleted, because we've experienced a tangible connection. The relational connection produces its own energy, giving amps to each subject in the discourse. In such conversations our own actions connect us to something bigger than us that nevertheless fully includes us.

Rosa explains that the Latin etymology of "resonance is first and foremost an acoustic phenomenon—'re-sonare' meaning *to resound*" (2019, 165; emphasis in the original). Resonance is a form of action that is a kind of reverberating word-event. This acoustic analogy is helpful for a few reasons. First, it shows that resonance is not a word-event in a sense of necessitating actual words or even cognitive abilities. We've all felt spoken to by a piece of music, an ocean breeze, an infant's smile, or a kind dog. Second, the acoustic analogy helps us recognize that resonance as a form of action—in the shape of a word-event, in the form of a conversation—produces a connection without enmeshment, domination, or cut-off. Conversations that lack mutuality are exhausting and therefore lack resonance. When we sense the conversation is not free of instrumental objectives, when the conversation is for winning our vote or buying a product, we feel our energy stolen. In such moments we may not enter the discourse for instrumental purposes, but we may leave it unable to evaluate the conversation in any other way. We say to ourselves, "That was a waste of time," meaning that was a waste of the resources of my energy. That was energy that won me "zero having." We feel this because our otherness, as a mutual dialog partner, has been overlooked (as the opposite of friendship). Yet when we experience something that speaks to us—with or without words—we can only do so if we encounter this interlocutor as other, recognizing our own otherness, made aware of the other's and our own being.

To show this, and draw further from the Latin etymology, Rosa uses a tuning fork as metaphor. When a tuning fork vibrates and it meets another fork, this other fork will begin to also vibrate. The vibrating action of the one fork leads the other fork to come to life and vibrate as well. But this other fork does so, at least at the start, at its own frequency. This other fork is allowed to have its own voice, if you will. It is brought to life, but never by losing its own unique pitch. Yet, eventually, if the two forks stay in communion, the freedom of the mutual responsive resonance will result in a synchronous resonance.

Eventually the two tuning forks will join frequencies and become stronger. But not because they've produced, in themselves, more energy to expend in *having* a louder frequency. Rather, the stronger frequency is produced by harmony, not competition. The power of the action of resonance is bound up in the mystery of plurality and unity. Resonance's power is in harmony. It is in its weakness, as Paul would say (2 Cor 12:9), to recognize harmony, not victory, as resonance's transformational power. Action as the expenditure of energy creates its power in an opposite way. Its power as a form of action rests not in harmony but the singular victory in competition. The great tragedy of late modernity is that the church (at least in practical terms) has assumed that the only form of action available to it is the expenditure of energy in the having mode. The church then has seen itself invariably in competition with the world. Or the church has seen it as necessary to adapt modernity's strategies of competition in the having mode to survive, racing for capitalist business approaches over the waiting of theological contemplation.

Yet resonance is a very different form of action than the competition inherent within the having mode of action as the expenditure of energy. In resonance the agent doesn't have to produce his or her own energy from within him or herself. The energy that feeds the action of resonance is delivered by the harmony of the union itself. In competition the energy is produced within the actor or by the resources owned and possessed by the actor. It is the actor's genius, or bank account, or fame or reputation that produces the energy.

In resonance, energy is found within relationality itself. Energy is found through the event of encounter with otherness, not through the possession of having resources. It's the conversation—the word-event—that creates the energy in resonance. And it's always as gift. The actor finds this energy not through skill or victory bound inside him or herself, but through a waiting to be addressed by something or someone who encounters her as friend.

WORKS CITED

Fromm, Erich. 2018. *To Have or to Be?* London: Bloomsbury.

Hochschild, Arlie Russell. 1997. *The Time Bind: When Work Becomes Home and Home Becomes Work.* New York: An Owl Book.

Root, Andrew. 2021. *The Congregation in a Secular Age.* Grand Rapids: Baker Academic.

Rosa, Hartmut. 2019. *Resonance: A Sociology of Our Relationship to the World.* Cambridge, UK: Polity.

Swinton, John. 2000. *Resurrecting the Person: Friendship and the Care of People with Mental Health Problems.* Nashville: Abingdon.

———. 2016. *Becoming Friends of Time: Disability, Timefullness, and Gentle Discipleship.* Waco, Tex.: Baylor University Press.

14

The Practice of Health Care and the Gentleness of Jesus

Warren Kinghorn and Stanley Hauerwas

Amid attention to the virtues in and of medical practice, there has been very little attention paid to gentleness. Pellegrino and Thomasma (1993) recommend for physicians the virtues of trust, compassion, *phronesis*, justice, fortitude, temperance, and integrity. Curiously, they omit gentleness. The widely cited "Physician Charter on Medical Professionalism" makes no mention of gentleness (ABIM Foundation et al. 2002). Medical school curricula frequently feature courses aimed at fostering compassion, empathy, courage, and a commitment to justice, but not gentleness. The expansive MEDLINE database of articles in medical journals features more than thirty thousand articles on the subjects of "compassion" and "justice," respectively, but fewer than 150 on "gentleness"—most of which refer to surgical or wound-care practices or to medical adhesives, not to health care as a whole.

Gentleness, indeed, may seem a poor candidate for a virtue of clinical practice. In a medical culture increasingly focused on equity, inclusivity, and dismantling historical structures of oppression, the English term *gentle*, like its French counterpart *gentil*, is marked by a chauvinistic history, carried forward in words like *gentleman* and *genteel*. To be "gentle" is to be well born, well bred, well mannered. In a medical culture that often frames care of the sick in the language of war, and clinicians as "front-line" combatants, gentleness carries unwelcome connotations of passivity and weakness in the face of threat. In a patriarchal medical culture ambivalent at best about associating the work of clinicians (especially physicians) with traditionally feminine images, gentleness evokes images of caregiving and care-receiving that are traditionally associated with women.

Those who look primarily to classical sources for understanding virtue might also be forgiven for overlooking gentleness. Aristotle considers gentleness (*praótes*) a relatively minor virtue dealing with the regulation of anger. Gentleness is the mean between excessive expression of anger (irascibility) on the one hand and the inability to summon appropriate anger (lack of spirit) on the other—though Aristotle says that gentleness is closer to the deficiency than to the excess (Aristotle 1999, IV.5). Being gentle, according to Aristotle, "means to be unruffled and not to be driven by emotion, but to be angry only under such circumstances and for as long a time as reason may bid." Later Christian interpreters of Aristotle such as Thomas Aquinas largely followed this concept of gentleness (*mansuetudo*), as a virtue pertaining to anger (*ST* IaIIae q. 60 a. 2; IaIIae q. 69 a. 3). Seen in this perspective, however, gentleness would seem to be primarily about self-regulation and self-control—a necessary virtue for clinicians, to be sure, but not one that breaks much new ground.

John Swinton has convinced us, though, that gentleness is an underrated virtue that must be central to the practice of any health care practitioner—especially those who claim to be Christian. We have learned much from John's writing, and from John himself, about gentleness. But, of course, John Swinton did not invent gentleness. He learned about the importance of gentleness from Jesus, but also through his experience with the L'Arche network of communities where people with and without intellectual disabilities live together in relationships of mutual care, dependence, and friendship. In this essay, therefore, we explore what we can learn from Jesus about gentleness, what we can learn from L'Arche about gentleness, and what we can learn from John Swinton about gentleness. We then consider the difference that a gentle medicine would make for the way that clinicians do their work.

LEARNING FROM JESUS ABOUT GENTLENESS

Jesus shows us what it means to be gentle. Variants of *praus*, the Greek word most commonly translated as "gentle" or "meek," are used only four times in the New Testament—once in 1 Peter and three times in the Gospel of Matthew. In the controversial text of 1 Peter, *praus* applies to women, who are encouraged to display "the lasting beauty of a gentle and quiet spirit, which is very precious in God's sight" (1 Pet 3:4). But in Matthew's Gospel, *praus* applies to Jesus.

Matthew's three uses of *praus* make clear that Jesus and gentleness must always be understood in the light of each other. First, Jesus tells his disciples that "blessed are the meek [gentle], for they will inherit the earth" (Matt 5:5). Jesus' understanding of gentleness, however, is not Aristotle's. Jesus is quoting Psalm 37, with its strong encouragement for those who are oppressed by "the wicked" to

> commit your way to the Lord;
>> trust in him and he will act.
> He will make your vindication shine like the light,
>> and the justice of your cause like the noonday. (37:4–6)

"The Lord loves justice" (37:28), and when the righteous wait for the Lord,

> yet a little while, and the wicked will be no more;
>> though you look diligently for their place, they will not be there.
> But the meek shall inherit the land,
>> and delight themselves in abundant prosperity. (37:10–11)

The "meek/gentle" persons in the psalm that Jesus quotes are the oppressed and powerless who are given the promise of land not through their own power but through God's just action (Domeris 2016).

Second, as John Swinton frequently notes, Jesus claims that he himself is *praus*: "Take my yoke upon you, and learn from me; for I am gentle and humble in heart, and you will find rest for your souls" (Matt 11:29). To be sure, at this point in the gospel, Jesus has not *acted* according to common standards of gentleness. He has warned his disciples of coming persecution and has told them that he has "not come to bring peace, but a sword" (Matt 10:34). He has responded cryptically to the imprisoned John the Baptist and has denounced several Galilean communities, including his own hometown, comparing them unfavorably to powerful, wicked gentile cities (Matt 11:20–24). But then he says, echoing the third Beatitude, "I am gentle."

What does Jesus mean by this? Having just spoken publicly against the ruling powers of his day, he cannot mean that he is passive or weak. Although he was kind to the poor, he was not being "nice." He certainly was not speaking in the well-bred, "genteel" cadence of a "gentleman." Nor, in the context of the gospel, does it make any sense to interpret Jesus' gentleness as an Aristotelian moderation of anger. When Jesus said, "I am gentle," he was drawing not on Aristotle but rather on the psalms and the prophets. To those in his time who were "weary" and "carrying heavy burdens" (Matt 11:28)—the first-century descendants of the "poor and needy" of Psalm 37—Jesus offers a yoke of rest, a yoke far lighter than that laid on them by the religious, economic, and political leaders of the day. But he does not do so in the mode of a ruler on a pedestal who throws down crumbs of sustenance to his subjects. Jesus, rather, says, "*I* am gentle and humble in heart" (Matt 11:29). Like you who are weary and carrying heavy burdens, like you who are *praus* and humble in heart, so also *I* am *praus*. I see you, I feel your burdens, because I myself am one of you.

In this statement, Jesus turns the classical, chauvinistic notion of gentleness—still present in our time—on its head. No longer, as in Aristotle's concept of *praótes*, is gentleness a virtue of the self-sufficient, great-souled man (*megalópsūkhos*) who achieves virtuous moderation of his anger. There is great power in gentleness, but it is not the power that derives from being well-born, well-heeled, or well-spoken. Gentleness in the way of Jesus, rather, is a grace-enabled, habit-formed way of life that comes from living in such solidarity with those who are weary and who are carrying heavy burdens that one can act in a way that releases these burdens rather than compounding them. This gentleness is strong, but the source of its strength is not the self-sufficient excellence of the Aristotelian great-souled man. Its strength is rather the justice of God, incarnate in Jesus, that promises that it is the gentle, not the self-sufficiently strong, who will inherit the earth. Christians are gentle in the way of Jesus only when we participate, in the Son by the Spirit, in this justice-seeking.

Jesus' revolutionary gentleness—or, as Jason Byassee (2016) frames it, Jesus' "strong-weakness"—is displayed even more publicly during his final entry into Jerusalem. Here, using *praus* a third time by quoting the prophet Zechariah, the gospel writer makes clear that to understand gentleness, we must see Jesus:

> Tell the daughter of Zion,
> "Look, your king is coming to you,
> *praus* and mounted on a donkey,
> and on a colt, the foal of a donkey." (Matt 21:5)

The immediate context of Zechariah's oracle is one of unmitigated military victory for Israel, including against Greece (Zech 9:13), with the king entering Jerusalem "triumphant and victorious," though riding on a donkey to signify peace (Zech 9:9). But Matthew notably leaves out "triumphant and victorious" from his quotation of Zechariah. Jesus was not coming to Jerusalem having achieved military victory over Israel's colonizing enemies. He was coming to Jerusalem to die. It would take Jesus' resurrection and ascension, and even then considerable time, for Jesus' followers to understand how that horrible week was in fact a decisive site of triumph and victory—but such is the revolutionary gentleness of Jesus. As Byassee puts it, "God's own strong-weakness is a cross" (2016, 52).

Jesus' early followers took strong note of Jesus' gentleness (*praótes*) and made it a cornerstone virtue of the evolving Christian community. Sometimes, as in a frustrated Paul's blunt question to the Corinthians, "Am I to come to you with a stick, or with love in a spirit of gentleness?" (1 Cor 4:21), there are hints of the older pagan concept of *praótes* as a virtue of moderating anger. But most writers frame gentleness in a specifically Christological and Trinitarian way. Paul later appeals to the Corinthians "by the meekness and gentleness of Christ" (2 Cor 10:1) and counts gentleness a fruit of the Spirit (Gal 5:22–23). Multiple New Testament writers also make clear that Jesus' gentleness is not only an individual virtue but also a communal virtue that should inform the life of the church. Christians are to display Jesus' gentleness in the execution of church discipline (Gal 6:1), in hearing and living according to the word of truth (Jas 1:21, 3:13), and in correcting opponents (2 Tim 2:25). The gentleness of Jesus, communally embodied and displayed, is indeed central if Christians are to "maintain the unity of the spirit in the bond of peace" (Eph. 4:1–3; cf. Col 3:12–15).[1]

LEARNING FROM L'ARCHE ABOUT GENTLENESS

Perhaps nowhere in our time is the revolutionary gentleness of Jesus more vividly displayed than in the global network of L'Arche communities, where people with and without intellectual disabilities live together and cultivate a common life where all belong, all are valued, all are honored, all have a vocation. Just as John Swinton learned about gentleness not only from Jesus but also from L'Arche, so we have also. L'Arche is, as Swinton (2003) has said, "a revelation of the way that God loves" (67). Faithfully reflecting Jesus' gentleness, the L'Arche communities understand impairments and disabilities

> not . . . as problems to be solved, but rather as particular ways of being human which need to be understood, valued, and supported. The focus is on discovering ways of loving and living together that recognize the naturalness and beauty of difference and the theological significance of weakness and vulnerability. The L'Arche communities "seek to offer not a *solution*, but a *sign*—a sign that a society, to be truly human, must be founded on welcome and respect for the weak and downtrodden." (Swinton 2003, 68, quoting the L'Arche Charter)

---

[1]   In his work, John Swinton cites an essay by David Ford that makes a similar set of connections in Young 1997, cited in Swinton 2016 and other essays of Swinton's.

Central to L'Arche are practices such as eating together, praying together, celebrating together, and footwashing, which encourage the "transvaluation" of socially inscribed hierarchies of worth and value that stigmatize and isolate persons with disabilities (Swinton 2003, 67; Grieg 2015; Hauerwas and Vanier 2008). L'Arche communities reject the shaping values of productivity, power, and consumption that drive so much of modern life. L'Arche communities help everyone—"core members" and "assistants" alike—to take time for peace and to become friends with time as they work to befriend each other (Swinton 2016; Hauerwas and Vanier 2008). L'Arche is a modest proposal that the gentleness of Jesus is possible even in a violent world.

But the example of L'Arche carries with it a note of sobering caution about how we are to embody Jesus' gentleness. The L'Arche communities would not exist in their present form apart from the life and work of Jean Vanier, who founded the first L'Arche community in 1964 and who at the time of his death in 2019 was widely admired as a "living saint." We, too, admired Jean Vanier, and learned a great deal from him. One of us even coauthored a brief book with him—on gentleness, no less (Hauerwas and Vanier 2008). When Jean related to others, he had a way of conveying that they mattered and were valued, that they belonged in his presence and on earth. To us, and to many others who were moved by the witness of L'Arche, Jean seemed to embody the revolutionary gentleness of Jesus.

We were therefore distressed and saddened to learn that an independent inquiry commissioned by L'Arche International and published in February 2020, months after Jean Vanier's death, concluded that Jean Vanier had engaged in "manipulative sexual relationships" with at least six nondisabled women associated with L'Arche communities between 1970 and 2005. The report disclosed a deeply disturbing pattern of abuse, consistent with prior abusive practices of his mentor Father Thomas Philippe, in which Vanier would develop close relationships with women in psychologically vulnerable moments, sometimes under the guise of spiritual direction, would establish a "psychological hold" on them, and then would engage in various sexual practices that they described to investigators as nonconsensual. Sometimes in these moments, Jean Vanier would directly place himself in the role of Jesus. The six women who were willing to speak with investigators about Jean Vanier's conduct all described "how the behavior had a subsequent long-lasting, negative impact on their personal lives and inter-personal and/or spousal relationships" (L'Arche International 2020).

Jean Vanier's behavior as described in this report is, needless to say, a deep betrayal of the gentleness of Jesus. We do not know how Jean justified these behaviors to himself, or what demons in his own soul made him vulnerable to such sin—though that he lied repeatedly about his knowledge of the behaviors of his mentor Thomas Philippe suggests that he both knew and feared the consequences of discovery. But here again, the L'Arche communities are teaching us about gentleness precisely in their courageous truth-telling about the violence of their founder. Gentleness, as the New Testament makes clear, is a virtue expressed in community. Secrecy, on the other hand, corrodes community and makes impossible the truthfulness that is central for any community that seeks to be gentle in the midst of the violence of the world. The gentleness that others perceived in Jean Vanier became, in secret, a pretense for violence.[2] By telling the truth about Jean Vanier and also by their embrace of transparent "safeguarding" practices (https://www.larcheusa.org/about/safeguarding/), the L'Arche communities are preserving the possibility of gentleness in their courageous attention to a deeply painful wound.

LEARNING FROM JOHN SWINTON ABOUT GENTLENESS

Just as John Swinton learned about gentleness from Jesus and from L'Arche, we have learned about gentleness from John Swinton as he has made God's gentleness a central theme of his life's work. John has always emphasized that his work is an expression of practical theology, defined in his first book as "critical reflection on the actions of the church in the light of the gospel and Christian tradition"—though we would add that this is also the task of Christian ethics (Swinton 2000a, 7). John's practical theology has always drawn him to the concrete, lived experiences of real people and real communities—including the structured attention that he gives to the complexity of lived experience through in-depth qualitative interviews. We suspect that this is, in part, what has conferred on John the remarkable ability to communicate complex theological concepts in a pastorally responsive and humanly effective way. But as a Christian theologian, it is central to John's work to consider humans in theological

---

[2]   Jean Vanier's conduct also provides a vivid reminder that those who seek to inhabit the gentleness of Christ must allow their relationships to be transparent to the broader community lest they fall into damaging self-deception. Although we will never know for sure, the L'Arche investigative report leaves open the possibility that Jean Vanier convinced himself that like his mentor, he was embodying Christ when he engaged in the behaviors outlined in the report. If so, he was badly wrong, with devastating consequences for his victims.

perspective, as beloved creatures of God who are made in the image of God, called to friendship with God and others, and invited by God's grace into the possibility of shalom. Shalom is an inextricably theological concept, more determinative for Christians' good than anything else, including "health."

> Shalom is not the *absence* of illness. Rather it is the *presence* of God. Shalom means righteousness and holiness; right relationship with God. To experience shalom is to be in right relationship with God irrespective of the state of our bodies or minds. *To be healthy is to love God in all things and at all times.* (Swinton and Vanier 2014, 78)

Indeed, "the test of good theology is not simply its intellectual coherence but the way it enables the people of God to see God more clearly and love God more dearly" (Swinton 2020, 212).

To inhabit God's shalom, however, humans must learn to inhabit God's time, which turns out to be gentle time, because God is gentle. Inhabiting God's gentle time, in turn, leads to a radical reconfiguration of the way that we live with each other, especially in the context of mental illness and disability.

> The ethos and movement of time and history is Christ shaped. Jesus *is* time in the sense that in Christ human beings can see clearly what time looks like and what time is for. If this is so, then God's time not only contains gentleness, it *is* gentleness. Gentleness is written into the heart of the universe. God's time is gentle time. The gifts of time and the practices of timefullness I am suggesting accompany the experience of certain forms of disability reveal different facets of living in God's time, because they are all facets of God. All of these gifts coalesce within the practices of gentle timefullness. God's time is gentle time because God is gentle; God's time is imbued with trust because God *is* trust; God's time is slow, loving time because God *is* love and the coming of the kingdom takes time. When we slow down and pay attention to the slowness of God's time, we encounter one another differently. (Swinton 2016, 75)

We resonate with John Swinton's connection of peace, friendship, and time. Time must be for Christians a theological category. We live in God's time, and as one of us has frequently said, God has given us all the time we need to become friends with one another, and in becoming friends with one another we learn to become friends with God (Hauerwas 2018).

Beyond connecting gentleness, time, and friendship, however, Swinton's work helps us to appreciate how gentleness might operate as a virtue not only for Christians generally, but specifically for health care practitioners. Swinton came to value gentleness in part through his experience as a psychiatric nurse within institutions that were not gentle. He recalls, as a trainee nurse, "being ordered to tell thirty patients to strip and line up in the bathroom in rows of ten, in order that they could be shaved and bathed by nursing assistants"—a practice, among others, that he came to understand "not [as] an act of care but [as] a method of control" (Swinton 2000b, 57). His appreciation of gentleness was further shaped by his subsequent training as a registered nurse for persons with disabilities, and then even more when he left nursing and began working as a community mental-health chaplain. He learned as a nurse, and perhaps even more as a chaplain, to *listen* for the deep and profound experiences of the human beings before him. His clinical and ministerial formation, along with his practical-theological commitments, have given rise to a scholarly body of work that not only *speaks of* the gentleness of God but also displays it. Swinton's theology emerges from questions that people encounter in their lived experience, and like Jesus and L'Arche, he prefers to focus on the details of specific people and specific communities rather than to engage in abstractions about humanity or the church as a whole. But just as he resists any reduction of human beings to theological abstractions, Swinton also writes against all forms of mental-health care or care of persons with disabilities that reduce persons to *clinical* abstractions. For example, in a clinical mental-health world full of thin descriptions that flatten the experience of human beings into efficient names such as "schizophrenia" or "bipolar disorder," Swinton rightfully insists on thick descriptions that honor the complexity of humans as God's beloved creatures, created in God's image, and called to the shalom that is right relationship with God and others. "There are no 'schizophrenics' in the kingdom of God," John rightfully insists, "just people who love Jesus" (Swinton 2020, 161). A central task of the church with respect to mental-health problems is, therefore, "to give people back their names."

> In John 15:15 Jesus once again draws our attention to the importance of naming: "I no longer call you servants, because a servant does not know his master's business. Instead, I have called you friends, for everything that I learned from my Father I have made known to you." Here the disciples are given a whole new identity. No longer are they servants. Now they are friends of Jesus. Friendship is the nature of discipleship in God's coming kingdom. Perhaps the most radical way we can counter the pathological culture [of depersonalized mental health care] is quite simple: make Christlike friendships with people. Sometimes the simplest things in life turn out to be the most profound. (Swinton 2020, 161)

GENTLENESS AS A VIRTUE FOR HEALTH CARE PRACTITIONERS

L'Arche and John Swinton have helped us better to understand the character of gentleness in the way of Jesus. But how might Jesus' gentleness, as displayed and described by L'Arche and by Swinton, help us to understand how modern health care practitioners might seek to be gentle, and how gentleness might be a virtue for health care practitioners?

It should be clear by now what gentleness in the way of Jesus is *not*. Contra Aristotle, Jesus' gentleness is not simply the effective moderation of anger. It is not weakness or passivity in the face of need. It is not kindness, empathy, compassion, respect, beneficence, or altruism, though it entails some degree of all of these. Rather, Jesus' gentleness is the capacity to encounter those who are oppressed and rendered powerless by disease, by mental-health problems, or by oppressive social structures and conditions—those who are weary and who are carrying heavy burdens—and to *see* them not as problems or diagnoses or as objects of charity, but rather as God's beloved creatures whom God knows and loves, who are called against all odds to God's *shalom*. It is to be able to say, "It's good that you exist; it's good that you are in this world!"—and really to believe it (Pieper 1997, 164). And it is then, in this space of recognition, to enter in faith into a deep solidarity that seeks the others' good as one's own. This gentleness will certainly require clinicians to inhabit time and space differently. God's time is different, and may indeed be slower, than the time of the clinic and hospital. But this is the healing gentleness of Jesus to which L'Arche and John Swinton both direct us.

This time-full gentleness is not easy. We conclude by offering five observations about the conditions needed for the seeds of gentleness to grow in the lives and work of health care practitioners.

First, gentleness requires *witnesses*. Just as John Swinton learned about gentleness from Jesus and from L'Arche, so also clinicians need those who witness to Jesus' gentleness. Such witnesses, to be sure, include L'Arche and John Swinton. But clinicians need more proximate witnesses also—those whose lives are so marked by encounter with the gentle Jesus that word and act are united in the person of the witness. Witnesses to Jesus understand that they have been given a gift that has made their lives possible, and therefore their message "points past them, or through them, to the God they believe they have met in Christ Jesus" (Hauerwas and Pinches 2013, 45).

Some health care practitioners may be fortunate to encounter such witnesses among other clinicians. But it is more likely that clinicians will need to leave the regimented, time-starved space of medical institutions to find witnesses to Jesus' gentleness—and they may have to learn to inhabit time and space very differently. Indeed, those who witness gentleness might not be who we expect. One of us recalls a former student, a wise physician who pursued theological study after decades of medical practice. During her study at Duke University, she worked as a volunteer chaplain at a local Methodist retirement community, where she befriended an older, educated woman living with dementia. Week after week they would talk about God, life, family, or nothing in particular. Slowly, our student experienced not only her experience of time but also her appreciation of the woman's humanness shifting and expanding. One day she reported with excitement, "We walked today on a trail around a pond, talking and talking—and I realized afterward that I hadn't had a single medical thought!" For a physician who had long been formed to see people through the lens of diagnosis and disease—in this case, the ugly lens of *dementia*—this was extremely liberating. She had walked around the pond not with a diagnosis but with a human being. Our student's friend, inviting her to a different inhabitation of time, served as a powerful witness to Jesus' gentleness.

Second, consistent with our student's story but unlike Aristotle's concept of *praótes*, Jesus' gentleness requires that clinicians work to overcome and to dismantle boundaries of class, culture, education, and ability that separate them from their patients. Contrary to many contemporary interpretations of the Beatitudes, the "meek" (or gentle) of Jesus' day were not privileged middle-class people who had mastered the virtue of humility. They were, rather, the "poor and needy" of Psalm 37 who, through God's righteous overthrow of their oppressors, stood to inherit the earth. Jesus' affirmation that "*I* am gentle" was likewise not feigned humility; it was a radical affirmation of solidarity with the *praus* of his time. While gentleness would not require clinicians to forgo all professional structures and customs, since many structures and customs serve to empower patients and clinicians alike and to facilitate effective therapeutic relationships, it would require clinicians, like Jesus, to enter the lives of their patients as closely as possible—starting with attentive, focused listening in conversation, and then very possibly through more radical practices that would involve clinicians working in solidarity with their patients to improve the material conditions of their lives.

Third, Jesus' gentleness requires *practice*, but this practice must not give way to self-sufficient pride in one's own gentleness. Gentleness, like most virtues, is a matter both of practice and of gift. Like humility—another overlooked virtue—gentleness often fades just to the degree that one takes pride in being gentle. If you try to be humble or gentle, you probably are not. Indeed, genuinely gentle people often seem to come from nowhere. They did not try to be gentle; somehow they just *are* gentle.

We suspect that the practice required for cultivating gentleness is not focused on improving oneself and one's own gentleness. Rather, practices that lead to gentleness are focused on others. One becomes gentle in the way of Jesus insofar as one learns to see others as Jesus sees them, which is to say, as those created in the image of God who need to be seen, known, and loved, no matter who they are. This is why gentleness in children is cultivated in practices that encourage children to exercise their power with and over other creatures in a way that respects the dignity of these creatures and learns how to respond to them. Children can be terribly cruel, particularly with other children, but some children seem to be born gentle and others learn to be gentle in the context of practices of knowing others and being known, caring for others and being cared for. That children must learn to be gentle is found in those learned behaviors that often seem insignificant. One of us has previously called attention to the everyday behavior of learning how to pet a pet, which is a reminder that animals can display a gentleness that is not to be dismissed as insignificant (Hauerwas 2018). Gentleness may well be one of the ways we see that human animals and nonhuman animals have more in common than is often acknowledged. Put more strongly, gentleness is the characteristic that should make us think twice about the assumed difference between us and God's creatures that is the assumed basis of our cruel treatment of animals.

But gentleness is not entirely an acquired virtue. It is also, in part, a gift of God's grace. Some who are gentle are created with natural temperaments that render them more able to see others and to respond to them with gentleness. And many who are gentle, including some who lack this natural temperament, have been graced to live into a story of cross and resurrection, of strong-weakness that triumphs over death, that runs contrary to the violence of the world. We fear such gentleness because we think we can survive only if we use violence. We are subtle, often using gentleness in a passive-aggressive way, to get what we think we must have to survive. But that is not true gentleness. Those who are gentle have learned that God's gentleness ended on a cross, refusing to resort to violence to save us from our violence. As Karl Barth has made clear, nowhere is God's humanity more evident than in Jesus' crucifixion. Gentleness might put one at the mercy of those who are violent. But there is courage in gentleness: the gentle have a strength that makes them able to persevere in the face of danger. Those who are gentle in the way of Jesus have a strength that comes from God.

Fourth, as the haunting example of Jean Vanier makes clear, Jesus' gentleness requires transparency and accountability. It is the church, not any individual, that is the body of Christ. Just as one of us has written that "friendship must be communal because only a community that is made of those aware of their limits can create the peaceful space for all to flourish," so also gentleness is a communal virtue, not solely an individual one (Hauerwas 2022, 153). This is important, because gentle practices create powerful experiences of vulnerability. Most human beings have many relationships with many people, but many of these relationships—even within families—are ordered by utility and productivity, and layered with expectation and shame. The busyness of late-modern consumer culture encourages such shallow, utilitarian relationships (cf. Andrew Root's chapter in this volume). Even for people with many social connections, it is often rare to feel deeply known, seen, loved, *valued* by someone else—and yet this is what gentleness evokes. Gentleness often leads to surprising intimacy. Intimacy, in turn, can be a site of deep healing, when the experience of being known by another enables a secure base of belonging and a subsequent flowering of agency. But it can also, especially when kept secret, be a site of abuse and of deep pain. Those who would seek to be gentle in the way of Jesus must be surrounded by a community of accountability and support, lest gentleness serve as an insidious front for violence.

Finally, clinicians who would be gentle in the way of Jesus must cultivate habits that enable them to listen and to *see*.[3] John Swinton's focus on the particularity of human lived experience is here deeply formative and instructive for us. One cannot be gentle in general; one is always gentle *with someone*, in a particular place and time. The capacity for gentleness requires the capacity for seeing, sensing, discerning, and experiencing the beauty and complexity of the humans and other creatures who are before us. And this requires a continual openness to wonder. John Swinton, who witnesses the gentleness of Jesus to us, continues to inspire us with his capacity for wonder. Swinton's way of helping us to see the healing power of gentleness is remarkable. In the final meditation of a recent book, he writes:

> My kids often ask me what superpower I would like to have. I always tell them I'd like to have the power to be gentle and kind . . . at all times.

[3] "Seeing" is here meant as metaphor; those who are not sighted will often "see" in nonvisual ways that are equally, if not more, discerning.

They just laugh, and I can understand why. But I am serious. Such a superpower seems rather weak in the face of the ability to fly, to shoot spider webs from your wrists, to scale tall buildings, or to defeat the powers of darkness while talking to your beautiful girlfriend on your state-of-the-art mobile! But I think my superpower . . . is more interesting. Imagine a world where people didn't judge one another, a world where gentleness, kindness, and tenderness were our priorities. Within such a world, being different or seeing the world differently would not be an occasion for rejection, humiliation, demonization, and loneliness. Rather, such experiences would be seen as an opportunity to practice kindness. It seems to me that is precisely the superpower that is given us by the Holy Spirit and is manifested so beautifully and movingly in the life of Jesus: "Take my yoke upon you and learn from me, for *I am gentle* and humble in heart, and you will find rest for your souls" (Matt 11:29). Jesus is gentle. Wow! (Swinton 2020, 214–15)

We agree entirely. Sometimes, "Wow!" is all that witnesses can say.

WORKS CITED

ABIM Foundation, ACP-ASIM Foundation, European Foundation of Internal Medicine. 2002. "Medical Professionalism in the New Millennium: A Physician Charter." *Annals of Internal Medicine* 136, no. 3: 243–46.

Aristotle. 1999. *Nicomachean Ethics*. Translated and with an introduction and notes by Martin Ostwald. Upper Saddle River, N.J.: Prentice-Hall.

Byassee, Jason. 2016. "Gentleness Rules." *Journal for Preachers* 39, no. 4: 49–54.

Domeris, W. 2016. "Meek or Oppressed? Reading Matthew 5:5 in Context." *Acta Theologica* 23 suppl.: 131–49.

Grieg, Jason Reimer. 2015. *Reconsidering Intellectual Disability: L'Arche, Medical Ethics, and Christian Friendship*. Washington, D.C.: Georgetown University Press.

Hauerwas, Stanley. 2018. *The Character of Virtue: Letters to a Godson*. Grand Rapids: Eerdmans.

———. 2022. "To Be Befriended: A Meditation on Friendship and the Disabled." In *Fully Alive: The Apocalyptic Humanism of Karl Barth*, 152–64. Charlottesville: University of Virginia Press, 2022.

Hauerwas, Stanley, and Charles Pinches. 2013. "Witness." In *Approaching the End: Eschatological Reflections on Church, Politics, and Life*, by Stanley Hauerwas, 37–63. Grand Rapids: Eerdmans.

Hauerwas, Stanley, and Jean Vanier. 2008. *Living Gently in a Violent World: The Prophetic Witness of Weakness*. Downers Grove, Ill.: IVP Books.

L'Arche International. 2020. "Summary Report." www.larcheusa.org/news_article/summary-report-from-larche-international/.

Pellegrino, Edmund, and David C. Thomasma. 1993. *The Virtues in Medical Practice*. New York: Oxford University Press.

Pieper, Josef. 1997. *Faith, Hope, Love*. San Francisco: Ignatius.

Swinton, John. 2000a. *From Bedlam to Shalom: Towards a Practical Theology of Human Nature, Interpersonal Relationships, and Mental Health Care*. New York: Peter Lang.

———. 2000b. *Resurrecting the Person: Friendship and the Care of People with Mental Health Problems*. Nashville: Abingdon.

———. 2003. "The Body of Christ Has Down's Syndrome: Theological Reflections on Vulnerability, Disability, and Graceful Communities." *Journal of Pastoral Theology* 13, no. 2: 66–78.

———. 2016. *Becoming Friends of Time: Disability, Timefullness, and Gentle Discipleship*. Waco, Tex.: Baylor University Press.

———. 2020. *Finding Jesus in the Storm: The Spiritual Lives of Christians with Mental Health Challenges*. Grand Rapids: Eerdmans.

Swinton, John, and Jean Vanier. 2014. "A Place to Belong—Understanding and Being alongside People with Mental Health Problems." In *Mental Health: The Inclusive Church Resource*, 53–102. London: Darton, Longman & Todd.

Young, Frances, ed. 1997. *Encounter with Mystery: Reflections on L'Arche and Living with Disability*. London: Darton, Longman & Todd.

15

Peace

Medi Ann Volpe

Where does peace come into John Swinton's work? Everywhere. Even though it isn't a prominent theme, all of what John does is deeply irenic. That's not because he's interested in peace; it is because he's interested in *Jesus*. All the strands of peacefulness, gentleness, patience, and timefullness in John's work meet in the person of Jesus. The connection between Jesus and peace, however, needs some teasing out. While my main interlocutors in what follows are St. Paul and St. Augustine, John Swinton has shaped the lens through which I read them both.[1]

To draw out the connection between Jesus and peace, which I find woven throughout John's work, I consider how and why St. Paul can write that "[Jesus] is our peace" (Eph 2:14). There, Paul is writing to gentiles, who were alienated, hopeless strangers, to remind them of the good news.

> But now in Christ Jesus you who once were far off have been brought near in the blood of Christ. For he is our peace, who has made us both one, and has broken down the dividing wall of hostility, by abolishing in his flesh the law of commandments and ordinances, that he might create in himself one new man in place of the two so making peace and might reconcile us both to God in one body through the cross, thereby bringing the hostility to an end. And he came and preached peace to those who were far off and peace to those who were near; for through him we have access in one Spirit to the Father. (Eph 2:13–18, RSV)

[1]   In fact, without Swinton 2016, I never would have considered writing about Augustine. Because I found John's reliance on secondary sources so frustrating, I returned to *Confessions* and began reading it anew, with John's then-new book alongside it. See https://syndicate.network/symposia/theology/becoming-friends-time/.

Paul uses the word *peace* in three different ways. First, peace is something that Jesus is. Second, peace is something that Jesus makes. And third, peace is something that Jesus preached. The passage also tells us something about the content of peace (especially as it is preached): the ending of enmity and the restoration of access through one Spirit to the Father.

A series of questions emerge from this passage. First, what does it mean to say that Jesus "is our peace"? We think of peace as a state of affairs, the cessation of hostilities, perhaps, or an inner attitude of calm repose—and we're not wrong. But the state of affairs called "peace," whether that peace is political, cosmic, or "inner" peace, consists in a person. To see why, we need to go back to the beginning, to the doctrine of creation. Creation comes into being out of nothing, which is to say, from God alone, who is eternal peace. Second, if Jesus *is* peace, and the creation has its origin and *telos* in peace, then how can it also be the case that Jesus *makes* peace? How *can* Jesus make something that already exists and cannot be destroyed?

The final question for us is about the preaching of peace. How did Jesus preach peace, and how do we continue to preach peace? We live and tell the story of Jesus' peace-making. The story also implies a way of being in the world. Because Jesus *is* peace, *makes* peace, and *preaches* peace (now by his body, the church), the way to becoming people of peace is by following Jesus. These three questions structure the chapter, and I take each of them in turn.

IN THE BEGINNING

"In the beginning, God created the heavens and the earth": so Genesis 1 recounts the start of everything that is (see, for example, Oliver 2017, 7–59, and Anderson 2018). The Gospel according to John opens with an echo of Genesis: "In the beginning was the Word, and the Word was with God, and the Word was God. He was in the beginning with God and all things were made through him, and without him was not anything made that was made" (John 1:1–2, RSV).[2] When we talk about creation, we use relational terms involving space and time. But to talk about God "apart from" creation or "before" creation is not quite right. That would give the impression that God exists as we do, just in a much bigger space and a much longer time. Since we employ spatial and temporal terms in talking about God, we need to be clear at the outset about their limitations. Augustine explains nicely why "before" won't do, and his reasoning

---

[2]   This theme runs through the Bible from Genesis to the Gospel according to John. See, for example, Ps 32 [33]:6, etc.

applies to the spatial terms as well. Augustine suggests that the person who "is astonished that you, all powerful, all creating, and all sustaining God, artificer of heaven and earth, abstained for unnumbered ages from this work before you actually made it," should "wake up and take note that his surprise rests on a mistake." He explains:

> How would innumerable ages pass, which you yourself had not made? You are the originator and creator of all ages. What times existed which were not brought into being by you: or how could they pass if they never had existence? Since, therefore, you are the cause of all times, if any time had existed before you made heaven and earth, how can anyone say that you abstained from working. You have made time itself. Time could not elapse before you made time. But if time did not exist before heaven and earth, why do people ask what you were doing? There was no "then" when there was no time. (*Confessions* X.xiii.15)

However we think about God behind the curtain of creation, we must not think about God as existing in time. The same is true of space. We think of space as vast and populated by celestial bodies separated by immense distances. We describe what's between those distances as "nothing" and imagine that's what there was before God created it. But the nothing between all the somethings is coeval with the things. Before God created the heavens and the earth, the space between them did not exist, either. Only *in* creation do we talk about space and time. God is no-place, no-time, and God is all there is. Because God is all there is, and God is One, in the beginning there was peace.

So when we talk about creation ex nihilo, we might just as easily call it creation *in pacem*. God created the heavens and the earth without subduing some primordial enemy, and without imposing form on a substance that existed before God created it. It ought to go without saying that God has no rivals or competitors: nothing in creation can challenge God. The heart of creation is peace, and this peace is God. John 1 and Colossians 1 add some detail to this picture: everything is created through the Word (Logos) of God (John 1:3). In Colossians, St. Paul elaborates: "In him all things were created, in heaven and on earth, visible and invisible, whether thrones or dominions or principalities or authorities—all things were created through him and for him. He is before all things, and in him all things hold together" (1:16–17; see also 1:18, "He is the beginning"). The one who is peace is also the one above all the created powers, and the one who holds all things together; all things were created through the one who is peace, *for* the one who is peace. The one who is peace is also *logos*: the *reason* of creation is peace.

Two further things help to fill out this account of God's peace. The first has to do with the relationship between creator and creation. Augustine has explained for us why we needn't wonder about God's activity (or lack thereof, as it might seem to us) "before" creation; it's worth considering briefly the "where" question as it relates to God and creation. We use a lot of spatial terms in describing our relationship with God: God is "in" us; we are "in" God (in him we live and move and have our being, like fish in water); yet God transcends us—as high as the heavens are above the earth.[3] So where is God when God creates the heavens and the earth? Augustine warns, "Do not think of him being in the world in the same way as . . . trees, cattle, people are in the world." He explains:

> He did not make it, you see, in the way an artisan makes things. The chest an artisan makes is outside him and is in a different place from him while it is being fashioned . . . But God is present in the world he is fashioning, he does not stand aside from it and handle the matter he is working on, so to say, from the outside. He makes what he makes by the presence of his majesty; by his presence he governs what he has made. (*Tractates on John* 2.10).

So God is entirely, continuously making and holding the world together from the inside; the organizing principle of creation is God, who is peace. It follows that creation is dependent on God moment by moment, for its existence and its shape. For us human creatures, this is humbling news: we're not the creator, totally not in charge of anything, and, when it comes down to it, we're absolutely unnecessary (Swinton 2012, 161–65). "Human beings," as John reminds us, "are creatures who are wholly dependent on God" (Swinton 2012, 161). This is also great news, because it means that creatures "can never be defined by the job of meeting God's needs" (Williams 2000, 275).

The second point has to do with evil.[4] Whatever evil is, it cannot destroy the peace of creation, because creation is made in peace, for peace, and is held together continuously by peace. That's why Augustine says, somewhat audaciously to our ears, "For you evil does not exist at all, and not only for you but for your created universe, because there is nothing outside it which could break in and destroy the order which

---

[3]   See Isa 55 and Ps 102 [103], for example.

[4]   Deeper engagement with classical Christian teaching on evil would have bolstered the definition of evil in Swinton 2007.

you have imposed on it" (*Confessions* VII.xiii.19). However tangible and tragic the effects of evil may be, the only way properly to speak of evil is as a privation of good. Creation should be always at peace. The sabbath rest that John talks about in *Becoming Friends of Time* happens when God's majestic, peaceful presence governs us: "Sabbath is not only a day; it is a way of being within creation, a way of living time*fully* and faith*fully* with God" (Swinton 2016, 77–81; quotation 80). Why we do not submit to the yoke of the gentle, peaceful One is a mystery.

This all begs the question why creation doesn't exist in perfect peace. Nobody knows why God created human beings with the ability to resist the gentle government of the peaceful One in our souls. But I want to offer something I've found very suggestive for thinking about the fall and all the human sin that has been committed in its wake. Bill McKibben, looking at the vast and wonderful array of life on our planet, observes that

> the most curious of all those lives are the human ones, *because we can destroy, but also because we can decide not to destroy.* The turtle does what she does, and magnificently. She can't not do it, though, any more than the beaver can decide to take a break from building dams or the bee from making honey. But if the bird's special gift is flight, ours is the possibility of restraint. We're the only creature who can decide *not* to do something we're capable of doing. That's our superpower, even if we exercise it too rarely. (McKibben 2019, 255; emphasis in the original)

I wonder whether we might think about the commandment not to eat of that one tree as offering human beings the opportunity to exercise our superpower. Slowing down is one way do to just that (see Swinton 2016, 80–83). We could go faster and achieve more, and we live in a culture that seems to think the worst sin is not to do all we can as well as we can possibly do it. Slowing down requires being okay with untapped potential. I know something about that: I have a teenager whose innate athletic ability I recognized when he was a toddler; when he was a preschooler, it became clear that he was musically gifted. He has a wonderful ear and a lovely singing voice. But he doesn't sing, he doesn't play, and he doesn't do any sports. I said to him once that he was a bundle of untapped potential. Is that such a bad thing, though? In our achievement-obsessed world, every talent ought to be honed, perfected, and showcased. What if not developing every one of our talents is the modern analog for leaving that forbidden fruit untasted?

FROM RESTLESSNESS TO PEACE

If Jesus *is* peace, and creation's beginning and organizing principle is peace, then how can it also be the case that Jesus *makes* peace? In the first place, Jesus makes peace between human beings; second, he makes peace between human beings and God.[5] The movement from enmity to peace mirrors an internal transformation from restlessness to peace, a transformation Augustine traces in *Confessions*. He opens with theological anthropology.

> Man, a little piece of your creation, desires to praise you, a human being "bearing his mortality with him" (2 Cor 4:10), carrying with him the witness of his sin and the witness that you "resist the proud" (1 Pet 5:5). Nevertheless, to praise you is the desire of man, a little piece of your creation. You stir man to take pleasure in praising you, because you have made us for yourself, and our heart is restless until it rests in you. (*Confessions* I.1)

Augustine echoes Colossians 1: creation is made "for him"—that is, the Word of God, the Son of God, the one who is our peace. And he reminds us creatures who we are: "a little piece of you creation"; mortal and sinful. Human beings, Augustine asserts, "desire to praise [God]." This is the proper orientation for human creatures, but it no longer comes naturally as it ought. Never mind; God stirs us, little pieces of God's creation, to take pleasure in praising God. It seems that's the only cure for our restless heart; only God can stir the desire. "You touched me," Augustine writes in Book X, "and I am set on fire to attain the peace which is yours" (X.xxvii.38).

This movement from restlessness to peace must be set in the context of the account of creation I outline above. Because God is transcendent—wholly other, and not another "thing" among created things—God doesn't compete with anything. Every created thing has its nature. Most of creation grows unwaveringly toward its end and need only worry about disruption from outside. So an acorn grows into an oak tree—never an ash or a maple—given the right conditions, and provided the acorn isn't eaten by a squirrel, or the seedling browsed by a deer. God gives every creature—continuously—the power to perfect its nature; every creature, including human creatures. It isn't a giant leap to the conclusion that God stirs human creatures to praise God because resting in God is the perfection of our nature. It follows that God's will

---

[5]   There definitely remains a question about peace and the rest of creation, which St. Paul describes as "groaning" and which seems to me to be suffering because of humans' lack of restraint. But I haven't the space to get into that here!

is never in competition with our will because God wills for us what is best for us. When we stray, it is because our will deviates from its *natural* orientation—which is to adhere to God's will and grow toward the perfection of our nature.

To map this path toward rest in God, I turn to Augustine; my warrant for doing so comes from Book XIII of his *Confessions*.

> Of [the Holy Spirit] alone is it said that he is your "gift" (Acts 2:38).

> In your gift we find our rest. There you are our joy. Our rest is our peace.

> Love lifts us there, and "your good Spirit" (Ps 142:10) exalts "our humble estate from the gates of death" (Pss 9, 15). In a good will is our peace. A body by its weight tends to move towards its proper place. The weight's movement is not necessarily downwards, but to its appropriate position: fire tends to move upwards, a stone downwards. They are acted on by their respective weights; they seek their own place. Things which are not in their intended position are restless. Once they are in their ordered position, they are at rest.

> My weight is my love. Wherever I am carried, my love is carrying me. By your gift we are set on fire and carried upwards: we grow red hot and ascend . . . Lit by your fire, your good fire, we grow red-hot and ascend, as we move upwards "to the peace of Jerusalem" (Ps 121:6).

Augustine suggests at the very beginning of *Confessions* that the restless heart finds rest only in God; in the final paragraphs, he returns to this language, making explicit the connection I have assumed in the last few pages: "Our rest is our peace." The heart is restless because it has not been in its "ordered position"—the "natural" place God created it to occupy. By the Spirit (in whom "we have access to the Father"), the restless heart is set on fire and carried "upwards 'to the peace of Jerusalem'" (XIII.xi.10). Let's trace a bit of the narrative as it unfolds between these two points.

In Book VII Augustine makes an important distinction.

> It is one thing from a wooded summit to catch a glimpse of the homeland of peace and not to find the way to it, but vainly to attempt the journey along an impracticable route surrounded by the ambushes and assaults of fugitive deserters with their chief, "the lion and the dragon" (Ps 90:13). It is another thing to hold on to the way that leads there, defended by the protection of the heavenly emperor. There no deserters from the heavenly army lie waiting to attack. For this way they hate like a torture. (VII.xxi.27)

This is a journey, and it runs through dangerous territory.[6] It's not the strong and courageous who make it, it seems. Those who make it are those who take refuge under "the protection of the heavenly emperor."

What might it look like to travel under this protection? Augustine speaks approvingly of Victorinus—an example of one who did not "disdain to learn from [Jesus, who is . . .] meek and humble of heart" and "was not ashamed to become the servant of your Christ, and an infant born at your font, to bow his head to the yoke of humility and to submit his forehead to the reproach of the cross" (VIII.ii.3). More could be said here, more evidence heaped up from *Confessions*, to show that the way from restlessness to peace is humility. I will restrict myself to a few lines. "To possess my God, the humble Jesus, I was not yet humble enough. I did not know what his weakness was meant to teach," Augustine writes. In retrospect, he sees more clearly.

> Your Word, eternal truth . . . raises those submissive to him to himself . . . They are no longer to place confidence in themselves, but rather to become weak. They see at their feet divinity become weak by his sharing in our "coat of skin" (Gen 3:21). In their weariness they fall prostrate before this divine weakness which rises and lifts them up. (VII.xvii.24)

Self-reliance takes a variety of forms, but I want to focus on one in particular here—for reasons which will become evident in the final section of the chapter—confidence in our own self-understanding. Augustine describes his state of mind before his conversion.

> I was in conflict with myself and was dissociated from myself. The dissociation came about against my will. Yet this was not a manifestation of the nature of an alien mind but the punishment suffered in my own mind. And so it was "not I" that brought this about "but sin which dwelt in me" [Rom 7:17–20], sin resulting from the punishment of a more freely chosen sin, because I was a son of Adam. (VIII.x.22)

Following his conversion, Augustine tries to untangle the knot that prevented him from giving himself to Jesus (as we might call it) for so long. "The nub of the problem," he observes, "was to reject my own will and to desire yours." The change came "in a moment," the moment when

---

[6]   "There are no safe paths in this part of the world," as Gandalf observes as the company prepares to enter Mirkwood in *The Hobbit*. In that story, also, it is not the strong and courageous who are chosen: strength and courage are given as needed along the way.

Augustine "submitted [his] neck to [the Lord's] easy yoke and [his] shoulders to [the Lord's] light burden" (IX.i.1). Augustine delights in the transformation but doesn't answer the questions he raises, including "where through so many years was my freedom of will?" (IX.x.1) Not for nothing does he admit, in Book X, "I find my own self hard to grasp,"[7] and add (a few pages later), with respect to his "state of mind" that "I know myself less well than I know you" (X.xxxvii.62; and see discussion below).

The unity of Augustine's mind, of his whole self, lies not in himself, but in God. In the next book, near the conclusion of his discussion of time, Augustine casts his scattered self on God's mercy, saying "see how my life is a distension in several directions. 'Your right hand upheld me' (Pss 17:36; 62:9)" and longing for the experience of being "not stretched out in distension but extended in reach" toward the things which are eternal.

> You are my eternal Father, but I am scattered in times whose order I do not understand. The storms of incoherent events tear to pieces my thoughts, the inmost entrails of my soul until that day when, purified and molten by the fire of your love, I flow together to merge into you. (XI.xxix.39)

It seems like I've strayed rather a long way from "making peace." But I haven't. Let me complete the passage from Colossians. After telling us that "in him all things hold together," St. Paul continues.

> He is the head of the body, the church; he is the beginning, the first-born from the dead, that in everything he might be pre-eminent. For in him all the fulness of God was pleased to dwell, and through him to reconcile to himself all things, whether on earth or in heaven, making peace by the blood of his cross.

> And you, who once were estranged and hostile in mind, doing evil deeds, he has now reconciled in his body of flesh by his death, in order to present you holy and blameless and irreproachable before him, provided that you continue in the faith, stable and steadfast, not shifting from the hope of the gospel which you heard. (Col 1:18–23, RSV)

Jesus opens up a way of being in the world that is at once new—having created "one new man in place of the two"—and perfectly consonant with the peace in which creation came into being and toward which it

---

[7]   I am leaving aside here the question whether this difficulty has to   ʼth
understanding memory in particular; to the extent that the question he ask
IX about the hidden location of his free will is about memory, this obse
Book X is about himself, not just his memory.

tends (see Ayres 2009). Jesus makes peace by restoring humanity and the rest of creation to its "intended position": at rest in God. People are created to share God's peace; sin blocks our participation in and reception of that peace; Jesus removes the obstacle and restores us to communion with God.

Jesus, the Incarnate Logos of God, is the peace-principle of the cosmos: "in him all things hold together"; he is thus the principle that holds each of us together. This is important, in a world that values keeping it all together and curating "it"—our whole selves, our histories—in a kind of ongoing autobiographical performance. The advice to "be yourself" presupposes a firm grasp on the self and requires us to remain in character as we play the role of ourselves in the drama of our lives. This is a tough task for us since we are scripting it—or so it seems—as we go. But if Jesus is the Logos of everything, including each of us, then our lives unfold differently. The integrity of our self-identity comes not from our careful crafting of our stories but security in Christ. The fractured self is not fractured in Christ, however broken and scattered it may seem to us. As John Swinton explains:

> Human beings' value and their identity are held and assured by the God who created them, who inspired them with God's *nephesh*, who sustains them in the power of the Holy Spirit, and who continues to offer the gift of life and relationship to all of humanity. (Swinton 2012, 185)

So we can see why Augustine writes, "I find no safe place for my soul except in you" (*Confessions* X.xl.65). Something else happens, though, when we let our souls rest in Jesus: Jesus takes up residence and comes to rest in our souls (see John 15:5 and Rev 3:20). John tells the story of a L'Arche core member who went to see the cardiologist.

> One of his friends asked him where he had been. "To see the doctor," replied Danny. "And what did the doctor do?" his friend asked. Danny replied, "He looked into my heart." His friend smiled. "And what did he see there, Danny?" Danny paused and looked intently at his friend. "He saw Jesus," replied Danny. "And what was Jesus doing?" Danny paused, smiled and looked away. Then he said, "He was resting." (Swinton 2016, 80)

Just like that. Jesus was resting in Danny's heart. When the heart finds its safe place in Jesus, the heart sees Jesus at rest there. What this means for us is perfect freedom, perfect peace. "The pure heart enjoys absolute concord and unity in the unshakeable peace of holy spirits, the citizens of your city in the heavens above the visible heavens" (Augustine, *Confessions* XII.xi.12). When the peace of God—Jesus!—comes to rest in our hearts, then we enter into that peace for which we were created. This is the peace of the Logos of God; this is the way of being in the world for which human beings are made. Our hearts are restless until Jesus rests in them.

For most of us, however, it is not so simple. Few of us with the usual number of chromosomes and a typically functioning brain would recount a trip to the cardiologist in the way that Danny did. Watching over the technician's shoulder as my daughter's heart was examined—she, too, lives with an extra copy of chromosome 21 and has heart trouble—I saw the movement of the heart, and the shifting of oxygen-poor blood through one side and out; on the other side, the oxygenated blood flows in and is pumped out to the body. When my daughter was a small baby, holes between the atria and ventricles allowed the blood to slosh back and forth, mixing oxygen-poor blood with freshly oxygenated blood. I was amazed at her little body's capacity to cope with that for the first four months of her life. Then she had surgery. The cardiothoracic surgeon opened up that tiny heart and fixed it, as best he could. (That was the first of three surgeries she would have by the time she was six.) And though I am certain that Jesus is resting in my daughter's heart (she knows God: he's the one who is "bounding in love"!), neither I nor any of the professionals who examined her have seen him there. This, I submit, is a failure of imagination: it is not that Danny sees something that isn't there; it's that we do not perceive what *is* there. For us to see Jesus resting in our hearts, we need to learn a new way of being in the world: the way of peace, "living trustfully, patiently, and gently" (Swinton 2018, 103).

LIVING PEACEFULLY IN 'THE TIME THAT IS GIVEN US'

The essence of practicing peace is humility. I want to note at the outset, however, that those who have already been humbled by station or situation have less need of this instruction; hence Jesus insists that unless his followers turn again and become like little children, they will not enter into the kingdom of heaven. All speculation about the specific childlike trait(s) Jesus might have in mind can be swept aside. Children have only one real advantage in the economy I have been describing: they have no choice but to be humble. In Matthew 18, little children are *being brought* to Jesus to be blessed (one ought to be reminded of the paralytic, who is the only grown-up to be brought to Jesus). These are the members of society, often forgotten in theology, who have no choice but to trust;[8] they are not autonomous or self-sufficient, and their autobiographical self is nascent at best. If people with disabilities point us to a peaceful way of being in the world, it is at least in part because of the social location they share with these "little ones." The way of peace woven through John Swinton's theological work depends upon humility that is instinctual, humility that becomes the visceral response of the follower of Jesus.

In what follows, I want to explore the humility that Jesus displayed and which grounds our practice of Christian life. John writes in *Becoming Friends of Time*:

> If we are to have the same attitude as Christ, we need to allow God's time to come upon us; we cannot assist it; all we can do is receive it. As it is received, we are allowed to enter into a quite different relationship with time. To be humble, contingent, obedient and faithful requires that we inhabit God's time in ways that match the nature of the time within which we live . . . To try to master time is to try to master Jesus, and that can never end well. When we try to master time, violence becomes inevitable. (Swinton 2016, 64)

Before I begin to unfold the characteristics of peaceful being, I need to be reminded what "the same attitude as Christ" entails; I need to reread Philippians 2 (RSV).

> So if there is any encouragement in Christ, any incentive of love, any participation in the Spirit, any affection and sympathy, complete my joy by being of the same mind, having the same love, being in full accord and of one mind. Do nothing from selfishness or conceit, but in humility count others better than yourselves. Let each of you look not only to his own interests, but also to the interests of others. Have this mind among yourselves, which is yours in Christ Jesus, who, though he was in the form of God, did not count equality with God a thing to be grasped, but emptied himself, taking the form of a servant, being born in the likeness of men. And being found in human form he humbled himself and became obedient unto death, even death on a cross.

This is the attitude of the one who is our peace: humility. Not only that: remember humans' superpower? Earlier I called it restraint; in Philippians 2 we find it as "not grasping." The Word of God, equal with God, did the ultimate feat of self-restraint: the power that made the universe took the form of "a little piece of . . . creation," adopting the littleness and mortality that go with it. Restraint doesn't just mean not sinning—though it does of course mean that—it means, for example, not insisting on our rights, and allowing for untapped potential, as I describe above. God commands landowners to leave some fruit on the vine, some corn in the fields. Not taking all that we might claim as ours is exactly parallel to not counting equality with God a thing to be grasped.

This is the example that Christ gives us; having "the same attitude as Christ" means, above all, humility. But why does being humble require "that we inhabit God's time"? Accepting our finitude is essential to the humility appropriate to creaturehood, a humility deeper and more pervasive than most feeble practices of Christianity reflect. The human longing to be in another time and place, away from peril and pain, natural as it is, is also always a temptation. To lament, as Frodo does, "I wish it need not have happened in my time," is common enough. Gandalf is sympathetic and wise, as usual: "So do I . . . and so do all who live to see such times. But that is not for them to decide. All we have to do is to decide what to do with the time that is given us" (Tolkien 1966a, 60). None of us is a time lord. That title belongs to the creator of time.

Part of learning to "inhabit God's time" is receiving time as a gift. Time—this present moment and all the moments stretching out behind us and before us—"is *given* us." The way of being in the world suggested by Danny's visit to the cardiologist, "a way of being in the world without anxiety," is made possible by casting off time as a burden and receiving it as a gift (See Swinton 2016, 78–79; and Matt 11:28–30). In this way of being in the world, we can take the time to listen. The refusal to take time is prevalent in a world that often communicates on social media; it is difficult to envision a more impatient form of exchange than the one that limits the would-be "speaker" to 280 characters. And the whole array of similar forms of social exchange falls into the problem Stanley Hauerwas says besets academics: the inability to listen, and the tendency instead to predict what other people are going to say and respond to our own preconceived notions rather than what our interlocutors said (Hauerwas 2018). All this serves to distort our differences, either erasing them (in the case of people whom we believe to be "like us") or raising them to insurmountable obstacles (in the case of people whom we believe to be opposed to us). The former we count our friends, and the latter we come to regard as enemies. There is very little middle ground. But when we receive time from God, we discover that

patience creates the time necessary for people to come to reconciliation and knowledge of one another . . . We have all the time we need
in a world that doesn't think it's got much time at all to draw on God's
love, to enact that love, that the world might see what it means to be
chosen by God. (Swinton 2012, 252)[9]

We might think that overcoming enmity depends upon forgiveness, or at
least forbearance, and this is probably right. But we should not underes-
timate the role of taking time.

The stone we stumble over as we try to accept "the time that is
given us" is that we want to tell our own stories, we want to decide what
time is for. But we've already seen that time is that dimension in which
God perfects creation. We are not the authors of that story: God is.[10]
Yet our stories each have a place within the story of the redemption of
the world—indeed all our moments (De Caussade 1921). Accepting our
place in the story requires—once again, we find—humility.

Returning to "the time that is given us" in *The Fellowship of the Ring*,
we find two competing stories. Let's hear the story that Frodo wants to
hear. Wants to hear, yes, because he would rather be hearing about the
downfall of Sauron than living in "such times." Upon hearing that "Bilbo
was *meant* to find the Ring, and *not* by its maker. In which case you
also were *meant* to have it. And that may be an encouraging thought,"
Frodo replies, "It is not" (Tolkien 1966a, 65). He would rather not be a
character—and certainly not the protagonist—in the story of the One
Ring in the Third Age of Middle Earth. Finding himself implicated in the
story despite his protestations, Frodo wishes to make an adjustment or
two to the narrative. Most notably, he would rather have a story in which
Bilbo had dispatched the creature, Gollum, by whose agency Sauron discovered that the Ring was in the Shire, in the possession of a Baggins.
"But this is terrible!" Frodo exclaims—the situation is worse than Frodo's
worst-case scenario. "What am I to do?" he laments; then immediately
wishes the story were different. "What a pity that Bilbo did not stab that
vile creature, when he had a chance!" Gandalf's response to this comes
into the unfolding story, which we will hear below. Frodo laments again:
"Even if Bilbo could not kill Gollum, I wish he had not kept the Ring. I
wish he had never found it, and that I had not got it!"[11] That is as much
as to say: I do not wish to be in this story!

---

[9]   Swinton is quoting an unpublished paper by Stanley Hauerwas.
[10]   See, e.g., Swinton 2012, 164. This is an observation that John makes more
than once.
[11]   Tolkien 1966a, 69.

Yet Frodo begins to accept "the time that has been given [him]": "I do really wish to destroy it . . . Or, well, to have it destroyed. I am not made for perilous quests. I wish I had never seen the Ring! Why did it come to me? Why was I chosen?" Of course Gandalf has no answers to these questions, and his reassurance is not very reassuring. "You may be sure that it was not for any merit that others do not possess: not for power or wisdom, at any rate. But you have been chosen, and you must therefore use such strength and heart and wits as you have" (Tolkien 1966a, 70). In Frodo's final attempt to alter the story, he asks Gandalf to take the Ring, which Gandalf will not do. Frodo would very much like to hear some story about the Ring and its fate that did not involve him in danger, nor threaten the Shire. His choices of alteration would, however, have spelled disaster for the story as it unfolded with him in the midst of it.

Frodo considered it "a pity that Bilbo did not stab that vile crea-ture," Gollum. Gandalf's response suggests something about why Bilbo might have been *meant* to find the Ring. "Pity? It was pity that stayed his hand. Pity, and Mercy: not to strike without need. And he has been well rewarded, Frodo. Be sure that he took so little hurt from the evil, and escaped in the end, because he began his ownership of the Ring so. With Pity" (Tolkien 1966a, 68–69). Gandalf adds, "My heart tells me that he has some part to play yet, for good or ill, before the end." Gandalf allows the story of the Ring to unfold: "Even the very wise," he observes, "cannot see all ends" (Tolkien 1966a, 69). Gollum did indeed have a part to play. Frodo's revision of the narrative—writing Gollum out of it, that is—would have ruined everything.

The second point I want to make is about Frodo's place in the story. He only finds his place in the story when he is well into the middle of it. Sam observes that "we shouldn't be here [a place with a wicked feeling about it] at all, if we'd known more about it before we started" (Tolk-ien 1966c, 320). He goes on to compare their situation with the stories about "wonderful folk"—like Frodo and Sam, they did not go looking for adventure; "that's not the way of it with the tales that really mattered, or the ones that stay in the mind. Folks seem to have been just landed in them, usually—their paths were laid that way, as you put it" (Tolkien 1966c, 321). Not only that, but the characters in the stories, like Sam and Frodo, had many chances to turn back—to get out of the story, as it were—but they didn't. Some of the stories Sam has in mind (which may be found in *The Silmarillion*) did not have a happy ending; "I wonder what sort of a tale we've fallen into?" he wonders. We are all, like Sam and Frodo, in the middle of stories, and we don't know how they'll turn out.

But that is not all. As Sam recounts a part of one of the stories, he realizes something. "We've got—you've got some of the light of [the Silmaril] in that star-glass that the Lady [Galadriel] gave you! It's still going on. Don't the great tales never end?" Frodo agrees that they do not, not "as tales . . . But the people in them come, and go when their part's ended. Our part will end later—or sooner" (Tolkien 1966c, 321). Sam and Frodo find their place in a much larger narrative—in fact, in a narrative that encompasses the whole tale of *The Lord of the Rings* and stretches back to the foundation of Middle Earth.

The story of redemption is like that. Although we do not know, any more than Frodo and Sam did, whether we will come "to a good end," those who believe in the gospel know how the story ends: "When all things are subjected to Him, then the Son Himself will also be subjected to the One who subjected all things to Him, so that God may be all in all" (1 Cor 15:28 NASB). Stanley Hauerwas is fond of reminding us that folks in the modern world like to think that we have no story except the story we gave ourselves when we had no story, and of explaining why this is nonsense (Hauerwas 2018). It *is* nonsense, but for people who have difficulty telling their own stories, it is dangerous nonsense. If "personhood is defined in terms of a capacity for self-awareness, identity, continuity of thinking, a sense of self over time, consciousness, and above all, memory" (Swinton 2012, 123), to lack the capacity to tell your story is to be a defective human. Not only that; if a judgment is made before you're born that you might not develop that capacity, you might not be born at all. Dangerous nonsense indeed, as John explains in *Becoming Friends of Time* (Swinton 2016, 35–53).

The good news is that God's peace, which is before all things and in all things, has come to us in Jesus. In Jesus the grace and peace of God comes to oppose the dangerous nonsense that threatens the weakest and most vulnerable members of society. Jesus is our peace: in him and through him, our hearts find the way to their "intended position" at rest in God.

WORKS CITED

Anderson, Gary. 2018. "*Creatio ex nihilo* and the Bible." In *Creation* ex nihilo: *Origins, Development, Contemporary Challenges*, edited by Gary Anderson and Markus Bockmuehl, 15–35. Notre Dame, Ind.: University of Notre Dame Press.

Augustine. 1989. *Tractates on John*. Translated by John W. Rettig. Washington, D.C.: Catholic University of America Press.

———. 1992. *Confessions*. Translated by Henry Chadwick. Oxford: Oxford University Press.

Ayres, Lewis. 2009. "Into the Poem of the Universe: *Exempla*, Conversion, Church in Augustine's *Confessions*." *Zeitschrift für Antikes Christentum* 13, no. 2: 263–81.

De Caussade, Jean. 1921. *Abandonment to Divine Providence*. Translated by H. Ramiere. Exeter: Catholic Records Press.

Hauerwas, Stanley. 2018. "The Politics of Gentleness." In *Living Gently in a Violent World: The Prophetic Witness of Weakness*, by Stanley Hauerwas and Jean Vanier, 55–76. Downers Grove, Ill.: IVP Books.

McKibben, Bill. 2019. *Falter: Has the Human Game Begun to Play Itself Out?* London: Wildfire/Hachette.

Oliver, Simon. 2017. *Creation: A Guide for the Perplexed*. London: Bloomsbury.

Swinton, John. 2007. *Raging with Compassion: Pastoral Responses to the Problem of Evil*. Grand Rapids: Eerdmans.

———. 2012. *Dementia: Living in the Memories of God*. Grand Rapids: Eerdmans.

———. 2016. *Becoming Friends of Time: Disability, Timefullness, and Gentle Discipleship*. Waco, Tex.: Baylor University Press.

———. 2018. "Conclusion: L'Arche as a Peace Movement." In Stanley Hauerwas and Jean Vanier, *Living Gently in a Violent World: The Prophetic Witness of Weakness*, 77–80. Downers Grove, Ill.: IVP Books.

Tolkien, J. R. R. 1966a. *The Fellowship of the Ring*. London: Allen & Unwin.

———. 1966b. *The Hobbit*. New York: Ballantine.

———. 1966c. *The Two Towers*. London: Allen & Unwin.

Williams, Rowan. 2000. *On Christian Theology*. Oxford: Blackwell.

Afterword

On Following Jesus into the Shadows

Brian Brock

It is not easy to write about a friend. Put more directly, it is hard for me to write about someone who taught me what it means to be a friend, who slowly and gently made a friend out of me. What makes it hard is that there is too much to say. Anytime something or someone is right up close in our field of vision, description becomes harder. There's too much detail, too much going on, and we are implicated. This makes it all too easy to fall into describing the thing or person before us with the wrong words, the easy words, the words everyone else uses for them. Sometimes being too close to the particularities of our lives traps us. But if we are given different words, better words, they can help us to see things and situations anew, and so to act differently toward them. New and better words can unveil marvelous unseen richness. The essays in this volume are an eloquent testimony of how many of us have experienced John's life and work as leading us to that richness. The richness, that John sees in the world and the church, is finally the work of a living and active Jesus.

I take the richness of the chapters in this volume as a sign of the importance and fertility of John's work, as well as a drawing attention to the witness embodied in the unique way he wears the mantle of the academic. This afterword is an attempt to draw some of that richness together in one place, by picking out a few connections between the different facets of John's work and life recounted by the authors of this volume that, when combined, might reveal one or two new facets of the complex person most people know as the eminent Reverend Professor John Swinton.

I've been blessed to know a few more sides of John than most people. (I am not sure I would call it a blessing to have discovered that at home

John "dresses down" from what he wears to work, which those who know what he wears to the office probably won't believe. The man does like to be comfortable, and who can blame him?) In the last few years, we've fallen into the delightful habit of occasionally meeting up after work for a pint (or two) and a curry. Knowing I needed to write this chapter but not having the slightest idea where to begin, I decided to surprise John by showing up for one evening out with my audio recorder. "I can't tell you what this is for," I told him, "I just have to write something about you, and I don't want to take notes." I take it as a sign of a long-built trust that, despite not knowing what I was going to use his answers for, he trusted me enough to let me ask him about his life, his faith, his theology, and his view of his impact in the academy. John also gave me permission to use his comments in what I was writing. After a little tag-team transcription with my wife, Stephanie, I was delighted and a little bit envious to discover that even when John has had a pint (or two), his thoughts came out with sparkling clarity. His self-descriptions also converged in remarkable and illuminating ways with the many insights presented by the contributors to this volume, who have clearly found his work rewarding enough that they have studied it in sufficient depth to genuinely understand his theological impulses.

I will not attempt a comprehensive overview of the chapters in this volume. Instead, I offer a bricolage construction tracing out points of thematic convergence between the chapters in this volume and John's own self-description as he saw it one fine September evening in Aberdeen in 2021. As there is as yet very little secondary literature specifically devoted to John's corpus of writing—despite his very broad influence on a wide range of discussions in several fields—I also hope this afterword might offer a few guideposts for future readers and scholars who want to understand the continuity of John's work as a whole. For me, gleaning some insights from the chapters of this volume is a gift, giving me a way to acknowledge a character whose stature has loomed impressively large in the professional and intellectual landscapes I've been privileged to live within for the last fifteen years of my life.

INTEGRATING THE THEOLOGICAL AND PASTORAL

A scholarly consensus is already emerging that John's most visible contribution to practical theology in general, and disability theology in particular, is his closing the gap between systematic and practical theology. As Bill Gaventa highlights in his chapter, John has let us see what it looks like to bring theological and pastoral reasoning together. Over the last fifty years, the division between systematic theology and pastoral theology has continuously widened. Practical theologians, activists, and practitioners almost never talked constructively to one another, let alone engaged constructively to delve into the real-life problems of Christians (205).

When I asked John how he might characterize his scholarly contribution his answer paralleled Gaventa's assessment.

> The questions that I ask of the tradition come from my experience in nursing and chaplaincy. I came into academia with a certain set of questions that seemed to have opened up space for discussion in areas that weren't being discussed before. There is plenty of discussion going on about dementia, for example, but it tends to be either overly pastoral or overly theological in the sense of types of theology that most people can't associate with. It's not that theology is wrong or that there's anything wrong with the theology, it's just the way that it's communicated. And I think probably one of my contributions is to take complicated theological ideas and communicate them in a broad way so that people can get to the heart of what is being said and to begin to think differently in the light of the language of theology. So with something like dementia, much of what you can find on that topic is either overly theological or overly pastoral, and I've maybe helped to join these two things together by showing the way that theology and pastoral practice are inexplicably intertwined. I don't think I've democratized theology, but I think I've made it accessible to people that couldn't access it before.

This impulse was not one that John invented but learned from his teachers, most influentially the Irish practical theologian and ethicist Stephen Pattison. It was from Pattison, John said, that he gained a political perspective on theology. A group of Edinburgh theologians were similarly formative during John's training in promoting a vision of practical theology beyond, as John likes to put it, "handy household hints for ministers." These include the practical theologians Duncan Forrester and William Storrar, the systematic theologian David Fergusson, the bioethicist-chaplain Alastair Campbell, and the missiologist David Lyon. Several of these figures had deeply shaped the field of practical theology in Britain in the 1970s and 1980s, so that, in John's words, "when I came into that field in the 90s when I left nursing, I think I resonated with them because there's a lot of connection between nursing and theology, or at least pastoral theology, and they were capturing some of these dynamics."

After John became an academic in his own right, colleagues in practical theology such as Elaine Graham continued to inspire John to further refine his methods as a practical theologian. But it was a new circle of theologians engaging with the theme of disability who were to shape his approach to the topics for which his work has become so well known: mental health, disability, dementia, friendship, and suffering. Some of these were theologians with disabilities themselves, such as the theologians Nancy Eiesland and John Hull, and others were theologians who had a special interest in disability, such as Hans Reinders and Stanley Hauerwas. It may have been from this last figure that John acquired what has become one of the sharpest tools in his already formidable toolbox: theological criticism as language critique.

CHANGING PRACTICES BY DEFAMILIARIZING LANGUAGE

If cultural values are embodied in language, then one of the most potent ways to invite alternative ways of living together is to challenge a widely accepted label. Grant Macaskill's chapter very helpfully traces why John's attentiveness to the implications of the labels we put on people is so central to the challenge he mounts to the value systems carried by those labels (80). To attend to labels as a domain of social ordering is a theologically crucial beginning point for practical theology, Michael Mawson points out, simply in revealing hegemonic secular descriptions of reality as open for discussion. Questioning commonly accepted labels is liberative and politically subversive resistance to the status quo because their power resides in their unquestioned status (151). Who could imagine, for instance, that some people don't consider being deaf a disability? (Deaf people have taught us that this can indeed be true.) Elahe Hessamfar's chapter puts living flesh on this theoretical insight. John's sensitivities to the dynamics of labeling people raised for her productive questions about what is entailed in accepting the medical labeling of her daughter as "schizophrenic." Simply asking this question allowed productive questions to emerge about how this label is connected to a medical system that regularly deploys unsettling violence toward the mentally ill, a violence that is intrinsic to it being involuntarily committed (177).

It is a significant contribution for Macaskill to provide us with such a subtle conceptual description of how John's theology springs from his attraction to situations in human life and society that are not satisfactorily described within the terms of current thinking (82–83). John constantly seeks ways to reshape contemporary practices by defamiliarizing commonly used language. When I asked him how he knows that some particular topic is one that he needs to write about, his answer helpfully confirmed and elaborated Macaskill's description of his mode of theological working.

If you take something like *Raging with Compassion*, it begins with an experience that I had whereby one of my neighbor's kids, who was twelve years old, was walking down the beach and just died. To this day nobody knows why. They were friends of ours, and I ended up ministering to them. It was my first funeral. It was a rough first funeral. Looking back, what I did at the service was full of mistakes. But the questions that were asked by the family at that time, "Why does this happen?" and "Where is God?" were very sharp, and very difficult. I didn't even try to answer them at the time, because I didn't have anything to say. The experience led me to think about *why* it is that I had nothing to say. And whether or not I had nothing to say was a good or a bad thing. That led me in turn to think about issues around theodicy and then to the realization that theodicy was a pretty hopeless and even dangerous endeavor. The thing that would have brought healing in that situation was prayer. I don't mean supernatural intervention, I mean the words that you speak, I mean the words of comfort, the words of hope, the words of possibility in an impossible situation. This took me into the psalms of lament. That's how that particular biblical book came into existence. Experience is not illustrative of the points I want to make in my books; it's not "here's a case study that illustrates a point," it's actually formative. Experience gives me the questions and the perspectives that I want to begin to explore. Likewise with a book like *Resurrecting the Person*, which comes directly out of my experience in chaplaincy. That experience led me to ask certain questions, which leads to different theological and practical outcomes. And I would say that was the case for all of my single author monographs.

To defamiliarize the labels that hold our lives in shape is a risky proposition, stripping us of comforting certainties, false though they may be. John nevertheless insists that theology venture into the zone that seems to contain nothing but questions nobody seems to be able to answer. If it is life and not our own intellectual or moral certainties that should shape theological questions, the crucial theological moments will be those in which we are confronted by questions that we normally do not see or actively suppress because they will raise questions about our most basic theological beliefs. Human beings cannot stand much reality.

Pain and disorientation are necessary gateways to new knowledge and can become generative when we allow that pain to provoke reconsideration of our beliefs. Only a theology willing to face the loss of old certainties can be alive, because theology that aims at nothing more than self-protection can only produce more of the same. It is a sign of the bravery embodied in John's work that he dares to ask questions that have the potential to dismember his certainties. The experiences that do not promise to demand transformation, which only solidifies our certainty that we know God and the world, are not of interest to John. He enacts a seeking of truth aware that reality is often hard and unyielding. But because the reality of human life is unyielding, if we let it in, it will transform us. This is why not shying away from pain allows thinking to become profound and alive. We might even put this more strongly. John displays a commitment to the neighbor that keeps theology living and growing, but only because it does not shy away from the angularity of real, present neighbors and their demands and problems.

Walking with open eyes into this twilight is as likely to produce frustration and disappointment as theological insight, as Aileen Barclay's story of living with her husband's dementia so eloquently displays (158). Barclay warns us, taking away what few words we feel we have in life passages in which we already have precious few words to describe what is going on seems tailor-made to make our failures feel more painful and obvious than whatever few fleeting successes we might encounter there (162). John clearly finds such a risky and potentially costly investigative strategy personally indispensable, and the chapters of this volume help us to understand why.

LOOKING FOR GOD IN THE SHADOWS

Marcia Webb's description of "God in the shadow" seems to grasp something essential (and previously unnoticed) about John's theological instincts (106–7, 110–11). We might describe John's mode of theological investigation in terms of a practice of looking in a concentrated way into the shadows cast by our thought schemas and lived experiences. John's working procedure suggests that he approaches these shadows as embodied refusals of peace and intimacy with God. "Stigma" is the secular label used to indicate that these refusals have become culturally elaborated. Stigma is aptly called a darkness or a shadow because to find oneself there is to discover oneself as having been given a social death sentence. In diving into these shadow zones, John understands himself to be following Jesus' resurrecting love into these zones of social death. His theology enacts a refusal of stigmatization that "resurrects the person" (as the title of one of his early works emphasized), but it can only do so by beginning with the battle with our own impulses to reject or ostracize everything or everyone who reminds us that this shadow zone exists—and that we are the ones who produce and sustain it.

Seeking God in the shadows with the stigmatized sounds like a description that many would apply to the life-project of Jean Vanier, as Hans Reinders and Christina Gangemi point out. Questions are thus raised about whether John is labeling some lives as especially shadowed by human sin. I would suggest that if we compare John's work with that of Vanier, the latter with all his now-obvious failures, we can better see what John's engagement with the shadows has refused. First, John has never presented his seeking God in the shadows as a method or principle, as Vanier and other theologies have sometimes done under a slogan like "Go to where disabled (or poor, or ostracized) people are, if you want to find God." For John, the example of Jesus propels us toward those who are ostracized. We do not find God in the shadows because we try to preserve our lives by staying away from the shadows. Despite the very understandable instincts for self-preservation that cause us to shun the shadows, the Jesus who has sought and found us leads us toward those who our society casts into the shadows of inattention.

Second, John has never taken up the Aristotelian virtue tradition which carries in its DNA the suggestion that a lifegiving individual exemplar or community is by definition something that others should emulate. This is important because it means that John's work has never been the expression of a strategy or a project. He has initiated many practical projects, some of which have failed, some of which have succeeded, though as regards the latter none spectacularly and in a way that might be held up as a "model community." John cares about community, but he is not the product of a "virtuous community." Rather, he has practiced a generative attentiveness, and it is through his attentiveness that God has invited us all into shadow zones very often avoided by Christians. Christina Gangemi articulates this point with great clarity: John ventures into the shadow zones of our social world not because there are people there who are especially weak or vulnerable (which they often are), but because Jesus' love reveals them to us as valuable (122, 125, 130).

THE VENTURE OF FAITHFULNESS

In the light of this account of John's propensity to look for God in the shadows, chapters 9 and 10 might be usefully read as exemplifications of how this theological procedure has been carried out in practice. Let us call them ventures in faithfulness catalyzed by John's inversion of the normal ways of configuring theological questions. Paralleling Aileen Barclay's sometimes grueling narrative of caring for a husband as he slowly becomes someone very hard indeed to love, Elahe Hessamfar articulates how her daughter Helia showed her "how difficult it was to love the unlovable, as God had loved us" (189). The shadows are populated by people who may be stigmatized because we have to change to love them well, or who have been contorted to become grating personalities in having to live for so long under the withering pressure of the excluding gaze. While Barclay's story offers a crucial reminder that venturing into these shadow domains may not end with a happy ending, the story of Hessamfar and Helia shows how a measure of healing and new life may indeed emerge as Christians venture faithfully patient presence to those consigned to the shadows.

Stephen Judd's chapter gives us a different angle on the new life that might emerge from such ventures in patient attentiveness. New institutional forms and cultures may be birthed when a collective sense is fostered that shadow zones must be seriously resisted. Judd's reflections on dementia also follow the track John has laid out. Our society says that people with dementia are "losing themselves" or "going away." John resists this labeling, insisting instead that right relationship with God is not based on our remembering God but God's faithfulness to *us*. John's emphasis on God's action and love liberates people facing frightening and uncomfortable life experiences to weather them with grace and practical care, rather than replaying the script that demands they gear up for the war against the existential threat that can be more violent against sufferers than the condition itself. It is ultimately our fear that leads us to build institutions in which people like Helia are drugged and forcibly restrained for hearing voices in their heads, or those who are losing their memories are euthanized. As Judd points out, these are examples of how theological insights not only can but in fact already have produced real institutional change by reconfiguring how carers understand what they are doing and who they are serving. When the object of care is changed, the alteration of the manner of carers in their approach to their work calls in turn for a reordering of institutions to better support the provision of such attentive care (197–98, 200–202).

THE GENTLENESS OF THE CARER

The scholarly community has not yet appreciated the full implications of the origins of John's work in the practices of nursing, social care, and chaplaincy. What most people notice upon meeting John, as Warren Kinghorn and Stanley Hauerwas point out, is that gentleness is one of the obvious and defining characteristics of his character. Kinghorn and Hauerwas observe in passing that within Western culture, gentleness has most often been considered a feminine virtue (263, 271), an insight which becomes more intriguing if linked to the reality that nursing has been a medical specialty overwhelmingly populated by women almost since its inception. There is a politics associated with the dominance of women investing in bodily care in the institutions of early- and late-modern medicine that is distinguishable from the drive to "fix" or "cure" often associated with the medical practices of medicine and surgery. The hint provided by Kinghorn and Hauerwas thus provokes further reflection on the connections between John's theological emphases and their roots in practical experiences in a medical field predominantly populated by women.

The presumption of patriarchal moral cultures that caring actually is an eternally feminine virtue obscures the more interesting truth that there may be a wisdom carried in caring professions clearly and explicitly organized around bodily caregiving. We can thank second-wave feminists for highlighting that feminism raises important ethical questions about who does the dishes and washes the clothes, and who cares for children or the elderly (Held 2003; Fine 2015; Noddings 2003; Nussbaum 2006, chaps. 2–3). These feminist thinkers developed a theoretical framework that allowed them to make sense of the wide range of human experiences that had been treated as inconsequential in traditional patriarchal societies. As Eva Feder Kittay observes:

> Dependents require care. . . . Questions of who takes on the responsibility of care, who does the hands-on care, who sees to it that caring is done and done well, and who provides the support for the relationship of care and for both parties to the caring relationship—these are social and political questions . . . How a social order organizes care of these needs is a matter of social justice. (Kittay 1999, 1)

There is a moral seriousness and hermeneutic of listening that is necessary for good hands-on care of dependent human beings, whether the sick in hospitals, children, or those with disabilities. John is a fellow traveler with these feminist ethicists in his acute awareness of the political import of taking this care seriously. From the beginning of his career as a mental-health nurse, he had literally hands-on experience of the difference in ethos between those who are simply providing a set of services to an individual "care user" and those whose investment goes deeper and so becomes a potent form of political engagement.

Kinghorn and Hauerwas describe L'Arche as "a modest proposal that the gentleness of Jesus is possible even in a violent world" (268). This formulation acknowledges that L'Arche exists as a counter-politics, an enclave ruled by gentleness amid a world outside its borders organized according to very different priorities. I want to propose that nursing be understood as a practice of gentleness carried out *within* the very institutions where people may be forcibly restrained or drugged, and where the language of "invasive surgery" and "the war on cancer" are common, even dominant discourses.

This is why it is profoundly important to notice, as Kinghorn and Hauerwas observe, that,

> Swinton came to value gentleness in part through his experience as a psychiatric nurse within institutions that were not gentle. He recalls, as a trainee nurse, "being ordered to tell thirty patients to strip and line up in the bathroom in rows of ten, in order that they could be shaved and bathed by nursing assistants"—a practice, among others, that he came to understand "not [as] an act of care but [as] a method of control" (Swinton 2000b, 57). His appreciation of gentleness was further shaped by his subsequent training as a registered nurse for persons with disabilities, and then even more when he left nursing and began working as a community mental-health chaplain. He learned as a nurse, and perhaps even more as a chaplain, to *listen* for the deep and profound experiences of the human beings before him. (271)

It is not sufficient to simply say that John is gentle because of his biographical experiences, observes Medi Volpe: instead, John is peaceful and gentle because he is "interested in *Jesus*" (279). Being in mental hospitals as one paid to care can just as easily harden as make one gentle, and that has probably made at least as many who worked there hard as gentle. That is why it is so important, says Volpe, to notice how "the way of peace woven through John Swinton's theological work depends upon humility that is instinctual, humility that becomes the visceral response of the follower of Jesus" (290).

Volpe leads us further, all the way back to the Fall, understood as the desire of the first couple's desire to "do it all." Adam and Eve are not content to embrace the limits of their contingency, but they want to do more, to express more, to experience more. In contrast, as presented in the Christus Hymn of Philippians 2, God's kenotic love in Jesus Christ did not grasp to "have it all" but instead embodied a joyful contentment with the goodness of the life course that he alone could live (290–91). With this insight Volpe opens up a new vista for thinking about the vocation of nursing. No nurses worth their salt would chafe at not having the skills and role of surgeons or consultant doctors who are so obviously feted by society. To be a nurse demands coming to terms with the activity of caring as true and good in itself. To be a good nurse thus depends on thoroughly internalizing this truth. The gentleness and peace of the nurse thus points toward the life of the One who gave his life for us when he was at the height of his powers, refusing to shirk this divinely appointed work in favor of actualizing all his possibilities. In the leaning in to care for the bodies of those who are ill and in need—and who in falling ill are, if not yet officially stigmatized, at least beginning to fall out of social relevance—nurses display crucial aspects of God's kenotic leaning into the worlds of sinful creatures. To grasp the gentleness demanded of the nurse is thus to glimpse something important about those whose bodies we call disabled, whose peaceableness can only be achieved by owning their limitations in a world full of people obsessed with maximizing their potential.

Even if John's kids might snicker at the suggestion that John is "gentle and kind at all times" (275–76), speaking as John's longest-serving colleague in Aberdeen, I can't think of a single instance of his not fitting this description, even in the face of my own often distinct lack of gentleness.

LIVING AND THEOLOGIZING

In raising the question of what it might mean that John was first a nurse and then a theologian, I take up a theme investigated by Henk de Roest (31–34) and Doug Gay (64). Both contributors pick up hints in John's work that suggest answers to the question of what John hopes the contribution of his life and work might be. As someone who has seen John's work grow and evolve over many years, I have found this a particularly interesting question, since he is evidently not the sort of person whose next moves are easily predicted. Like any genuinely creative thinker, he keeps us on the edge of our seats, wondering what will come next.

Bill Gaventa testifies in chapter 11 that "my vocation found me" (212). When I asked John how he would describe the relationship between his life and his work, he offered an uncannily similar answer. There were no epiphanies involved.

> The disability thing just happened. It's only when somebody asks me that question that I think about it. It was a natural progression. Through all my theological education, it's just been there. I'm a firm believer that a good deal of theology begins with autobiography. I don't mean theology *as* autobiography. But I do think that these autobiographical dimensions shape and form the way that we approach the theological task. And for me that's clearly the case. I wouldn't have even noticed the way I came to disability until you asked the question. It's just "me."

Sensing that there might be more to it than this explanation admitted, I pressed for more, asking, "Why then did you go into mental health nursing?" John replied:

> I didn't have a job! I was driving a van! I didn't know what to do! I had just been sacked as a marine scientist. I was seventeen, and I was driving a van, and quite enjoying it! But I knew I couldn't do that forever. Then one of my friends, David Adams, decided to become a nurse. So I thought, "Hmm, I'll try that!" And I did. In those days you trained either as a mental health nurse or a learning disability nurse or as a general nurse, and I chose to be a mental health nurse, though I also worked in general nursing.

"I chose to be a mental health nurse." "My vocation chose me." "The disability thing was always there." The puzzle does not quite fit. There is one more missing piece. Jesus does not lead us into community in general, but into a specific community, the body of Christ.

IN LOVE WITH THE DIVERSITY OF CHRIST'S BODY

Only those who are not disabled can "develop an interest" in disability, observes Bill Gaventa. Those of us who work in disability theology have probably not thought hard enough about the implication of this fact. We ought do so, however, because those who "develop an interest" are formed very differently in their theological thinking than those who carry the label "disabled" and very often find their lives tracing a diametrically opposed journey. Those who discover themselves in the shadow zone demarcated by the label "disability" often desperately desire to escape the parts assigned to them in the social scripts available to the disabled person. Every Christian should be on one of these two journeys—into or out of the shadow zone—because the church should be a community in which, as Bill so nicely puts it, we are encouraging and helping each person to "find their place in the choir" (213). To find our place in the community of worship will for some be a movement toward grasping something of the limits of their able-bodiedness, while for others it will trace the opposite trajectory, moving toward the discovery of what is erased or overlooked by our society's focus on their bodily or intellectual limits.

Bill Gaventa recounts the powerful story of where such transitions take us when Christ's body takes concrete form in local churches. Chris was an altar boy in a Catholic parish in New Jersey, who also happened to have the genetic palette that medicine labels as Down syndrome. One

Sunday his parents could not find him after church, and when they did, he was speaking to an older couple. To their surprise, that couple wanted to talk to Chris specifically because they had come to church wrestling with a burden of pain, grief, and uncertainty around a newly born grand-child who shared his genetic palette. Seeing Chris and his ministry at the church, they felt compelled to talk to him. In talking to him, they received a profound form of pastoral care from a priest in the kingdom of priests (214). Chris was living out what they could not imagine. Chris was speaking out of a mouth with a shape that signaled to many his life in the shadow zone what their own consciences could not: May the peace of the Lord be with you. Only a church that knows itself as the body of Christ and loves its diversity is capable of living up to such a reality.

I asked John how he arrived at this countercultural vision of the church, and his first answer pointed to his teacher Duncan Forrester, who as Doug Gay points out, was prone to inverting the words of Jesus: "No us without them" (64). It is an insight that John certainly developed much more fully by rooting this insight in a robust account of the body of Christ. John's account of the discovery of the beauty of the body of Christ begins with the theme that we have highlighted in the title of this volume.

> The question of what it means to be human has always fascinated me. To notice the diversity of humanity really opens up a space to recognize—it democratizes humanity, if you like. Very often we think about issues of normality in mathematical sense. If you've got two arms or two legs, then you're normal. That may or may not be the case for a statistician, but for me as a theologian that's not the way a conversation about normalcy ought to run. I was always very influenced by a British practical theologian called John Hull. I knew him. A good guy, very interesting guy, who went blind in his early fifties. He uses Merleau-Ponty's phenomenology to explore the experience of going blind. First of all, you go inwards, you're trapped inside because sighted people always look outwards—if you hear a sound you're looking out, to see any colors you have to look out. Suddenly all that was taken from him, so he had to rethink almost everything about the world. He eventually came to the conclusion that sighted people tend to colonize the word "normal." If you are not sighted, you're expected to act in ways that are as close an approximation as possible of what sighted people think of as normality. And he says, No! The way in which human beings understand the world is through our bodies, from a phenomenolog-ical perspective. And your body is different from mine, my body is different from yours, so we all experience the world differently. The only way we can really understand what it means to be human is by

experience, not by colonizing one another. This leads him ̄usion that to be human is a wide range of possibilities, and ̄ical task is to work out the nature of these possibilities, and ̄ kind of revelation it then gives to us. And I think that's probably now I understand my own perception of what it means to be human. It's that sense of diversity, unity, and diversity, but respecting the diversity. The body of Christ is marked by diversity rather than homogeneity.

We might say that this is an ontological description based on a phenomenological insight. Human beings have bodies that shape their experience of the world. Because we all have subtly different bodies, we literally experience different worlds, to a greater or lesser extent. Given this reality, we will never be properly responding to human diversity by attempting to impose a single vision of the world on every other human being. Humanity is diverse, and the body of Christ is diverse. I am calling this an ontological description because it is an account of the beings that make up the church, how they fit together and how we might describe them from the outside. Swinton's genius is not to stop at this point, but to go on to ask, What does it mean to live in this truth?

CHURCH AS A COMMUNITY OF ATTENTION

John's answer to this question is to call the church to be a "community of attention," as Bill Gaventa notes (209). John's own formulations of this point have become increasingly precise over the years. As he put this point in his 2012 book, *Dementia* (226):

> To be attentive is to pay close attention to the other. The church is called first of all to become a community that is attentive to God, the Rememberer and Bearer and Sustainer of our true identities. It is here that the church's worship finds its focus and goal. But the members of Christ's body are also called to become attentive to one another, and in particular, to those who may be considered weak and vulnerable. (1 Cor 12:21–31)

Such attentiveness is the seedbed of practices of hospitality, notes Benjamin Conner. When Christians are oriented toward those among us whose value is questioned by society, asking what it means to have them as friends becomes an expression of a desire to be hospitable that is indispensable to true Christian mission. This hospitality is not that of the magnanimous man of Greek ethics, whose hospitality is intended to display the free hand with which he dispenses the bounty of his wealth.

Instead, hospitality in the body of Christ is the work of opening a space in which those who are stigmatized experience themselves not as strangers but as friends. As with the Friendship House project recounted by the authors of chapter 1, this is intrinsically difficult and politically charged work, since opening a space where those stigmatized in a social domain that valorizes power and production is by definition a desacralizing and dethroning of those values (235–40).

Grant Macaskill has well described John's theological account of the dynamics of inclusion and their rooting in a fundamentally theological description of reality (90–91). And as Ben Conner points out, John understands baptism as the practice through which the church both announces and continuously reactivates its unique form of belonging. The baptismal form of belonging is infinitely deeper than all secular accounts of inclusion (231–32). John unpacked for me in more detail how the practice of baptism provokes questions about what it means to live as a Christian that point toward the furthest reaches of what it means to live as a human with other humans.

> When you listen to peoples' different experiences, it raises all kinds of questions about what it looks like to be church, to belong to each other in the body of Christ. What does it mean to engage in a holy embrace when you don't have arms? What does it mean to engage in the sacrament when you can't swallow the bread or the wine? And again, what does it mean to know Jesus when you can't know who Jesus is? I think those are really good questions because they remind us of the diversity of our humanness, but at the same time challenge us to listen, to a hermeneutic of generosity in life. That's something we could all do with, not just in the context of disability, but just if people were just a bit more generous with their time and with their listening and with their desire to be with one another, we'd have a different world.

That is the nub of the matter for John and, I would suggest, the font of his creativity. The church is the beginning of a different world, a beachhead of an alternative social universe, which is as close as the baptismal font and the bodies of our fellow worshipers.

This alternative social universe is as close as the worshiping community, but it must be received. John's label for the form of action that draws us into divine action is "friendship," Andrew Root observes (247). Our salvation is very near, but it may come in the form of a hug that we do not know how to respond to from someone with no arms, or a pastoral chat from someone who cannot "understand" what it means to have a grandchild with Down syndrome. To patiently let such interactions unfold is to embrace our training in the faith, our catechesis, Root continues. Relaxing into such unfamiliar exchanges forms us to see the action of a living God who liberates human beings from the limits of their sinful views of others (251). In the body of Christ, such waiting for one another is distinguishable from the waiting of the world which is vacant and beset by the sense of time being wasted. The waiting of faith is full and replete, a hopeful waiting to find our ways into a living together different in kind from the busyness of modern life. In Christ we are waiting for encounter, not for something to "happen" or "get done." This is attentive waiting, waiting saturated with affection, flowing from affection and evoking affection. Root touches on one of the fecund sources of John's work when noting that this account of the drive of love toward friendship is ultimately an elaboration of John the Evangelist's understanding of God's love for the world. In Jesus, God's love is revealed to be affectionate, patient, and straining toward rendering us friends of God (253–57).

LEGACIES: AN INVITATION INTO THE PATIENT AND PEACEFUL WELCOME OF JESUS' KINGDOM

The Friendship House Christmas carol service at the University of Aberdeen narrated in chapter 1 (22–26) offers a concrete example of an incursion of this different peace and of John's place in inviting its realization. This is a service that makes it obvious and palpable that those who normally live as outsiders to society have become very much a living part and know themselves as friends. For me the joy of this service is the vigorous cacophony of the singing. It never fails to give me those giggles that are somewhere between nervousness and pure, tear-inducing eschatological joy. Everyone has a place in this choir, and the place of one or two is to bawl out their carols at such volume and with such evident joy that their imperviousness to the pace and tone of John's leadership appears not so much a breach of decorum but a questioning the very notion of there being a human leader at all.

John loves music, he has toured professionally as a musician, and he still writes songs. Yet it is paradigmatic of his witness that even when the braying of the celebrants reaches its most cacophonous crescendos, he neither winces nor attempts to correct singers who would in any other carol service be considered to be engaged in a hostile takeover of the service. John lives among us the patience of God, and hence the hospitality opened by God's patient friendship as he deploys his musical skill not to correct the singers in this worshiping community, but to fill in and help us all find the rhythm together that only this particular group of singers will have. The contrast could not be starker with the day-to-day happenings in that space. In a chapel that regularly hosts musicians and concerts regulated for utmost precision and performance, this is nothing less than a subversive act, as John understood it to be from the inception of the formation of Friendship House, sited as it is within a university designed to seek out and train only the best and the brightest.

I present this elaboration of the story told in chapter 1 as my testimony of how John has served to reveal the wondrous works of the Lord among us. He has showed us the way into the ethos of the psalmists, whose constant refrain is: "O give thanks to the Lord, call on his name, make known his deeds among the peoples. Sing to him, sing praises to him; tell of all his wonderful works" (Ps 105:1–2). John is so at peace in situations like the Friendship House carol service that it tempts me to speak up, to say what I see, to try on being at ease with him in what feels at first like an eardrum-rattling cacophony.

This is perhaps the most important legacy of John's work and witness: its inviting and tempting us all a little bit further out into the open of God's working among us. All of us need to be invited out beyond our own prejudices, both those with and without disabilities, as Bill Gaventa observes (208–9). John has played a central role in fostering an academic community that is free, welcoming, and supportive enough (166) to provide a safe space for Grant Macaskill to publicly announce for the first time his diagnosis of being on the autistic spectrum, as he has done in his essay in this volume (94). Michael Mawson's chapter is another such testimony, in bringing to speech how John's descriptions of God's care for those with dementia allowed him "to actively affirm and attend to God's presence and work in the context of the many changes that my father underwent . . . to be less anxious and fearful in the face of such changes" (151). These are powerful displays of how a community can invite that vulnerable living into truth that John has in his works so often and in so many different ways invited us all into.

WORKS CITED

Fine, Michael. 2015. "Eva Feder Kittay: Dependency Work and the Social Division of Care." In *The Palgrave Handbook of Social Theory in Health, Illness and Medicine*, edited by F. Collyer, 628–43. London: Palgrave Macmillan.

Held, Virginia. 2003. *The Ethics of Care: Personal, Political, Global.* Oxford: Oxford University Press.

Kittay, Eva Feder. 1999. *Love's Labor: Essays on Women, Equality, and Dependency.* Thinking Gender. New York: Routledge.

Noddings, Nel. 2003. *Caring: A Feminine Approach to Ethics and Moral Education*. 2nd ed. Berkeley: University of California Press.

Nussbaum, Martha C. 2006. *Frontiers of Justice: Disability, Nationality, Species Membership*. Cambridge, Mass.: Belknap Press of Harvard University Press.

Contributors

Aileen Barclay is an experienced educationalist and practical theologian. She completed her PhD under the supervision of Professor John Swinton entitled "Becoming Educators of the Cross: a faithful Christian response to pupil disaffection in state schools" while lecturing in Inclusive Education in the School of Education at the University of Aberdeen. She lives in the Northeast of Scotland and although retired remains active in theological activities and church life.

Brian Brock is Professor of Moral and Practical Theology at the University of Aberdeen, Scotland. He has written scholarly works on the use of the Bible in Christian ethics, the ethics of technological development, and the theology of disability. He is founder and managing editor of the academic monograph series *T&T Clark Enquiries in Theological Ethics*, and a managing editor of the *Journal of Disability & Religion*.

Benjamin T. Conner is Professor of Practical Theology and Director of the Center for Disability and Ministry at Western Theological Seminary in Holland, Michigan. His most recent book is *Disabling Mission, Enabling Witness: Exploring Missiology through the Lens of Disability Studies* (IVP Academic, 2018) and his current projects include vocation and disability and a practical theology of therapeutic horsemanship.

Henk de Roest is Professor of Practical Theology at the Protestant Theological University, Groningen. Earlier he held the chair of practical theology at Leiden University and served twelve years as minister in parishes north of Amsterdam. In 1998 he defended his dissertation on the relationship between the philosophy of Jürgen Habermas and the discipline of practical theology. He is editor-in-chief of *Ecclesial Practices: Journal of Ecclesiology and Ethnography*.

Topher Endress earned his PhD in Theological Ethics from the University of Aberdeen in 2021, where he focused on the spatial aspects of disability theology. He is an ordained minister in the Christian Church (Disciples of Christ) and is primarily focused on bringing the idealism of academic pursuits into the lived experience of faith communities. His other projects have included qualitative research on autistic experiences of liturgy and a manual outlining inclusion processes for churches seeking to combat ableism.

Cristina Gangemi holds a Master's degree in Pastoral Theology and Lay Ministry, with a special focus on disability. She is director of The Kairos Forum, which focuses on enabling communities to be places of belonging for people with a disability. She is currently working as a study skills teacher in an international school in Rome, where she is studying for a professional doctorate in disability, theology, and the writings of Edith Stein. Cristina is a "formator" and researcher. She is the author of numerous articles, book chapters, pastoral programs, and the book set *Because I AM*.

Bill Gaventa is an author, speaker, trainer, and consultant in the arena of faith and disability. He is the founder/director emeritus of the Institute of Theology and Disability. He was the Director of Community and Congregational Supports at the Boggs Center on Developmental Disabilities in New Jersey from 1995 to 2013 and served as the president of the American Association of Intellectual and Developmental Disabilities from 2016 to 2017. Bill was editor of the *Journal of Religion, Disability & Health* for fourteen years, and is author of *Spirituality and Disability: Recovering Wholeness* (Baylor University Press, 2018).

Doug Gay is a Lecturer in Practical Theology at the University of Glasgow, where he is also Principal of Trinity College. He is a Church of Scotland minister.

Stanley Hauerwas is Gilbert T. Rowe Professor Emeritus of Divinity and Law at Duke Divinity School. He is the author of many books including *A Community of Character: Toward a Constructive Christian Social Ethic*, selected by *Christianity Today* as one of the one hundred most important books on religion of the twentieth century, and most recently of *Fully Alive: The Apocalyptic Humanism of Karl Barth*.

Elahe Hessamfar is a former business and technology executive from corporate America. For years, she stood at the helm of innovation and technology development, leading major global companies toward the most advanced information systems of the time. Hessamfar has a PhD in Divinity from the University of Aberdeen in Scotland, an MA in Biblical Studies from the Reformed Theological Seminary, an MS in Computer Science from the George Washington University, and a BS in Electrical Engineering from the University of Kansas. She has a ministry to support and care for families faced with challenges of mental illness.

Stephen Judd AM was Chief Executive of HammondCare, an Australian independent Christian charity from 1995 to 2020, a period in which HammondCare became recognized nationally and internationally for its innovation and leadership in dementia and palliative care. Since stepping down as CEO in 2020, Stephen has been a Senior Visiting Fellow in the School of Population Health, University of New South Wales. Stephen has authored books on church history, dementia care, aged care design, and the role of charities and is currently writing and advising on how organizations avoid mission drift and remain faithfully Christian.

Warren Kinghorn is Associate Professor of Psychiatry at Duke University Medical Center; Esther Colliflower Associate Professor of the Practice of Pastoral and Moral Theology at Duke Divinity School; co-director of the Theology, Medicine, and Culture Initiative at Duke Divinity School; and staff psychiatrist at the Durham VA Medical Center.

Julie Marie Land is a PhD Candidate in Theological Ethics at the University of Aberdeen, and a University of Aberdeen Friendship House fellow. Her research explores friendship and Eucharist in the Gospel of John within the context of disability theology.

Grant Macaskill is the Kirby Laing Chair of New Testament Exegesis at the University of Aberdeen. He previously taught at the University of St Andrews, where he also earned his PhD. He is the author of *Autism and the Church: Bible, Theology, and Community* (Baylor University Press, 2019), *The New Testament and Intellectual Humility* (Oxford University Press, 2017) and *Union with Christ in the New Testament* (Oxford University Press, 2013).

Michael Mawson is Senior Lecturer in Theology at Charles Sturt University, Australia, and Research Fellow for the Theology for Southern Africa Initiative at the University of the Free State, South Africa. He is the author of *Christ Existing as Community: Bonhoeffer's Ecclesiology* (2018) and co-editor of *The Oxford Handbook of Dietrich Bonhoeffer* (2019).

Johannes (Hans) S. Reinders received his PhD from VU University Amsterdam. From 1995 to 2016 he served his *Alma Mater* as Professor of Ethics, and Professor of Disability and Ethics in Long Term Care. He has been a visiting scholar in philosophy at the University of Notre Dame and a resident scholar at the Center for Theological Inquiry in Princeton. He was general editor of the *Journal of Disability & Religion* from 2010 to 2016, and author of many publications.

Andrew Root is the Carrie Olson Baalson Professor of Youth and Family Ministry at Luther Seminary in St. Paul, Minnesota.

Armand Léon van Ommen is Senior Lecturer in Practical Theology at the University of Aberdeen and Co-Director of the Centre for Autism and Theology. His current research focuses on autism and liturgy. His publications include *Suffering in Worship: Anglican Liturgy in Relation to Stories of Suffering People* (Routledge, 2016) and various articles and book chapters on liturgy, lament, joy, autism, mental health, and disability.

Medi Ann Volpe is Director of Research at Wesley House, Cambridge, and Assistant Professor of Theology and Ethics at Durham University. As a Catholic moral theologian and mother of four children, including an adult daughter with Down syndrome, she is interested in the intersection of ecclesiology, disability, and the spiritual formation of children and adults. Her first book, *Rethinking Christian Identity* (Wiley, 2013), began to explore this intersection, and she has continued work on these themes in writing and speaking. Her current book project (*Living as the Body of Christ*) considers ecclesiology from the perspective of disability.

Hannah Waite earned her PhD in Practical Theology from the University of Aberdeen in 2021, where she studied the lived experience of stigma in Christians with a clinical diagnosis of bipolar disorder. While she was in Aberdeen Hannah was a Friendship House fellow. Hannah continues to research mental health, disability theology, and how to create loving communities within the Church. She currently works as the Science and Religion researcher at Theos Think Tank.

Marcia Webb earned an MDiv and a PhD in clinical psychology from Fuller Theological Seminary in 1995. She has taught at Seattle Pacific University for approximately twenty-five years. Her scholarship has focused upon the potential interplay between Christian religiosity and clinical psychology. She has studied trauma and religiosity; psychological maltreatment, guilt, shame, and forgiveness; and religious stigma about mental illness. She is the author of *Toward a Theology of Psychological Disorder* (Eugene, Ore.: Cascade, 2017).

Index